FINANCIAL INSTITUTIONS AND SERVICES

THE STATE OF COMMUNITY BANKS AND CREDIT UNIONS AND THE POTENTIAL ROLE OF THE DODD-FRANK ACT

Financial Institutions and Services

Additional books in this series can be found on Nova's website under the Series tab.

Additional E-books in this series can be found on Nova's website under the E-book tab.

Economic Issues, Problems and Perspectives

Additional books in this series can be found on Nova's website under the Series tab.

Additional E-books in this series can be found on Nova's website under the E-book tab.

FINANCIAL INSTITUTIONS AND SERVICES

THE STATE OF COMMUNITY BANKS AND CREDIT UNIONS AND THE POTENTIAL ROLE OF THE DODD-FRANK ACT

JEFFREY R. HOLMAN
EDITOR

nova publishers
New York

For permission to use material from this book please contact us:
Telephone 631-231-7269; Fax 631-231-8175
Web Site: http://www.novapublishers.com

Additional color graphics may be available in the e-book version of this book.

Library of Congress Cataloging-in-Publication Data

ISBN: 978-1-62417-227-4

Published by Nova Science Publishers, Inc. † New York

CONTENTS

PREFACE

The Dodd-Frank Act includes numerous reforms to strengthen oversight of financial services firms and consolidate certain consumer protection responsibilities within the Consumer Financial Protection Bureau (CFPB). To help minimize its regulatory burden on small institutions, including community banks and credit unions, the act exempts such institutions from several of its provisions. However, the act also contains provisions that impose additional requirements on small institutions. Historically, community banks and credit unions have played an important role in providing credit to small businesses and other local customers. This book examines the significant changes community banks and credit unions have undergone in the past decade and the factors that have contributed to such changes with a focus on the Dodd-Frank Act provisions that regulators, industry associations, and others expect to impact community banks and credit unions, including their small business lending.

Chapter 1 – The Dodd-Frank Act includes numerous reforms to strengthen oversight of financial services firms and consolidate certain consumer protection responsibilities within CFPB. To help minimize its regulatory burden on small institutions, including community banks and credit unions, the act exempts such institutions from several of its provisions. However, the act also contains provisions that impose additional requirements on small institutions. Although no commonly accepted definition of a community bank exists, the term often is associated with smaller banks. Historically, community banks and credit unions have played an important role in providing credit to small businesses and other local customers.

This report examines (1) the significant changes community banks and credit unions have undergone in the past decade and the factors that have contributed to such changes, and (2) Dodd-Frank Act provisions that regulators, industry associations, and others expect to impact community banks and credit unions, including their small business lending. GAO analyzed regulatory and other data on community banks and credit unions; reviewed academic and other relevant studies; and interviewed federal regulators, community banks, credit unions, state regulatory and industry associations, academics, and others.

CFPB, federal banking regulators, and the Securities and Exchange Commission provided technical comments on this chapter, which GAO incorporated as appropriate. CFPB and the National Credit Union Administration generally agreed with the chapter.

Chapter 2 – This is a statement of Maryann F. Hunter, Deputy Director, Division of Banking Supervision and Regulation, Board of Governors of the Federal Reserve System.

Chapter 3 – This is a statement of Sandra L. Thompson, Director of Risk Management Supervision, Federal Deposit Insurance Corporation.

Chapter 4 – This is a testimony of Jennifer Kelly, Senior Deputy Comptroller for Midsize and Community Bank Supervision, Office of the Comptroller of the Currency.

Chapter 5 – This is a testimony of John P. Ducrest, Commissioner, Louisiana Office of Financial Institutions.

Chapter 6 – This is a testimony of William A. Loving, President and CEO of Pendleton Community Bank.

Chapter 7 – This is a testimony of Paul Reed, Chairman of the Ohio Bankers League.

Chapter 8 – This is a testimony of Tommy G. Whittaker, CEO, The Farmers Bank.

In: The State of Community Banks … ISBN: 978-1-62417-227-4
Editor: Jeffrey R. Holman

Chapter 1

COMMUNITY BANKS AND CREDIT UNIONS: IMPACT OF THE DODD-FRANK ACT DEPENDS LARGELY ON FUTURE RULE MAKINGS*

United States Government Accountability Office

WHY GAO DID THIS STUDY

The Dodd-Frank Act includes numerous reforms to strengthen oversight of financial services firms and consolidate certain consumer protection responsibilities within CFPB. To help minimize its regulatory burden on small institutions, including community banks and credit unions, the act exempts such institutions from several of its provisions. However, the act also contains provisions that impose additional requirements on small institutions. Although no commonly accepted definition of a community bank exists, the term often is associated with smaller banks. Historically, community banks and credit unions have played an important role in providing credit to small businesses and other local customers.

This report examines (1) the significant changes community banks and credit unions have undergone in the past decade and the factors that have

* This is an edited, reformatted and augmented version of the Highlights of GAO-12-881, a report to congressional requesters, dated September 2012.

contributed to such changes, and (2) Dodd-Frank Act provisions that regulators, industry associations, and others expect to impact community banks and credit unions, including their small business lending. GAO analyzed regulatory and other data on community banks and credit unions; reviewed academic and other relevant studies; and interviewed federal regulators, community banks, credit unions, state regulatory and industry associations, academics, and others.

CFPB, federal banking regulators, and the Securities and Exchange Commission provided technical comments on this chapter, which GAO incorporated as appropriate. CFPB and the National Credit Union Administration generally agreed with the chapter.

What GAO Found

While the number of community banks and credit unions has declined in recent years, they have remained important lenders to small businesses and other local customers. From 1985 through 2010, the number of banks under $10 billion in assets and credit unions declined by over 50 percent to 7,551 and 7,339, respectively. The decline resulted largely from consolidations, which were facilitated by changes in federal law that made it easier for banks and credit unions to expand geographically. Another factor that may have contributed to consolidations is economies of scale, which refer to how an institution's size is related to its costs. Although the existence of economies of scale in banking has been subject to debate, some recent research suggests that banks can save costs by expanding. Despite the decline in their number, community banks and credit unions have maintained their relationship-banking model, relying on their relationships with customers and local knowledge to make loans. Such institutions can use their relationship-based information to make loans to small businesses and other borrowers that larger banks may not make because of their general reliance on more automated processes. About 20 percent of lending by community banks can be categorized as small business lending (based on a commonly used proxy), compared to about 5 percent by larger banks. Community banks and credit unions also play an important role in rural areas, using relationship-based lending to serve customers with limited credit histories.

Although the Dodd-Frank Wall Street Reform and Consumer Protection Act's (Dodd-Frank Act) reforms are directed primarily at large, complex U.S. financial institutions, regulators, industry officials, and others collectively identified provisions within 7 of the act's 16 titles that they expect to have positive and negative impacts on community banks and credit unions. Industry officials told us that it is difficult to know for sure which provisions will impact community banks and credit unions, because the outcome largely depends on how agencies implement certain provisions through their rules, and many of the rules implementing the act have not been finalized. Thus, regulators and industry officials also have noted that the full impact of the Dodd-Frank Act on these institutions is uncertain. Nonetheless, some regulators and industry officials expect some of the act's provisions to benefit community banks and credit unions and other provisions to impose additional requirements on community banks and credit unions that could affect them disproportionately relative to larger banks. GAO analyzed a number of the Dodd-Frank Act provisions that regulators, industry officials, and others expect to impact community banks and credit unions. Several of the act's provisions, including its deposit insurance reforms, exemption from Section 404(b) of the Sarbanes-Oxley Act, and the Bureau of Consumer Financial Protection's (CFPB) supervision of certain nonbanks, could reduce costs and/or help level the playing field for community banks and credit unions. Other provisions, such as the act's mortgage reforms, may impose additional requirements and, thus, costs on generally all banks and credit unions, but their impact will depend on, among other things, how the provisions are implemented. Finally, industry officials generally told us that it is too soon to determine the Dodd-Frank Act's overall impact on small business lending and identified only one provision that contains a data collection and reporting requirement as potentially having a direct impact on such lending.

ABBREVIATIONS

CFPB	Bureau of Consumer Financial Protection
CFTC	Commodity Futures Trading Commission
DIF	Deposit Insurance Fund
Dodd-Frank Act	Dodd-Frank Wall Street Reform and Consumer Protection Act
FDIC	Federal Deposit Insurance Corporation
Federal Reserve	Board of Governors of the Federal Reserve System
FHFA	Federal Housing Finance Agency
HMDA	Home Mortgage Disclosure Act
JOBS Act	Jumpstart Our Business Startups Act

NCUA	National Credit Union Administration
OCC	Office of the Comptroller of the Currency
OTC	over-the-counter
OTS	Office of Thrift Supervision
QM	qualified mortgage
QRM	qualified residential mortgage
RMBS	residential mortgage-backed securities
SBA	Small Business Administration
SEC	Securities and Exchange Commission
TILA	Truth in Lending Act

September 13, 2012

The Honorable Olympia Snowe
Ranking Member
Committee on Small Business and Entrepreneurship
United States Senate

The Honorable Mark Kirk
United States Senate

In 2008, the U.S. financial system and broader economy faced the most severe financial crisis since the Great Depression. The crisis threatened the stability of the financial system and contributed to the failure of numerous financial institutions, including some large, complex financial institutions. For example, 414 banks and 90 credit unions failed between 2008 and 2011, with such failures peaking in 2010. In response to the crisis, Congress passed the Dodd-Frank Wall Street Reform and Consumer Protection Act (Dodd-Frank Act), which became law on July 21, 2010.[1] The act includes numerous reforms to strengthen oversight of financial services firms and consolidate certain consumer protection responsibilities within the Bureau of Consumer Financial Protection, commonly known as the Consumer Financial Protection Bureau (CFPB).[2] Although the Dodd-Frank Act exempts small institutions, such as community banks and credit unions, from several of its provisions, and authorizes federal regulators to provide small institutions with relief from certain regulations, it also contains provisions that will impose additional restrictions and compliance costs on these institutions.[3] Historically, community banks and credit unions have played an important role in serving their local customers, including providing credit to small businesses.

This report examines

- the significant changes community banks and credit unions have undergone in the past decade, and the factors that have contributed to such changes; and
- Dodd-Frank Act provisions that regulators, industry associations, and others expect to impact community banks and credit unions, including their small business lending.

To examine changes in community banks and credit unions, we analyzed data from SNL Financial, a private financial database that contains publicly filed and financial reports, including Consolidated Reports on Condition and Income (Call Reports) submitted to the Federal Deposit Insurance Corporation (FDIC), Thrift Financial Reports submitted to the Office of Thrift Supervision (OTS), and 5300 Call Reports (Call Reports) submitted to the National Credit Union Administration (NCUA).[4] We used SNL Financial data to identify changes in the total number, profitability, lending activities, expenses, and other metrics of community banks and credit unions from 2002 through 2011.[5] We reviewed the SNL Financial data and found the data to be sufficiently reliable for our purposes. We also reviewed and analyzed relevant academic, regulatory, and industry studies. We interviewed officials from FDIC, the Board of Governors of the Federal Reserve System (Federal Reserve), the Office of the Comptroller of the Currency (OCC), and NCUA, and the Small Business Administration (SBA); officials from two state regulatory associations (Conference of State Bank Supervisors and National Association of State Credit Union Supervisors); representatives of industry associations, including the American Bankers Association, Credit Union National Association, Independent Community Bankers of America, and National Association of Federal Credit Unions; and academics to obtain their perspectives on industry changes.

To assess the Dodd-Frank Act's impact on community banks and credit unions, we reviewed the act and related materials, including relevant congressional hearings; comment letters on proposed rules; and studies and analyses prepared by federal and state regulators, industry associations, law firms, and academics. We used Call Report and other data compiled by SNL Financial to assess the extent to which community banks and credit unions may be subject to or otherwise impacted by various Dodd-Frank Act provisions. We reviewed the SNL Financial data and found the data to be sufficiently reliable for our purposes. To help identify Dodd-Frank Act provisions applicable to community banks and credit unions and assess their impact on those institutions, we interviewed the federal agencies, state regulatory and industry associations, and others identified above, and CFPB. We discussed public comments that some regulators received about proposed rules, but regulators generally do not disclose how they will respond to such comments until after the rules are finalized. In addition, based on demographic factors, we interviewed four state banking and credit union associations, and we randomly selected and interviewed 12 community banks and credit unions to obtain information on the Dodd-Frank Act's provisions. Our interviews with this small sample of institutions provided further insights on the expected impact of the Dodd-Frank Act, but the responses are not generalizable to the population of community banks and credit unions. Although we analyzed the impact of a number of specific Dodd-Frank Act provisions on community banks and credit unions, assessing the extent to which these provisions or their related regulations should apply to such institutions was beyond the scope of our work. Appendix I contains additional information on our scope and methodology.

We conducted this performance audit between February and September 2012, in accordance with generally accepted government auditing standards. Those standards require that we plan and perform the audit to obtain sufficient, appropriate evidence to provide a reasonable basis for our findings and conclusions based on our audit objectives. We believe that the evidence obtained provides a reasonable basis for our findings and conclusions based on our audit objectives.

BACKGROUND

In the banking industry, the specific regulatory configuration for a banking institution depends on the type of charter the institution chooses. Depository institution charter types include:

- commercial banks, which originally focused on the banking needs of businesses but over time have broadened their services;
- thrifts, which include savings banks, savings associations, and savings and loans, and were originally created to serve the needs—particularly the mortgage needs—of those not typically served by commercial banks; and

- credit unions, which are member-owned cooperatives run by member-elected boards with an historical emphasis on serving people of modest means.

These charters may be obtained at the state or federal level. State regulators charter institutions and participate in their oversight, but all institutions that offer federal deposit insurance have a prudential regulator. The prudential regulators—which generally may issue regulations for and take enforcement actions against industry participants within their jurisdiction—are identified in table 1.

As shown in table 2, almost 7,400 (about 99 percent) of all banks had less than $10 billion in assets in 2011 and thus fell within our definition of a community bank. The majority of community banks have $250 million or less in total assets. Although community banks comprise the vast majority of all banks, they held in aggregate about 20 percent of the industry's total assets (about $2.8 trillion) in 2011.

Similarly, table 3 shows that the vast majority of credit unions (over 99 percent) had $10 billion or less in total assets in 2011. Furthermore, around 80 percent of the credit unions had $100 million or less in total assets.

Table 1. Prudential Regulators and Their Basic Functions

Agency	Basic function
Office of the Comptroller of the Currency	Charters and supervises national banks and federal thrifts
Board of Governors of the Federal Reserve System	Supervises state-chartered banks that opt to be members of the Federal Reserve System, bank holding companies, thrift holding companies, and the nondepository institution subsidiaries of those institutions
Federal Deposit Insurance Corporation	Supervises FDIC-insured state-chartered banks that are not members of the Federal Reserve System, as well as federally insured state savings banks and thrifts; insures the deposits of all banks and thrifts that are approved for federal deposit insurance; and resolves all failed insured banks and thrifts and certain nonbank financial companies
National Credit Union Administration	Charters and supervises federally chartered credit unions and insures savings in federal and most state-chartered credit unions

Source: GAO.

Table 2. Numbers of Banks by Asset Class, 2011

Asset size	Number of banks	Percentage of total banks
Community Banks		
< $100 million	2,504	33%
$100 - $250 million	2,418	32
$250 million - $1 billion	1,907	25
$1- $10 billion	556	7
Large Banks		
> $10 billion	109	1
Total	**7,494**	**100%**

Source: GAO analysis of SNL Financial data.

Note: Community banks can be defined based on a number of criteria, but for the purpose of this chapter, we use size (less than $10 billion in assets) as the sole criterion to distinguish community banks from their larger counterparts.

Table 3. Numbers of Credit Unions by Asset Class, 2011

Asset size	Number of credit unions	Percentage of total credit unions
Small Credit Unions		
< $5 million	1,676	24%
$5 - $20 million	1,936	27
$20 - $100 million	2,080	29
$100 million - $1 billion	1,219	17
$1- 10 billion	180	3
Large Credit Unions		
> $10 billion	3	0
Total	**7,094**	**100%**

Source: GAO analysis of SNL Financial data.

Note: We use under $10 billion in total assets as our criteria for a small credit union, because the Dodd-Frank Act exempts small institutions from a number of its provisions based on that threshold.

The Dodd-Frank Act made important and fundamental changes to the structure of the U.S. financial system to strengthen safeguards for consumers and investors and to provide regulators with better tools for limiting risk in the major financial institutions and the financial markets. According to the Financial Stability Oversight Council, the core elements of the act are designed to build a stronger, more resilient financial system—less vulnerable to crisis, more efficient in allocating financial resources, and less vulnerable to fraud and abuse.[6] Under the Dodd-Frank Act, federal financial regulatory agencies are directed or have the authority to issue hundreds of regulations to implement the act's reforms. The Dodd-Frank Act directs agencies to adopt regulations to implement the act's provisions and, in some cases, gives the agencies little or no discretion in deciding how to implement the provisions. However, other rule-making provisions in the act are discretionary in nature, stating that (1) certain agencies may issue rules to implement particular provisions or that the agencies may issue regulations that they decide are "necessary and appropriate," or (2) agencies must issue regulations to implement particular provisions but have some level of discretion as to the substance of the regulations. As a result, the agencies may decide to promulgate rules for all, some, or none of the provisions, and often have broad discretion to decide what these rules will contain. Many of the provisions in the Dodd-Frank Act target the largest and most complex financial institutions, and regulators have noted that much of the act is not meant to apply to community banks. As such, the act directs regulators in a number of areas to consider whether to exempt small banks and credit unions. However, the act is comprehensive and far-reaching and will impact smaller institutions, specifically those that undertake activities thought to be precipitating factors in the 2007 through 2009 financial crisis.

Community Banks and Credit Unions Have Declined in Number but Remain Important for Small Businesses and Agriculture

The number of community banks and credit unions has declined in recent decades, as smaller institutions have expanded, merged with, or been purchased by larger institutions. The trend of consolidation in banks and credit unions has been facilitated by statutory and regulatory changes and may have resulted, in part, from advantages in efficiency at larger institutions. However, community banks and credit unions still play an important role in the economy. Community banks and credit unions allocate more of their lending to small businesses and rural areas than large banks, which research suggests is due to their focus on relationship-based lending.

Changes in Regulation and Other Factors Have Led to the Consolidation of Many Community Banks and Credit Unions

The number of community banks and credit unions has continued to decline significantly since at least the mid-1980s. According to FDIC research presented in 2012, the number of banks with less than $10 billion in assets declined from 17,997 to 7,551, or by about 58 percent, between 1985 and 2010.[7] Similarly, according to NCUA annual reports, the number of federally insured credit unions declined from 15,045 to 7,339, or by about 51 percent, between 1985 and 2010. Despite the decline in the number of credit unions, our analysis of Census data found that membership in credit unions doubled over the same period. Our analysis of SNL Financial data shows that the number of community banks and credit unions declined further in 2011, to 7,385 and 7,094, respectively.[8]

The decline in the number of community banks and credit unions has resulted largely from consolidations, in which two or more institutions generally merge into one larger institution. In their 2012 research, FDIC staff found that of the banks that exited the market between 1985 and 2010, 16 percent failed but 80 percent merged with another financial institution or consolidated within a single holding company. FDIC staff also found that the smallest banks (those with less than $100 million in assets) experienced the largest decline in number, decreasing by 81 percent. Consistent with a pattern of consolidation and expansion, the number of midsize banks (those with $250 million to $1 billion in assets) and large banks (those with over $10 billion in assets) increased by 47 percent and 197 percent, respectively.

Changes in Regulation

Two key statutory and regulatory changes have facilitated consolidation by removing regulatory barriers to geographic and membership expansion by banks and credit unions, respectively. First, the Riegle-Neal Interstate Banking and Branching Efficiency Act of 1994 authorized interstate mergers between banks starting in June 1997, regardless of whether the transaction would be prohibited by state law.[9] Previously, most banks that wanted to operate across state lines had to establish a bank holding company and, with certain restrictions, acquire or charter a bank in each state in which they wanted to operate. With the advent of interstate branching, banks that previously were not permitted to expand across state lines could do so by acquiring existing banks, and some multistate bank holding companies could consolidate their operations into a single bank with multistate branches.[10] Second, after the passage of the Credit Union Membership Access Act in 1998, NCUA revised its regulations to make it easier for federal credit unions to qualify for community charters that allowed people to qualify for membership in a credit union based on their geographic location (e.g., such as a county) rather than based on their employer or affiliation in an organization.[11] As a result, community-chartered credit unions were able to expand, according to one expert we interviewed, by consolidating with other local credit unions, whose members resided in their geographic area. As we previously reported, the total number of federally chartered credit unions declined from 2000 through 2005, but the number of federal community-chartered credit unions more than doubled.[12]

Economies of Scale

Another factor that may have contributed to consolidation is economies of scale, which refer to how a bank's or credit union's scale of operations, or size, is related to its costs. Increasing returns to scale are created when an increase in size leads to a less than proportionate increase in cost and, therefore, a decline in average cost. Banks and credit unions that can take advantage of economies of scale can generate revenues at lower costs by increasing their size through expansion and consolidation. For example, a bank could reduce the average cost in its technology investment by increasing the volume of its goods and services, and thereby increase its profitability. Importantly, the existence of economies of scale in banking has been subject to debate. Studies using data from the 1980s failed to find scale economies beyond very small banks, but later studies have found scale economies in various sized banks.[13] For example, a 2009 study covering all commercial banks from 1984 to 2006 found that banks had increasing returns to scale throughout the distribution of banks, and the authors concluded that industry consolidation had been driven, at least in part, by scale economies.[14] Similarly, in a 2008 study of credit union consolidation presented at FDIC's Mergers and Acquisitions of Financial Institutions Conference, researchers found that smaller and less profitable credit unions were more likely to merge with other credit unions, and that the assets of a small credit union might be used more efficiently if the credit union were acquired and its assets were absorbed into a larger institution.[15]

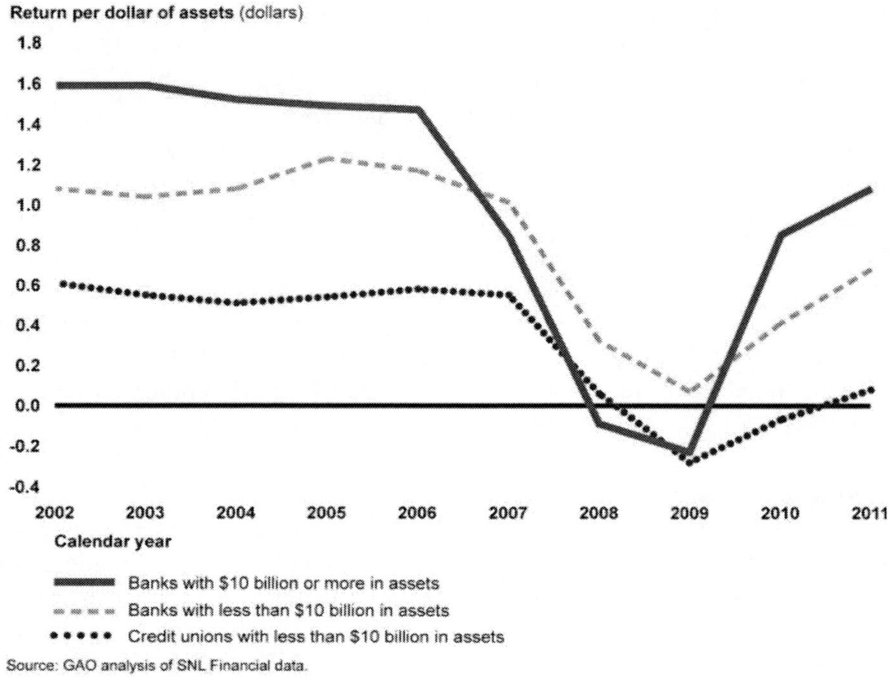

Figure 1. Return on Assets at Large Banks, Community Banks, and Credit Unions from 2002 through 2011.

The results of our analysis are consistent with research finding that larger banks generally are more profitable and efficient than smaller banks, which may reflect increasing returns to scale.[16] For example, in a 2004 study that compared performance between smaller and larger banks, FDIC staff found that smaller banks earned more on their assets than larger banks but that the earnings did not translate into a higher return on assets because smaller institutions also had higher costs.[17] Our analysis of SNL Financial data also found that community banks and credit unions generally have lower rates of return on their assets.[18] As shown in figure 1, banks with more than $10 billion in assets had higher rates of return on their assets than community banks and credit unions from 2002 through 2006.[19] However, returns on assets at large banks declined sharply in 2007 and turned negative in 2008 and 2009, coinciding with the financial crisis. During this period, returns on assets at community banks were higher than at large banks—declining but remaining positive. From 2010 through 2011, returns on assets increased more quickly at large banks than at community banks and credit unions. Returns on equity at community banks, credit unions, and large banks have followed a trend similar to that of returns on assets, with large bank earning higher returns on equity than small financial institutions from 2002 through 2006. Moreover, the gap in returns on equity between large and small financial institutions was greater than the gap in returns on assets before the financial crisis. In their 2004 study, FDIC staff also found that smaller institutions tend to have higher capital ratios than large banks, which also leads to lower returns on equity at a given level of earnings.[20]

Our analysis also indicates that community banks and credit unions have generated revenues at higher average costs than large banks since 2002.[21] As of the end of 2011, large banks earned $1.71 per dollar of operating costs, while community banks earned $1.27 and credit unions earned $1.09. We also found that larger community banks and credit unions were more efficient than smaller institutions by this measure, suggesting that those institutions may have benefited from some economies of scale. As shown in figure 2, the difference in efficiency between community banks and credit unions and large banks generally remained consistent between 2002 and 2010. However, recent declines in revenue per dollar of overhead cost at large banks, along with gains in efficiency at community banks, decreased the difference in 2011. Although community banks with less than $100 million in assets were the least efficient in each year between 2002 and 2011, they (unlike the other banks) experienced an overall increase in their efficiency over the period. These measures of efficiency and profitability also can be influenced by other factors outside of economies of scale, such as increased competition. In April 2011, an OCC official testified that declines in net interest margins have played a major role in decreasing community bank profits.[22]

Some research suggests that one area in which large banks are able to take advantage of economies of scale is regulatory compliance, which contributes to their advantage in terms of operational efficiency. Federal regulators and state regulatory association and industry officials that we interviewed stated that regulatory compliance costs are not regularly tracked in Call Reports, and these costs have not been studied recently in the research literature. Thus, information on economies of scale in this area is limited. However, in a 1998 study, Federal Reserve staff reviewed statistical studies that empirically examined possible economies of scale in regulatory compliance at banks, noting that "if regulatory costs exhibit economies of scale, smaller banks would face higher average costs in complying with regulations than larger banks."[23] The studies found statistical evidence that indicated economies of scale in compliance costs for several regulations, which suggested that smaller banks, relative to larger banks, have a cost disadvantage that may discourage the entry of new firms into banking, may stimulate consolidation of the industry into larger banks, and may inhibit competition among institutions in markets for specific financial products. Additionally, several experts that we spoke with said that smaller institutions are disproportionately affected by increased regulation, because they are less able to absorb additional costs.

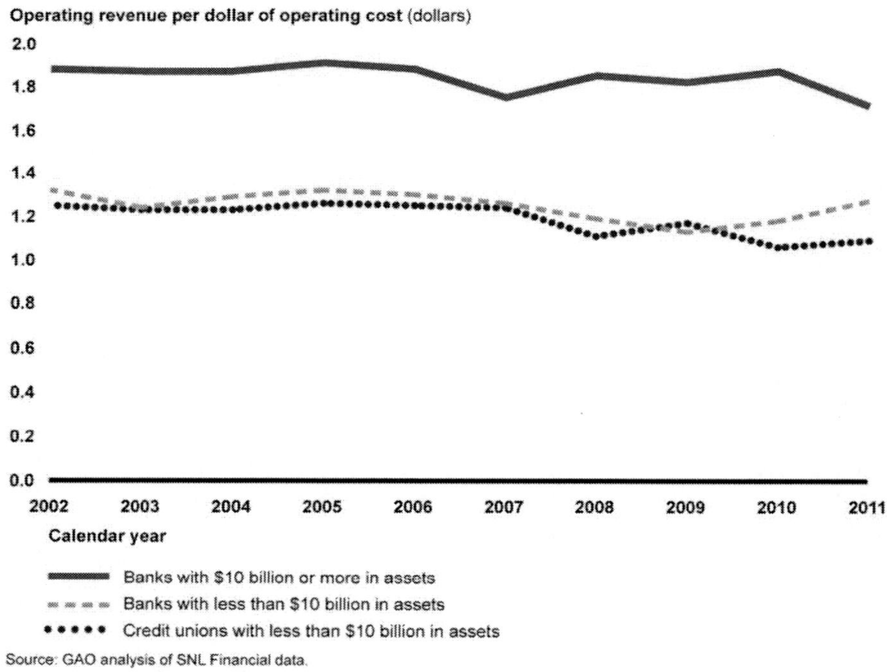

Figure 2. Efficiency at Large Banks, Community Banks, and Credit Unions from 2002 through 2011.

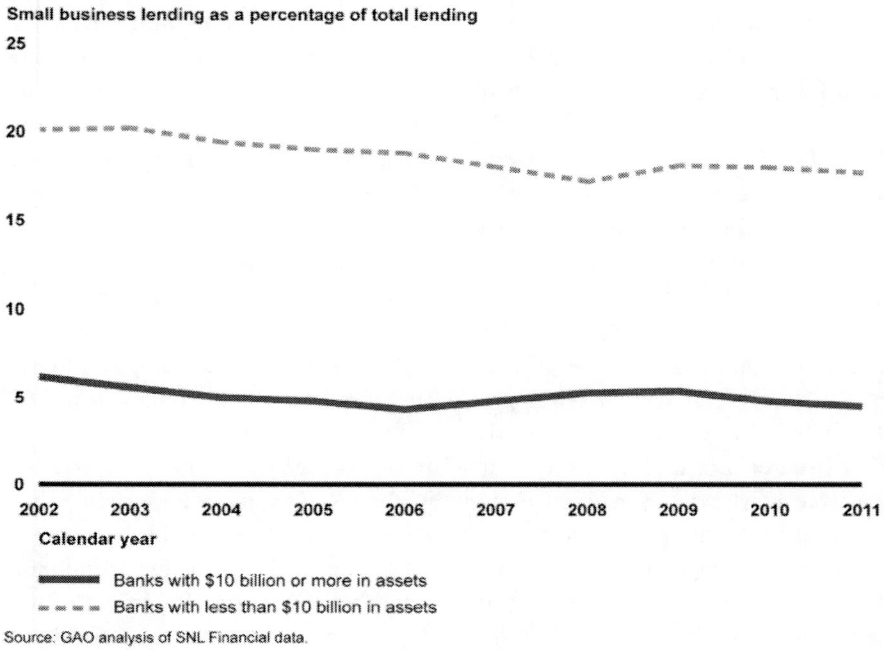

Figure 3. Small Business Lending at Large Banks and Community Banks from 2002 through 2011.

Compared with Larger Banks, Community Banks and Credit Unions Allocate More of Their Lending to Small Businesses and Agriculture

Our analysis suggests that community banks have done more small business and agricultural lending as a percentage of their total lending than large banks over the past decade. To examine small business lending, we used business loans of $1 million or less as a proxy for small business loans at banks, though these loans were not necessarily made to small businesses. As shown in figure 3, our analysis of SNL Financial data found that about 18 percent of total lending at community banks was small business loans, compared to about 5 percent at larger banks in 2011. Figure 3 also shows that while the difference between small business lending at community banks and large banks has remained fairly consistent over the past decade, small business lending as a percentage of total lending declined at both community banks and large banks by about 2 percent from 2002 through 2011. Despite allocating less of their lending to small business loans, banks with more than $10 billion in assets still made about 45 percent of all small business loans in 2011, while accounting for about 1 percent of the total number of banks.

Community banks also have done significantly more agricultural lending as a percentage of total lending than large banks, with the smallest community anks allocating the highest percentage of lending to agricultural loans. Our analysis found that banks with less than $100 million in assets had allocated about 14 percent of their lending to agricultural loans on average from 2002 through 2011, while banks with over $10 billion in assets had allocated less than 1 percent of their loans to agriculture on average. In a 2003 study, Federal Reserve staff also found that community banks played an important role in rural areas generally, where they represented a much higher percent of branches and deposits than in urban areas.[24] The study found that community banks represented nearly 58 percent of bank branches and 49 percent of total deposits in rural areas, compared to 24 percent of branches and around 14 percent of deposits in urban areas.

Some credit unions also make small business and agricultural loans, but differences in regulation and structure make comparisons to banks difficult. We found that small business lending at credit unions with less than $10 billion in assets increased from about 2 percent to about 7 percent of their total lending from 2002 through 2011.[25] A recent study conducted on behalf of SBA found that credit union lending may have offset some of the decrease in small business lending at banks.[26] We recently reported that such loans can be risky for credit unions and have contributed to the failure of a number of credit unions.[27] Specifically, we reported that our analysis of NCUA and its Office of Inspector General's data indicated that member business loans contributed to 13 of the 85 credit union failures from January 2008 to June 2011. The Credit Union Membership and Access Act of 1998 contains a provision that limits business lending by credit unions to the lesser of 12.25 percent of total assets or 175 percent of net worth.[28] Experts and credit union officials told us that smaller credit unions may not be able to engage profitably in small business lending due in part to the lending cap. To engage in such lending, these officials told us a credit union has to develop business lending expertise and resources and may need to hire additional staff, but the cap may not allow them to make the volume of loans needed to cover these costs. Larger credit unions are able to make more loans under the cap and thus are better able to develop the necessary resources. Our analysis found that small business lending increased much more dramatically at credit unions with at least $100 million in assets from 2002 through 2011. Figure 4 shows that small business lending at these large credit unions increased from about 2 percent of total loans in 2002 to nearly 8 percent in 2011. While most credit unions do little or no agricultural lending, some credit unions have been chartered specifically to provide agricultural credit, and industry officials told us that these institutions play key roles in their communities.

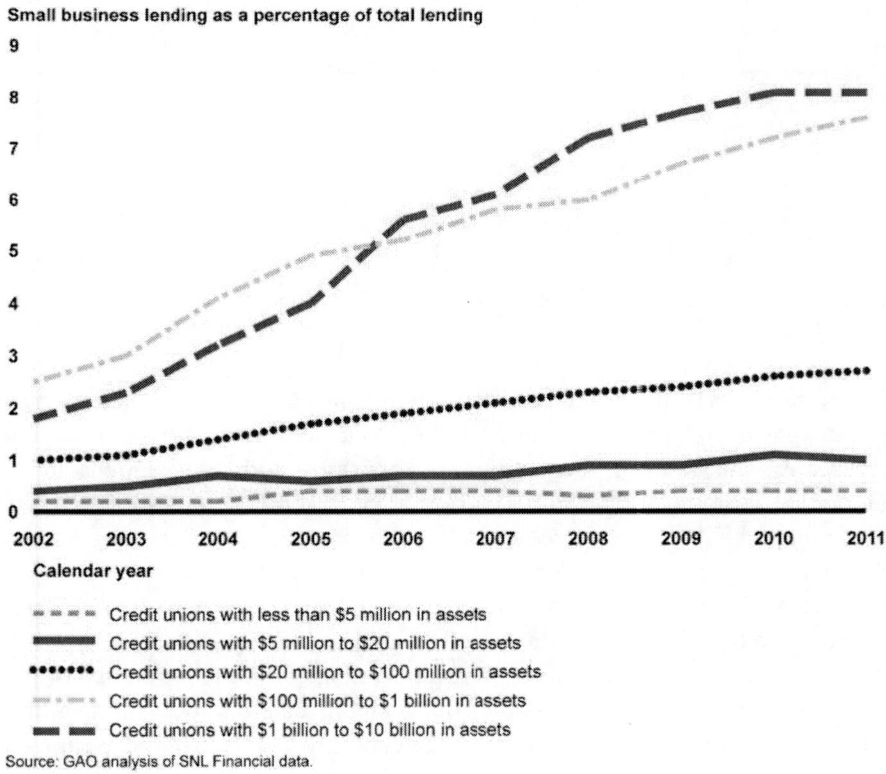

Figure 4. Credit Union Small Business Loans as a Percentage of All Loans from 2002 through 2011.

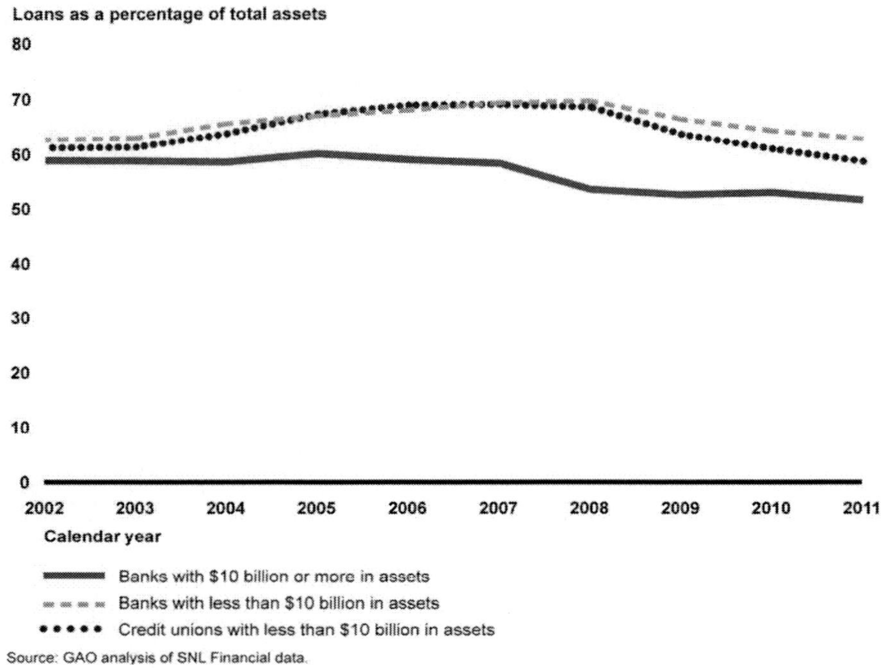

Figure 5. Loans as a Percentage of Total Assets at Banks and Credit Unions from 2002 through 2011.

Research has indicated that community banks and credit unions have advantages over larger banks in providing small business loans and loans in rural areas because of their direct relationships with and knowledge of individual customers. The 2003 study by Federal Reserve staff found that community banks have focused on “relationship banking,” basing lending decisions on personal knowledge of their customers and an understanding of their local economies. The study contrasted this approach to that of large banks, which often rely on data, credit scoring, and centralized decision making. FDIC staff noted that relationship lending gives community banks the ability to lend to borrowers without long credit histories, because it allows them to use nonstandard information to make profitable loans to customers who are seen as high risk by large banks. Experts we spoke with noted that small businesses often do not have audited financial statements and other data that may be used by large banks in credit scoring models. One expert stated that loans to small business and rural residents tend to have nonstandard terms and require knowledge of the personal or professional history of the business or person seeking the loan. As shown in figure 5, we found that loans make up a slightly greater proportion of their total assets, which suggests that community banks and credit unions may be more focused on traditional lending services than large banks.

MANY DODD-FRANK ACT PROVISIONS MAY AFFECT COMMUNITY BANKS AND CREDIT UNIONS, BUT THE FULL EXTENT OF THEIR IMPACT IS UNCERTAIN

The Dodd-Frank Act's reforms are directed primarily at large, complex U.S. financial institutions, and the act exempts small institutions, including community banks and credit unions, from several of its provisions. However, federal regulators, state regulatory associations, and industry associations collectively identified provisions within 7 of the act's 16 titles that they expect to impact community banks and credit unions. (See app. II for the Dodd-Frank Act provisions identified by the above entities.) We analyzed the impact of a number of these Dodd-Frank Act provisions and, in brief, found that:

- some provisions, including the depository insurance reforms and CFPB supervision of nonbank providers of financial services and products, have benefited or may benefit community banks and credit unions;
- certain of the act's mortgage reforms are expected to impose additional costs on community banks and credit unions, but their impact depends on future rule makings;
- the act's risk retention provision for securitizations is expected to initially have a limited impact on community banks and credit unions; and
- other provisions, including those covering proprietary trading, remittance transfers, and executive compensation, are expected to impose additional requirements on community banks and credit unions, but their impact depends partly on future rule makings.

Industry officials told us that determining which provisions will affect small institutions is difficult, because the impact may depend on how agencies implement certain provisions through their rules, and many of the rules needed to implement the act have not been finalized.[29] For the same reason, regulators and industry officials have noted that the full impact of the Dodd-Frank Act on community banks and credit unions is uncertain. Nonetheless, regulators and industry officials have noted that they expect that some of the act's regulations will increase regulatory requirements on community banks and credit unions and disproportionately affect them relative to larger banks because of their size. Moreover, some industry officials have expressed concern that the reforms targeting only large banks eventually will be applied to small institutions in varying degrees, for example, through industry best practices. In our interviews with officials from community banks and credit unions, several told us that they may reduce certain business activity or exit certain lines of business as a result of the new regulations. However, some also have cited benefits of particular provisions for smaller institutions.

As recognized by federal regulators, industry officials, and others, the Dodd-Frank Act contains several provisions to help minimize certain regulatory requirements on small institutions. For example, the act includes provisions that generally exempt (1) small bank holding companies from certain leverage and risk-based capital requirements, (2) small banks and credit unions from supervision by CFPB, (3) small debit card issuers from the debit interchange fee standards, and (4) small financial institutions from disclosure and reporting requirements for incentive-based compensation arrangements.[30] The Dodd-Frank Act also provides federal agencies with the authority to provide small institutions with relief from certain regulations. For example, the act and certain of the federal consumer financial laws provide CFPB with the authority to exempt covered persons or transactions from certain CFPB rules, and it directs the Commodity Futures Trading Commission (CFTC) and the Securities and Exchange Commission (SEC) to consider exempting small banks and credit unions from their swap clearing requirements.

CFPB, FDIC, the Federal Reserve, OCC, and NCUA have undertaken various efforts to reach out to community banks and credit unions outside of the examination process, in part to understand challenges being raised for them by the Dodd-Frank Act. Examples of such outreach efforts include the following:

- CFPB has created the Office of Small Business, Community Banks, and Credit Unions, to help it incorporate the perspectives of these institutions in its policy-making process, communicate relevant policy initiatives to them, and work with them to identify areas for regulatory streamlining. According to CFPB officials, CFPB has convened three small business panels in conjunction with SBA's Chief Counsel for Advocacy and the Office of Management and Budget's Office of Information and Regulatory Affairs.[31]

- FDIC has held roundtable discussions with community banks in each of its regions and a community bank conference. It is researching a variety of issues involving community banks and expects to issue its study by the end of 2012. In 2009, FDIC established the FDIC Advisory Committee on Community Banking to provide it with advice and guidance on policy issues affecting community banks, and the committee's meetings have included discussions of the Dodd-Frank Act.
- In October 2010, the Federal Reserve formed the Community Depository Institutions Advisory Council to provide the agency with direct insight and information from community bankers about supervisory matters and other issues of interest to community banks. In a recent testimony, a Federal Reserve official noted that the agency expects these ongoing discussions to provide a useful and relevant forum for improving its understanding of the effect of legislation, regulation, and examination activities on small banking organizations.[32]
- OCC has conducted a variety of outreach activities, including Meet the Comptroller events, chief executive officer roundtables, and teleconferences on topical issues. In preparation for the transfer of federal savings associations to OCC supervision, OCC presented numerous programs for thrift executives around the country to provide information and perspective on OCC's approach to supervision and regulation. OCC also has chartered advisory committees for federal savings associations with mutual charters and minority-owned institutions similar to those OTS had chartered.
- NCUA officials told us that to assist credit unions in complying with the Dodd-Frank Act, they have posted articles on their website, conducted a webinar with the CFPB director, and issued letters to credit unions on any rule changes.

As presented below, we analyzed a number of the Dodd-Frank Act provisions that regulators, industry officials, and others expect to impact community banks and credit unions. While several of these provisions have been implemented through finalized rules, most have not. The impact of those provisions will depend, in part, on how they are implemented by federal agencies through their regulations. As the act's impact on individual banks and credit unions will depend on their organizational form, mix of activities, or other factors, our analysis focused on assessing, where data were available, which of these institutions may be subject to the selected provisions. As part of our analysis, we also document industry and other views on the potential impact of the provisions and the status of regulations needed to implement the provisions. As noted above, assessing whether such provisions or their related regulations should apply to community banks and credit unions was beyond the scope of our work.

Some Provisions Have Reduced Costs or Provided Other Benefits

Some of the Dodd-Frank Act provisions that we analyzed have benefited or may benefit community banks or credit unions, such as by reducing costs.

Depository and Share Insurance Reforms

The Dodd-Frank Act's depository and share insurance reforms have reduced costs for community banks and increased consumer confidence to the benefit of community banks and credit unions. Title III of the Dodd-Frank Act includes several provisions reforming the Deposit Insurance Fund (DIF) and National Credit Union Share Insurance Fund.[33] For example, section 331 revised the method used to calculate DIF assessments.[34] Section 335 permanently increased the standard deposit and share insurance coverage amount from $100,000 to $250,000. Section 343 provided temporary unlimited deposit and share insurance coverage for non-interest-bearing transaction accounts, such as consumer checking accounts.

Section 331 required FDIC to redefine the DIF assessment base, generally basing it on average consolidated total assets rather than domestic deposits, on which it was previously based. According to FDIC, the change in the assessment base shifted some of the overall assessment burden from community banks to the largest institutions, which rely less on domestic deposits for their funding than smaller institutions, but without affecting the overall amount of assessment revenue collected. As shown in table 4, after the rule became effective on April 1, 2011, DIF assessments for community banks (those with less than $10 billion in assets) decreased in aggregate by $342 million, (33 percent) from the first to second quarter of 2011.[35] According to FDIC, this rule has resulted in a sharing of the DIF assessment burden that better reflects each group's share of industry assets. Officials from industry associations told us that they viewed this change as positive for community banks overall. In addition, officials from the two community bank state associations told us that assessments likely have decreased for their member institutions. Also, officials from five community banks told us that their assessments have either decreased or stayed about the same, but officials from three community banks told us that that their assessments had increased (one of these banks has between $1 billion to $10 billion in assets).

Section 335 made permanent the temporary increase of the maximum deposit and share insurance amounts from $100,000 to $250,000. Beginning in October 2008, the deposit and share insurance coverage had been increased temporarily to $250,000 to help consumers maintain confidence in the banking system and the marketplace.[36] These increases were made permanent and effective in August and September 2010, respectively.[37] According to FDIC, the higher insurance coverage level should help community banks attract and retain core deposits. Industry associations and officials from the community banks and credit unions we spoke with generally viewed the increase in insurance coverage as beneficial to community banks and credit unions.

Table 4. Change in Quarterly Insurance Assessments Primarily Due to the Change in the Assessment Base

Dollars in millions			
Asset size group	**First quarter 2011 assessments**	**Second quarter 2011 assessments**	**Percentage change**
Less than $100 million	$51	$33	-36
$100 million - $250 million	147	96	-35
$250 million - $500 million	160	104	-35
$500 million - $1 billion	180	123	-32
$1 billion - $10 billion	499	340	-32
Total of less than $10 billion	**$1,037**	**$695**	**-33**
Over $10 billion	2,423	2,836	17
Total of asset size groups	**$3,460**	**$3,531**	**2**

Source: FDIC.

Note: According to FDIC officials, at the same time the new assessment base was implemented, other assessment changes also were implemented that had a minor effect on the quarterly change in total assessments and the distribution of assets (e.g., a new large bank pricing scorecard and changes in bank ratings, assets, and capital during the quarter).

Section 343 provided temporary unlimited deposit and share insurance coverage for non-interest-bearing transaction accounts from December 31, 2010, through December 31, 2012.[38] According to FDIC, the 10.7 percent increase in insured deposits during 2011 was primarily attributable to growth in non-interest-bearing transaction account balances receiving temporary coverage.[39] However, according to an NCUA official, non-interest-bearing transaction accounts typically are held by businesses for payroll and accounts payable and, therefore, are less common at credit unions than at banks. Although this insurance program was designed to be a temporary response to financial instability, several industry associations representing banks are advocating for this provision to be extended. In addition, officials from two state associations representing community banks we spoke with said they expect the termination of the coverage to have a negative or very negative impact on their member institutions. In contrast, officials from the two state associations representing credit unions said they expect the termination would have no impact. But the responses from the individual community banks and credit unions were more mixed. Officials from five of the eight community banks and two of the four credit unions we spoke with said that they expect the termination of the coverage to have a negative or very negative impact on their institution. Officials from the other three community banks and two credit unions said that the termination would have no impact on their institution or it was too soon to determine the impact.

Exemption from Section 404(b) of the Sarbanes-Oxley Act

Section 989G of the Dodd-Frank Act eliminates an audit requirement for a number of small community banks and bank holding companies that are public companies.[40] In response to numerous corporate failures arising from corporate mismanagement and fraud, Congress passed the Sarbanes-Oxley Act of 2002 to help protect investors, in part by improving the accuracy, reliability, and transparency of corporate financial reporting and disclosures.[41] Specifically, section 404(a) of the Sarbanes-Oxley Act requires a public company's management to assess and report on the effectiveness of its internal controls over financial reporting. In turn, section 404(b) requires an independent auditor to attest to and report on management's assessment. Under SEC rules, non-accelerated filers (generally defined as public companies with a public float under $75 million) have been required to comply with section 404(a) for fiscal years ending on or after December 15, 2007.[42] However, before the passage of the Dodd-Frank Act, these filers were not required to comply with section 404(b) for fiscal years ending before June

15, 2010. SEC had provided such issuers with several extensions to the compliance dates in response to concerns about compliance costs and management's preparedness.

Section 989G of the Dodd-Frank Act amended the Sarbanes-Oxley Act to exempt non-accelerated filers from section 404(b).[43] Using SNL Financial data, we found that around 630 publicly traded financial institutions, including community banks and bank holding companies, identified themselves as non-accelerated filers.[44] These financial institutions may qualify for the exemption and not have to incur the audit-related costs to comply with section 404(b). In a 2009 survey, which included 99 public companies with a public float under $75 million, SEC's Office of Economic Analysis found that these companies had incurred a median (average) annual cost of $157,500 ($259,004) to comply with section 404(b) following reforms SEC made in 2007.[45] In our prior work, we found that smaller public companies faced disproportionately higher costs (as a percentage of revenues) in complying with section 404.[46]

Debit Interchange Fee Provision

Unlike large banks, community banks and credit unions generally have not, on average, experienced a significant decline in their debit interchange fees as a result of the Federal Reserve's implementation of section 1075 of the Dodd-Frank Act. Debit cards can be used to make noncash purchases at merchants. When a consumer uses a debit card to make a purchase, the merchant does not receive the full purchase amount. Part of the amount (called the merchant discount fee) is deducted and distributed among the merchant's bank, debit card issuer, and payment card network processing the transaction. Historically, the majority of the merchant discount fee was paid from the merchant's bank to the debit card issuer in the form of an interchange fee. Debit card interchange fees are established by card networks and ultimately paid by merchants to debit card issuers for each electronic debit transaction.

In July 2011, the Federal Reserve adopted Regulation II (Debit Card Interchange Fees and Routing) to implement section 1075 of the Dodd-Frank Act.[47] Regulation II establishes standards for assessing whether debit card interchange fees received by issuers are reasonable and proportional to the costs incurred by issuers for electronic debit transactions. The rule sets a cap on the maximum permissible interchange fee that an issuer may receive for an electronic debit transaction at $0.21 per transaction, plus 5 basis points multiplied by the transaction's value.[48] The fee cap became effective on October 1, 2011. However, the rule exempts from the fee cap issuers that have, together with their affiliates, less than $10 billion in assets, and transactions made using debit cards issued pursuant to government-administered payment programs or certain reloadable prepaid cards. In addition, Regulation II prohibits issuers and card networks from restricting the number of networks over which electronic debit transactions may be processed to less than two unaffiliated networks.[49] The rule further prohibits issuers and networks from inhibiting a merchant from directing the routing of an electronic debit transaction over any network allowed by the issuer.

Initial data collected by the Federal Reserve indicate that card networks largely have adopted a two-tiered interchange fee structure after the implementation of Regulation II, to the benefit of exempt issuers. According to the Federal Reserve, over 14,300 banks, credit unions, savings and loans, and savings banks qualified for an exemption from the debit card interchange fee cap during 2011.[50] Data collected by the Federal Reserve from 16 card networks show that all but 1 network provided a higher interchange fee, on average, to exempt issuers than nonexempt issuers after the rule took effect. The data also show that the average interchange fee received by exempt issuers declined by $0.02, or around 5 percent, after the rule took effect—declining from $0.45 over the first three quarters of 2011 to $0.43 in the fourth quarter of 2011.[51] During the same period, the interchange fee as a percentage of the average transaction value for exempt issuers declined from 1.16 percent to 1.10 percent.[52] In comparison, the average interchange fee received by issuers subject to the fee cap (nonexempt issuers) declined from $0.50 to $0.24, or by 52 percent, between the two periods. Our analysis of SNL Financial data shows that interchange fee income received by around 6,450 exempt banks increased, in aggregate, on a quarterly basis after the rule became effective, but the data do not allow us to determine why fee income increased, such as because of an increase in transaction volume. The aggregate interchange fee income reported quarterly by these banks from the second quarter of 2011 through the first quarter of 2012 was about $532 million, $547 million, $575 million, and $585 million, respectively.[53]

Although Regulation II has had a limited impact on exempt issuers to date, concerns remain about the potential for their interchange fees or fee income to decline over the long term. For example, industry officials and others have noted that (1) some merchants may steer customers to lower-cost payment options, even if networks maintain a two-tiered fee structure, (2) the prohibition on network exclusivity and routing restrictions may lead networks to lower their interchange fees, in part to encourage merchants to route debit card transactions through their networks, or (3) economic forces may cause networks not to maintain a two-tiered fee structure that provides a meaningful differential between fees for exempt and other issuers. Some merchants and others have noted that major card networks have adopted a two-tiered fee structure and have an incentive to maintain that structure to attract exempt issuers.[54] According to Federal Reserve officials, the agency plans to collect data annually that analyze the rule's impact on exempt issuer fees. It also plans to survey exempt issuers in 2012 to determine how much it cost them to comply with the network exclusivity prohibition and whether any merchants are refusing to accept their debit cards.

CFPB Provisions May Help Level the Regulatory Playing Field but also May Result in Additional Compliance Requirements

According to some regulators and industry officials, subjecting certain nonbank providers of financial services or products (nonbanks) to federal consumer protection laws and CFPB supervision may benefit community banks and credit unions by helping to level the regulatory playing field. Although community banks and small credit unions are not supervised by CFPB, they generally are subject to its regulations. CFPB's implementation of the Dodd-Frank Act's mortgage-related and other provisions are expected to impose additional requirements on community banks and credit unions. However, the impact of these regulations will depend on how CFPB implements such provisions and exercises its exemption authority. The Dodd-Frank Act established CFPB and authorized it to supervise certain nonbank financial companies and large banks and credit unions with over $10 billion in assets and their affiliates for consumer protection purposes. Before the Dodd-Frank Act, responsibility for administering and enforcing consumer financial laws for these entities was spread across several federal agencies. The act transferred supervisory and enforcement authority over a number of consumer financial institutions and services, as well as rule-making and enforcement authority (for those institutions it supervises) over many previously enacted consumer protection laws, to CFPB.[55]

CFPB Supervision of Nonbanks

To promote consistent enforcement of consumer protection laws, sections 1024, 1053, and 1054 of the Dodd-Frank Act provided CFPB with authority to supervise, examine, and take enforcement action against nonbanks, such as payday lenders and mortgage lenders and servicers.[56] Before the passage of the Dodd-Frank Act, there was no federal program to supervise nonbanks for compliance with consumer financial protection laws. The Federal Trade Commission had enforcement authority, but did not have the supervisory authority to regularly examine these entities or impose reporting requirements on them with respect to consumer financial protection law.[57] Nonbanks were primarily supervised by state regulators, whose authority and level of supervision varied. Under the Dodd-Frank Act, CFPB is authorized to supervise, based on statutory factors that focus on risk to consumers, nonbanks engaged in the residential mortgage industry, private education lending, and payday lending. For other financial services or product markets, CFPB's authority applies only to a "larger participant."[58] CFPB's supervisory authority also covers nonbanks that it has reasonable cause to determine are engaging, or have engaged, in conduct that poses risks to consumers with regard to the offering or provision of consumer financial products or services.[59] In January 2012, CFPB launched its nonbank supervision program, under which it examines such entities for, among other things, compliance with federal consumer financial laws.[60] According to CFPB, nonbanks will be identified for examination based on risks to consumers, including consideration of the company's asset size, volume of consumer financial transactions, extent of state oversight, and other relevant factors.[61]

Regulators and industry representatives expect CFPB supervision of nonbanks to benefit community banks and credit unions by leveling the regulatory playing field. For example, in 2011, an FDIC official testified that CFPB will likely reduce the unfair competitive advantage that nonbanks have long enjoyed as under-regulated—and often unregulated and unsupervised—financial services providers.[62] Industry officials have testified that community banks and credit unions did not engage in abusive lending practices and were not the cause of the financial crisis, and urged CFPB to focus its efforts on regulating nonbanks as many of the problems that led to the financial crisis began outside the regulated banking industry.[63] Officials from half of the 16 state associations, community banks, and credit unions we interviewed told us that they expect CFPB supervision of nonbanks to have a positive impact. Officials from three of these entities expect CFPB supervision to have no impact, three thought it was too soon to tell, and two thought it could have a negative impact.

CFPB Rule Making

The Dodd-Frank Act grants broad rule-making authority to CFPB, but requires it to coordinate with other federal agencies to ensure consistency in its regulation of consumer products and services. Although CFPB does not directly supervise community banks and small credit unions, its regulations generally apply to all banks and credit unions (and most nonbanks). According to CFPB, its rule-making activities have focused on two main areas: implementing protections required by the Dodd-Frank Act and streamlining inherited regulations. Pursuant to the Dodd-Frank Act, CFPB has proposed or finalized various regulations involving the mortgage market and international money transfers (discussed below). In December 2011, CFPB issued a notice requesting public comment on how to streamline existing regulations implementing federal consumer financial laws.[64]

Section 1022 of the Dodd-Frank Act permits CFPB to exempt any class of product or institution, including small institutions, from its regulations issued under Title X of the act. In issuing any such exemption, CFPB must take into account several factors, including the existing provisions of law applicable to the consumer financial product or service and the extent to which such provisions provide consumers with adequate protections. Furthermore, other federal consumer financial laws provided CFPB with varying degrees of exemption authority, generally with respect to classes of transactions where certain conditions are met. In a recent testimony, the CFPB Director said that when it is appropriate to treat smaller institutions differently from larger institutions, CFPB will consider doing so.[65] Similarly, CFPB staff told us that they will need to determine how much regulatory relief the agency will provide small institutions on a rule-by-rule basis.[66] For example, in early July 2012, pursuant to sections 1032(f), 1100A, and 1098 of the Dodd-Frank Act, CFPB proposed a rule to integrate mortgage disclosures required by two different mortgage-lending-related statutes into one form.[67] In the proposed rule, CFPB is considering exempting small entities (including some banks and credit unions with $10 billion or less in assets) from electronic data retention requirements to reduce their burden. In addition, CFPB is seeking comment on how much time industry needs to make any changes required in implementing the rule and whether small entities should have more time.[68]

While many consumer protection and mortgage reforms are not yet finalized, CFPB staff told us that they are in the process of proposing several additional regulations to provide guidance to the mortgage industry in implementing new reforms under the Dodd-Frank Act. As mandated by the statute, most of these rules are due in final form by January 21, 2013. However, industry representatives and others have expressed concern about the potential impact of CFPB regulations on community banks and credit unions. In congressional testimony and our interviews, industry representatives have said that they are hopeful that CFPB will be able to consolidate and simplify rules for all financial institutions. They also have noted that CFPB has conducted outreach efforts to obtain input on CFPB's activities. However, industry representatives expressed concern that the numerous new regulations from CFPB will impose additional regulatory burden and compliance costs on small institutions, potentially causing them to exit certain lines of business. Specifically, they cited concerns about the additional time, resources, and effort it would take their institutions to address new regulatory requirements. In particular, they were concerned about having to comply with numerous regulations issued around the same time by CFPB. Industry representatives also were concerned that the standardization of processes through CFPB regulations could reduce the ability of community banks and credit unions to offer differentiated products to better serve their communities. In congressional testimony and our interviews, community bank and credit union associations and representatives have emphasized that they believe these entities have a long history of serving customers fairly. Some commented that it is their opinion that CFPB regulations should not apply to them as they did not engage in the types of abuses that prompted the passage of the Dodd-Frank Act. Credit union representatives added that credit unions are owned by their members and, thus, have a strong incentive to treat their consumers well.

Mortgage Reforms Are Expected to Impose Additional Costs, but Their Impact Depends on Future Rule Makings

The Dodd-Frank Act's mortgage reform provisions are expected to impose additional costs on a large percentage of community banks and credit unions. However, the full cost to these entities will depend on the extent to which CFPB (and other agencies where appropriate) exercises its authority, where available, to exempt small institutions from any of its regulations and how it implements specific provisions that provide more limited relief to small institutions, particularly those operating in rural or underserved communities. The act's mortgage reforms include (1) additional origination and servicing requirements; (2) minimum standards for mortgage loans (including determining a borrower's ability to repay the loan); (3) limits on charges for mortgage prepayments; (4) expanding the definition of "high-cost mortgages" and protections that apply to such loans; (5) new disclosure requirements; (6) establishing various appraisal standards; and (7) requiring additional data elements to be reported under the Home Mortgage Disclosure Act (HMDA) reporting requirements.[69] The Dodd-Frank Act's mortgage reforms generally seek to address substandard residential mortgage lending practices that contributed to spikes in foreclosures and the 2007 through 2009 financial crisis. A key challenge in implementing these reforms is balancing the goals of protecting consumers from abuse and maintaining broad access to credit. Authority for implementing these reforms generally was transferred from the Federal Reserve to CFPB in July 2011.[70] CFPB has the rule-making authority for most of these regulations, and in other cases agencies are jointly responsible for rule making. While federal agencies have proposed a number of rules to implement the act's mortgage reforms, most of the required rules have not been finalized.

The Dodd-Frank Act's mortgage reforms could apply to and impact the vast majority of community banks and credit unions, given their involvement in mortgage lending. On the basis of our analysis of SNL Financial data, over 97 percent of community banks and over 70 percent of credit unions held residential mortgage loans in 2011. Over the past 5 years, community banks within different asset-sized categories generally dedicated about 30 percent of their lending portfolios to mortgage lending. However, mortgage lending by credit unions was more varied by asset size. As a percentage of a credit union's total lending portfolio in 2011, mortgage lending comprised, on average, over 50 percent for credit unions holding more than $100 million in assets, about 44 percent for those with $20 million to $100 million in assets, about 26 percent for those with $5 million to $20 million in assets, and about 7 percent for those with less than $5 million in assets.

Although the Dodd-Frank Act's mortgage reforms may affect the majority of community banks and credit unions, precisely how or to what extent the reforms will affect these institutions is uncertain. Many of the reforms have not yet been implemented; therefore, data do not exist to assess their impact. However, some regulators and industry representatives expect the potential cumulative effect of the mortgage reforms to increase the regulatory burden for smaller institutions, potentially leading them to decrease certain mortgage lending activities or, at the extreme, exit the mortgage business. In our interviews with state associations, community banks, and credit unions, officials from 9 of the 16 entities told us that they expected the act's mortgage reforms to decrease their or their member institutions' lending, but officials from seven of the entities told us it was too soon to determine the reforms' potential impact. Some officials also told us that the mortgage reforms may reduce community banks' and credit unions' advantage not only in serving niche markets (e.g., rural communities) by standardizing mortgage terms but also in making loans based on "soft information" by increasing the cost of providing these loans. Evaluating these concerns is difficult, especially given the CFPB's regulatory flexibility. As discussed in the previous section, the Dodd-Frank Act and federal consumer financial protection laws provide CFPB with varying amounts of exemptive authority with regard to particular transactions and circumstances. In addition, the Dodd-Frank Act's provisions that establish minimum standards for mortgage underwriting ("ability-to-repay" provision), additional escrow requirements, and appraisal standards provide some exceptions and regulatory relief for small institutions. These particular provisions were identified by regulators and industry representatives as potentially having a significant impact on community banks and credit unions.

Ability-to-Repay and Escrow Provisions

Sections 1411 and 1412 of Title XIV of the Dodd-Frank Act amended the Truth in Lending Act (TILA) by prohibiting creditors from making mortgage loans without regard to consumers' ability to repay them and establishing standards for making a reasonable and good faith determination based on verified and documented information. This reform was enacted to address the loosening of underwriting standards, which was partly responsible for the dramatic increase in mortgage delinquencies and foreclosures beginning in 2006. A creditor can meet the ability-to-repay requirement by satisfying certain underwriting factors, or the creditor may also be presumed to have satisfied the ability-to-repay requirement and receive some protection from liability if it originates a "qualified mortgage" (QM) as defined by criteria in the Dodd-Frank Act and implemented by CFPB. In other sections of subtitle B of Title XIV, the act sets steeper penalties for noncompliance with the requirements and allows consumers to cite ability-to-repay violations as a set off in foreclosures.

In a 2011 report, we examined five of the nine QM criteria specified in the Dodd-Frank Act for which sufficient data were available and generally found that most mortgages likely would have met the individual criteria for each year from 2001 through 2010.[71] However, we noted that the impact of the full set of QM criteria was uncertain, partly because data limitations made analysis of the other four criteria difficult and partly because CFPB could establish different criteria in developing final regulations. Consumer and industry groups indicated that the criteria specified in the act would likely encourage sound underwriting, but could also restrict the availability of and raise the cost of mortgage credit for some homebuyers. Provisions in the act and proposed regulations attempt to address some of these issues, in part by providing exemptions for certain loan products in certain locales, such as rural areas.

Within subtitle E of Title XIV, sections 1461 and 1462 of the Dodd-Frank Act amended TILA to expand escrow requirements for certain types of mortgage loans to enhance consumer protection.[72] Before the Dodd-Frank Act, regulations issued under TILA required that creditors establish escrow accounts for taxes and insurance for higher-priced residential mortgage loans.[73] The Dodd-Frank Act substantially codified these requirements and lengthened the time during which a mandatory escrow account established for a higher-priced mortgage loan must be maintained from 1 to 5 years. In addition, the act established additional disclosure requirements for escrow accounts.

Both the ability-to-repay and escrow provisions may provide some relief to creditors operating in predominantly rural or underserved communities. As discussed previously, smaller banks generally have higher levels of agricultural loans as a percentage of their total lending portfolios. In addition, some credit unions are chartered specifically to serve agricultural communities. Community banks and credit unions may make balloon loans to help ensure access to credit in rural or underserved communities where consumers may be able to obtain credit only from these institutions offering such loans and to hedge against interest rate risk. Section 1412 of the Dodd-Frank Act defines a balloon payment as a scheduled payment that is more than twice as large as the average of earlier scheduled payments. Under this provision, CFPB may by regulation allow some creditors, including those operating in predominantly "rural or underserved" areas, to make balloon-payment QMs that meet certain criteria. In other cases, balloon-payment loans may not be considered QMs, and creditors making these loans would not be protected from certain liabilities. The act provides a similar exemption from mandatory escrow requirements for similar types of creditors. To qualify for these exemptions, in both cases, creditors must operate in predominately rural or underserved areas, be under total annual asset and mortgage loan origination limits to be set by CFPB (initially set by the Federal Reserve, see following discussion), and retain their mortgage loans in their portfolios. The intent behind these exemptions is to preserve access to credit for consumers located in rural or underserved areas, where creditors may originate balloon loans to hedge against interest rate risk or higher-priced mortgages, but in volumes too small to justify the expense of establishing and maintaining escrow accounts for loans held in portfolio.

Before the transfer of rule-making authority for TILA to CFPB, the Federal Reserve proposed rules to implement both the ability-to-repay and escrow requirements. In May 2011, the Federal Reserve proposed regulations for compliance with the ability-to-repay provisions.[74] Its proposal provided a definition for a QM and, in accordance with the act, proposed that creditors with under $2 billion in assets operating predominantly in "rural or underserved" areas may make a balloon-payment QM that meets certain conditions. Due to the lack of available data, the agency requested comment on how to set a mortgage loan origination limit.[75] In March 2011, the Federal Reserve proposed rules for implementing the act's escrow requirements.[76] With respect to the exemption, the agency proposed a threshold of no more than 100 total mortgage loan originations a year and chose not to propose an asset-size threshold. In both rules, the Federal Reserve defined "underserved" areas as counties where not more than two creditors may make five or more mortgages a year and "rural" areas as counties classified by the U.S. Department of Agriculture as representing the most remote rural areas—where access to the resources of more urban communities and mobility is limited.[77]

In their comment letters on these proposed rules, community bank and credit union associations supported the intent of the reforms but were concerned about regulatory burden. One community bank association noted that the additional requirements could lead to an economic environment where only larger creditors would continue doing business, as they generally are better equipped to absorb increased regulatory costs. Industry representatives added that community banks and credit unions had not engaged in the abusive lending practices or substandard underwriting practices the mortgage provisions sought to address. For example, a community bank association noted that community banks have provided balloon loans in small communities for decades without problems and that these types of loans may be the only available credit option for consumers in rural communities. They also noted that many balloon loans would fall under the definition of higher-priced loans and, therefore, would be covered by the mandatory escrow requirement. In our interviews with state associations, community banks, and credit unions, officials from 8 of the 16 entities expected the ability-to-repay provisions to decrease their or their member institutions' mortgage lending, four thought the provisions would have no impact, and four thought it was too soon to tell.

For both of the proposed rules, a state regulatory association and several industry associations emphasized the importance of the exemptions for small institutions, but disagreed with how "underserved" and "rural" areas were defined and, in turn, proposed that their definitions be expanded. They said the proposed definitions were too narrow and complicated, and would exclude many community banks and credit unions that should be covered. A state regulatory association and industry associations also supported expanding these exemptions to cover all creditors holding loans in portfolio, maintaining that these institutions have an incentive to ensure higher standards of underwriting and retain the risk associated with consumers failing to pay taxes and insurance. With respect to the escrow requirements, industry representatives suggested increasing the proposed threshold of 100 loans.

As of August 2012, CFPB has not finalized either rule. In early June 2012, CFPB reopened the comment period for the proposed ability-to-repay rule. In particular, CFPB requested additional data on mortgage lending underwriting criteria and loan performance, as well as estimates of litigation costs and liability risks associated with claims alleging ability-to-repay requirement violations. CFPB expects to issue final rules for the ability-to-repay provisions and the escrow requirements by the end of this year. According to the Dodd-Frank Act, these provisions become effective 18 months after rule-making authority was transferred to CFPB (that is, January 21, 2013) if implementing regulations have not been issued. Where implementing regulations are issued by the deadline, the statutory provisions take effect when the rules take effect. In some cases, implementing rules must take effect within 12 months of issuance.

Appraisals

Subtitle F of Title XIV established additional appraisal requirements for mortgage lending. Among other provisions, section 1471 establishes additional requirements for "higher risk" mortgages.[78] Section 1472 of the act amends TILA to require that appraisers be independent to reduce any conflicts of interests. It declared the Home Valuation Code of Conduct, the previous standard for appraisal independence for loans purchased by Fannie Mae and Freddie Mac (the enterprises), to no longer be in effect but codified several of the code's provisions.[79] The intent of section 1472 is to better ensure that real estate appraisals used to support creditors' decisions are based on the appraiser's independent judgment, free of any influence from parties that may have an interest in the transaction. Among other requirements, section 1472 (1) prohibits coercion and bribery to influence the value of an appraisal, (2) prohibits appraisers from having a financial interest in property they are appraising, (3) prohibits a creditor from extending credit if it knows that a violation of appraisal independence has occurred, (4) mandates that the parties involved in the transaction report appraiser misconduct to state appraiser licensing authorities, and (5) mandates the payment of reasonable and customary compensation for appraisals.

CFPB, FDIC, the Federal Reserve, the Federal Housing Finance Agency (FHFA), OCC, and NCUA are jointly responsible for implementing the act's appraisal provisions. Section 1471 of the act provides the rule-making agencies discretion in exempting certain loans from its requirements.[80] In their August 2012 proposed rule, the agencies sought comment on whether the final rule should provide an exemption for certain appraisal requirements for higher-risk mortgage loans made in rural areas.[81] They also sought comment on whether the final rule should define "rural" areas as proposed in the ability-to-repay rule.[82] In October 2010, the Federal Reserve issued an interim final rule implementing section 1472.[83] The Federal Reserve included a safe harbor for compliance with prohibitions on conflicts of interest for employees and affiliates of creditors holding less than $250 million in assets. According to our analysis of SNL Financial data, about 65 percent of community banks and about 90 percent of credit unions held less than $250 million in assets in 2011. The agency noted that without allowances for staff and other limitations of smaller creditors, smaller creditors may decrease their lending, which could reduce credit availability and harm many consumers. Further, the agency stated that the federal banking agencies have long recognized that small institutions may be unable to achieve strict separation between valuation and loan underwriting staff, and the rule provides special guidance taking this limitation into account. Specifically, the interim final rule provides that the appraiser can be employed or affiliated with the creditor as long as (1) their compensation does not depend on the value of the appraisal and (2) the appraiser does not participate in the decision as to whether to make a loan or not.

In their comment letters on the interim final rule, several bank and credit union associations supported the intent and key aspects of the rule.[84] However, both a banking and a credit union association suggested that the safe harbor be expanded to include institutions with less than $1 billion in assets and that hold their loans in portfolio. Specifically, they noted that many smaller community banks are predominately portfolio creditors and often make lending decisions based on long-term relationships and experience in their communities, which would extend to any valuation activity. CFPB, FDIC, the Federal Reserve, FHFA, OCC, and NCUA share responsibility for jointly issuing any further final rules on appraisal requirements under section 1472, as well as implementing section 1471 and other appraisal provisions.

Risk Retention Provision Initially May Have a Limited Impact

The Dodd-Frank Act's risk retention provision for securitizations, found in section 941 of the act, is expected to have a limited initial impact on community banks and credit unions largely because of the limited nature of their current involvement in securitizations. However, as we recently reported, the implications of section 941 with respect to residential mortgage lending will depend on a variety of regulatory decisions and potential changes in the mortgage market that could affect the availability and cost of mortgage credit and the viability of a private mortgage securitization market.[85] In turn, such market changes could affect community banks and credit unions. As discussed in the previous section, our analysis of SNL Financial data found that over 97 percent of community banks and over 70 percent of credit unions held residential mortgage loans in 2011. To securitize residential mortgage loans, lenders may, in some cases, sell their loans to third parties, generating funds that they can use to make more loans. The third parties, or securitizers, bundle mortgages and sell them as investment products, called residential mortgage-backed securities (RMBS). Securitizers include investment banks, commercial banks, mortgage companies, and real estate investment trusts.[86] Types of RMBS sold in the secondary market are (1) Ginnie Mae-RMBS backed by cash flows from federally insured or guaranteed mortgages, (2) enterprise RMBS backed by mortgages that meet the criteria for purchase by the enterprises, and (3) private-label RMBS, which are backed by mortgages that may not meet some aspect of enterprise underwriting criteria.[87] Securitization typically is less expensive for lenders than raising funds directly, and it transfers some or all of the credit and interest rate risk from the lender to the investors. At the height of the mortgage boom, as demand for securitization of mortgage loans grew, lenders and securitizers were increasingly compensated based on loan volume rather than loan quality, contributing to a decline in underwriting standards.

Section 941 of the Dodd-Frank Act requires, in part, that mortgage securitizers retain a financial exposure of no less than 5 percent of the credit risk of any securitized residential mortgage that is not a "qualified residential mortgage" (QRM)—that is, one that does not meet certain underwriting criteria to be defined by the rule-making agencies (FDIC, the Federal Reserve, OCC, SEC, FHFA, and the Department of Housing and Urban Development).[88] The requirement mandates that securitizers of RMBS have an economic stake in the assets included in the securitizations they sponsor and, thus, an incentive to help ensure that lenders originate well-underwritten mortgages. In addition to the securitization of loans that meet the QRM criteria, the act exempts securitizations of government-insured or government-guaranteed mortgages (and certain other assets) from the risk retention requirement (excluding mortgages backed by the enterprises, which are currently in government conservatorship).[89] Although the purpose and scope of the QM and QRM provisions are somewhat different, they could be expected to work together by increasing lenders' and securitizers' exposure to the risks that are associated with mortgages whose features and terms may put borrowers at a higher risk of default and foreclosure.

Section 941 requires the rule-making agencies to jointly prescribe regulations for the risk retention requirement. The Dodd-Frank Act requires that in crafting the risk retention regulations, the rule-making agencies must specify, among other things,

- criteria for QRMs, taking into consideration underwriting and product features that historical loan performance data indicate result in a lower risk of default;[90]
- permissible forms of risk retention and the minimum duration for meeting the requirement;
- whether credit risk is to be allocated from securitizers to loan originators; and
- the possibility of permitting a lower risk retention requirement (less than 5 percent) for any non-QRM that meets underwriting standards that the agencies develop in regulations.

Federal banking and other agencies issued a proposed rule for the risk retention requirement in April 2011 but have not finalized the rule.[91] In the proposed rule, the agencies established criteria for QRMs, including that the mortgage, if made in connection with a purchase, must have a loan-to-value ratio of 80 percent or less.[92] The agencies also proposed that the full guarantee provided by the enterprises would satisfy the risk retention requirement for securitizations sponsored by the enterprises while they are under conservatorship with the capital support of the U.S Department of the Treasury. Although the Dodd-Frank Act places the responsibility for retaining risk on securitizers, it permits the agencies to require lenders to share the risk retention obligations. The proposed rule permits but does not require a securitizer to allocate a portion of its risk retention requirement to any lender that contributed at least 20 percent of the underlying assets to the asset pool underlying a securitization transaction.

In the proposed rule, the agencies, pursuant to the Regulatory Flexibility Act, estimated that the proposed requirement would not have a significant impact on a substantial number of small banking institutions (as defined by SBA as those with assets less than or equal to $175 million), at least under current market conditions.[93] Based on their analysis of Call Report data for the third quarter of 2010, FDIC, the Federal Reserve, and OCC identified over 6,200 small banking organizations under their supervision, of which 329 originated loans for securitization.[94] FDIC and OCC noted that they were aware of only six small banking organizations that sponsored securitizations. The regulators also noted that the small banks making securitized loans usually sell their loans to the enterprises, which retain credit risk through agency guarantees; thus, the banks would not be allocated credit risk under the proposed rule. In the proposed rule, for the purposes of their Regulatory Flexibility Act analysis, regulators estimated that most RMBS are collateralized by a pool of mortgages with aggregated balances of at least $500 million. Accordingly, under the proposed rule, a securitizer could allocate a portion of the risk retention requirement to a small banking organization only if the bank originated at least 20 percent ($100 million based on the above estimate) of the securitized mortgages. According to the regulators, only one small banking organization reported an outstanding principal balance of over $100 million in assets sold and securitized as of September 30, 2010. Using SNL Financial data, we expanded this analysis to include banks with less than $10 billion in total assets (our definition of "community bank") at year-end 2011. We found that over 890 of these banks originated loans for securitization, of which 9 reported an outstanding principal balance of over $100 million in assets sold and securitized, primarily residential mortgages.[95] NCUA officials said that there is limited Call Report data on credit unions' securitization of mortgage loans and stated that credit unions that do securitize mortgage loans usually sell their loans to the enterprises. Therefore, under the proposed rule, such credit unions would not be allocated credit risk because it has been transferred to the enterprises. Also, under the proposed rule, the enterprises would be required to retain the risk (and while under conservatorship, the enterprise guarantee would satisfy the risk retention requirement).

In our 2011 report, we reported that many industry stakeholders and consumer groups noted that the implications of the proposed risk retention rule depend on a variety of regulatory decisions and potential changes in the mortgage market.[96] These include decisions on the characteristics of QRMs that would be exempt from the risk retention requirement, the forms of risk retention that would be allowed, the percentage that securitizers would be required to hold, and the risk-sharing arrangements between securitizers and lenders. They noted that these factors could affect the availability and cost of mortgage credit and the future viability of the private-label RMBS market, which could impact all institutions involved in mortgage lending. In addition, several mortgage industry representatives indicated that smaller lenders, such as independent mortgage companies and small community banks, could lack sufficient capital resources to share risk retention obligations or hold non-QRMs that were not securitized on their balance sheets. As we reported, a few mortgage and securitization market participants told us that large lenders had the financial capacity to share risk retention obligations with securitizers or hold non-QRMs on their balance sheets, giving them an advantage over smaller lenders that could ultimately reduce competition in mortgage lending. Finally, a number of market participants noted that even if lenders were not required to share risk in the manner prescribed by the Dodd-Frank Act, securitizers could be expected to take steps to transfer the cost of risk exposure by paying lenders less for the mortgages they sold or requiring additional collateral to ensure the underwriting quality of the mortgages. But others noted that creditors would pass this cost on to borrowers and that the cost would likely be marginal.

In our interviews with state associations, community banks, and credit unions, officials from 8 of the 16 entities said that the QRM proposed rule would have a negative impact on community banks and credit unions and may cause them to decrease their mortgage lending. Five said that it was too soon to discern the impact of the proposed QRM rule, and three said the rule would have no impact. One bank noted that the risk retention requirement would likely curtail the availability of securitizers because of tighter guidelines for them and limit the bank's potential market. Officials from several banks and credit unions said that the risk retention requirement would not have any impact on their institution because they did not securitize any of their mortgage loans. One bank official said that his bank sells its loans in the private market and that its portion of the securitization is less than 20 percent; thus, the bank would not be affected by the provision as proposed.

Other Provisions May Impose Additional Costs or Other Compliance Requirements, but Their Impact Depends Partly on Future Rule Makings

A number of provisions are expected to impose additional costs or other requirements on certain community banks or credit unions. However, the extent to which these small institutions will be affected is largely uncertain, in part because the rules implementing the provisions have not been finalized.

Prohibitions against Proprietary Trading and Ownership of Certain Funds

Few community banks may be directly affected by the Dodd-Frank Act's proprietary trading prohibitions, but the federal regulators' proposed rules implementing this provision would create additional compliance responsibilities for community banks. Section 619 of the Dodd-Frank Act, also known as the Volcker Rule, amends the Bank Holding Company Act to prohibit banking entities from engaging in proprietary trading and having ownership interests in hedge funds and private equity funds (covered funds).[97] The provision's prohibitions are designed to restrain risk-taking and reduce the potential for federal support of entities covered by the provision. To implement the provision, four agencies proposed a joint rule that was published in the *Federal Register* in November 2011.[98] The restrictions and prohibitions in section 619 were to be effective the earlier of either a year after the issuance of final rules or July 21, 2012. As final rules have not yet been issued, the prohibitions became effective on July 21, 2012. Banking and nonbank entities covered by the provision generally will have 2 years to bring existing activities into conformance.[99] The act defines proprietary trading as the purchase or sale of securities, derivatives, commodities futures, or options on these instruments (covered positions) for the trading account of a banking entity or nonbank financial entity, as opposed to on behalf of a customer. The act further defines a trading account as any account used principally with the intent to profit from short-term price movements. The proposed rule implements statutory exemptions from the prohibition on proprietary trading for certain government securities, and for hedging, market-making, and underwriting activities. The proposed rule also provides guidance on the types of interests that are considered to be ownership interests in hedge funds, which commonly are understood to be investment vehicles that engage in active trading of securities and other financial contracts, and private equity funds, which commonly are understood to be funds that use leverage or other methods to invest in companies or other less-liquid investments.

Our analysis found that few community banks may be affected by the proposed rule's prohibitions, but data on proprietary trading and involvement with covered funds at community banks are limited. Thus, the exact number of institutions that may be affected by the proposed rule is unknown. Using SNL Financial data, we found that about 1 percent of banks with more than $100 million and less than $10 billion in assets reported having financial instruments that may fall under the definition of a covered position in their trading accounts at the end of 2011. In previous analysis conducted on proprietary trading in July 2011, we found that most proprietary trading has been conducted by the largest bank holding companies.[100] However, because banks with less than $100 million in total assets or less than $2 million in trading assets are not required to report their trading assets in Call Reports by the type of financial instrument, not all community banks involved in proprietary trading may be captured in the data.[101] Further, Call Reports do not require banks to report ownership stakes in covered funds, so we could not estimate the number of community banks that may be affected by this prohibition.

Despite the small percentage of community banks that may be affected by the Dodd-Frank Act's proprietary trading and covered fund prohibitions, the proposed rules could have an impact on community banks due to their compliance requirements. The proposed rules have a tiered compliance program, which was not expressly part of the act but could apply to all banks. Under the proposed rules, banks that do not engage in any covered trading or fund activities must ensure that their existing investment policies and procedures include measures that are designed to prevent them from becoming engaged in prohibited activities in the future, for example, by limiting their authorized investments to those exposures exempt from the prohibition.[102] Banks engaging in covered activities under the proposed rules must establish a six-part compliance framework to demonstrate that their activities are allowed by one of the rules' exemptions.[103] Specific exemptions also have additional compliance requirements. For example, to use the exemption for risk-mitigating hedging, banks must be able to demonstrate that their hedging positions are reasonably correlated with specific risks. Our analysis of SNL Financial data on over-the-counter (OTC) derivatives found that about 15 percent of community banks held derivatives for purposes other than trading, such as hedging risk. The extent to which the risk mitigating hedging provision may affect community banks will depend on the requirements or standards that the regulators establish for demonstrating that a hedge is reasonably correlated with specific risks and whether such correlations must be on a transaction or portfolio basis. The proposed rule did not include any specific exemptions from the compliance requirements for small institutions, so if the proposed rules were adopted, these banks may have to expand their compliance frameworks to accommodate any additional hedging requirements imposed by the rule.

Although the impact of the proposed rules' compliance requirements on community banks still is unknown, industry associations have expressed concern that the rules will impose an undue burden on small banks. As part of the proposed rules, the regulators considered the impact of the rules on small entities in accordance with the Regulatory Flexibility Act, and concluded that the compliance requirements in the proposed rule would not result in a significant economic impact on a substantial number of small entities. However, one industry association expressed concerns in its comment letter that the proposed rule will adversely affect community banks. The association noted that it would be costly for banks with no covered activities to amend their compliance policies and procedures, but did not estimate the anticipated increase in compliance costs for these institutions. The industry association also recommended that community banks that occasionally engage in interest rate swaps to hedge their interest rate risk be able to do so without meeting the compliance requirements for that exemption because these requirements are more extensive. However, the level of compliance burden may be relatively small for most community banks, given that the proprietary trading provisions do not apply to types of exposures that comprise the investment portfolio of most of the smaller community banks.

Swap Provisions

The Dodd-Frank Act's swap provisions under Title VII may impose additional costs on the fraction of community banks currently using swaps, but CFTC and SEC have taken steps to help minimize the burden. A swap is a type of derivative that involves an ongoing exchange of one or more assets, liabilities, or payments for a specified period.[104] Unlike exchange-traded derivatives, swaps traditionally have been traded in the OTC market and generally have not been cleared through clearinghouses.[105] Financial and nonfinancial firms use swaps and other OTC derivatives to hedge risk, speculate, or for other purposes, but the market is dominated by a limited number of dealers.[106] According to the Financial Stability Oversight Council, OTC derivatives, with the exception of credit risk transfer products, generally were not a central cause of the recent financial crisis but were a factor in the propagation of risks, as their complexity and opacity contributed to excessive risk taking and a lack of clarity about the ultimate distribution of risks.[107]

Title VII of the Dodd-Frank Act establishes a new regulatory framework for swaps to reduce risk, increase transparency, and promote market integrity in the financial system. The act authorizes CFTC to regulate "swaps," and SEC to regulate "security-based swaps" (hereafter collectively referred to as swaps).[108] Among other things, Title VII (1) provides for the registration and regulation of swap dealers and major swap participants; (2) imposes clearing and trade execution requirements on swaps, subject to certain exceptions; and (3) creates record-keeping and real-time reporting regimes. CFTC and SEC are continuing to implement Title VII through their rule makings. According to Davis Polk, CFTC, SEC, and other regulators have finalized 43 of the 90 rules required under Title VII (as of July 2, 2012).

As shown in table 5, Call Report data aggregated by FDIC show that 1,101 of the 7,250 community banks (15 percent) held derivatives in 2011. According to industry officials, community banks typically use swaps to manage their exposure to interest rate risk or to help customers meet their risk management needs. Indeed, banks with $10 billion or less in total assets held nearly $88.8 million (notional amount) in derivatives at year-end 2011, of which $82.4, nearly 93 percent, was interest rate derivatives. Table 5 also shows that a considerably higher percentage of larger community banks hold derivatives than smaller community banks, but the use of derivatives within each asset-size class increased over the past 5 years. In 2011, for instance, over 50 percent of banks with over $1 billion to $10 billion held derivatives, but around 3 percent of banks with less than $100 million in assets held derivatives. In contrast to community banks, federally chartered credit unions have been prohibited by NCUA from engaging in derivatives, except through a pilot program.[109] In view of the Dodd-Frank Act's clearing requirements and its pilot program experience, NCUA is reconsidering whether to permit credit unions to engage in derivatives to hedge risk.[110]

Table 5. Number of Banks with $10 Billion or Less in Total Assets and Number of These Banks Holding Derivatives from 2007 through 2011

Reporting institutions	2007		2008		2009		2010		2011	
	Number	Percentage	Number	Percentage	Number	Percentage	Number	Percentage	Number	Percentage
Less than $100 million in total assets										
Reporting banks	3,440		3,131		2,845		2,622		2,416	
Reporting banks with derivatives	67	2	82	3	86	3	95	4	84	3
$100 million to $1 billion in total assets										
Reporting banks	4,425		4,499		4,495		4,368		4,284	
Reporting banks with derivatives	632	14	663	15	663	15	702	16	723	17
Over $1 billion to $10 billion in total assets										
Reporting banks	549		561		565		560		550	
Reporting banks with derivatives	264	48	273	49	295	52	290	52	294	53
All banks with $10 billion or less than total assets										
Reporting banks	8,414		8,191		7,905		7,550		7,250	
Reporting banks with derivatives	963	11	1,018	12	1,044	13	1,087	14	1,101	15

Source: GAO analysis of FDIC's Banking Quarterly Profile, Fourth Quarter 2007 through Fourth Quarter 2011.

Community bank and other industry officials have raised concerns about the potential for Title VII provisions or related regulations to impede the ability of community banks to use swaps. One concern is that community banks entering into swaps with customers could be required to register as swap dealers, unless they qualify for an exemption, and therefore be subject to capital, margin, business conduct, and other regulations. CFTC and SEC finalized their rule defining, among other things, a swap dealer.[111] The final rule excludes persons engaged in a *de minimis* amount of swap-dealing activity from the definition of a swap dealer.[112] Based on our analysis of SNL Financial data, we identified over 1,000 community banks that held OTC derivatives at year-end 2011. The data provided a snapshot of the notional amount of a bank's derivatives activity, but did not indicate the value of derivatives entered into in the previous year, which is needed to determine whether any of the banks we analyzed met the definition of a swaps dealer. However, the bank with the highest notional amount of OTC derivatives held around $4.1 billion, which is considerably below the *de minimis* amounts set by CFTC and SEC for CFTC-regulated swaps and SEC-regulated credit default swaps. In addition, as directed by the Dodd-Frank Act, CFTC and SEC's rule excludes from the swap dealer definition banks that enter into a swap with a customer in connection with originating a loan with that customer and meet other conditions specified under the rule.

Another concern raised by industry officials is that community banks, unless exempted, could be required to clear their swaps through a clearinghouse, which would impose additional costs on them. Title VII requires those swaps that CFTC or SEC determines must be cleared to be cleared through a clearinghouse, but provides an exception from the clearing requirement to end-users that are not financial entities and use these swaps to hedge or mitigate commercial risk. CFTC and SEC are required to consider whether to except, among others, small banks and credit unions from the definition of financial entity and thereby provide them with an exception from the mandatory requirement. In July 2012, CFTC adopted a final rule that exempts banks, savings associations, farm credit system institutions, and credit unions with total assets of $10 billion or less from the definition of "financial entity," making such "small financial institutions" eligible for the end-user exception.[113] As noted above, community banks' derivatives activities are limited largely to interest rate derivatives, which are regulated by CFTC. In December 2010, SEC proposed rules that would allow small banks and credit unions to use the end-user exception from mandatory clearing created by the Dodd-Frank Act.[114]

Even if community banks were provided with an exception from the mandatory swap clearing requirements, community bank officials are concerned that their noncleared swaps could be subject to margin requirements set by CFTC, SEC, or prudential regulators.[115] According to an industry association, margin requirements could make it difficult or impossible for many community banks to continue using swaps. CFTC and the prudential regulators have issued proposed regulations for noncleared swaps.[116] CFTC's proposal would not impose margin requirements on nonfinancial entities.[117] The prudential regulators' proposal would impose margin requirements on nonfinancial entities but categorize them as lower-risk, requiring the dealer to collect margin from a nonfinancial entity only when the dealer's exposure to the entity exceeded whatever credit limit the dealer has established for that particular customer, after evaluation of the customer's particular financial repayment capacity.[118]

According to FDIC staff, under long-standing banking agency guidance that predates the Dodd-Frank Act, a dealer bank engaging in an interest rate or other derivative with a community bank would not be expected to collect margin as long as the dealer bank's exposure to the community bank was below the credit exposure limits that the dealer bank had established under its credit assessment processes and procedures. FDIC staff noted that the joint margin rule proposed by the prudential regulators reiterates this long-standing interagency safety and soundness guidance and that the proposed rule would effectively maintain the status quo with respect to commercial banks that are end-users of interest rate or other derivatives.[119]

Remittance Transfer Provision

Section 1073 of the Dodd-Frank Act imposes new requirements on remittance transfers (typically money transferred from consumers to their families or friends in other countries) that likely will increase costs for community banks and credit unions, but it also provides some temporary regulatory relief.[120] This provision established new consumer protections for remittance transfers, including most electronic wire transfers sent by consumers in the United States to individuals and businesses in other countries. In February 2012, CFPB issued a final rule to implement section 1073 and provided a 1-year implementation period, making the rule effective in February 2013.[121] The rule generally requires transfer providers to provide disclosures and receipts to consumers who provide the exact price of the remittance transfer, exchange rate, amount of currency to be delivered, and date of the funds' availability. In addition, the rule generally provides that consumers have 30 minutes to cancel a transaction after payment and the ability to dispute errors related to the transfer.[122] NCUA analysis of Call Report data estimated that about 10 percent of all credit unions offered remittance services in the fourth quarter of 2011. Although comparable data on remittance services do not exist for community banks, a recent Federal Reserve study found that most U.S. depository institutions process international wire transfers on behalf of their customers.[123]

Industry associations have questioned the ability of institutions that use open networks to make remittance transfers, such as community banks and credit unions, to continue to provide such services because of their difficulty in complying with the rule's disclosure requirements.[124] These associations suggested that open network transfer providers be given regulatory relief. In addition, two industry associations commented that the final rule does not level the playing field for consumer financial products, as it favors remittance transfer providers that use closed networks, such as nonbank institutions. In the February final rule, CFPB noted that it does not plan to provide an exemption for open network transfers, because the Dodd-Frank Act clearly covers these types of transfers.[125] However, insured depository institutions, including community banks and credit unions, are provided with a temporary statutory exemption that allows them to provide estimated disclosures for certain information, including exchange rates and foreign fees and taxes, in certain circumstances rather than exact pricing. This exemption expires on July 21, 2015, but CFPB may extend the exemption for an additional 5 years. In addition, to reduce the compliance burden for institutions that provide remittance services outside of their normal course of business, CFPB has excluded from disclosure requirements those institutions that provide 100 or fewer remittance transfers per year.[126]

Officials from 5 of the 12 community banks and credit unions we spoke with said their institutions offer remittance services, and officials from two of the four state associations we spoke to said that they have members that offer remittance services. Of this group, officials from five of the entities expect that the new remittance transfer rule to decrease their (or their member institutions') remittance transfer business. In particular, one credit union official told us that his institution may exit this line of business due to the increased disclosure requirements.

Executive Compensation Provisions

Subtitle E of Title IX of the Dodd-Frank Act will provide investors with more input on executive compensation practices, but may impose additional compliance requirements on certain publicly traded community banks and publicly traded companies that hold community banks. According to the Dodd-Frank Act's legislative history, Subtitle E of Title IX is intended to address executive compensation practices that promoted excessive risk taking.[127] The title contains a number of provisions intended to provide shareholders with greater influence over, and insight into, the activities of publicly traded companies. For example, section 951 requires shareholder advisory votes on executive compensation and "golden parachutes." Section 953 requires disclosure of pay versus performance and the ratio between the chief executive officer's total compensation and median total compensation for other employees. Section 954 requires listed companies to develop and implement clawback policies for incentive-based compensation.[128] Based on our analysis of SNL Financial data, we identified approximately 200 publicly traded community banks and approximately 1,200 community banks held by public companies, some of which may be affected by these provisions.[129]

Section 951 amends the Securities Exchange Act of 1934 to require public companies subject to the proxy rules to conduct a separate shareholder advisory vote on compensation for executives ("say-on-pay") at least every 3 years and a vote on the frequency of these votes at least every 6 years ("say-on-frequency").[130] The amendment also requires a shareholder advisory vote on whether to approve certain golden parachute compensation arrangements in connection with a business combination.[131] Section 951 provides that SEC may exempt an issuer from the advisory voting requirements. In determining whether to make an exemption, SEC is to take into account, among other considerations, whether the requirements disproportionately burden small issuers.

SEC issued a final rule implementing section 951, which became effective in April 2011.[132] In commenting on the proposed rule, two industry associations recommended that community banks be exempted from the rule because they believe it will add significant burdens. While SEC did not exempt community banks from the rule, it extended the compliance date for the say-on-pay and say-on-frequency advisory votes for smaller reporting companies and newly public companies that qualify as smaller reporting companies, so that they will not be required to comply until the first annual or other shareholder meeting occurring on or after January 21, 2013.[133] According to SEC, this deferral served, in part, to allow those companies to better prepare for implementation of the rules.

Section 953(a) requires public companies subject to the proxy rules to provide disclosure about pay versus performance, and section 953(b) requires reporting companies to disclose the ratio between the chief executive officer's total compensation and the median total compensation for all other company employees.[134] An industry association commented that the provision would require complex financial calculations and potentially expand the universe of persons subject to executive compensation disclosure requirements. In addition, the association suggested that SEC should exempt community banks from this provision, in light of SEC's recognition that the compensation arrangements at smaller reporting companies generally are less complex than at other public companies. SEC has not yet proposed a rule to implement this provision.

Section 954 prohibits securities exchanges from listing securities of issuers that have not developed and implemented incentive-based compensation clawback policies. In addition, it prohibits exchanges from listing securities of issuers that have not disclosed incentive-based compensation policies. According to the Dodd-Frank Act's legislative history, the purpose of this provision is to prevent executives from retaining compensation that they were awarded erroneously.[135] An industry association has commented that this provision could make it more difficult for community banks to attract and retain qualified officers and could make privately held community banks reluctant to become publicly traded companies. The industry association suggested that SEC should exempt community banks from this provision. SEC has not yet proposed a rule to implement this provision.

Incentive-Based Compensation Provision

The Dodd-Frank Act's incentive-based compensation provision, section 956, will require a small percentage of community banks and credit unions to report incentive-based compensation. Specifically, section 956 requires that financial institutions with $1 billion or more in total assets disclose the structures of all incentive-based compensation arrangements to their federal regulators.[136] The required disclosures will be used to determine whether the compensation structure provides excessive compensation, fees, or benefits, or could lead to a material financial loss to the institution, which section 956 also requires the regulators to prohibit. According to our analysis of SNL Financial data, most community banks and credit unions would not be subject to this provision. Our analysis indicates that, as of year-end 2011, around 7 percent of community banks and around 3 percent of credit unions have between $1 billion and $10 billion in assets and, therefore, could be subject to the provision.[137]

The responsible rule-making agencies jointly issued a proposed rule to implement section 956 in April 2011, but a final rule has yet to be issued as of August 2012.[138] Under the proposed rule, financial institutions with $1 billion or more in assets would be required to report incentive compensation arrangements annually to their appropriate regulators. However, pursuant to section 956, specific compensation to individuals will not be disclosed. Incentive compensation arrangements that encourage inappropriate risks through excessive compensation or pose a risk of material financial loss to an institution would be prohibited. Incentive compensation would be considered excessive when amounts paid are unreasonable or disproportionate to, among other things, the amount, nature, quality, and scope of services performed. In addition, larger financial institutions—such as banks with $50 billion or more in assets and credit unions with $10 billion or more in assets—would be subject to additional incentive compensation rules. Incentive compensation would be deemed to lead to material financial loss unless the arrangement fulfills certain requirements, including balancing risk and financial rewards and involving effective risk management and strong corporate governance.

In their comment letters, industry associations suggested changes to the proposed rule to benefit community banks and credit unions. One industry association suggested that the final rule be phased in over a longer time period for institutions with assets between $1 billion and $10 billion. Another industry association suggested that institutions with $15 billion or less in assets with few incentive compensation arrangements should be required to disclose incentive-based compensation plans once every 2 years, rather than annually, to relieve excessive disclosure requirements for smaller institutions. Also, several industry associations commented that the definition of excessive incentive compensation was overly broad and should be narrowed. Of the 12 banks and credit unions we interviewed, three of these institutions had more than $1 billion in assets and may be subject to this rule, and officials from all three of these institutions told us that they offer incentive compensation. Two officials expect the proposed rule, if adopted, to have no impact on their institutions, and the other official said that it was too soon to judge what the impact would be.

Required Registration of Municipal Advisors

Section 975 of the Dodd-Frank Act requiring the registration of municipal advisors may or may not affect the majority of community banks, depending on how SEC interprets "municipal advisor" in its final rule. Section 975 amended section 15B of the Securities Exchange Act to require municipal advisors, who previously were largely unregulated, to register with SEC like investment advisers. Before the Dodd-Frank Act, some municipal advisors were involved in, among other abuses, "pay-to-play" scandals—that is, influencing the award of business through political contributions—and recommended unsuitable investments to small municipalities. Section 975 also authorizes the Municipal Securities Rulemaking Board to develop professional standards, continuing education requirements, and business conduct requirements for municipal advisors. SEC proposed a rule to implement section 975 but has not yet finalized the rule.[139] The proposed rule requires institutions that meet the definition of a "municipal advisor" to submit registration documents to SEC detailing their organizational structure, business activities, and other information. Further, the proposed rule would require employees at institutions that meet the definition of a municipal advisor to register with SEC.

The definition of "municipal advisor" in the proposed rule could cover many community banks. SEC noted in the proposed rule that the statutory definition of a "municipal advisor" in the Dodd-Frank Act is "broad and includes persons that traditionally have not been considered to be financial advisors.[140]" The rule identifies three general types of municipal advisors: (1) financial advisors that provide advice to municipal entities with respect to their issuance of municipal securities and municipal financial products, (2) investment advisers that advise municipal pension funds and other municipal entities on the investment of funds held by or on behalf of municipal entities, and (3) third-party marketers and solicitors.

The proposed rule noted that while some types of financial advisors were exempted in the statutory language, banks were not included in the exemptions. The proposed rule also notes that every bank account of a municipal entity is comprised of funds held by or on behalf of a municipal entity. Thus, if the rule is finalized as proposed, community banks that provide advice to municipal entities with respect to traditional depository services could be considered municipal advisors. If community banks providing such advice to municipal entities are included in the definition of municipal advisors, community banks and the individual employees that provide these services would need to register with SEC, who may be a new regulator for many community banks.

We used SNL Financial data to estimate the number of community banks with deposits from municipal entities and found that around 82 percent of banks with less than $10 billion in assets had deposits from municipal entities at the end of 2011. In the proposed rule, SEC analyzed the anticipated initial compliance burden for the registration requirement, and estimated that the institutions would spend 6.5 hours completing the registration, on average, and individuals would spend 3 hours, on average.

In the proposed rule, SEC sought comment on whether the definition of a municipal advisor should exclude banks to the extent that the bank provides advice to a municipal entity about traditional banking products, such as deposit accounts. Industry associations commented that banks should be explicitly exempted in the proposed rule because their activities are already supervised by federal and state banking regulators. However, SEC noted that federal and state banking regulators supervise banks for safety and soundness purposes and not the quality of the investment advice they provide to their municipal entity clients. SEC also received several comment letters from members of Congress who noted that it was not the intent of Congress to include traditional banking in the definition of municipal advice. SEC is reviewing the comments it has received as it develops a final rule, and SEC staff commented that the agency expects to implement its new oversight responsibilities for municipal advisors after careful consideration of the comments received.

Too Early to Determine the Impact of the Dodd-Frank Act on Community Banks' and Credit Unions' Small Business Lending

Regulators and industry officials have noted that the full impact of the Dodd-Frank Act on community banks and credit unions remains uncertain. Industry officials also have noted that it generally is too soon to determine the act's overall impact on community banks' and credit unions' ability to lend to small businesses. According to our analysis of SNL Financial data, almost 90 percent of community banks and about one-third of credit unions held loans to small businesses in 2011. Although any provision in the Dodd-Frank Act that affects these institutions could impact their customers (including small businesses), officials from federal agencies, state regulatory associations, and industry associations we interviewed identified only one provision in the Dodd-Frank Act (discussed below) that may directly impact community banks' and credit unions' ability to lend to small businesses. As discussed above, community banks are important lenders to small businesses. Over the past decade, community banks have done more small business lending as a percentage of their total lending than large banks, although large banks have done more small business lending overall. Small business lending by credit unions with less than $10 billion in assets has increased over the past decade from 2 percent to about 7 percent of their total lending.

Although a number of provisions may ultimately impact lending by smaller institutions, section 1071 was the only Dodd-Frank Act provision identified by regulators and industry representatives as potentially having a direct impact on small business lending by community banks and credit unions. Section 1071 amends the Equal Credit Opportunity Act to require financial institutions to collect and report information concerning credit applications made by women-owned, minority-owned, and small businesses. The provision serves, among other purposes, to facilitate the enforcement of fair lending laws. CFPB expects to undertake action to implement section 1071 in June 2013.

Industry officials and others have expressed concerns about section 1071. According to industry and regulatory officials, the reporting requirements will increase the costs associated with small business lending. Industry officials also have noted that the reporting requirements could lead community banks and credit unions to develop standardized criteria for their small business lending to avoid being criticized or penalized by regulators for being discriminatory. They added that such standardization could then result in less lending to small businesses. Officials from 12 of the 16 state associations, community banks, and credit unions we spoke with expect this provision to negatively affect their institutions or member institutions, and four officials said it was too soon to tell how this provision would affect their institutions.

We also asked officials from the 16 state associations, community banks, and credit unions if they expected the Dodd-Frank Act generally to impact the amount of small business lending conducted by their institutions. Officials from 11 of these entities told us it was too soon to tell, although two officials said the Dodd-Frank Act would have no impact. Officials from three of the entities said that they expected the act to decrease their small business lending. In our interviews, industry officials also said that the Dodd-Frank Act provisions cumulatively could increase their compliance and other costs and adversely affect their competitiveness in the small business lending market.

AGENCY COMMENTS AND OUR EVALUATION

We provided a draft of this chapter to CFPB, FDIC, the Federal Reserve, OCC, NCUA, SBA, and SEC for review and comment. CFPB and NCUA generally agreed with our report. In addition, CFPB, FDIC, OCC, and SEC staff provided technical comments, which we have incorporated, as appropriate. The Federal Reserve and SBA did not provide any comments.

In its comment letter, CFPB generally agreed with the report's analysis of the role played by community banks and credit unions in the economy and discussion of CFPB's responsibilities in implementing Dodd-Frank Act reforms. CFPB further elaborated on the status of its rule makings related to mortgage reforms and efforts to seek input from small businesses, community banks, and credit unions about the impacts and potential alternatives for its rule-making initiatives.

Although generally agreeing with our report, NCUA commented on a finding that we cited from a GAO report issued in January 2012.[141] NCUA noted that it does not believe there is sufficient evidence to suggest that member business loans pose a higher risk to credit unions or that a key driver in credit union failures is commercial loans. In our prior report, our analysis of NCUA's and its Office of Inspector General's data indicated that member business loans contributed to 13 of the 85 credit union failures from January 2008 to June 2011.

Lawrance L. Evans, Jr.
Acting Director, Financial Markets and Community Investment

APPENDIX I. SCOPE AND METHODOLOGY

Our objectives in this chapter were to examine (1) significant changes that community banks and credit unions have undergone in the past decade, including the factors that have contributed to such changes, and (2) the Dodd-Frank Wall Street Reform and Consumer Protection Act (Dodd-Frank Act) provisions that regulators, industry associations, and others expect to impact community banks and credit unions, including their small business lending.[142]

To address our first objective, we reviewed and analyzed studies by regulators, industry associations, and academics. We conducted searches of social science, economic, and federal research databases, including EconLit, Fed-in-Print, Google Scholar, and JSTOR, to identify relevant studies on community banks and credit unions, including their lending to small businesses. To help us identify relevant studies, we also relied on federal agencies, including the Board of Governors of the Federal Reserve System (Federal Reserve), Federal Deposit Insurance Corporation (FDIC), Office of the Comptroller of the Currency, National Credit Union Administration (NCUA), and Small Business Administration; state regulatory associations (the Conference of State Bank Supervisors and National Association of State Credit Union Supervisors); industry associations (the American Bankers Association, Credit Union National Association, Independent Community Bankers of America, National Association of Federal Credit Unions, National Federation of Independent Business, and Main Street Alliance); and academic or other experts.[143] Although we found these studies to be sufficiently reliable for the purposes of our report, the results should not necessarily be considered as definitive, given the potential methodological or data limitations contained in the studies individually and collectively. Moreover, the studies investigating economies of scale and consolidation generally address the relationship in a manner that limits the ability to make definitive causal claims. In addition, we analyzed data from SNL Financial, a private financial database that contains publicly filed and financial reports, including Consolidated Reports on Condition and Income (Call Reports) submitted to FDIC, Thrift Financial

Reports submitted to the Office of Thrift Supervision, and 5300 Call Reports (Call Reports) submitted to NCUA. We used SNL Financial data to identify changes in the total number, profitability, lending activities (including small business lending), expenses, and other metrics of community banks and credit unions from 2002 through 2011. As regulators do not collect data specifically on small business lending, we created a proxy for small business lending using Call Report data on commercial real estate and commercial and industrial loans for under $1 million for community banks and member business lending by credit unions. As a result, what we characterize as small business lending also may include, to some degree, small loans to larger businesses. We analyzed the data for different asset classes of community banks (assets of $10 billion or more, $1 billion to $10 billion, $250 million to $1 billion, $100 million to $250 million, and less than $100 million) and credit unions (assets of $10 billion or more, $1 billion to $10 billion, $100 million to $1 billion, $20 million to $100 million, $5 million to $20 million, and less than $5 million). We reviewed the SNL Financial data and found the data to be sufficiently reliable for our purposes, and we have relied on the data in our previous reports. We also interviewed the federal agencies and associations identified above and four academic and industry experts about trends in the community bank and credit union sectors and their causes.

To address our second objective, we reviewed the Dodd-Frank Act and related materials, including relevant congressional hearings; comment letters on proposed rules; and studies or analysis prepared by federal and state regulators, industry associations, law firms, and academics. To help us identify the Dodd-Frank Act provisions applicable to community banks and credit unions and assess their impact on such institutions, we interviewed and obtained documentation, when available, from the federal agencies, state regulatory associations, and industry associations identified above, and the Bureau of Consumer Financial Protection. Appendix II contains a table of the provisions identified collectively by these groups. We also analyzed a number of the Dodd-Frank Act provisions that regulators, industry officials, and others expect to impact community banks and credit unions. We used Call Report and other data compiled by SNL Financial to assess the extent to which community banks and credit unions may be subject to or otherwise affected by various Dodd-Frank Act provisions. We took steps to ensure consistency in data analyses for the various provisions within this reporting section and determined that any differences in data due to the date on which we downloaded them from SNL Financial did not have a material impact on our analysis.[144] Our review of the SNL Financial data also found the data to be sufficiently reliable for making judgments about the institutions likely impacted. To obtain further insights into the expected impact of the Dodd-Frank Act, we conducted semistructured interviews with a sample of four state associations and a sample of 12 community banks and credit unions. We interviewed two state banking associations and two credit union associations from Georgia, Illinois, Minnesota, and Pennsylvania, based on the number and uniformity of community banks and credit unions within the states. We randomly selected and interviewed eight community banks and four credit unions from California, Florida, Massachusetts, Michigan, Ohio, Oklahoma, South Dakota, Texas, Virginia, and Wisconsin. For selected associations and institutions that were unavailable to participate, we substituted other similar institutions. In conducting our interviews, we first sent structured questions by e-mail and then followed up with in-depth telephone interviews. These interviews were conducted, in part, to confirm whether the state-level bank and credit union associations and individual community banks and credit unions generally considered the same Dodd-Frank Act provisions identified by regulators, industry associations, and others as potentially impacting their institutions (or member institutions). These interviews also provided further insights on the expected impact of the Dodd-Frank Act, but their responses are not generalizable to the population of community banks and credit unions.

We conducted this performance audit between February and September 2012, in accordance with generally accepted government auditing standards. Those standards require that we plan and perform the audit to obtain sufficient, appropriate evidence to provide a reasonable basis for our findings and conclusions based on our audit objectives. We believe that the evidence obtained provides a reasonable basis for our findings and conclusions based on our audit objectives.

APPENDIX II. PROVISIONS OF THE DODD-FRANK ACT EXPECTED BY FEDERAL REGULATORS, STATE REGULATORY ASSOCIATIONS, AND INDUSTRY ASSOCIATIONS TO IMPACT COMMUNITY BANKS AND CREDIT UNIONS

The following table lists the Dodd-Frank Act provisions that are expected to impact some or all community banks and credit unions. These provisions were identified primarily based on information we collected from federal regulators, state regulatory associations, and industry associations.[145] Industry officials also told us that it is difficult to identify all of the provisions that may impact small institutions because such outcomes may depend on how agencies implement certain provisions through their rules, and many rules have not been finalized. For the same reason, regulators and industry officials also have noted that enough time has not passed to assess the full impact of the Dodd-Frank Act on community banks and credit unions. In particular, the table identifies provisions that are expected to impact community banks and credit unions or a subset of these institutions. The table also includes provisions with explicit exemptions for community banks and credit unions or that provide regulators with the authority to exempt certain entities or financial products from a provision.

As discussed in the chapter, some provisions or exemptions in the act are expected to have an indirect impact on community banks and credit unions. For example, section 1024 is expected to have an indirect impact on community banks and credit unions because it authorizes the Bureau of Consumer Financial Protection (CFPB) to supervise nonbank financial institutions. Before the Dodd-Frank Act, nonbank financial institutions generally were not subject to supervision at the federal level with respect to the federal consumer financial laws, and CFPB's supervision is expected to help level the playing field between these institutions and regulated institutions, such as community banks and credit unions.

Table 6. Dodd-Frank Act Provisions Expected by Federal Regulators, State Regulatory Associations, and Industry Associations to Impact Community Banks and Credit Unions

Title and subtitle	Provisions expected to impact community banks and credit unions
Title I—Financial Stability	
Subtitle C—Additional Board of Governors Authority for Certain Nonbank Financial Companies and Bank Holding Companies	Section 165, Enhanced supervision and prudential standards for nonbank financial companies supervised by the Board of Governors of the Federal Reserve System (Federal Reserve) and certain bank holding companies. Section 165(h)(2)(B) permits the Federal Reserve to require publicly traded bank holding companies with less than $10 billion in assets to establish a risk committee.
	Section 171, Leverage and risk-based capital requirements. This section requires federal banking agencies to establish minimum leverage and risk-based capital requirements on a consolidated basis for insured depository institutions, depository institution holding companies, and systemically important nonbanks. Section 171(b)(4)(C) exempts from capital deductions otherwise required by this section debt or equity instruments issued before May 19, 2010, by bank holding companies with less than $15 billion in assets and mutual holding companies. Moreover, section 171(b)(5)(C) exempts from section 171 bank holding

Title and subtitle	Provisions expected to impact community banks and credit unions
	companies subject to the Federal Reserve's Small Bank Holding Company Policy Statement in effect on May 19, 2010.
Title II—Orderly Liquidation Authority	
Title III—Transfer of Powers to the Comptroller of the Currency, the Corporation, and Board of Governors	
Subtitle A—Transfer of Powers and Duties	Subtitle A of Title III abolishes the Office of Thrift Supervision and provides for the transfer of its functions and authorities to the Office of the Comptroller of the Currency (OCC), Federal Deposit Insurance Corporation (FDIC), and Federal Reserve.
Subtitle C—Federal Deposit Insurance Corporation	Subtitle C of Title III contains provisions that make changes to the federal deposit insurance regime, including (1) redefining the assessment base against which deposit insurance premiums are calculated (section 331) and increasing the standard maximum deposit and share insurance amount from $100,000 to $250,000 (section 335).
	Section 334, Transition reserve ratio requirements to reflect new assessment base. This provision exempts banks with less than $10 billion in assets from the increase in the minimum reserve ratio.
Subtitle D—Other Matters	Section 341, Branching. Section 341 permits any thrift that converts to a bank charter to continue to operate branches and agency offices in existence prior to the charter conversion.
	Section 343, Insurance of transaction accounts. Section 343 provided temporary unlimited deposit and share insurance coverage for non-interest-bearing transaction accounts from December 31, 2010, through December 31, 2012.
Title IV—Regulation of Advisers to Hedge Funds and Others	
Title V—Insurance	
Title VI—Improvements to Regulation of Bank and Savings Association Holding Companies and Depository Institutions	
	Section 613, De novo branching into states. Section 613 expands the de novo interstate branching authority of national and state banks by eliminating the requirement that a state expressly opt-in to de novo branching.
	Section 619, Prohibitions on proprietary trading and certain relationships with hedge funds and private equity funds. This section prohibits banking entities from engaging in proprietary trading and private fund management activities, subject to certain exemptions.
	Section 627 Interest-bearing transaction accounts authorized. This section eliminates the prohibition against the payment of interest on demand deposits (e.g., commercial checking accounts).
Title VII—Wall Street Transparency and Accountability	
	Title VII contains provisions that authorize Commodity Futures Trading Commission (CFTC) and Securities and Exchange Commission (SEC) to regulate the OTC derivative markets and subject various market participants to capital, margin, business conduct, and other requirements.
Subtitle A—Regulation of Over-the-Counter Swaps Markets	Section 721, Definitions. Section 721 amends the Commodity Exchange Act to require CFTC to exempt an entity that engages in de minimis derivatives from the swap dealer definition.
	Section 723, Clearing. This section provides CFTC with the authority to exempt from the mandatory clearing requirement community banks and credit unions with less than $10 billion in assets.

Table 6. (Continued)

Title and subtitle	Provisions expected to impact community banks and credit unions
	Section 737, Position limits. This section provides CFTC with the discretionary authority to exempt community banks or credit unions, among other entities and transactions, from the position limits.
Subtitle B—Regulation of Security-Based Swap Markets	Section 761, Definitions under the Securities Exchange Act of 1934. Section 761 amends the 1934 act to require SEC to exempt an entity that engages in de minimis quantity of security-based swap dealing from the swap dealer definition.
	Section 763, Amendments to the Securities Exchange Act of 1934. This section amends the 1934 act to authorize SEC to exempt from the mandatory clearing requirement community banks and credit unions with less than $10 billion in assets. The amendment also provides SEC with the discretionary authority to exempt entities from position limits.
Title VIII—Payment, Clearing, and Settlement Supervisor	
Title IX—Investor Protections and Improvements to the Regulation of Securities	
Subtitle C—Improvements to the Regulation of Credit Rating Agencies	Section 939A, Review of reliance on ratings. Section 939A requires federal banking and other agencies to review their regulations requiring the use of credit ratings with a goal of modifying those regulations by substituting for such use the standard of creditworthiness they deem appropriate.
Subtitle D—Improvements to the Asset-Backed Securitization Process	Subtitle D of Title IX contains provisions that require federal agencies to jointly issue rules requiring a securitizer of an asset-backed security (other than a residential mortgage-backed security) to retain at least 5 percent of the credit risk in any asset that the securitizer, through the issuance of an asset-backed security, transfers, sells, or conveys to a third party.
	Section 941, Regulation of credit risk retention. This section includes language providing regulators with the discretionary authority to exempt entities from the risk retention requirements.
Subtitle E—Accountability and Executive Compensation	Subtitle E of Title XI contains provisions that require additional executive compensation-related disclosures by public companies, including requiring such companies to hold a non-binding vote to approve the compensation of certain executives (Section 951).
	Section 956, Enhanced compensation structure reporting. This section requires financial institutions to report incentive compensation to their regulator and prohibits incentive compensation that is "excessive" or "could lead to material financial loss" at an institution. Financial institutions with less than $1 billion in assets are exempted from this provision.
Subtitle G—Strengthening Corporate Governance	Section 971, Proxy access. Subsection 971(c) provides SEC with the authority to exempt certain issuers from the proxy access requirement.
Subtitle H—Municipal Securities	Section 975, Regulation of municipal securities and changes to the board of the Municipal Securities Rulemaking Board. Section 975 amends section 15B of the Securities Exchange Act, 15 U.S.C. § 78o-4, to require municipal advisors, who were largely unregulated, to register with SEC like other financial advisors.
Subtitle I—Public Company Accounting Oversight Board,	Section 989G, Exemption for nonaccelerated filers. Section 989G exempts smaller issuers from section 404(b) of the Sarbanes-Oxley Act, 15 U.S.C. § 7262(b).

Title and subtitle	Provisions expected to impact community banks and credit unions
Portfolio Margining, and Other Matters	
Title X—Bureau of Consumer Financial Protection	
Subtitle A—Bureau of Consumer Financial Protection	Subtitle A of Title X contains provisions that create CFPB to regulate financial products or services provided by insured depository institutions, finance companies, mortgage lenders, and a broad range of nontraditional financial services entities, and provides CFPB with the authority to prevent covered institutions from engaging in unfair, deceptive, or abusive acts or practices in the provision of consumer financial products and services.
Subtitle B—General Powers of the Bureau	Subtitle B of Title X contains provisions that provide CFPB the authority to prescribe rules and issue orders and guidance, as may be necessary or appropriate to enable the Bureau to administer federal consumer financial laws.
	Section 1022, Rule-making authority. Section 1022(b)(3) grants CFPB broad authority to exempt entities from the provisions of Title X or any rule under Title X. This could include community banks and credit unions.
	Section 1024, Supervision of nondepository covered persons. Provides CFPB with supervisory and enforcement authority for federal consumer financial protection laws for certain nonbank institutions such as nonbank institutions that provide origination, brokerage, or servicing of residential real estate loans.
	Section 1025. Supervision of very large banks, savings associations, and credit unions. This provision generally excludes banks and credit unions with $10 billion or less in assets (other than affiliates of large banks) from CFPB supervision.
	Section 1026, Other banks, savings associations, and credit unions. This section provides CFPB with certain authority over small banks and credit unions with less than $10 billion in assets. This authority allows CFPB to require reports, as necessary, from small banks and credit unions and CFPB, at its discretion, may include its examiners on a sampling basis in small banks and credit union examinations conducted by their prudential regulator.
Subtitle C—Specific Bureau Authorities	Subtitle C of Title X contains sections that provide CFPB with the authority to prescribe rules identifying as unlawful, unfair, deceptive, or abusive acts or practices for a consumer financial product or service and to ensure that the features of any consumer financial product or service are fully, accurately, and effectively disclosed to consumers. In addition, it requires the CFPB to establish reasonable procedures to provide a timely response to consumers to complaints against or inquiries concerning a financial institution.
	Section 1032, Disclosures. This section includes a provision (section 1032(f)) that requires CFPB to combine disclosures required under the Truth in Lending Act (TILA) and sections 4 and 5 of the Real Estate Settlement Procedures Act of 1974 into a single disclosure.
Subtitle G—Regulatory Improvements	Section 1071 Small business loan data collection. This section requires that lenders collect and report to CFPB certain women-owned, minority-owned, and small business loan data. In addition, this provision provides CFPB with the discretionary authority to exempt any financial institution from the data collection and reporting requirements.

Table 6. (Continued)

Title and subtitle	Provisions expected to impact community banks and credit unions
	Section 1073 Remittance transfers. This section requires disclosures to consumers that send money remittance transfers in accordance with rules to be prescribed by CFPB.
	Section 1075 Reasonable fees and rules for payment card transactions. This section requires the Federal Reserve to prescribe regulations regarding any interchange transaction fee that an issuer may receive or charge for an electronic debit transaction. This provision includes an exemption for institutions with less than $10 billion in assets from the cap on debit card interchange fees.
Subtitle H—Conforming Amendments	Section 1094 Amendments to the Home Mortgage Disclosure Act of 1975 (HMDA). This section amends HMDA to expand the scope of information relating to mortgage loans to add a number of new data elements.
	Section 1098 Amendments to the Real Estate Settlement Procedures Act of 1974. This section requires CFPB to issue rules that combine two different mortgage loan disclosures, one required by the TILA and the other by the Real Estate Settlement Act.
Title XI—Federal Reserve System Provisions	
Title XII—Improving Access to Mainstream Financial Institutions	
Title XIII—Pay it Back Act	
Title XIV—Mortgage Reform and Anti-Predatory Lending Act	
Subtitle A—Residential Mortgage Loan Origination Standards	Subtitle A of Title XIV contains provisions that establish certain origination standards to be applied by lenders in the underwriting of residential mortgage loans, including registration and licensing requirements for mortgage originators and a prohibition on steering and certain mortgage originator compensation.
	Section 1405. Regulations. CFPB may, by rule, exempt from or modify disclosure requirements, in whole or in part, for any class of residential mortgage loans for which it determines that such exemption or modification is in the interest of consumers and in the public interest.
Subtitle B—Minimum Standards For Mortgages	Subtitle B of Title XIV contains provisions that establish minimum standards for mortgage loans.
	Section 1411, Ability to Repay. This section amends the TILA to provide that no creditor may make a residential mortgage loan unless the creditor makes a reasonable and good faith determination based on verified and documented information that the consumer has the reasonable ability to repay the loan at the time the loan is consummated.
	Section 1412, Safe Harbor and Rebuttable Presumption. This section provides the “qualified mortgage” criteria under which a creditor or assignee may presume the ability-to-repay requirements have been met. It also provides regulators with the authority to consider certain loans as qualified mortgages as long as they meet certain criteria, including balloon loans being extended by a lender that operates in a predominantly rural or underserved area.
	Section 1422, State attorney general enforcement authority. This section provides state attorneys general with increased enforcement

Title and subtitle	Provisions expected to impact community banks and credit unions
	authority for certain provisions of TILA including steering prohibitions; ability to repay; minimum standards for residential mortgage loans; appraisal independence; prompt crediting of mortgage payments; requests for payoff amounts; and property appraisal requirements.
Subtitle C—High-Cost Mortgages	Subtitle C of Title XIV contains provisions that expand the definition of high-cost mortgage, enhance existing protections regarding prepayment penalties and balloon payments, and prohibit certain practices.
Subtitle E—Mortgage Servicing	Subtitle E of Title XIV contains provisions that require the establishment of escrow or impound accounts for the payment of taxes and insurance in connection with certain first lien mortgage loans.
	Section 1461, Escrow and impound accounts relating to certain consumer credit transactions. This section includes a provision authorizing CFPB to exempt from the escrow requirements entities that operate in predominantly rural or underserved areas; have total annual mortgage loan originations that do not exceed a certain limit; retain their mortgage loan originations in portfolio; or meet any asset-size threshold and any other criteria established by CFPB.
	Section 1462, Disclosure notice for consumers who waive escrow services. This section amends TILA to add a requirement that creditors provide specified disclosures to consumers who waive escrow services.
Subtitle F—Appraisal Activities	Subtitle F of Title XIV contains provisions regarding appraisals in connection with residential mortgage loans.
	Section 1471, Property appraisal requirements. This section provides regulators with discretionary authority to exempt, by rule, a class of loans from the appraisal requirements in this section if they determine that the exemption is in the public interest and promotes the safety and soundness of creditors.
	Section 1472, Appraisal Independence Requirements. This section amends TILA by adding appraisal independence requirements. These requirements include, among other things, a description of acts or practices that violate appraisal independence a list of actions that an appraiser can take at the request of an interested party but do not violate independence, and mandatory reporting of appraisers that do not comply with Uniform Standards of Professional Appraisal Practice to state appraiser certifying and licensing agencies.
Title XV—Miscellaneous Provisions	
Title XVI—Section 1256 Contracts	

Source: GAO analysis of information collected from federal regulators (the Federal Deposit Insurance Corporation, the Federal Reserve, National Credit Union Administration, Office of the Comptroller of the Currency, and the Bureau of Consumer Financial Protection); state regulatory associations (Conference of State Bank Supervisors and National Association of State Credit Union Supervisors); and industry associations, including the American Bankers Association, Independent Community Bankers of America, Credit Union National Association, and National Association of Federal Credit Unions.

End Notes

[1] Pub. L. No. 111-203, 124 Stat. 1376 (2010).

[2] Title X of the Dodd-Frank Act, also called the Consumer Financial Protection Act of 2010, creates CFPB as a new executive agency to enforce certain existing federal consumer protection laws and promulgate new rules regarding federal consumer financial laws.

[3] Although no commonly accepted definition of a community bank exists, the term often is associated with smaller banks (e.g., under $1 billion in assets) that provide relationship banking services to the local community and have management and board members who reside in the local community. In this chapter, we generally define community banks as banks (insured depository institutions that are not credit unions) with under $10 billion in total assets. We also include in our analysis federally insured credit unions with under $10 billion in total assets. We use under $10 billion in total assets as our criterion because the Dodd-Frank Act exempts small institutions from a number of its provisions based on that threshold.

[4] The Dodd-Frank Act eliminated OTS, which chartered and supervised federally chartered savings institutions and savings and loan companies. Rule-making authority previously vested in OTS was transferred to the Office of the Comptroller of the Currency (OCC) for savings associations and to the Board of Governors of the Federal Reserve System (Federal Reserve) for savings and loan holding companies. Supervisory authority was transferred to OCC for federal savings associations, to FDIC for state savings associations, and to the Federal Reserve for savings and loan holding companies and their subsidiaries, other than depository institutions. The transfer of these powers was completed on July 21, 2011, and OTS was officially dissolved 90 days later (Oct. 19, 2011).

[5] Call Reports are a primary source of financial data used for the supervision and regulation of banks and credit unions. They consist of a balance sheet, an income statement, and supporting schedules. Every national bank, state member bank, insured state nonmember bank, and federally insured credit union is required to file a consolidated Call Report, normally as of the close of business on the last calendar day of each calendar quarter. The specific reporting requirements depend on the size of the institution and whether it has any foreign offices. As of March 31, 2012, savings associations no longer filed Thrift Financial Reports and instead were required to file Call Reports.

[6] Financial Stability Oversight Council, *Financial Stability Oversight Council 2011 Annual Report* (Washington, D.C.: July 26, 2011).

[7] Richard Brown, Chief Economist, FDIC, "Community Banking by the Numbers" (paper presented at FDIC's Future of Community Banking Conference, Feb. 16, 2012). FDIC plans to issue additional research on the community banking sector by the end of 2012.

[8] For this objective, our analysis of SNL Financial data includes commercial banks, savings banks, savings institutions, and credit unions.

[9] Pub. L. No. 103-328, 108 Stat. 2338 (1994).

[10] Section 613 of the Dodd-Frank Act further reduced restrictions on interstate branching. Before the passage of the Dodd-Frank Act, states could opt not to allow national banks and out-of-state banks to open new branches. The Dodd-Frank Act allows national and out-of-state banks to open branches in any state, only restricted by the laws that apply to in-state banks.

[11] Pub. L. No. 105-219, 112 Stat. 913 (1998). By federal statute, credit unions may not serve the general public.

[12] GAO, *Credit Unions: Greater Transparency Needed on Who Credit Unions Serve and on Senior Executive Compensation Arrangements*, GAO-07-29 (Washington, D.C.: Nov. 30, 2006).

[13] See, for example, Loretta J. Mester, "Optimal Industrial Structure in Banking," *Handbook of Financial Intermediation*, Arnoud Boot and Anjan Thakor, eds. (2008).

[14] David C. Wheelock and Paul W. Wilson, "Do Large Banks have Lower Costs? New Estimates of Returns to Scale for U.S. Banks," Working Paper 2009-054E, Federal Reserve Bank of St. Louis, Revised (May 2011).

[15] John Goddard, Donal McKillop, and John Wilson, *Consolidation in the US Credit Union Sector: Determinants of the Hazard of Acquisition* (2008), accessed June 15, 2012, www.fdic.gov/bank/analytical/cfr/Goddard_McKillop_Wilson.pdf .

[16] NCUA officials noted that while banks and credit unions often collect the same data, comparisons between the two are limited because of differences in organizational structure and regulation. Specifically, credit unions operate as not-for-profit institutions and have limited fields of membership.

[17] Tim Critchfield, Tyler Davis, Lee Davison, Heather Gratton, George Hanc, and Katherine Samolyk, "The Future of Banking in America, Community Banks: Their Recent Past, Current Performance, and Future Prospects," *FDIC Banking Review*, vol. 16, no. 3 (2004).

[18] Return on assets and return on equity are both measures of bank profitability. Return on assets represents the income banks earned per dollar of loan or investment, while return on equity represents the income earned per dollar of capital. Differences between a bank's return on equity and return on assets depend on the bank's use of leverage, which can be measured by its capital ratio.

[19] We adjusted each bank's and credit union's total assets in each year for inflation to 2011 dollars using the U.S. gross domestic product deflator.

[20] For a given return on assets, lower capital ratios imply higher returns on equity because leverage magnifies returns on equity.

[21] Operating expenses as a percentage of operating revenues is a standard measure of bank efficiency in the literature. For clarity, we have provided the inverse of this measure, operating revenues per dollar of operating costs, so that a higher number indicates greater efficiency.

[22] *The State of Community Banking: Opportunities and Challenges, Before the Senate Committee on Banking, Housing, and Urban Affairs*, 112th Cong. (2011) (statement of Jennifer Kelly, Senior Deputy Comptroller for Midsize and Community Bank Supervision, OCC).

[23] Gregory Elliehausen, " The Cost of Banking Regulation: A Review of the Evidence ," Staff Study 171, Federal Reserve (Washington, D.C.: April 1998).

[24] The Role of Community Banks in the U.S. Economy," Federal Reserve Bank of Kansas City, *Economic Review*, Second Quarter (2003).

[25] We used business lending data compiled by SNL Financial as a proxy for small business lending for credit unions. Business lending at credit unions is referred to as member business lending because credit unions are owned by their depositors, or members, and credit unions may extend credit only to their members. One expert noted that nearly all member business lending is done to small businesses.

[26] James Wilcox, *The Increasing Importance of Credit Unions in Small Business Lending*, prepared for the SBA, Office of Advocacy, 2011.

[27] GAO, *National Credit Union Administration: Earlier Actions Are Needed to Better Address Troubled Credit Unions*, GAO-12-247 (Washington, D.C.: Jan. 4, 2012).

[28] Credit unions designated as low income are exempt from the 12.25 percent statutory cap on member business loans. A low-income credit union is one that serves predominantly low-income members as defined in NCUA regulations. A recent NCUA initiative streamlined the process for federal credit unions to receive a low-income designation.

[29] According to Davis Polk & Wardwell (a law firm that has been tracking the implementation of the Dodd-Frank Act), 119 of the 398 rulemakings required under the Dodd-Frank Act, about 30 percent, had been finalized as of July 2, 2012.

[30] These exemptions are based on specific asset thresholds, and the exemptions do not use the same asset threshold. For example, the exemption from CFPB supervision applies to banks and credit unions with $10 billion or less in assets, and the exemption from disclosure and

reporting requirements for incentive-based compensation arrangements applies to financial institutions with less than $1 billion in assets.

[31] Section 1100G of the Dodd-Frank Act requires CFPB to convene panels to seek direct input from small businesses before proposing certain rules.

[32] *The State of Community Banking: Opportunities and Challenges. Before the Subcommittee on Financial Institutions and Consumer Protection of the Committee on Banking, Housing, and Urban Affairs*, U.S. Senate (2011) (statement of Maryann F. Hunter, Deputy Director of Division of Banking Supervision and Regulation, Board of Governors of the Federal Reserve System).

[33] DIF insures deposits at banks and the National Credit Union Share Insurance Fund insures deposits, referred to as shares, at credit unions.

[34] DIF assessments are insurance assessments collected from its member depository institutions.

[35] 76 Fed. Reg. 10,672 (Feb. 25, 2011). For more information on this rule, see GAO, *Dodd-Frank Act Regulations: Implementation Could Benefit from Additional Analyses and Coordination,* GAO-12-151 (Washington, D.C.: Nov. 10, 2011).

[36] The Emergency Economic Stabilization Act of 2008, Pub. L. No. 110-343, 122 Stat. 3765, temporarily increased the deposit and share insurance amount from $100,000 to $250,000 from October 3, 2008, through December 31, 2009. The Helping Families Save Their Homes Act of 2009, Pub. L. No. 111-22, 123 Stat. 1632, extended the temporary increase through December 31, 2013, and the Dodd-Frank Act made the increase permanent.

[37] 75 Fed. Reg. 53,841 (Sept. 2, 2010); 75 Fed. Reg. 49,363 (Aug. 13, 2010).

[38] Temporary unlimited insurance coverage for non-interest-bearing transaction accounts initially was provided for federally insured banks through FDIC's Transaction Account Guarantee program. The temporary unlimited insurance coverage for non-interest-bearing transaction accounts differs from the Transaction Account Guarantee program in that it applies to all insured depository institutions with non-interest-bearing accounts, it does not cover low interest negotiable order of withdrawal accounts, and FDIC does not charge a separate assessment for the insurance of non-interest-bearing transaction accounts. The Transaction Account Guarantee program expired on December 31, 2010, and section 343 for federally insured banks became effective on that same date. Section 343 was effective for federally insured credit unions on July 21, 2010. 75 Fed. Reg. 69,577 (Nov. 15, 2010).

[39] FDIC, *FDIC Quarterly,* vol. 6, no. 1 (2012).

[40] Credit unions are member-owned cooperatives, rather than public companies, and so are not subject to section 404 of the Sarbanes-Oxley Act of 2002, which was amended by section 989G of the Dodd-Frank Act.

[41] Pub. L. No. 107-204, 116 Stat. 745 (2002).

[42] Although the term non-accelerated filer is not defined in SEC rules, it refers to a reporting company that does not meet the definition of either an "accelerated filer" or a "large accelerated filer" under Exchange Act Rule 12b–2. The public float is the aggregate market value of the issuer's outstanding voting and nonvoting common equity held by nonaffiliates of the issuer. An accelerated filer generally is a public company that, among other things, had at least $75 million but less than $700 million in public float as of the last business day of its most recently completed second fiscal quarter, and filed at least one annual report with SEC. A large accelerated filer generally is a public company that, among other things, had a public float of $700 million or more as of the last business day of its most recently completed second fiscal quarter and filed at least one annual report with SEC.

[43] SEC amended its rules and forms to conform them to section 404(c) of the Sarbanes-Oxley Act of 2002, as added by section 989G of the Dodd-Frank Act. Section 404(c) provides that section 404(b) of the Sarbanes-Oxley Act shall not apply with respect to any audit report prepared for an issuer that is neither an accelerated filer nor a large accelerated filer as defined in Rule 12b–2 under the Securities Exchange Act of 1934. *See* 75 Fed. Reg. 57,385 (Sept. 21, 2010).

[44] We also found other banks and bank holding companies that identified themselves as non-accelerated filers but were traded on the Over-the-Counter Pink market. We excluded these companies, because the data did not allow us to determine whether they were subject to reporting requirements under the federal securities laws.

[45] SEC, Office of Economic Analysis, *Study of the Sarbanes-Oxley Act of 2002 Section 404 Internal Control over Financial Reporting Requirements* (Washington, D.C.: September 2009). The study noted that these companies voluntarily complied or were required to comply in the past as accelerated filers and must continue to do so because their float had not since dropped below $50 million. The study noted that to the extent that these factors affect companies' experience with section 404(b) compliance, care should be taken when extrapolating the results to non-accelerated filers that had yet to comply.

[46] See GAO, *Sarbanes-Oxley Act: Consideration of Key Principles Needed in Addressing Implementation for Smaller Public Companies*, GAO-06-361 (Washington, D.C.: Apr. 13, 2006). In addition, pursuant to section 989I of the Dodd-Frank Act, GAO is required to conduct a study on the impact of the section 404(b) amendments under the Dodd-Frank Act on smaller issuers and to submit a report not later than 3 years after the date of enactment of the act.

[47] 76 Fed. Reg. 43,394 (July 20, 2011).

[48] An issuer also is allowed to receive an upward adjustment of 1 cent to its interchange transaction fee, if the issuer, among other things, develops, implements, and updates policies and procedures reasonably designed to identify and prevent fraudulent electronic debit transactions. See 76 Fed. Reg. 43,478 (July 20, 2011).

[49] The prohibition on network exclusivity, which applies to all issuers regardless of size, took effect on April 1, 2012, with respect to most types of debit cards.

[50] Institutions that qualified for the exemption during 2011 were those institutions that had, together with affiliates, assets of less than $10 billion as of December 31, 2010.

[51] The Federal Reserve collected data from 16 payment card networks. Eight networks reported a decline in their average interchange fee per transaction for exempt issuers—ranging from $0.01 to $0.04—after the rule took effect. Three networks reported no change in their average interchange fee for exempt issuers. Five networks reported an increase in their fee for exempt issuers—ranging from $0.01 to $0.03—after the rule took effect.

[52] The interchange fee as a percentage of the average transaction value is calculated by dividing the total interchange fees by the value of settled purchase transactions.

[53] The totals include both debit and credit card interchange fee income reported by banks that were exempt from the debit interchange fee cap. Credit card interchange fees are not subject to the Regulation II limitations. The reporting of bank card and credit card interchange fees in Call Reports is required only if that amount exceeds $25,000 or 3 percent of other noninterest income. As a result, not all banks report a value for this variable. In addition, savings institutions historically did not report interchange fee income in their Thrift Financial Reports. Finally, the totals exclude interchange fee income reported by credit unions. Although credit unions report their interchange fee income, they aggregate that income with other sources of operating income.

[54] A number of merchant associations have brought a lawsuit against the Federal Reserve, alleging that it failed to follow the intent of Congress regarding the amount of an interchange fee that an issuer could charge or receive.

[55] Section 1021 of the Dodd-Frank Act established the following goals for CFPB: (1) ensure that consumers have timely and understandable information to make responsible decisions about financial transactions, (2) protect consumers from unfair, deceptive, or abusive acts or practices, and from discrimination, (3) reduce unwarranted regulatory burdens due to outdated, unnecessary, or unduly burdensome regulations, (4) promote fair competition by enforcing the federal consumer financial laws consistently, and (5) ensure that markets for consumer financial products and services operate transparently and efficiently to facilitate access and innovation.

[56] Section 1024 of the Dodd-Frank Act authorizes CFPB to supervise certain entities and individuals that engage in offering or providing a consumer financial product or service and their service providers that are not covered by sections 1025 or 1026 of the act. Specifically, section 1024 applies to those entities and individuals who offer or provide mortgage-related products or services and payday and private student loans as well as larger participants of other consumer financial service or product markets as defined by a CFPB rule, among others, plus their service providers. Section 1025 authorizes CFPB to supervise, with respect to consumer finance laws, large insured depository institutions and credit unions with more than $10 billion in total assets and all their affiliates (including subsidiaries), as well as service providers for such entities. Under section 1026, CFPB has the authority to require reports, as necessary, from banks and credit unions under $10 billion, and CFPB, at its discretion, may include its examiners on a sampling basis in examinations conducted by their prudential regulator for these entities. Under sections 1026 and 1061(c), CFPB has supervisory authority over a service provider to a substantial number of smaller depository institutions.

[57] The Federal Trade Commission has enforcement authority over most nonbank entities for numerous consumer protection statutes, including, for example, the Truth in Lending Act, 15 U.S.C. §§ 1601-1666j and the privacy provisions of the Gramm-Leach Bliley Act, 15 U.S.C. §§ 6801-6809. The Commission generally retains its enforcement authority under the Dodd-Frank Act, although in some instances its authority may be concurrent with CFPB's enforcement authority.

[58] In February 2012, CFPB issued a proposed rule defining a larger participant in certain consumer product and finance markets. 77 Fed. Reg. 9,592 (Feb. 17, 2012). In its proposal, CFPB proposed to define larger participants in the markets for consumer debt collection and consumer reporting. CFPB intended that this proposal and subsequent initial rule would be followed by a series of rule makings covering additional markets for consumer financial products and services. In July 2012, CFPB issued a final rule to define larger participants in a consumer reporting market as a nonbank-covered person with more than $7 million in annual receipts resulting from consumer reporting activities. 77 Fed. Reg. 42,874 (July 20, 2012).

[59] In May 2012, CFPB proposed a rule establishing the procedures by which it may subject a nonbank to this authority. 77 Fed. Reg. 31,226 (May 25, 2012).

[60] CFPB's supervision program has two parts that operate under common procedures and shared staff. The large bank supervision program began operations in July 2011 and focuses on compliance at banks, thrifts, and credit unions with assets over $10 billion, their affiliates, and certain service providers.

[61] *Implementing Wall Street Reform: Enhancing Bank Supervision and Reducing Systemic Risk. Before the Senate Banking Committee*, 112th Cong. (2012) (statement of Richard Cordray, Director, CFPB).

[62] *The State of Community Banking: Opportunities and Challenges. Before the Subcommittee on Financial Institutions and Consumer Protection of the Committee on Banking, Housing, and Urban Affairs*, U.S. Senate (2011) (statement of Sandra L. Thompson, Director of Risk Management Supervision, FDIC).

[63] *The Effect of Dodd-Frank on Small Financial Institutions and Small Businesses, Before the House Committee on Financial Services*, 112th Cong. (2011) (statements of Albert Kelly, Chairman and Chief Executive Officer, Spiritbank on Behalf of the American Bankers Association; James D. MacPhee, Chief Executive Officer, Kalamazoo County State Bank, on Behalf of the Independent Community Bankers of America; and John P. Buckley, Jr. President and Chief Executive Officer, Gerber Federal Credit Union, on behalf of the National Association of Federal Credit Unions).

[64] 76 Fed. Reg. 75,825 (Dec. 5, 2011).

[65] *Implementing Wall Street Reform: Enhancing Bank Supervision and Reducing Systemic Risk, Before the Senate Banking Committee*, 112th Cong. (2012) (statement of Richard Cordray, Director, CFPB).

[66] The Dodd-Frank Act also requires CFPB to comply with the Small Business Regulatory Enforcement Fairness Act panel process. This act requires CFPB to convene a Small Business Review Panel before proposing a rule that may have a significant economic impact on a substantial number of small entities. *See* Pub. L. No. 104-121, tit. II, 110 Stat. 847, 857 (1996) (as amended by Pub. L. No. 110-28, § 8302 (2007)).

[67] 77 Fed. Reg. 51,116 (Aug. 23, 2012).

[68] Pursuant to the Small Business Regulatory Enforcement Fairness Act, CFPB must convene a panel to obtain feedback from small business representatives before proposing rules that may affect them. Throughout the proposed rule to integrate mortgage disclosures, CFPB discussed how it is addressing issues considered by this panel, including the timing of implementation.

[69] The Home Mortgage Disclosure Act of 1975 (HMDA), Pub. L. No. 94-200, 89 Stat. 1124, requires certain creditors to collect, disclose, and report data on the personal characteristics of mortgage borrowers and loan applicants (for example, their ethnicity, race, and gender), the type of loan or application (for example, if the loan is insured or guaranteed by a federal agency), and financial data such as the loan amount and borrowers' incomes. Institutions that provide mortgage lending, have over $41 million in assets, and have a home office or branch office in a metropolitan statistical area must report HMDA data. The purposes in collecting these data are to aid in determining whether financial institutions are serving the housing needs of their communities, identifying areas where additional investment is needed, and identifying possible discriminatory lending patterns.

[70] In July 2011, pursuant to the Dodd-Frank Act, rulemaking, supervision, and enforcement authority for consumer protection laws were generally transferred to CFPB. This includes responsibility for implementing the Truth in Lending Act (TILA) and the Home Ownership Equity Protection Act, which are among the primary federal laws governing consumer credit, including mortgage lending. TILA was intended to provide consumers with more information about the costs of credit, and the Home Ownership Equity Protection Act amended TILA to regulate and restrict certain "high cost" mortgage loans.

[71] GAO, *Mortgage Reform: Potential Impacts of Provisions in the Dodd-Frank Act on Homebuyers and the Mortgage Market*, GAO-11-656 (Washington, D.C.: July 19, 2011).

[72] The act generally requires that mandatory escrow accounts be established for mortgages secured by a first lien on a customer's primary residence if (1) the escrow account is required by federal or state law; (2) the mortgage is made, guaranteed, or insured by a state or federal government lending or insurance agency (e.g., the Federal Housing Administration or the Department of Veterans Affairs); or (3) the mortgage is a close-ended "higher priced" mortgage loan.

[73] On July 30, 2008, the Federal Reserve published a final rule amending Regulation Z (TILA) to establish new regulatory protections for consumers in the residential mortgage market. 73 Fed. Reg. 44,522 (July 30, 2008). Among other things, the final rule defined a class of higher-priced mortgage loans that are subject to additional protections, including mandatory escrow accounts for certain loans. Different aspects of the rule were to be effective as of October 2009 and April 2010; however, in August 2009 the Federal Reserve published a proposed rule to amend this Regulation Z requirement due to concerns about the rate used in determining whether a loan is higher-priced. No final action had been taken on this rule prior to the Dodd-Frank Act.

[74] 76 Fed. Reg. 27,390 (May 11, 2011).

[75] In its proposed rule, the Federal Reserve requested comment on whether the mortgage loan origination limit should be set by the aggregate principal amounts of relevant loans extended by the creditor and its affiliates or by the total number of such loans.

[76] 76 Fed Reg. 11,598 (Mar. 2, 2011). On the same date, the Federal Reserve issued a final rule implementing part of section 1461 that amended Regulation Z to provide a separate, higher threshold for determining when the escrow requirement applies to higher-priced mortgage loans that exceed the maximum principal obligation eligible for purchase by Freddie Mac, or "jumbo" loans. The final rule was effective on April 1, 2011. 76 Fed. Reg. 11,319 (Mar. 2, 2011).

[77] The Economic Research Service of the U.S. Department of Agriculture maintains "urban influence codes" that reflect factors such as counties' relative population sizes, degrees of urbanization, access to larger communities, and commuting patterns.

[78] Section 1471 defines a "higher risk" mortgage as one that is not a "qualified mortgage" (to be defined by CFPB pursuant to section 1412) and whose annual percentage rate exceeds average rates (specified in the act) for a comparable transaction. This report section focuses primarily on section 1472. However, Subtitle F of Title XIV of the act includes other appraisal provisions. For example, section 1473 includes amendments relating to the Appraiser Subcommittee of the Federal Financial Institutions Examination Council, appraisal independence monitoring, appraisal management companies, automated valuation models, and broker price opinions. For additional GAO work relating to the Dodd-Frank Act appraisal provisions, see GAO, *Residential Appraisals: Opportunities to Enhance Oversight of an Evolving Industry*, GAO-11-653 (Washington, D.C.: July 13, 2011) and *Real Estate Appraisals: Appraisal Subcommittee Needs to Improve Monitoring Procedures*, GAO-12-147 (Washington, D.C.: Jan. 18, 2012).

[79] The Dodd-Frank Act stated that the Home Valuation Code of Conduct ceased to be effective as of the date the Federal Reserve issued interim final rules covering appraiser independence. Dodd-Frank Act § 1472(a) (codified at 15 U.S.C. § 1639e(j)). The Federal Reserve issued that rule on October 28, 2010. 75 Fed. Reg. 66,554.

[80] The act allowed rule-making agencies to jointly exempt, by rule, a class of loans from the requirements of this provision if the agencies determine that the exemption is in the public interest and promotes the safety and soundness of creditors.

[81] 77 Fed. Reg. 54,722 (Sept. 5, 2012).

[82] On August 15, 2012, the rule-making agencies issued a proposed rule for implementing section 1471. They sought comment as to whether higher-risk mortgage loans made in rural areas should be exempt from the requirement that creditors obtain two appraisals prior to extending a higher-risk mortgage loan to finance a consumer's acquisition of property. In the proposed rule, the agencies requested any data to be submitted supporting whether exempting any classes of higher-risk mortgage loans from the additional appraisal requirement would be in the public interest and promote safety and soundness of creditors. Comments on the proposed rule are due in October 2012.

[83] 75 Fed. Reg. 66,554 (Oct. 28, 2010).

[84] One national credit union association did not support the rule due to its requirement that credit unions report violations of the rule, suggesting that the requirement would require credit unions to become experts in rules, laws, and standards regarding appraisers.

[85] See GAO-11-656 .

[86] Real estate investment trusts are companies that own income-producing real estate and in some cases engage in the financing of real estate. To qualify as a real estate investment trust, a company must have most of its assets and income tied to real estate investment and must distribute at least 90 percent of its taxable income to shareholders annually in the form of dividends. For more detailed information on securitization processes, see GAO-11-656.

[87] Government-insured or government-guaranteed mortgages primarily serve borrowers who may have difficulty qualifying for mortgages. The Federal Housing Administration and the Department of Veterans Affairs operate the two main federal programs that insure or guarantee mortgages. Fannie Mae and Freddie Mac (the enterprises) purchase mortgages that meet specified underwriting criteria from approved lenders. Most of the mortgages are made to prime borrowers with strong credit histories. The enterprises bundle the mortgages

into securities and guarantee the timely payment of principal and interest to investors in the securities. On September 6, 2008, the enterprises were placed under federal conservatorship because of concern that their deteriorating financial condition and potential default on $5.4 trillion in outstanding financial obligations threatened the stability of financial markets.

[88] The Dodd-Frank Act's risk retention requirement also applies to securities backed by other asset classes, such as commercial loans, commercial real estate mortgage loans, credit cards, and automobile loans.

[89] In addition to mortgages backed by the enterprises, this section of the act also does not apply the exemption for government-insured or government-guaranteed mortgages to mortgages backed by Federal Home Loan Banks, which form a system of regional cooperatives that support housing finance through advances and mortgage programs, among other activities.

[90] The Dodd-Frank Act specifies that the QRM definition cannot be broader than the QM definition described previously (i.e., the QRM criteria can be more restrictive than the QM criteria but not less restrictive).

[91] 76 Fed. Reg. 24,090 (Apr. 29, 2011). FDIC, the Federal Reserve, OCC, SEC and, in cases of residential mortgage assets, the Department of Housing and Urban Development and FHFA, are responsible for jointly prescribing the risk retention rules. The Chairperson of the Financial Stability Oversight Council is tasked with coordinating the risk retention rule-making effort.

[92] The proposed rule also established other QRM criteria, including: (1) the debt to income ratio must be 36 percent or less; (2) the loan term must not exceed 30 years; (3) the loan cannot include negative amortization or payment deferral features; (4) points and fees cannot exceed 3 percent of the total loan amount; (5) the borrower can neither be 30 or more days past due on any debt obligation at the time of the loan nor have been 60 or more days past due on any debt obligation within the preceding 24 months; and (6) the originator must incorporate into the mortgage documents certain requirements regarding policies and procedures for servicing the mortgage.

[93] The Regulatory Flexibility Act generally requires that an agency, in connection with a notice of proposed rulemaking, prepare and make available for public comment an initial regulatory flexibility analysis that describes the impact of the proposed rule on small entities or certify that the rule will not have a significant economic impact on a substantial number of small entities (defined in regulations promulgated by SBA to include banking organizations with total assets of less than or equal to $175 million).

[94] In its analysis, the Federal Reserve included over 2,400 small bank holding companies.

[95] This analysis does not include data for thrift institutions. This finding assumes that no portion of the assets originated by these banks was sold to the enterprises or securitizations that qualify for an exemption from the risk retention requirements under the proposed rule. OCC officials commented that because no private-label RMBS transactions closed in 2011, none of the 2011 securitization activity would have been in residential mortgages sold to a securitizer, where the securitizer might have attempted to allocate the risk retention back to the lender. They noted that the residential mortgages were either government-insured mortgages or sold to the enterprises.

[96] See GAO-11-656 .

[97] This section's prohibitions apply to banking entities and do not apply to credit unions. The section does not prohibit nonbank financial companies supervised by the Federal Reserve from engaging in proprietary trading or having ownership interests in a covered fund. However, the provision allows the Federal Reserve or other agencies to impose additional capital charges and quantitative limits on nonbank financial companies supervised by the Federal Reserve that are engaged in those activities. OCC officials noted that no such nonbank entities have been designated as of August 13, 2012.

[98] 76 Fed. Reg. 68,846 (Nov. 7, 2011). The responsible rule-making agencies are OCC, the Federal Reserve, FDIC, and SEC. CFTC also has rule-making authority under section 619 of the Dodd-Frank Act and proposed a substantively similar rule in February 2012. The

rules proposed by SEC and CFTC will not apply to community banks, as these agencies are not the primary financial regulatory agency for banks.

[99] The Federal Reserve, Statement of Policy Regarding the Conformance Period for Entities Engaged in Prohibited Proprietary Trading or Private Equity Fund or Hedge Fund Activities, 77 Fed. Reg. 33,949 (June 8, 2012). *See also* the Federal Reserve's conformance period final rule, which was issued in February 14, 2011, 76 Fed. Reg. 8,265.

[100] GAO, *Proprietary Trading: Regulators Will need More Comprehensive Information to Fully Monitor Compliance with New Restrictions When Implemented*, GAO-11-529 (Washington, D.C.: July 13, 2011).

[101] Other banks that report total average trading assets of less than $2 million in each of the four preceding quarters also are not required to provide a breakdown of their trading assets by type of financial instruments.

[102] Banks currently are required to have investment policies that identify acceptable instruments for purchase. The Supervisory Policy Statement on Investment Securities and End-User Derivatives Activities (63 Fed. Reg. 20,191 (Apr. 23, 1998)) specifies that banks should identify, measure, monitor, and control the risks of investment activities as a matter of sound banking practice. This includes maintaining policies that set limits on the purchase of securities and other investment vehicles. These policies can be used to identify instruments that the bank may purchase, such as U.S. Treasuries, municipal obligations, and Government Sponsored Enterprise debt, that are exempt from the proposed Volcker Rule.

[103] Banks with more than $1 billion in covered positions or covered fund activities must also meet minimum standards in the compliance program.

[104] A derivative is a financial instrument created from, or whose value depends upon, the value of one or more separate assets or indexes of asset values.

[105] A derivatives clearinghouse or similar organization enables each party to a derivatives transaction to substitute the credit of the clearinghouse for the credit of the parties, provides for the settlement or netting of obligations from the transaction, or otherwise provides services mutualizing or transferring the credit risk from the transaction.

[106] Dealers participate in the derivatives market by quoting prices to, buying derivatives from, and selling derivatives to end users and other dealers.

[107] Financial Stability Oversight Council, *Financial Stability Oversight Council 2011 Annual Report* (Washington, D.C.: July 26, 2011).

[108] Swaps include interest rate swaps, commodity-based swaps, and broad-based credit swaps. Security-based swaps include single-name and narrow-based credit swaps and equity-based swaps.

[109] Although permitted by law, NCUA currently allows only a limited number of credit unions, on a case-by-case basis, to engage in such transactions under an investment pilot program.

[110] 76 Fed. Reg. 37,030 (June 24, 2011).

[111] See 77 Fed. Reg. 30,596 (May 23, 2012).The Dodd-Frank Act instructed CFTC and SEC to exempt from designation as a dealer a person that engages in a *de minimis* quantity of swap or security-based swap dealing in connection with transactions with or on behalf of his or her customers.

[112] The rules provide for a phase-in of the *de minimis* thresholds to facilitate orderly implementation of swap dealer and security-based swap dealer requirements. The initial swap dealer and security-based swap dealer *de minimis* thresholds are, for the preceding year, no more than $8 billion in aggregate gross notional amount of dealing activity in CFTC-regulated swaps, $8 billion in notional amount of dealing activity for security-based swaps that are credit default swaps, and $400 million for other types of security-based swaps for security-based swap dealers. After the phase-in period ends and if CFTC or SEC have not otherwise determined to change the respective threshold amounts, the swap dealer *de minimis* threshold will be $3 billion in notional amount of dealing activity for all CFTC-regulated swaps, and the security-based swap dealer *de minimis* thresholds will be $3 billion

in notional amount of dealing activity for security-based swaps that are credit default swaps, and $150 million in notional amount of dealing activity for other security-based swaps.

[113] 77 Fed. Reg. 42,560 (July 19, 2012).

[114] 75 Fed. Reg. 79,992 (Dec. 30, 2010).

[115] Futures clearinghouses use initial and variation margin as a key part of their risk management programs. Initial margin serves as a performance bond against potential future losses. If a party fails to meet its obligation to pay variation margin, resulting in a default, the other party may use initial margin to cover most or all of any loss based on the need to replace the open position. Variation margin entails marking open positions to their current market value each day and transferring funds between the parties to reflect any change in value since the previous time the positions were marked. This process prevents losses from accumulating over time and thereby reduces both the chance of default and the size of any default should one occur.

[116] CFTC has proposed regulations for noncleared swaps (*see* 76 Fed. Reg. 23,732 (Apr. 28, 2011)). Also, the prudential regulators have jointly proposed corollary noncleared margin rules (76 Fed. Reg. 27,564 (May 11, 2011)).

[117] CFTC requested public comments on whether counterparties that are small financial institutions using derivatives to hedge their risks should be treated in the same manner as nonfinancial entities for purposes of the margin requirements.

[118] The prudential regulators requested public comments on whether counterparties that are small financial institutions using derivatives to hedge their risks be treated in the same manner as nonfinancial end users for purposes of the margin requirements.

[119] Under the proposed rule, most community banks would fall under the category of "low-risk financial end users." Under the proposal, such users would be required to post an initial margin only when the initial margin requirement, as calculated by the dealer, exceeds the lesser of $15 million or 0.1 percent of the dealer's capital.

[120] Section 1073 of the act amended the Electronic Fund Transfer Act (15 U.S.C. 1693 et seq.).

[121] 77 Fed. Reg. 6,194, 6,208 (Feb. 7, 2012).

[122] For example, if the remittance amount delivered is less than the amount stated on the disclosure and this error is successfully disputed, the provider (such as a bank or credit union), at no additional charge, must either refund the consumer or transfer to the recipient the portion of the funds that were not received.

[123] *Report to the Congress on the Use of the Automated Clearinghouse System for Remittance Transfers to Foreign Countries*, Federal Reserve (July 2011). The United States is the largest estimated source of international remittances. Historically, consumers have largely chosen to send remittance transfers through nonbank money transmitters, such as Western Union. Although less common, individuals may also send remittances using services provided by depository institutions, such as banks and credit unions. Banks and credit unions typically transmit funds through an open network, such as international wire transfers and automated clearing house transactions.

[124] Remittance transfer methods generally are described as closed network and open network systems. Closed network providers, such as Western Union, transfer remittances through a network of agents or other partners that help collect funds domestically and disburse funds abroad. Open network providers, such as banks and credit unions, may collect funds domestically and use the network to transfer remittances to an unaffiliated institution to disburse the funds abroad. In addition, national laws, individual contracts, and rules of various messaging, settlement, or payment systems may constrain certain parts of transfers sent through an open network system.

[125] 77 Fed. Reg. 6,208 (Feb. 7, 2012).

[126] 77 Fed. Reg. 50,244 (Aug. 20, 2012).

[127] U.S. Senate, Committee on Banking, Housing, and Urban Affairs. "The Restoring American Financial Stability Act of 2010," *Rep. 111-176*, 111th Congress, 2d Sess. (Apr. 30, 2010).

[128] Clawbacks are recovery by the company of amounts paid to an employee based on materially inaccurate financial statements or performance criteria. This is money that the executive would not have received if the accounting was done properly and to which the executive was not entitled.

[129] OCC staff commented that these numbers will likely be lower because of the Jumpstart Our Business Startups Act of 2012 (JOBS Act), Pub. L. No. 112-106, 126 Stat. 306. With the exception of section 956, all of sections in Title IX, subtitle E of the Dodd-Frank Act, are amendments to the Securities Exchange Act of 1934. Banks and bank holding companies must be registered under the Securities Exchange Act for these provisions to apply. The JOBS Act provides relief from the Securities Exchange Act's registration requirements for banks and bank holding companies.

[130] The JOBS Act further amended the Securities Exchange Act of 1934 to provide that emerging growth companies—issuers with less than $1 billion in total annual gross revenues—are not required to seek advisory votes related to executive compensation.

[131] Section 951 requires disclosure of any agreements or understandings that the person making a proxy or consent solicitation has with named executive officers of the acquiring issuer concerning any type of compensation that is based on or relates to the acquisition, merger, consolidation, sale, or other disposition of all or substantially all of the assets of the issuer and the aggregate total of all such compensation that may be paid or become payable to or on behalf of such executive officer.

[132] 76 Fed. Reg. 6,010 (Feb. 2, 2011).

[133] SEC generally defines smaller reporting companies as those with a public float of less than $75 million.

[134] Section 953(a) amends section 14 of the Securities Exchange Act of 1934. In addition, the JOBS Act further amended the Securities Exchange Act of 1934 to provide that emerging growth companies are not required to make these disclosures.

[135] *See* S. REP. NO. 111-176 (2010).

[136] Depending on the final rule and its implementation, subsidiaries of certain financial institutions with less than $1 billion in consolidated assets could also be affected.

[137] Under the proposed rule, total consolidated assets are calculated using the average of the total assets reported in a bank's or credit union's four most recent Call Reports.

[138] FDIC, the Federal Reserve, FHFA, OCC, OTS, NCUA, and SEC issued the proposed rule to implement section 956. 76 Fed. Reg. 21,170 (Apr. 14, 2011).

[139] 76 Fed. Reg. 824 (Jan. 6, 2011). In September 2010, SEC issued an interim final temporary rule establishing a temporary registration program to comply with section 975's requirement that municipal advisors register by October 1, 2010. 75 Fed. Reg. 54,465 (Sept. 8, 2010). SEC subsequently extended the expiration date for this temporary rule, and it will now expire on September 30, 2012. 76 Fed. Reg. 80,733 (Dec. 27, 2011).

[140] 76 Fed. Reg. 824, 828.

[141] See GAO-12-247.

[142] Although no commonly accepted definition of a community bank exists, the term often is associated with smaller banks (e.g., under $1 billion in assets) that provide relationship banking services to the local community, and have management and board members who reside in the local community. In this chapter, we generally define banks (insured depository institutions that are not credit unions) with under $10 billion in total assets as community banks. We also include in our analysis federally insured credit unions with under $10 billion in total assets. We use under $10 billion in total assets as our criterion because the Dodd-Frank Act exempts small institutions from a number of its provisions based on that threshold.

[143] The Main Street Alliance is a national network of state-based small business coalitions.

[144] As SNL Financial data are updated continually, data downloaded on different dates may differ.

[145] For some titles, we identified subtitles that included a number of sections that were expected to impact community banks and credit unions, but did not necessarily include every section within that subtitle in the table.

In: The State of Community Banks … ISBN: 978-1-62417-227-4
Editor: Jeffrey R. Holman

Chapter 2

STATEMENT OF MARYANN F. HUNTER, DEPUTY DIRECTOR, DIVISION OF BANKING SUPERVISION AND REGULATION, BOARD OF GOVERNORS OF THE FEDERAL RESERVE SYSTEM. HEARING ON "THE STATE OF COMMUNITY BANKING: OPPORTUNITIES AND CHALLENGES"*

Chairman Brown, Ranking Member Corker, and members of the subcommittee, thank you for the opportunity to testify today on the challenges and opportunities facing community banks. As a former examiner and former head of banking supervision at the Federal Reserve Bank of Kansas City, which has one of the highest numbers of community banks in the Federal Reserve System, I am keenly aware of the critical role that community banks play in their local communities. Community banks also provide valuable insights into the health of their local economies, which the Federal Reserve finds invaluable in determining the appropriate path of monetary policy and in taking actions to preserve the nation's financial stability. Accordingly, I and my colleagues at the Federal Reserve value our connection with community banks and take very seriously our responsibility for the supervision of these banks.

* This is an edited, reformatted and augmented version of the testimony given on April 6, 2011 before the Senate Committee on Banking, Housing, and Urban Affairs, Subcommittee on Financial Institutions and Consumer Protection.

The Federal Reserve, in conjunction with our colleagues at the state banking supervisory agencies, is responsible for supervising approximately 830 state member banks. The vast majority of these banks are community banks[1] that provide traditional banking services and loans to small businesses and consumers. In addition, the Federal Reserve supervises more than 4,700 community bank holding companies, which together control more than $2 trillion in assets and a significant majority of the number of commercial banks operating in the United States. Beginning in July 2011, the Dodd-Frank Wall Street Reform and Consumer Protection Act (Dodd-Frank Act) will transfer responsibility from the Office of Thrift Supervision to the Federal Reserve for the supervision of more than 425 savings and loan holding companies, most of which operate community thrifts. Given these supervisory responsibilities--as well as the Federal Reserve's need to fully understand regional economic conditions--we closely monitor the condition and performance of community banks and appreciate the opportunity to discuss with you today some of the factors affecting their operations.

We gain considerable insight into community banking through our supervisory, research, and outreach activities both at the Reserve Banks and at the Board of Governors. Moreover, the Federal Reserve has undertaken several recent initiatives to better understand the perspectives of community banks and the challenges they face. The Board recently established a special supervision subcommittee of Board members that provides leadership and oversight on a variety of matters related specifically to our supervision of community and smaller regional banks.[2] This subcommittee is chaired by Governor Elizabeth Duke, a former longtime community banker, and also includes Governor Sarah Bloom Raskin, previously the Maryland state banking commissioner. A key role of this subcommittee is to review policy proposals to better understand the effect that these policies and their implementation could have on smaller institutions, both in terms of safety and soundness and potential regulatory burden.

The Federal Reserve also has undertaken an initiative to formalize and expand its dialogue with community banks. In October 2010, the Board announced the formation of the Community Depository Institutions Advisory Council (CDIAC) to provide the Board with direct insight and information from community bankers about the economy, lending conditions, supervisory matters, and other issues of interest to community banks.[3] Council members share first-hand knowledge and experience regarding the challenges they and their communities face, as well as their plans to address these challenges. Each Reserve Bank has its own local advisory council comprising representatives from banks, thrift institutions, and credit unions, and one member from each local council serves on the national council that meets with the Board twice a year in Washington. Each of the local advisory councils has held its first meeting, and the first meeting of the CDIAC with all of the members of the Federal Reserve Board took place on Friday, April 1. We expect these ongoing discussions will provide a particularly useful and relevant forum for improving our understanding of the effect of legislation, regulation, and examination activities on small banking organizations.

STATE OF COMMUNITY BANKING

The economic downturn has had a significant impact on community banks and, unfortunately, many continue to struggle. Although community banks recorded an aggregate profit for 2010, one in every five community banks reported a loss. This weakness stemmed mainly from elevated loan losses and the need to bolster reserves in anticipation of future loan deterioration. Provisions for loan losses were down considerably from 2009 but remained near historically high levels. There are some positive signs, however. For example, the pace of deterioration in loan quality continued to slow during the fourth quarter of 2010 and nonperforming assets[4] fell for the third straight quarter. However, the nonperforming assets ratio is still higher than the levels that prevailed during the significant credit downturn in the early 1990s. Loans secured by real estate continue to be the main contributors behind poor asset quality, particularly loans for construction and land development.

Although community banks have sharply reduced exposures to commercial real estate lending--sometimes through heavy write-offs of problem loans--many remain vulnerable to further deterioration in real estate markets. The continued weaknesses in real estate markets offer particular challenges to community banks, which secure much of their lending with properties in their local markets. This has reduced a significant source of revenue and has caused many banks to rethink their operating models and seek alternative sources of revenue in new lending segments.

As they seek to work through loan problems with their borrowers and implement guidance issued by the supervisory agencies in 2009, community banks have continued to actively restructure loans to creditworthy borrowers who are experiencing financial difficulties. During the past year, loans restructured and in compliance with modified terms have increased more than 30 percent to $15.1 billion. This includes $3.5 billion in restructured residential mortgages. We believe these efforts will contribute to the recovery of many struggling banks and the preservation of many small businesses, but significant improvement in financial conditions will likely take considerable time for many community banks. Indeed, although banks have been aggressive in charging off losses on problem loans and restructuring loans to borrowers experiencing financial difficulties, the adequacy of loan loss reserves remains an ongoing supervisory focus. As a consequence, reserves may require further strengthening and loan loss provisions will likely continue to weigh on earnings in future quarters at many banks.

Disappointingly, outstanding loan balances have declined for nine consecutive quarters for community banks as a group, as they have for the banking system as a whole. However, we have seen evidence that many healthy community banks have continued to lend to creditworthy borrowers. While lending contracted overall from mid-2008 through 2010, this contraction was not uniform; a significantly higher proportion of smaller banks (in this case, those with assets of $1 billion or less) actually increased their lending during this period than was the case for larger banks.

Community banks have reported a number of potential causes for the low level of lending, including reduced loan demand, a tightening of underwriting standards, a lack of creditworthy borrowers, declining collateral values, and high levels of problem loans. They have also frequently raised concerns about what they characterize as heightened supervisory expectations for capital, liquidity, and the management of concentrations in loans secured by commercial real estate, which some bankers say are leading them to make fewer loans. We take these concerns seriously and have worked hard to ensure that examiners are well-trained and employ a balanced approach to bank supervision. For example, following the issuance of the interagency *Policy Statement on Prudent Commercial Real Estate Loan Workouts* in October 2009,[5] an intensive training effort was conducted for examiners across the Federal Reserve System to promote consistency and balance in reviewing bank workouts of troubled commercial real estate loans. We have also undertaken a number of initiatives through our community affairs functions across the Federal Reserve System to encourage lending to creditworthy small businesses and consumers.

On a final note, community bankers and their supervisors have also been increasing their attention to other areas where lending concentrations may exist. For instance, both the Federal Reserve and many community banks are monitoring developments in agricultural lending to ensure that underwriting standards are consistent with assessments of potential exposures to fluctuations in commodity prices and land values.

EFFECTS OF RECENT LEGISLATION

In our interactions with community bankers, we consistently hear that the changing regulatory environment is a key challenge and concern for community banks. Even though recent reforms are directed principally at the largest and most complex U.S. financial firms and explicitly exempt small banks from the most stringent requirements, community bankers remain concerned that expectations being set for the largest institutions will ultimately be imposed in a burdensome manner on smaller institutions or will otherwise adversely affect the community bank model.

For example, bankers have brought several provisions of the Dodd-Frank Act to our attention as particular areas of concern for community banks. One such provision is the requirement that the Federal Reserve issue a rule to limit debit card interchange fees and to prohibit network exclusivity arrangements and merchant routing restrictions. Many community bankers have also expressed a sense of uncertainty about the rulemaking authority of the new Consumer Financial Protection Bureau formed by the Dodd-Frank Act. Another concern is that the more-stringent prudential standards[6] that the Federal Reserve is required to develop for banking firms with assets greater than $50 billion and all nonbank financial firms designated as systemically important by the Financial Stability Oversight Council might ultimately filter down to smaller banks. In this regard, some concerns have been raised that the new, international Basel III prudential framework for large, globally active banks--which will require large banks to hold more and better-quality capital and more-robust liquidity buffers--may be applied to banks that are not systemic or internationally active. More generally, community banks have raised concerns that the cost of compliance with new regulations and requirements may fall disproportionately on smaller banks that do not benefit from the economies of scale of larger institutions, and that this may exacerbate consolidation of the banking sector.

In this regard, the Federal Reserve and the other federal financial supervisory agencies will be publishing all of the Dodd-Frank proposed rulemakings for public comment. For example, last week the Federal Reserve, in conjunction with other federal agencies,[7] issued a proposed rule that would require sponsors of asset-backed securities to retain at least 5 percent of the credit risk of the assets underlying the securities and would not permit sponsors to transfer or hedge that credit risk. We are aware that some community banks have expressed concerns about the potential impact this proposed rule might have on the availability of credit. We encourage public comments from community banks and other commenters on this and all proposals, and will carefully consider comments in drafting final rules.

Before concluding my remarks on the effects of recent legislation, let me say a few words about the transfer of savings and loan holding company supervisory authority to the Federal Reserve. We have been working in close coordination with the Office of Thrift Supervision, the Office of the Comptroller of the Currency, and the Federal Deposit Insurance Corporation to prepare for this transfer. Our intent--to the maximum extent possible and consistent with the Home Owners' Loan Act and other laws--is to create an oversight regime for savings and loan holding companies that is consistent with our comprehensive consolidated supervision regime for bank holding companies, and we intend to issue a public notice to this effect shortly. We appreciate that savings and loan and bank holding companies differ in important ways and will remain governed by different statutes. Federal Reserve staff have been engaged in an active and constructive outreach effort to savings and loan holding companies to better understand their unique features and to help them understand our supervisory approach to holding companies.

Resilience of Community Banks

These regulatory changes will provide a new set of challenges for community banks. However, community banks have faced similar challenges in the past and have performed effectively and continued to meet the needs of their communities. Indeed, while much of the focus in recent years has been on the inability of many community banks to withstand intense credit and liquidity pressures, it is important to note that many community banks supervised by the Federal Reserve remained in sound condition throughout the crisis. Most of these banks entered the crisis with moderate exposures to commercial real estate, moderate loan-to-deposit ratios, and ample investment securities. They tended to report solid earnings and net interest margins, very limited reliance on noncore funding, and generally strong capital levels throughout the crisis. In summary, the banks that weathered the crisis most effectively were those that adhered to the traditional community banking model.

The performance of these banks provides perhaps the best example of the resilience of the community bank model. Looking back over the crisis, these banks operated safely, soundly, and profitably despite the most challenging financial climate since the Great Depression. This speaks to the skill of their management and the soundness of their business models.

CONCLUSION

Community banks will continue to face a challenging environment for some time as they work through financial difficulties brought on by the economic downturn and face challenges that arise from a rapidly changing regulatory environment. The unique connection between community banks and the communities they serve is clear. The bankers who live and work in these communities know their customers and understand their local economies, and that knowledge is not easily replaced or replicated. This relationship banking is crucial to the community banking model and an important part of its viability. The Federal Reserve will continue to listen to the concerns of community banks and carefully weigh the impact of regulatory and policy changes on them, while at the same time working with them to address the future challenges they may face.

Thank you again for inviting me to appear before you today on this important subject. I would be pleased to answer any questions you may have.

End Notes

[1] For supervisory purposes, the Federal Reserve defines banking organizations with assets of $10 billion or less as community banking organizations.

[2] For supervisory purposes, the Federal Reserve generally considers banking organizations with assets between $10 billion and $50 billion to be regional banking organizations.

[3] The CDIAC replaces the former Thrift Institutions Advisory Council which provided the Board with information from the perspective of thrift institutions and credit unions.

[4] Defined as nonaccruing loans plus other real estate owned.

[5] See Board of Governors of the Federal Reserve System, Division of Banking Supervision and Regulation (2009), "Prudent Commercial Real Estate Loan Workouts," Supervision and Regulation Letter 09-7 (October 30), www.federalreserve.gov/boarddocs/srletters/2009/SR0907.htm.

[6] These more-stringent standards for large institutions will include stronger capital and leverage requirements, liquidity requirements, and single-counterparty credit limits, as well as requirements to periodically produce resolution plans and conduct stress tests.

[7] The other agencies are the Department of Housing and Urban Development, Federal Deposit Insurance Corporation, Federal Housing Finance Agency, Office of the Comptroller of the Currency, and Securities and Exchange Commission. For more information, see Board of Governors of the Federal Reserve System (2011), "Agencies Seek Comment on Risk Retention Proposal," joint press release, March 31, www.federalreserve.gov/newsevents/press/bcreg/20110331a.htm.

In: The State of Community Banks …
Editor: Jeffrey R. Holman
ISBN: 978-1-62417-227-4

Chapter 3

STATEMENT OF SANDRA L. THOMPSON, DIRECTOR OF RISK MANAGEMENT SUPERVISION, FEDERAL DEPOSIT INSURANCE CORPORATION. HEARING ON "THE STATE OF COMMUNITY BANKING: OPPORTUNITIES AND CHALLENGES"*

Chairman Brown, Ranking Member Corker, and members of the Subcommittee, I welcome the opportunity to speak with you today about the state of community banking.

Community banks provide vital services in their communities; making loans to customers they know, in markets they know. Community banks are essential providers of credit to small businesses, and through the recent financial crisis, community banks have maintained steadier levels of total loan balances than their larger competitors. As our economy recovers from the most severe recession since the 1930s, a thriving community banking sector is important to help support the credit needs of local households and business borrowers.

As the supervisor of 4,414 community banks,[1] the FDIC has a keen appreciation for the important role community banks play in the national

* This is an edited, reformatted and augmented version of the testimony given on April 6, 2011 before the Senate Committee on Banking, Housing, and Urban Affairs, Subcommittee on Financial Institutions and Consumer Protection.

economy. The FDIC's bank examiners work out of duty stations located in 85 communities across the country. They know the community banks in their areas and are familiar with the local conditions facing those banks. Many have seen more than one previous economic down cycle and recognize the critical role that community banks play in credit availability.

Over 90 percent of all FDIC-insured institutions are community banks, and they hold close to 11 percent of aggregate industry assets. Community banks have branches in nearly all towns and urban areas, and about two-thirds of all branches in rural areas are community bank branches. Through fast, localized decision-making, personal service, and a strong local presence, community banks serve the loan and deposit needs of consumers and small businesses in periods of both economic expansion and contraction.

In my testimony, I will describe the performance of community banks as of year-end 2010, identify some of the challenges and opportunities we see for community banks, and discuss some of the actions that the FDIC has taken to help smaller institutions navigate the downturn. Finally, I will discuss the effects of the Dodd-Frank Wall Street Reform and Consumer Protection Act (the Dodd-Frank Act) on community banks.

THE FINANCIAL PERFORMANCE OF COMMUNITY BANKS

After an extremely challenging 2009, community banks reported improving performance in 2010. Just as in the broader economy and in the aggregate performance of larger banks, 2010 shows signs of marking the beginning of a turnaround for community banks.

A number of community banks still face headwinds in the form of legacy problems in their real-estate loan portfolios. These headwinds are reflected in aggregate financial performance that continues to be weaker than pre-crisis levels. Thus, while community bank earnings rebounded from the aggregate loss reported in 2009, the average return on assets remained low and lags that of larger banks. Asset quality deterioration appears to have leveled off, but volumes of troubled assets and charge-offs remain high. In addition, community banks continue to have high concentrations of commercial real estate loans, a market segment that remains weak in many areas of the country. A more detailed discussion of community bank performance follows.

Earnings

Community banks earned $4.7 billion in 2010, in contrast to the net loss that was reported for 2009. Fewer institutions reported annual losses in 2010 than in the previous year, and two-thirds of community banks had earnings improvement in 2010, compared to only 40 percent in 2009. Most community banks set aside smaller provisions for loan loss in 2010 than they did the previous year, and lower funding costs helped net interest margins rise slightly.

The average return on assets (ROA) for community banks in 2010 was 0.33 percent. While this was a clear improvement over the prior year's loss, it was only half the overall banking industry's ROA of 0.66 percent, indicating that community bank performance continues to trail that of larger banks. The difference in performance may be attributable in part to large banks' more diversified revenue sources and to differences in asset composition – community banks are more dependent upon interest income from loans than their larger competitors are, and community banks have higher loan-to-asset ratios than large banks.

Asset Quality

Asset quality is not recovering as quickly at community banks as at larger banks. The ratio of noncurrent[2] loans to total loans for community banks fell very slightly during the fourth quarter, to 3.46 percent, and was flat compared to a year ago. Noncurrent rates and net charge-off rates for community bank loan portfolios remain lower than average industry rates, but this is a function of the differing mix of loans between small and large institutions. The retail loans that make up a larger portion of big banks' portfolios, such as credit card loans, have relatively high noncurrent rates. However, these loans are also recovering more quickly than the commercial real estate (CRE) loans that make up a larger part of community banks' portfolios.

The noncurrent rate for construction and development (C&D) loans at community banks remained stubbornly high at 12.88 percent in the fourth quarter and reflects the ongoing distress in the real estate development sector. Noncurrent rates also rose during the fourth quarter for one-to-four family residential real estate loans and nonfarm nonresidential real estate loans, but declined for commercial and industrial (C&I) loans.

Net charge-offs increased during the fourth quarter, but were lower than a year ago (net charge-offs are typically higher in the fourth quarter than in the preceding three quarters). Most community banks reported declines in net charge-offs compared to fourth quarter 2009. Community banks set aside more in provisions for loan losses than they charged off during the quarter, suggesting that community banks will continue to work through their asset quality problems in 2011.

As a result of the protracted credit quality problems, community banks' levels of other real estate owned (ORE) and restructured loans have increased. ORE represented 1.05 percent of assets at community banks and restructured loans made up another 1.19 percent. Troubled assets – ORE, restructured loans, delinquent, and noncurrent loans – represented about five percent of assets.

Commercial real estate markets have been hard-hit in the crisis, and it is no surprise that community banks with rapid growth or exceptionally high concentrations of CRE lending, and especially C&D lending, have suffered disproportionately. C&D loans and nonfarm nonresidential real estate loans comprise 38 percent of community bank loan balances, but during the fourth quarter represented 50 percent of their loans charged-off, almost 60 percent of their noncurrent loans, and close to three-fourths of their ORE. Given that real estate markets continue to struggle in many regions across the country, troubled CRE-related assets will continue to strain community banks' asset quality and earnings throughout this year.

Lending by Community Banks

As I stated earlier, community banks play a vital role in credit creation across the country and small businesses especially rely on community banks for loans when large institutions and non-banks curtail their lending activity. This has been borne out by loan originations over the past several years, as community bank loan balances have increased by about three percent on a merger-adjusted basis since second quarter 2008. Over the same period, overall industry loan balances *fell* by more than 7 percent. It is also noteworthy to point out that community banks held almost 39 percent of small loans to businesses (C&I and CRE loans in amounts under $1 million and agricultural and farmland loans under $500,000) at the end of 2010, which represents about three times the community banks' share of total industry loans.

Funding and Capital

Consistent with their focus on providing traditional banking services to retail customers, community banks rely heavily on deposits to fund their balance sheets. Fourth quarter domestic deposits were equal to more than 80 percent of assets at community banks, compared to less than 60 percent of industry assets. Close to three-fourths of community bank deposit accounts are in accounts under the insurance limit of $250,000. Community banks held $53 billion in non-interest bearing transaction accounts over $250,000 temporarily insured under the Dodd-Frank Act at the end of the fourth quarter. Again, the local focus and convenience offered by community banks provides them with a viable platform for gathering deposits, while delivering essential depository and payment services to consumers and small businesses.

Community banks have maintained capital ratios higher than the industry averages. Risk-based capital ratios rose for the fourth straight quarter and the community bank leverage ratio was just below the two-year high.

Consolidation

At year-end 2010, there were 874 fewer FDIC-insured institutions with assets under $1 billion than at year-end 2007, as continuing consolidation and a number of failures have reduced the community bank population. From year-end 2007 through year-end 2010, the share of industry assets represented by community banks has declined from 11.4 percent to 10.8 percent, while the share of industry assets represented by the largest banks (those with total assets greater than $100 billion) has increased from 54.6 percent to 59.1 percent. However, consolidation of community banks is not primarily a result of the recent crisis, but is the continuation of a long-term trend precipitated by competition, technological advances, and innovation in the financial services industry.

CHALLENGES AND OPPORTUNITIES FOR COMMUNITY BANKS

The most important challenge facing community banks at present is improving their operating performance amid the lingering effects of the financial crisis and recession. A large number of financial institutions have an elevated level of problem assets, which strains earnings and can divert management's attention from executing longer-term strategic initiatives. Moreover, communities across the country continue to suffer from high unemployment and slow job creation, and loan demand remains weak. According to the latest Federal Reserve Senior Loan Officers' Opinion Survey, only twelve percent of small banks in the survey reported increased demand for C&I loans. Tepid business expansion and continuing high unemployment are also making it difficult for businesses and consumers to service existing loans and for financial institutions to work out problems.

Many community banks remain vulnerable to additional real estate market declines as a result of their significant holdings of commercial real estate assets, both as loans and as ORE. Many institutions that relied heavily on C&D lending in the years leading up to the recession continue to be exposed to declining home prices. At the same time, commercial real estate markets remain weak in most areas.

In spite of the obstacles, and high concentrations of commercial real estate loans, many community banks weathered the financial storm well because of sound underwriting practices and corporate governance, in addition to a keen understanding of their local market and economy. As a result, those institutions are poised to respond quickly and prudently once credit demand returns. These banks know their customers well and in turn, their customers know them, trust them, and appreciate their personal attention and responsiveness at the local level.

Community banks could also begin to see a narrowing of the cost advantage that larger institutions had previously enjoyed. Many of the reforms that are being implemented in response to the financial crisis are aimed at improving lax underwriting practices, particularly in the residential mortgage lending field. Community banks for the most part, did not relax their standards. That made it difficult for them to compete during the years of expansion leading up to the crisis. As both nonbanks and larger institutions are required by the Dodd Frank Act to tighten standards, the community banks may see an improvement in their ability to originate good quality mortgage loans at competitive interest rates.

THE FDIC AND COMMUNITY BANKS

Throughout the real estate and economic downturn, the FDIC has advocated for policies that will help community banks and their customers navigate this challenging period and mitigate unnecessary losses. We share community banks' desire to restore profitability, strengthen asset quality, and serve the credit needs of local markets. The FDIC has worked closely with banks as they have taken steps to raise capital, enhance their loan workout functions, and revise strategic plans to remain competitive in the financial services industry. Through our regional and field offices, the Corporation actively communicates with the community banks we supervise and provides recommendations for addressing operational and financial weaknesses as appropriate.

The FDIC has joined several interagency efforts that encourage banks to originate and restructure loans to creditworthy borrowers, and to clarify outstanding guidance. For example, the federal bank regulatory agencies issued the *Interagency Statement on Meeting the Needs of Creditworthy Borrowers* on November 12, 2008, which encouraged banks to prudently make loans available in their markets. The agencies also issued the *Interagency Statement on Meeting the Credit Needs of Creditworthy Small Business Borrowers* on February 12, 2010, to encourage prudent small business lending and emphasize that examiners will apply a balanced approach in evaluating loans. This guidance was issued subsequent to the October 30, 2009 *Policy Statement on Prudent Commercial Real Estate Workouts* that encourages banks to restructure loans for commercial real estate mortgage customers experiencing difficulties making payments. The CRE Workouts Guidance reinforces long-standing supervisory principles in a manner that recognizes pragmatic actions by lenders and small business borrowers are necessary to weather this difficult economic period.

The FDIC also joined the other banking agencies in issuing the *Interagency Appraisal and Evaluation Guidelines* on December 2, 2010, to clarify expectations for real estate appraisals. Clarification of these guidelines was important for the industry given changes in property values over the past several years. We also actively engage with community banks at the state level and nationally through various trade associations, which helps our agency articulate its supervisory expectations on important issues through a variety of forums. We also sponsor training events for community banks including regional and national teleconferences on risk management and consumer protection matters, as well as Directors Colleges to help bank directors better understand the supervisory process.

POTENTIAL IMPACT OF THE DODD-FRANK ACT

Some community bankers have pointed to uncertainty about the effect of new regulations under the Dodd-Frank Act as a potential obstacle to their continued profitability.

However, much of the Dodd-Frank Act should have no direct impact on community banks, while certain changes in the Act provide real benefits. For example, those provisions of the Act that impose additional capital and other heightened prudential requirements on the largest financial institutions are aimed at reducing systemic risks. If properly implemented, those and other provisions of the Act should do much to return competitive balance to the marketplace by restoring market discipline; ensuring appropriate regulatory oversight of systemically important financial companies; and having rules that apply to all providers of financial services, not just insured depository institutions. In fact, as noted above, there are immediate, tangible benefits that the Dodd-Frank Act confers on community banks.

First, the deposit insurance coverage limit was permanently increased to \$250,000. In addition, the law provides a guarantee of all balances in non-interest bearing transaction accounts above \$250,000 until the end of 2012. These changes help to address one of the main sources of competitive imbalance, by giving community banks access to federally insured or guaranteed funding in larger amounts, without having to pay a fee to deposit brokers or consultants.

The Dodd-Frank Act also changes the assessment base used to calculate premiums paid to the Deposit Insurance Fund (DIF), from one based on deposits to one based on total assets. Because community banks generally rely more on deposits as a funding source than do larger banks, the Dodd-Frank Act effectively shifts a greater proportion of DIF assessments to larger banks. In aggregate, banks with assets under \$10 billion should see their assessments decline by 30 percent. The final rule implementing the new assessment base took effect on April 1st.

To provide for a more stable DIF going forward, the law increases the minimum DIF reserve ratio to 1.35 percent. But it extends the period in which the DIF must be recapitalized to 2020, and also requires that the assessments needed to increase the DIF from the old minimum ratio of 1.15 percent to the new minimum ratio of 1.35 percent should be collected entirely from banks with total consolidated assets of $10 billion or more. Thus, community banks' deposit insurance assessments will not need to rise in order to meet the new target.

There are other important, if less tangible, ways that the Dodd-Frank Act should help create a more level playing field between community banks and their larger competitors.

Most – but not all – of the high risk mortgage lending that precipitated the recent crisis originated outside of insured banks. The Dodd-Frank Act requires these non-bank lenders to adhere to federal consumer protection laws and places them under federal supervision for the first time. The Consumer Financial Protection Bureau established by the Dodd-Frank Act will likely reduce the unfair competitive advantage that non-bank competitors have long enjoyed as under-regulated – and often unregulated and unsupervised – financial services providers.

Importantly, section 171 of the Dodd Frank Act, the Collins Amendment, places a risk-based capital floor under the so-called advanced approaches. The floor will ensure that capital requirements for the largest banks and their bank holding companies are no lower than the level of capital required of community banks that hold similar exposures. In addition, under section 165 of the Act, large bank holding companies are subject to heightened capital standards (that is, beyond the standards required of smaller institutions), to account for the greater risk that large bank holding companies pose to the financial system. These provisions of the Dodd Frank Act are consistent with developments taking place in the Basel Committee on Banking Supervision which, with the support of the U.S. banking agencies, has announced its intention to develop heightened capital standards for the largest banks.

Finally, the most fundamental reform in the Dodd-Frank Act is the new orderly liquidation authority for large bank holding companies and systemically important non-bank financial companies, which ends "Too Big to Fail." The FDIC regularly carries out a prompt and orderly liquidation process using its receivership authority for insured banks and thrifts that are facing insolvency. The Dodd-Frank Act for the first time gives the FDIC a similar set of receivership powers to close and liquidate systemically-important financial firms that are failing. Just as important, the Act mandates that systemically important financial institutions maintain credible, actionable resolution plans that facilitate their orderly resolution if they should fail. If the FDIC and the Federal Reserve Board do not find an institution's resolution plan to be credible, we can compel the divestiture of activities that would unduly interfere with the orderly liquidation of the company. The FDIC Board adopted a proposed rulemaking for public comment last week and as Chairman Bair said at the Board meeting, "This is a big step forward in ending 'too big to fail.'"

It has been well-documented that the cost of funds for the largest banks has been lower than that for smaller banks. In fourth quarter 2010, the average cost of funding earning assets for banks over $100 billion in assets was 0.67 percent, compared to 1.24 percent for community banks. Not all of this difference is due to the perception that the largest banks are too big to fail. Their product mix and access to capital markets in the U.S. and overseas help to lower their funding costs in low interest rate environments, such as the one we are in.

Using the tools provided under the Dodd-Frank Act, we can break this cycle of subsidized risk taking and create a financial marketplace that is both more stable and more competitively balanced. Much of the regulatory cost of the Dodd-Frank Act will fall, as it should, directly on the large institutions that create systemic risk. The leveling of the competitive playing field will help preserve the essential diversity of our financial system, and prevent any institution from taking undue risks at the expense of the public.

The FDIC understands why community banks are wary. We recognize the concerns community bankers have in understanding how new legislation and regulations will affect their operations. The FDIC is required or authorized by Congress to implement some 44 regulations, including 18 independent and 26 joint rulemakings. Community banks should be, and are, taking an active interest in these new regulations as they are developed.

We are implementing the provisions of the Dodd-Frank Act as transparently and expeditiously as possible. Not only is the FDIC following the normal steps used in any rulemaking process, we are also holding public roundtables to discuss issues such as our systemic resolution authority and required resolution plans, the new deposit insurance assessment provisions and core/brokered deposits. In addition, we document meetings between senior

FDIC officials and outside parties that are related to the implementation of the Dodd-Frank Act.

The FDIC also is focused on how other provisions of the Dodd-Frank Act could impact community banks. For example, we are extremely concerned that, under proposed regulations, community banks may not actually receive the benefit of the interchange fee limit exemption explicitly provided for in the law. We sent a comment letter to the Federal Reserve Board detailing these concerns and encouraging the Federal Reserve to consider the practical implications of its proposed rule on community banks.

We also have engaged the FDIC's Advisory Committee on Community Banking on the Dodd-Frank Act and other issues. At the January 20 meeting of the committee, there was a discussion of ways to ease the regulatory burden on small institutions. Among the ideas discussed at that meeting were identifying which regulatory questionnaires and reports can be streamlined through automation, reviewing ways to reduce the total amount of reporting required of banks, and ensuring that community banks are aware that senior FDIC officials in the regions and in Washington are available and interested in receiving their feedback regarding our regulatory and supervisory process.

The FDIC is particularly interested in finding ways to eliminate unnecessary regulatory burden on community banks, whose balance sheets are much less complicated than those of the larger banks. We continuously pursue methods to streamline our supervisory process through the use of technology and other means to reduce any possible disruption associated with examination activity. While we maintain a robust examination process, we are sensitive to banks' business priorities and strive to be efficient in our work.

To this end, we have established as a goal for the first quarter of 2011 to modify the content of our Financial Institution Letters (FILs) - the vehicle used to alert banks to any regulatory changes or guidance - so that every FIL issued will include a section making clear the applicability to smaller institutions (under $1 billion). In addition, by June 30 we plan to complete a review of all of our recurring questionnaires and information requests to the industry and to develop recommendations to improve the efficiency and ease of use and a plan to implement these changes. The FDIC also has challenged its staff to find additional ways of translating some of these ideas into action. This includes launching an intensive review of existing reporting requirements to identify areas for streamlining.

At the beginning of this year, we initiated a dialogue with our field and regional staffs to reinforce the FDIC's balanced approach to bank supervision.

In this effort, we are reminding examiners to work cooperatively with financial institutions and to be aware of the great challenges that face community banks. Moreover, we will be engaging in a dialogue with bankers at each examination in 2011 to solicit bankers' views on aspects of the regulatory and supervisory process that may be adversely affecting credit availability.

CONCLUSION

Community banks remain an essential part of the financial system, and the FDIC is committed to a regulatory structure that will support a vibrant, competitive community banking sector and a level playing field between large and small banks. Throughout the financial crisis and recession, community banks continued providing credit even as larger banks pulled back. We need a thriving community banking sector to support an economic recovery and fulfill the credit and depository needs of households and businesses on Main Street.

Thank you. I am pleased to answer any questions.

End Notes

[1] Throughout this testimony, for purposes of data analysis, community banks are defined as banks and thrifts with total assets of less than $1 billion. The FDIC supervises a total of 4,715 banks. All data are as of December 31, 2010.

[2] Noncurrent loans are loans that are 90 or more days past due or have been placed on nonaccrual status.

In: The State of Community Banks …
Editor: Jeffrey R. Holman
ISBN: 978-1-62417-227-4

Chapter 4

TESTIMONY OF JENNIFER KELLY, SENIOR DEPUTY COMPTROLLER FOR MIDSIZE AND COMMUNITY BANK SUPERVISION, OFFICE OF THE COMPTROLLER OF THE CURRENCY. HEARING ON "THE STATE OF COMMUNITY BANKING: OPPORTUNITIES AND CHALLENGES"*

I. INTRODUCTION

Chairman Brown, Ranking Member Corker, and members of the Subcommittee, my name is Jennifer Kelly. I have been a commissioned national bank examiner for 27 years, and I am currently the Senior Deputy Comptroller for Midsize and Community Bank Supervision for the Office of the Comptroller of the Currency (OCC), reporting directly to the Comptroller. In this capacity, I serve as the senior OCC official responsible for community bank supervision. I appreciate this opportunity to discuss the current state of the community banks the OCC supervises and the impact of the Dodd-Frank

* This is an edited, reformatted and augmented version of a Testimony Presented April 6, 2011 before the Senate Committee on Banking, Housing, and Urban Affairs, Subcommittee on Financial Institutions and Consumer Protection.

Wall Street Reform and Consumer Protection Act (Dodd-Frank Act) on those institutions.

My testimony first presents an overview of the OCC's approach to the supervision of national community banks, then addresses the present state of community banks, and concludes by sharing our perspective on the likely effects of the Dodd-Frank Act on community banks.

Let me say first that community banks play a crucial role in providing consumers and small businesses in communities across the nation with essential financial services as well as the credit that is critical to economic growth and job creation. While we have been through an extremely difficult economic cycle that has been challenging for institutions of all sizes, I am pleased to report that conditions are beginning to stabilize for community banks, and we are seeing these institutions return to profitability. As a result, the vast majority of these banks will continue to play a vital role in supporting their communities and the nation's financial system.

II. OCC's Approach to Community Bank Supervision

The OCC supervises over 1,200 community banks with assets under $1 billion; more than 800 of those banks have less than $250 million in assets. On July 21, in accordance with the Dodd-Frank Act, the OCC will assume responsibility for the supervision of approximately 664 federal savings associations – including 220 mutuals – with total assets of just over $912 billion. Since the overwhelming majority of those thrifts are community institutions, the number of community institutions we supervise will increase by more than half later this year. These institutions are integral to local economies throughout the country, and we remain deeply committed to their safe and sound operation.

The OCC's community bank supervision program is built around our local field offices. Approximately 75 percent of our examination staff is dedicated to the supervision of community institutions. These examiners are based in over 60 cities throughout the United States in close proximity to the banks they supervise. Every national community bank is assigned to an examiner who monitors the bank's condition on an on-going basis and who serves as the focal point for communications with the bank. The primary responsibility for the supervision of individual community banks is delegated to the local

Assistant Deputy Comptroller (ADC), who is under the oversight of a district Deputy Comptroller who reports to me. When we assume responsibility for federal savings associations later this year, we will increase the number of ADCs by more than 20 and open additional field offices.

Our structure ensures that community banks receive the benefits of highly trained bank examiners with local knowledge and experience, along with the resources and specialized expertise that a nationwide organization can provide. While our bank supervision policies and procedures establish a common framework and set of expectations, our examiners are taught to tailor their supervision of each community bank to its individual risk profile, business model, and management strategies. As a result, our ADCs are given considerable decision-making authority, reflecting their experience, expertise and their "on-the-ground" knowledge of the institutions they supervise.

We have mechanisms in place to ensure that our supervisory policies, procedures, and expectations are applied to community banks in a consistent and balanced manner. Every report of examination is reviewed and signed off by the responsible ADC or Deputy Comptroller before it is finalized. In those cases where significant issues are identified and an enforcement action is already in place, or is being contemplated, additional levels of review occur prior to finalizing the examination conclusions. We also have formal quality assurance processes that assess the effectiveness of our supervision and compliance with OCC policies through periodic, randomly selected reviews of the supervisory record. This is done with oversight by the Enterprise Governance Unit that reports directly to the Comptroller.

A key element of the OCC's supervisory philosophy is open and frequent communication with the banks we supervise. In this regard, my management team and I encourage any banker that has concerns about a particular examination finding to raise those concerns with his or her examination team and with the district management team that oversees the bank. Our ADCs and Deputy Comptrollers expect and encourage such inquiries. Should a banker not want to pursue those chains of communication, our Ombudsman's office provides a venue for bankers to discuss their concerns informally or to formally request an appeal of examination findings. The OCC's Ombudsman is fully independent of the supervisory process, and he reports directly to the Comptroller. In addition to hearing formal appeals, the Ombudsman's office provides bankers with an impartial ear to hear complaints and a mechanism to facilitate the resolution of disputes with our supervisory staff.

The OCC recognizes the importance of communicating regularly with the industry outside of the supervision process to clarify our expectations, discuss emerging issues of interest to the industry, and respond to bankers' concerns. We participate in numerous industry-sponsored events, as well as conduct a variety of outreach activities, including Meet the Comptroller events, chief executive officer roundtables, and teleconferences on topical issues. We also offer workshops for bank directors to help them understand and effectively execute their fiduciary responsibilities. In preparation for the transfer of federal savings associations to OCC supervision next July, we recently presented 17 day-long programs for thrift executives in locations around the country to provide information and perspective on the agency's approach to supervision and regulation.

III. Current Condition of National Community Banks

The operating environment for community banks over the last three years has been particularly challenging. Lending activity – the primary revenue source for community banks – has been hampered by the overall economic climate. Although it is true that many bankers have adjusted and tightened some of their credit underwriting standards, most of the community bankers I talk to reiterate that lending is the backbone of their business and that they are seeking to make loans to creditworthy borrowers. We continue to encourage bankers to lend to such borrowers.

As shown in Chart 1, community bank profitability, as measured by return on equity, improved last year after a precipitous decline in the previous two years but remains sharply below historical experience.

A major factor contributing to the decline in profitability is the continued pressure on community banks' net interest margins. Tepid loan demand and the low interest rate environment are contributing to the decline in these margins: as loans and investments mature, banks are forced to replace them with lower yielding assets. While the rates banks pay for certificates of deposit and other funding sources have also declined, many core deposits are already at extremely low rates, leaving little room for further declines. As a result, community banks' margins are at historical lows (see Chart 2).

Elevated levels of problem loans are also hampering community banks' financial performance as banks have had to increase their loan loss reserve provisions to cover loan losses. As shown in Chart 3 on the next page, the net effect of these factors has been a strain on community banks' net income.

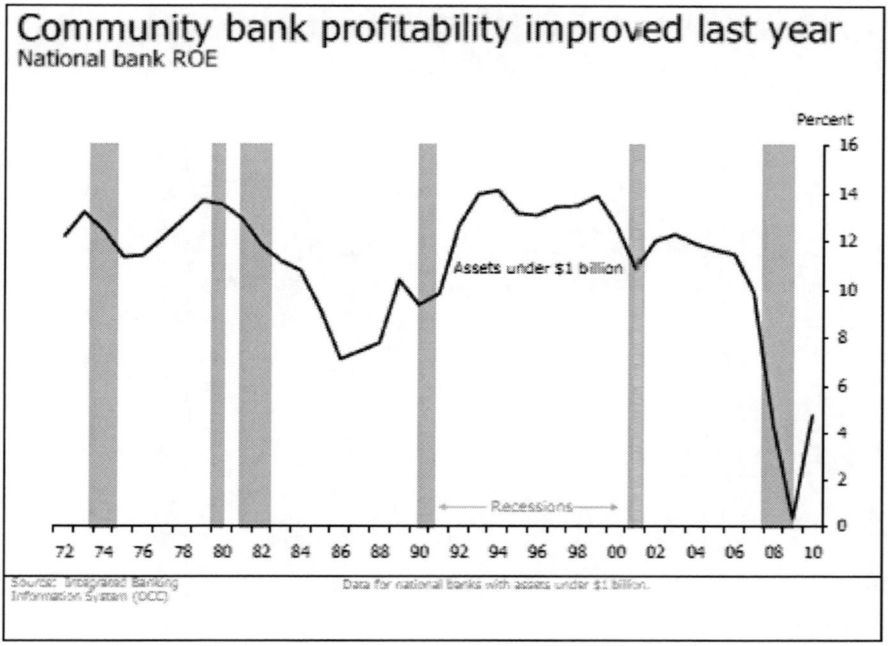

Chart 1.

Although similar trends are evident for the entire industry, they pose more difficult challenges for small institutions because large banks have more diverse revenue streams and greater economies of scale. When margins are under pressure, other sources of revenue take on greater prominence. But those other sources of income are also under pressure right now.

Notwithstanding these pressures, the vast majority of national community banks remain strong: three-quarters of the community banks we supervise have supervisory – or CAMELS – ratings of 1 or 2, reflecting their sound management and strong financial condition.[1] These banks have successfully weathered the recent economic turmoil by focusing on sound banking fundamentals: strong underwriting practices, prudent limits on loan concentrations, and stable funding bases.

There remains, however, a sizeable segment of community banks that are experiencing more severe financial strains, primarily due to their exposures to the commercial real estate (CRE) markets. As shown in Chart 4, although CRE concentrations as a percentage of capital have trended downward for all national banks, they are still significant for many community banks.

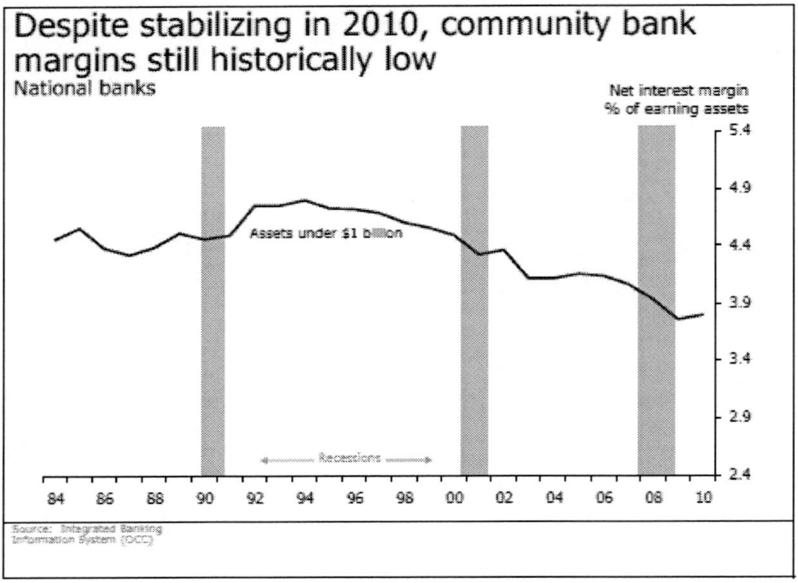

Chart 2.

Community bank profitability up in 2010 but provisions remain high

National banks

Assets under $1 B

$ billions

Major income components	2007	2008	2009	2010
Revenues				
Net interest income	8.4	8.7	8.8	9.0
Noninterest income	3.3	3.3	3.4	3.3
Realized Sec. G/L	-0.0	-0.3	0.0	0.1
Expenses				
Provisioning	0.5	1.4	2.3	1.6
Noninterest expense	8.0	8.5	9.2	9.1
Income Taxes	0.7	0.3	0.2	0.4
Net income	2.4	1.5	0.6	1.4

Source: Integrated Banking Information System (OCC)

Data are merger-adjusted and held constant for banks in operation from 1Q:06 to 4Q:10.

Chart 3.

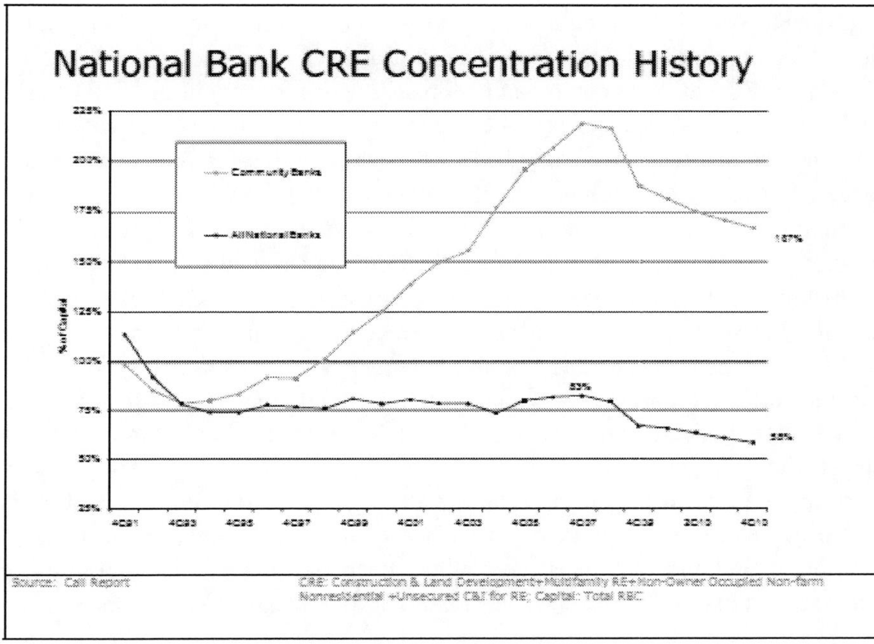

Chart 4.

CRE lending is an important product for both small banks and the communities they serve, but CRE concentrations have played a prominent role in most of the problem community banks that we supervise. The timing and effect of the distressed CRE market on individual banks' overall financial condition has varied by the size, location, and type of CRE exposure of the bank. For example, rapid deterioration of construction and development loans led the performance problems in the CRE sector and thus banks with heavier concentrations in this segment tended to experience losses at an earlier stage. Performance in this segment is expected to improve more rapidly as the pool of potentially distressed construction loans has diminished. Conversely, banks whose lending is more focused on income-producing commercial mortgages, including many smaller community banks, are continuing to experience an increase in problem loans and charge-off rates.

Although commercial property markets across the nation have begun to show signs of stabilization, net operating income (NOI), which is one of the key drivers for CRE property values and the primary source for loan repayment, continues to decline across most CRE sectors. This translates to potential for additional losses in income-producing CRE loans which is a significant issue for community banks since that loan category is twice as large as the construction and development portfolios in aggregate.

The OCC has been raising and addressing concerns about the CRE market and, in particular, the concentrated exposures that many community banks have to this market, since early 2004 when we initiated the first of a series of targeted examinations at banks that we believed were at significant risk due to the nature and scope of their CRE activities. These supervisory efforts have continued with various targeted examinations and reviews at national banks with significant CRE concentrations. Key objectives of our CRE examinations are to ensure that bank management recognizes and addresses potential problems at the earliest stage possible—when workout efforts are likely to be most successful—and that previously identified deficiencies and shortcomings in risk management practices have been addressed. In this regard, I want to stress that the OCC has and continues to encourage bankers to work constructively with borrowers who are facing difficulties. We firmly believe that prudent CRE loan workouts are often in the best interest of the financial institution and the borrower, and it has been our longstanding policy that examiners will not criticize prudent loan workout arrangements. This does not mean, however, that examiners will allow bankers to ignore loans with structural weaknesses or insufficient cash flows to support repayment. While we encourage bankers to work with troubled borrowers, we also insist that banks maintain the integrity of their financial reporting by maintaining appropriate loan loss reserves and capital and, when warranted, taking appropriate charge-offs.

IV. Challenges Presented for Community Banks by the Post-Crisis Regulatory Environment

As is commonly observed, the Dodd-Frank Act resulted in the most comprehensive reform of the United States financial system in decades. Some of the best-known changes will primarily affect the largest banking institutions – for example, the new requirements to be imposed on "systemically significant" institutions; the so-called "Volcker Rule" constraints on proprietary trading and investments in hedge funds and private equity funds; new restrictions on derivatives activities; and shifting more of the cost of deposit insurance to large banks. But other requirements within the Act broadly amend banking and financial laws in ways that affect the entire banking sector, including community banks.

The challenges banks face have several dimensions: new regulation – both new restrictions and new compliance costs – on businesses they conduct, limits on revenues for certain products, and additional regulators administering both new and existing regulatory requirements. In the context of community banks, a particular concern will be whether these combine to create a tipping point causing banks to exit lines of business that provide important diversification of their business, and increase their concentration in other activities that raise their overall risk profile.

For example, the Dodd-Frank Act imposes a range of new requirements on the retail businesses that are "bread-and-butter" for many community banks. The costs associated with small business lending will increase when new HMDA-style reporting requirements become effective. Longstanding advisory and service relationships with municipalities may cause the bank to be deemed a "municipal advisor" subject to registration with the Securities and Exchange Commission (SEC) and rules issued by the SEC and the Municipal Securities Rulemaking Board. And checking account relationships with customers are likely to be re-shaped to recover the costs associated with providing debit cards if debit interchange fees are restricted.

The new Consumer Financial Protection Bureau (CFPB) is charged with implementing new requirements that will affect banks of all sizes. These include new standards for mortgage loan originators; minimum standards for mortgages themselves; limits on charges for mortgage prepayments; new disclosure requirements required at mortgage origination and in monthly statements; a new regime of standards and oversight for appraisers; and a significant expansion of the current HMDA requirements for mortgage lenders to report and publicly disclose detailed information about mortgage loans they originate (13 new data elements).

The CFPB is also authorized to issue new regulations on a broad range of topics, including, but not limited to:

- additional disclosure requirements to "ensure that the features of any consumer financial product or service, both initially and over the life ofthe product, are fully, accurately, and effectively disclosed to consumers in a manner that permits consumers to understand the costs, benefits, and risks associated with the product or service, in light of the facts and circumstances";

- new regulations regarding unfair, deceptive or "abusive" practices; and
- standards for providing consumers with electronic access to information (retrievable in the ordinary course of the institution's business) about their accounts and transactions with the institution.

While we strongly support clearer, more meaningful, and accessible consumer disclosures, it is important to recognize that the fixed costs associated with changing marketing and other product-related materials will have a proportionately larger impact on community banks due to their smaller revenue base. The ultimate cost to community banks will depend on how the CFPB implements its new mandate and the extent to which it exercises its exemptive authority for community banks.

Community banks also may be particularly impacted by the Dodd-Frank Act's directive that Federal agencies modify their regulations to remove references to credit ratings as standards for determining creditworthiness. This requirement impacts standards in the capital regulations that are applicable to all banks. National banks are also affected because ratings are used in other places in the OCC's regulations, such as standards for permissible investment securities. As a result, institutions will be required to do more independent analysis in categorizing assets for the purpose of determining applicable capital requirements and whether debt securities are permissible investments – a requirement that will tax especially the more limited resources of community institutions.

The Dodd-Frank Act restrictions on corporate governance apply to community banks as well as larger institutions. Banks that are public companies will be subject to several new requirements on compensation, including shareholder "say on pay" votes, disclosures on performance-based compensation arrangements, and compensation clawbacks for accounting restatements.

Regardless of how well community banks adapt to Dodd-Frank Act reforms in the long-term, in the near- to medium-term these new requirements will raise costs and possibly reduce revenue for community institutions. The immediate effects will be different for different banks, depending on their current mix of activities, so it is not possible to quantify those impacts with accuracy. In the longer term, we expect to see banks adjust their business models in a variety of ways. Some will exit businesses where they find that associated regulatory costs are simply too high to sustain profitability, or they will decide how much of the added costs can, or should, be passed along to customers. Others will focus on providing products and services to the least risky customers as a way to manage their regulatory costs. Some will elect to concentrate more heavily in niche businesses that increase revenues but also heighten their risk profile. While we know there will be a process of adaptation, we cannot predict how these choices will affect either individual institutions or the future profile of community banking at this stage.

CONCLUSION

Community banks play a critical role in providing financial services to our nation's communities and businesses. The OCC is committed to providing balanced and fair supervision of nationally-chartered community banks and the federal savings associations that we assume responsibility for in July.

We are mindful of the economic challenges, and the regulatory and compliance burdens facing community banks, and that implementation of the Dodd-Frank Act may accentuate these challenges. It is our goal to implement the Dodd-Frank Act in a manner that accomplishes the legislative intent without unduly harming the ability of community banks to fulfill their role of supporting local economies and providing the services that their customers rely on. It will be extremely important that we hear from community banks during the notice and comment process of our rulemaking efforts to help determine whether we achieved this goal and whether additional changes or alternatives could be considered to lessen the burden on community banks.

End Note

[1] The Uniform Financial Institutions Rating System is commonly referred to as CAMELS. CAMELS is an acronym that is drawn from the first letters of the individual components of the rating system: Capital adequacy, Asset quality, Management, Earnings, Liquidity, and Sensitivity to market risk.

In: The State of Community Banks …
Editor: Jeffrey R. Holman

ISBN: 978-1-62417-227-4

Chapter 5

TESTIMONY OF JOHN P. DUCREST, COMMISSIONER, LOUISIANA OFFICE OF FINANCIAL INSTITUTIONS. HEARING ON "THE STATE OF COMMUNITY BANKING: OPPORTUNITIES AND CHALLENGES"*

INTRODUCTION

Good afternoon, Chairman Brown, Ranking Member Corker, and distinguished Members of the Subcommittee. My name is John Ducrest, and I serve as the Commissioner of Financial Institutions for the State of Louisiana. I am also the Chairman of the Conference of State Bank Supervisors (CSBS). It is my pleasure to testify before you today on behalf of CSBS.

CSBS is the nationwide organization of banking regulators from all 50 states, the District of Columbia, Guam, Puerto Rico, and the Virgin Islands. State banking regulators supervise, in cooperation with the Federal Deposit Insurance Corporation and Federal Reserve, over 5,600 state-chartered insured depositories. Further, the majority of state banking departments also regulate a variety of non-bank financial services providers, including mortgage lenders. For more than a century, CSBS has given state supervisors a national forum to coordinate supervision of their regulated entities and to develop regulatory policy. CSBS also provides training to state banking and financial regulators

* This is an edited, reformatted and augmented version of a Testimony Presented April 6, 2011 before the Senate Committee on Banking, Housing, and Urban Affairs, Subcommittee on Financial Institutions and Consumer Protection.

and represents its members before Congress and the federal financial regulatory agencies.

Today's hearing comes at a critical time for the community banking system. Community banks are currently operating in a very challenging business and regulatory environment. I thank you, Chairman Brown, and the Members of the Subcommittee for holding such a timely hearing. Understanding the current challenges and opportunities facing community banks is an important part of understanding the overall health of the economy. Even more importantly, the subject of today's hearing logically leads us to significant questions about the longer-term prospects for the community banking business model.

In my testimony I will discuss my perspectives as a state banking regulator on the critical role community banks play in economic development, job creation, and market stabilization. I will also address the current regulatory environment in which they operate. Additionally, my testimony will identify concerns that my state banking commissioner colleagues and I have about the impact of regulations and policies on community banks. Finally, I will provide some recommendations aimed at strengthening the community banking system.

Why Community Banking Still Matters

Over the past several months, my fellow state regulators and I have heard the very loud concerns of community bankers regarding their future. These concerns come from the feared trickle-down effect of the Dodd-Frank Wall Street Reform and Consumer Protection Act and other regulatory actions deemed necessary to address identified weaknesses in the banking system. This will undoubtedly add to the compliance burden being shouldered by the industry. While consumer compliance is significant, in this context, compliance also includes bank secrecy, corporate governance, accounting rules, and reporting requirements. In addition, community banks are facing an uncertain future as the structure and role of larger institutions in the economy is evolving and the future of mortgage finance is being debated.

We believe these concerns are very real and are worthy of our collective attention. This should be a serious, national concern. In our view, the viability of the community bank model has significant systemic consequences, which if left unaddressed will cause irreparable harm to local economies and erode critical underpinnings of the broader economy.

The challenges the community banking system is facing are already having an impact upon local economic development, as some local economies remain stalled or even eroded by more limited credit availability. As you meet with bankers in your office and in your state, I encourage you to ask them about the loans which are not being made. While some banks are not positioned to lend due to their financial condition, many banks are not making residential real estate loans due to the increased compliance burden. In addition, commercial real estate (CRE) loans are not being made due to the stigma of an entire asset class. We cannot accept this as collateral damage in the interest of consistency and national policy.

Small Business Lending

The vital role small businesses play in the national economy is widely recognized. Small businesses are often considered the "engine" of the U.S. economy and drive employment across the nation. Small firms:

- Represent 99.7% of all employer firms in the United States;
- Employ half of all private sector employees;
- Pay 44% of total U.S. private payroll;
- Generated 65% of net new jobs over the past 17 years;
- Made up 97.5% of all identified exporters and produced 31% of export value in FY 2008; and
- Produce 13 times more patents per employee than large patenting firms.[1]

Just as small businesses are recognized as critical to the health of our national economy, the U.S. banking system remains the most important supplier of credit to small businesses in the country. While the volumes are large, banks with over $50 billion in assets allocate only 24% of their loan portfolios to small business loans. Banks with less than $10 billion in assets invest 48% of their loans in small business (See Exhibit 1). There is a very significant difference in the type of small business lending conducted by the smaller banks. In general, lack of extensive financial data for smaller firms makes it more difficult for lenders to ascertain if a small business is "creditworthy." This makes community banks particularly well suited for small business lending. The largest banks tend to rely upon transactional

generally agreed upon, but rapidly approaching outdated, definition of a community bank is an insured depository institution with $1 billion or less in assets. Perhaps a better definition is an institution with a local focus and scope of activities, with the corresponding experience and expertise to excel at relationship lending. A community bank is to a local business what Wall Street is to a Fortune 50 company: not just a lender, but a financial and business adviser.

A strong community banking system is absolutely critical to the well-being of the United States economy. As discussed above, a diverse financial system characterized by strong community banks ensures local economic development and job creation, provides necessary capital for small businesses, and provides stability and continued access to credit during times of crisis. Therefore, it is critical that policies and decisions made in Washington, D.C. carefully consider the impact on smaller banks and the communities they serve. Put simply, how community banks are impacted by Dodd-Frank and other regulatory measures is too important not to understand.

THE CURRENT ENVIRONMENT FOR COMMUNITY BANKS

Despite indicators that the national economy and some of the nation's largest financial institutions are showing signs of improvement, community banks continue to operate — or in too many cases, struggle to survive — in a very challenging environment. The nation's biggest banks have returned to profitability faster than smaller banks. As of the 4th quarter of 2010:

- Only 12.15% of banks over $10 billion in assets remain unprofitable.
- In contrast, 21% of institutions under $1 billion in assets remain unprofitable.

During the collapse of the capital markets, the nation's largest institutions were granted unprecedented and extraordinary government assistance through a variety of programs and policies to not only remain solvent but to facilitate a return to economic health. Community banks have not received the same extraordinary assistance, and have been operating under an economic recession largely not of their making. In addition, the regulatory environment for community banks has proven unforgiving for miscalculations of risk. Since the start of the crisis in 2008, 348 banks have failed. The overwhelming majority of these banks have been community banks. Most of these failed institutions have been acquired by other community banks, while banks with assets greater than $100 billion have bought only 7% of the failed banks. While failures are disruptive at the local level, it is important to note that the regulatory and resolution process for this part of the industry worked. The community banking system is healing itself. We must ensure there is a structure and policies in place which encourage the active participation of community banks in the market. In my state and in my communities, I see needs that will not be met by the biggest institutions. Therefore, we must create an environment that does not drive people and capital away and attracts new entrants to the market. Increasingly, I am hearing a desire from community bankers to merge or sell their institution because they are overwhelmed by regulatory burden and the perception of a federal system which no longer supports their business model. The model of other concentrated banking systems, like Japan, where collapse was followed by long-term stagnation, should be better understood before we continue down the perhaps irreversible road of further consolidation.

CSBS appreciates that the Dodd-Frank Act was drafted with an eye to preserving the community banking system. CSBS views the Dodd-Frank Act as a reaffirmation of the importance of the dual-banking system and all that it entails: a system of regulatory checks and balances that serves as a counterweight to consolidation both of regulatory authority in Washington, D.C. and of influence into a handful of money-center banks; a diverse and competitive industry marked by charter choice and innovation; and access to credit for individuals and businesses in every corner of the country. However, we also understand that uncertainty about the impact of Dodd-Frank, especially when combined with a challenging business environment and general concerns about the direction of regulation, could create a sense of a crushing regulatory environment.

CSBS believes that community bank-oriented Dodd-Frank provisions such as the change in the deposit insurance assessment base which favors smaller, less-risky community banks and the elevation of deposit insurance coverage to $250,000 for individual accounts are critical for community banks. Additionally, the coordination that Dodd-Frank requires among state and federal regulators, such as the newly created Consumer Financial Protection Bureau (CFPB) and the Financial Stability Oversight Council (FSOC), serve the important goals of improving regulation efficiently and giving voice to a community bank regulatory perspective. Earlier this year, the CFPB signed its first information-sharing memorandum of understanding with CSBS and several state banking departments, a positive indicator that the CFPB intends to leverage the work of state regulators in protecting consumers and in bringing efficient compliance supervision to the community banking system.

Finally, CSBS appreciates the bill attempts to address the problems created by providing explicit government guarantees for a cadre of mega-banks considered "too big to fail." Addressing—and hopefully eliminating—the competitive advantages created by the perception and reality of being "too big to fail" has direct consequences for community banks. However, whether, and to what extent "too big to fail" has truly been rectified remains unclear. From the standpoint of state banking regulators, evaluating the success of efforts to eliminate "too big to fail" means looking at:

- Whether the cost of funds for institutions becomes more competitive, regardless of the institution's size. Currently, mega-banks enjoy a significant advantage in this area and are able to obtain funds at a much more affordable rate than
- community banks, giving them a clear operational advantage to the majority of the nation's banks. As demonstrated by Fannie Mae and Freddie Mac, a funding advantage and perceived federal guarantee can translate into market dominance.
- The efficacy of Dodd-Frank's resolution regime for large complex financial institutions. In a properly functioning, market-driven industry, bank resolutions must be allowed to occur when an institution becomes insolvent. Dodd-Frank did put a resolution regime in place, but until an institution that was once considered "too big to fail" is resolved in an orderly manner, such a regime will remain an empty threat to the biggest banks, and more importantly their investors and creditors, as they operate without fear of consequences for risky actions.
- Whether the banking industry in the United States remains diverse, with institutions of all sizes operating in communities around the nation by regular chartering of de novo institutions to fully serve the dynamic U.S. economy.
- Application of the Dodd-Frank concentration limit. This concentration limit, if implemented successfully, will do much to prevent banks from becoming "too big to fail" and will help ensure a competitive industry.
- Whether the ratings agencies consider being systemic or too big to fail a sign of strength and safety and a reason for a higher rating.

- Whether the cost of being systemic must be real and encourage an overall reduction in risk to the economy. Regulatory policy should clearly dissuade institutions from becoming too big to fail.

The Dodd-Frank Act was a sweeping overhaul of financial regulation and will require significant commitment, time and resources to fully implement. As a result, we are still unaware of the full scope of the impact of Dodd-Frank will have upon the industry as a whole, and community banks specifically. For example, we share our federal counterparts' concerns about the impact of the interchange fee provision could have upon community banks. As we discussed in a comment letter to the Federal Reserve Board, we do not fully understand the full impact this provision could have. In the near-term, given the condition of the industry, we fear near-term negative consequences for earnings and further impediments to the long term viability of the community banking model (See Exhibit 4).

The financial crisis and recession exposed weaknesses in risk management and supervisory practices which need to be addressed. These include:

- Concentrations;
- Loan underwriting;
- Funding sources, such as brokered deposits and wholesale funding;
- Capital standards; and
- Standards and expectations for de novo institutions.

Unfortunately, the potential solutions to these issues only increase the concern of community bankers. A broad brush approach, bright line limitations, and a checklist of risk management requirements will surely over-tax the industry. We need to ensure that regulatory policy in these areas does not further undermine the very industry it is attempting to strengthen. FDIC Chairman Bair's recent comments about community banks and CRE lending reflect this sentiment:

> "I believe that supervisory policies need to reflect the reality that most community banks are specialty CRE lenders and that examiners need to focus on assuring quality underwriting standards and effective management of those concentrations. Though hundreds of small banks have become troubled or failed because of CRE concentrations, thousands more have successfully managed those portfolios. We need to

learn from the success stories and promote broader adoption of proven risk-management tools for banks concentrated in CRE."[3]

RECOMMENDATIONS TO ADDRESS CONCERNS AND PRESERVE COMMUNITY BANKING SYSTEM

The economic crisis, the resulting recession, and now enhanced regulatory burden have combined to create an incredibly challenging operating environment for community banks. More consideration must be made by policymakers to understand the long-term impact our decisions and actions have upon the community banking system. To that end, I have a few suggestions for implementing a revamped regulatory regime while still encouraging the success of the community banking system.

First, there must be continued coordination and consultation between federal and state regulators to best understand how local and national economies will be impacted by new regulations. I believe the most effective system of financial supervision is one characterized by both state and federal financial regulation, what my colleague from New York, Superintendent of Banks Richard Neiman, refers to as "cooperative federalism." A system of supervision based on cooperative federalism allows for comprehensive, effective and efficient supervision of the banking industry. Key components of a state/federal supervisory system are the proximity of state regulators to the entities we supervise, and our ability to identify emerging threats or trends in the banking industry, as well as the ability of federal regulators to implement regulations on a national scale and applicable to all market participants.

Second, more analysis is needed to fully understand and appreciate the valuable relationship between community banks and small business. My fellow state regulators and I know anecdotally that the community banking system is at peril, and therefore the small business sector in the United States is also in jeopardy. However, the lack of data and analysis in this area has failed to provide a clear enough understanding to appreciate industry diversity and a viable and competitive community banking system. Significant resources at the federal level exist to perform such analysis and would provide tremendous benefit to the national economy, but also to your state and local economies. Across the country, different communities benefit from unique community banks that are specifically tailored to meet their needs. Gathering data to better understand and appreciate the business models of community banks will provide greater appreciation for this significant issue on a greater scale and will provide clear justification for a national priority to ensure public policy enables and does not overly burden community banking.

Finally, CSBS recommends that Congress and the federal regulators investigate ways to tailor regulatory requirements to institutions based upon their size, complexity, geographic location, management structure, and lines of business.

The current "one size fits all" approach to regulation, both in terms of safety and soundness and compliance supervision, has fallen harder on community banks and driven dramatic consolidation and bifurcation of the banking industry.

Perhaps it is time to explore a bifurcated system of supervision. After all, a bank with a single branch in one state has a dramatically different business model than Bank of America or Citigroup, so it should not be held accountable to the same supervisory structure as institutions which employ thousands of people and operate in hundreds of nations.

CONCLUSION

As I mentioned at the beginning of my testimony, addressing the challenges facing community banks now is very important and a meaningful exercise.

However, as important as understanding the current condition of community banking is, an awareness that decisions made and actions taken today will have a long-term impact on the viability of the community banking model is critical.

After the nation recovers from the recession and the provisions of the Dodd-Frank Act are implemented, what will our banking industry look like? We must ensure industry diversity and full access to credit across the country by creating an environment which benefits all institutions, but particularly the community banks which are so vital to providing stability, access to credit, and support for the small business sector.

CSBS stands ready to work with Members of Congress and our federal counterparts to create a regulatory regime which encourages industry diversity, creates a level playing field for all institutions, and will ultimately strengthen the local economies and the U.S. economy.

Thank you for the opportunity to testify today, and I look forward to answering any questions you may have.

End Notes

[1] U.S. Small Business Administration, Advocacy Small Business Statistics and Research, Frequently Asked Questions, http://web.sba.gov/faqs/faqindex.cfm?areaID=24.

[2] Hein, Scott E., Timothy W. Koch, and S. Scott MacDonald, "On the Uniqueness of Community Banks," Economic Review (First Quarter, 2005).

[3] Remarks by FDIC Chairman Sheila C. Bair to the ICBA National Convention, San Diego, California, March 22, 2011 http://www.fdic.gov/news/news/speeches/chairman/ spmar 2211.html.

In: The State of Community Banks …
Editor: Jeffrey R. Holman
ISBN: 978-1-62417-227-4

Chapter 6

TESTIMONY OF WILLIAM A. LOVING, PRESIDENT AND CEO OF PENDLETON COMMUNITY BANK. HEARING ON "THE STATE OF COMMUNITY BANKING: OPPORTUNITIES AND CHALLENGES"*

OPENING

Chairman Brown, Ranking Member Corker, and members of the subcommittee, my name is William A. Loving, Jr., and I am President and CEO of Pendleton Community Bank, a $250 million asset bank in Franklin, West Virginia. I am pleased to be here today to represent the nearly 5,000 members of the Independent Community Bankers of America. Thank you for convening this hearing on "The State of Community Banking: Challenges and Opportunities."

We appreciate your interest in the community banks of this country, which will undoubtedly play a significant role in any broad based economic recovery because we serve rural, small town, and suburban customers and markets, that are not comprehensively served by large banks. Our business is based on longstanding relationships in the communities in which we live. We make loans often passed over by the large banks because a community banker's personal knowledge of the community and the borrower gives him firsthand

* This is an edited, reformatted and augmented version of a Testimony Presented April 6, 2011 before the Senate Committee on Banking, Housing, and Urban Affairs, Subcommittee on Financial Institutions and Consumer Protection.

insight into the true credit quality of a loan, in stark contrast to the statistical model used by a large bank in another state or region of the country. These localized credit decisions, made one-by-one by thousands of community bankers, will restore our economic strength.

Community banks are prodigious small business lenders. We provide small business credit in good times as well as challenging times – supporting a sector responsible for more job creation than any other. In his recent speech before the ICBA annual convention, Federal Reserve Chairman Ben Bernanke shared new Federal Reserve Bank research that shows that while overall small business lending contracted during the recent recession, lending by a majority of small community banks (those of less than $250 million in assets) actually increased, and small business lending by banks with asset sizes between $250 million and $1 billion declined only slightly. By contrast, small business lending by the largest banks dropped off sharply. The viability of community banks is linked to our small business customers in the communities we serve, and we don't walk away from them when the economy tightens.

When community banks thrive they create a diverse, competitive financial services sector offering real choice, including customized products, to consumers and small businesses alike. An economy dominated by a small number of large banks wielding undue market power and offering commodity products would not provide the same level of competitive pricing and choice. Promoting a vibrant community banking sector is an important public policy goal.

Community Banks Remain Strong

The past few years have been tumultuous for community banks, but the vast majority of them are well capitalized and are helping to lead the economic recovery. Still, community banks were not unaffected by the financial collapse. The weakened economy has caused many consumers to tighten their belts and reduced the demand for credit. Despite the wave of failures and consolidations since the financial crisis, I fully expect the community bank business model will thrive in the future, to the benefit of consumers, small business, and the economy. Many ICBA members have been in business for more than 100 years and have survived the Great Depression and numerous other recessions. The community banking sector will remain vibrant, but policymakers must help by providing relief from overly-burdensome regulations.

Oppressive Examination Environment

In addition to contracting demand for credit and impairing asset quality, the financial crisis harmed community banks by provoking an overreaction among bank examiners. The most frustrating aspect of this exam environment is the disconnect between the examiners in the field and the directives from Washington.

A November 2008, Interagency Statement on Meeting the Needs of Creditworthy Borrowers established a national policy for banks to extend credit to creditworthy borrowers in order to help initiate and sustain an economic recovery. It stated, "The agencies expect all banking organizations to fulfill their fundamental role in the economy as intermediaries of credit to businesses, consumers, and other creditworthy borrowers." Unfortunately, this policy is often neglected by examiners in the field, especially in the regions most severely affected by the recession. Field examiners are second guessing bankers and independent professional appraisers and demanding unreasonably aggressive write-downs and reclassifications of viable commercial real estate loans and other assets. The misplaced zeal of these examiners is having a chilling effect on lending. Good loan opportunities are passed over for fear of examiner write down and the resulting loss of income and capital. The contraction in credit is having a direct, adverse impact on the recovery.

Community Banks Are Disproportionately Impacted by Regulation

Community banks have little in common with Wall Street firms, megabanks, or shadow banks and did not cause the financial crisis or engage in abusive consumer practices. Community banks have a much different risk profile because their business model is built on long-term customer relationships, and they cannot succeed without a reputation for fair treatment. For these reasons, ICBA believes it is appropriate to tier regulation of the financial services industry. Overly prescriptive regulation would only reduce community banks' flexibility in serving the unique needs of their customers. Moreover, regulation has a disproportionate impact on community banks because they have fewer resources to dedicate to compliance.

We are pleased the Dodd-Frank Act exhibits a clear preference for tiered regulation of the financial sector-- one of the most important precedents of that legislation. We believe Congress should further advance this trend by enacting legislation to provide much needed regulatory relief for community banks, their customers, and their communities. Such legislation should also reduce the tax burden on community banks and narrow the competitive gap between tax-paying community banks and tax-exempt credit unions.

Areas in which ICBA seeks relief include:

- Requiring FASB to conduct a cost/benefit analysis for any proposed accounting change;
- Lowering Small Business Administration origination and program fees for rural and small business borrowers;
- Restoring dividend payments on GSE preferred stock; Increasing the SEC shareholder registration threshold;

Amending the Dodd Frank Act to restore bank reliance upon external credit ratings; and Extending the 5-year net operating loss (NOL) carry back provision.

The Communities First Act (CFA), a bill meeting the broad objectives outlined above, was introduced and advanced during the 109th and 110th Congresses with bi-partisan support. In the 110th Congress, CFA was introduced in the House by then-Small Business Committee Chairwoman Nydia Velazquez (D-NY). The Senate version was introduced by then-Senator Sam Brownback (R-KS). The 2006 Financial Services Regulatory Relief Act (FSRRA) and other laws were welcome down payments on needed regulatory and tax relief for community banks. These laws have included provisions taken from prior versions of CFA, notably doubling to $500 million the asset size of banks eligible for the extended 18-month exam cycle. Our communities would benefit from the further relief provided by similar legislation in 2011.

THE DODD-FRANK ACT

The Dodd-Frank Act was generational legislation and will permanently alter the landscape for financial services. Every provider of financial services – including every single community bank – will feel the effects of this new law to some extent. Undeniably, it will result in additional compliance burden for community banks and will be challenging for them. The full and ultimate impact won't be known for years, depending on how the law is implemented and how the market adjusts to it. There's still an opportunity to improve some negative provisions in the law – with the help of this committee and Congress – and provisions that could be helpful to community banks are still at risk of being weakened in the implementation.

DEBIT INTERCHANGE

By a wide margin, the most troubling aspect of the Dodd-Frank Act is the debit interchange, or "Durbin," amendment. Despite the statutory exemption for institutions with less than $10 billion in assets, which many Senators thought would help community banks; we believe small financial institutions cannot be effectively carved out. Chairman Bernanke, the regulator charged with implementing the new law, conceded this point in a recent hearing before the Senate Banking Committee. Visa's announced two-tiered pricing system, however well-intentioned, also will not work. Small issuers will feel the full impact of the Durbin amendment overtime. It's too easy to focus on the large issuers and lose sight of the thousands of community bank issuers who will be harmed if the Federal Reserve proposal is implemented. Not only are small issuers not carved out in practice, they would be disadvantaged relative to large issuers, and a likely consequence of the Federal Reserve's proposed rule, if implemented, is further industry consolidation, higher fees and fewer choices for consumers.

Why won't the carve-out work? The reasons are twofold. First, in addition to the interchange price-fixing provisions of the law and the Federal Reserve proposal, other less-discussed provisions shift control of transaction routing from the card issuer to the merchant. These provisions apply to all financial institutions, regardless of size, and negate the benefit, if any; small financial institutions would gain from the interchange price-fixing exemption. Granting retailers the ability to route debit card transactions over the network of their choice – the card issuer currently designates the network on which its card is routed – will allow retailers to bypass the two-tier system. Further, large retailers will be able to incentivize customers to use the rate-controlled cards issued by the largest financial institutions, discriminating against community banks and their customers. Community bank cards will either be subject to the lower rate or their cards will be neglected by retailers.

There's a second way in which the carve-out fails to shield small issuers. In any two-tier system, the small issuer interchange rate, to the extent that small issuers actually receive it, will surely be lower than the current interchange rate. The payment card networks will be under considerable pressure from their clients with more than $10 billion in assets to narrow the gap between the two tiers.

For these reasons, a tiered system will not protect community banks. Overtime, community bank interchange revenue will drop sharply with a direct impact on community bank customers.

What would happen if the current Federal Reserve proposal were implemented? ICBA recently completed a survey of its members, and the results demonstrate that the Federal Reserve proposal would alter the economics of community banking and fundamentally and adversely change the nature of the relationship between a community bank and its customers. Among the survey results:

Community banks would be forced to charge their customers for services currently offered for free and that customers have come to expect and value – debit cards, checking accounts, online or mobile banking. Community banks will have difficulty offering their customers – both consumers and small businesses – competitive rates on deposits and loans. It will be harder to qualify for a debit card. Finally, twenty percent of survey respondents say they will have to eliminate jobs or halt plans to open new bank branches – extending the impact from individual consumers to communities. To use my bank as an example, in 2010 we had about 6,250 debit cards outstanding and our profit for the year was approximately $132,000 pre-tax. If the Federal Reserve proposal goes into effect, I estimate that we could lose, based upon the lowest proposed interchange rate, approximately $237,000 pre-tax on our debit card program – lost income that we would have to make up through higher fees on our products and services.

Our global payments system works so well that thousands of small community banks are able to stand toe-to-toe and offer services to consumers in direct competition with banks like Citigroup and Bank of America, while providing the quality of relationship service only a community banker can give. The new law and the Federal Reserve proposal would threaten the ability of community banks to compete with large issuers and would bring about further industry consolidation, to the detriment of consumers and small businesses in small town and rural America.

ICBA is grateful to Senators Tester and Corker for introducing S. 575, the Debit Interchange Fee Study Act, which would delay implementation of the Durbin amendment for two years.

MORTGAGE RISK RETENTION

Community banks make commonsense mortgages supported by sound, conservative underwriting. As the banking regulatory agencies implement Section 941 of the Dodd-Frank Act, which requires mortgage originators to retain credit risk on non-qualified residential mortgages, ICBA strongly urges them not to define "qualified residential mortgage", or QRM, too narrowly. An unreasonably narrow definition of QRM will drive thousands of community banks from the residential mortgage market, leaving it to only a few of the largest lenders. Too narrow a definition will also severely limit credit availability to many borrowers who are creditworthy though unable to make significant down payments. In ICBA's view, the definition of QRM should be relatively broad and encompass the largest portion of the residential mortgage market, consistent with the stronger underwriting standards called for by the Act. An unduly narrow definition of QRM will disadvantage community banks because they lack access to the increased capital needed to offset risk retention requirements, despite conservative underwriting. What's more, community banks operating in rural areas will be driven out of the market by Farm Credit System direct lenders who carry an exemption for the loans or other financial assets that they make, insure, guarantee or purchase.

We are currently reviewing the proposed rule released last week, which is over 300 pages and raises scores of questions. While I am sure we will offer many suggested changes, overall, for the community banking industry, there are many positive provisions in the proposal, notably, the exemption from the QRM standards and risk retention requirements for loans sold to Fannie Mae and Freddie Mac, as long as they have government capital. Because the vast majority of residential mortgages originated by community banks are conforming loans sold to Fannie Mae and Freddie Mac, the proposal would preserve the ability of community banks to continue to provide their customers with long-term mortgages. ICBA is also pleased that the proposed rule does not impact mortgage loans held in portfolio and focuses the risk retention requirement on securitizers, not originators.

CONSUMER FINANCIAL PROTECTION BUREAU

While we are pleased the Dodd-Frank Act allows community banks with less than $10 billion in assets to continue to be examined by their primary regulators, ICBA remains concerned about CFPB regulations, to which community banks will be subject. ICBA strongly opposed provisions in the Dodd-Frank Act that excluded the prudential banking regulators from the CFPB rule-writing process. Bank regulators are in the best position to balance the safety and soundness of banking operation with the need to protect consumers from unfair and harmful practices and provide them with the information they need to make informed financial decisions.

The Act gives the prudential regulators the ability to comment on CFPB proposals before they are released for comment and an extremely limited ability to veto regulations before they become final. This veto can only be exercised if, by a 2/3 vote, FSOC determines that a rule "puts at risk safety and soundness of the banking system or the stability of the financial system," an unreasonably high standard and one that should be amended. ICBA supports changing the standard so the FSOC is permitted to veto a CFPB rule that could adversely impact a subset of the industry in a disproportionate way. We believe this standard would give prudential regulators a more meaningful role in CFPB rule writing.

Absent such legislation, ICBA encourages the CFPB to reach out to community banks as they contemplate rules – before proposed rules are issued – to better understand how proposed rules would impact community bank operations and community bank customers. In particular, any rules that privilege "plain vanilla" products (credit cards, mortgages, etc.) would adversely impact community banks, who are frequently the only providers who are willing to customize products to meet customer needs.

Any enhanced consumer protection laws should focus on the "shadow" financial industry which has been most responsible for victimizing consumers while avoiding serious regulatory scrutiny. This segment of the financial services industry should be brought under the same regulatory and supervisory umbrella as commercial banks. ICBA supports a balanced regulatory system in which all financial firms that grant credit are subject to meaningful supervision and examination. Under Dodd-Frank, the CFPB has discretion in defining non-depository "covered persons" subject to CFPB rules, examination and enforcement. ICBA urges the CFPB to broadly define "covered persons."

Community banks are already required to spend significant resources complying with voluminous consumer protection statutes. CFPB rules should not add to these costs. The Dodd-Frank Act gives the CFPB authority to exempt any class of providers or any products or services from the rules it writes considering the size of the entity, the volume of its transactions and the extent to which existing law already has protections.

ICBA urges the CFPB to use this authority to grant broad relief to community banks and/or community bank products where appropriate.

The Dodd-Frank Act is a mixed outcome for community banks. I've noted some of our concerns, but the legislation also gave us an opportunity to advance long sought priorities.

Too Big To Fail

ICBA has long expressed concerns about too-big-to-fail banks and the moral hazard they pose, well before the financial crisis. Community banks are more finely tuned to these concerns because we and our customers feel the direct impact.

It's challenging for us to compete against mega-banks whose toobig-to-fail status gives them funding advantages. For this reason, we're pleased the Act takes steps to mitigate too-big-to-fail.

ICBA supported the creation of the Financial Stability Oversight Council (FSOC) whose duties include identifying and responding to risks to financial stability that could arise from the failure of a large, interconnected bank or nonbank.

We are pleased that Dodd-Frank provides for enhanced prudential standards for systemically risky firms, including higher capital, leverage, and liquidity standards, concentration limits and contingent resolution plans. Firms subject to these higher standards should include, but not necessarily be limited to, large investment banks, insurance companies, hedge funds, private equity funds, venture capital firms, mutual funds (particularly money market mutual funds), industrial loan companies, special purpose vehicles, and nonbank mortgage origination companies.

We also support the FDIC's new resolution authority to empower it to unwind large, systemically-risky financial firms. The government must never again be forced to choose between propping up a failing firm at taxpayer expense and allowing it to fail and wreak havoc on the financial system. Powerful interest groups are lobbying doggedly to undermine the too-big-to-fail provisions of Dodd-Frank, which are essential to creating a robust and competitive financial services sector to the benefit of consumers, businesses, and the economy. We urge this committee to ensure that these provisions are upheld and enforced.

Deposit Insurance

ICBA was a leading advocate for the deposit insurance provisions of the Act, including the change in the assessment base from domestic deposits to assets (minus tangible equity), which will better align premiums with a depository's true risk to the financial system and will save community banks $4.5 billion over the next 3 years. The deposit insurance limit increase to $250,000 per depositor and the two-year extension of the Transaction Account Guarantee (TAG) Program, which provides unlimited deposit insurance coverage for non-interest bearing transaction accounts, will help to offset the advantage enjoyed by the too-big-to-fail mega-banks in attracting deposits.

Small Business Lending Fund

ICBA fully supports the $30 billion Small Business Lending Fund (SBLF) program. This program will provide capital for interested community banks to increase small business lending in their communities and boost economic growth. With the private capital markets for small and mid-sized banks still largely frozen since the financial crisis, SBLF provides an important alternative source of capital for interested healthy banks, structured to incentivize increased lending. We urge Treasury to complete the term sheets for Subchapter S and Mutual banks so they too can have access to tier 1 SBLF capital as Congress intended.

Closing

Thank you again for your interest in and commitment to community banks and for the opportunity to testify today. I've outlined some of the more significant regulatory challenges we face in the months ahead. Negotiating these challenges will help us to serve our communities and promote the economic recovery – a goal we share with this committee. Thank you for hearing our concerns. We look forward to working with you.

In: The State of Community Banks … ISBN: 978-1-62417-227-4
Editor: Jeffrey R. Holman

Chapter 7

TESTIMONY OF PAUL REED, CHAIRMAN OF THE OHIO BANKERS LEAGUE. HEARING ON "THE STATE OF COMMUNITY BANKING: OPPORTUNITIES AND CHALLENGES"*

Mr. Chairman, Members of the Financial Institutions Subcommittee, my name is Paul Reed. I am president and chief executive officer of the Farmers Bank and Savings Company in Pomeroy, Ohio. Farmers is a community bank serving a largely Appalachian market. I was born and raised in my community. That same can be said of most of the other bankers in my market. We serve those we grew up with.

I appreciate your invitation to testify on behalf of the Ohio Bankers League. My association represents most of Ohio's commercial banks, savings banks, and savings & loan associations.

I hope to address three themes in my testimony:

- A good community bank plays a unique role in economic development important to public policy.
- The regulatory structure in 2008 unintentionally but effectively empowered abuse.
- Dodd Frank does too little to simplify and rationalize an extraordinarily complex and ineffective financial regulatory structure.

---

* This is an edited, reformatted and augmented version of a Testimony Presented April 6, 2011 before the Senate Committee on Banking, Housing, and Urban Affairs, Subcommittee on Financial Institutions and Consumer Protection.

I'll start my testimony with a question – why should community banking matter to Congress?

My answer is pretty simple. While larger financial institutions care about their customers, they do not care where they live. That doesn't make big guys bad. It does mean community banks are a critical element of economic redevelopment in many communities.

As a community bank I have a vested interest in the economic and social health of my local market. If my customer cannot find a good job in my community and leaves, I cannot follow him. So my bank's operations must closely sync with what my community needs.

The news media has become very sloppy with the term bank, so let me call myself a traditional bank. There is a difference, important to national policy, between a traditional bank and the various forms of investment companies. I need my customer to be successful. I want long term customers. I win if my customer is successful. Contrast that with the investment bank for which the deal is too often an end in itself rather than the means to the end.

Because I have a practical loan size limit, my bank has always focused on small business. That is our expertise. I am close to my customers which, if I do my job well, will give me added insight. I should be able to make more loans safely than my bigger, distant competitors. Many successful small businesses in Ohio, including those that have grown to be large, started with a close call on a loan, made by a community bank which could say yes safely because it knew its customer.

Recently, walking down a hallway in my bank, I overheard a customer talking to another bank officer. The customer said "I didn't know what to do; but knew if I came to see you, you would." Any good community bank hears that sentiment every day.

As we forge recovery from a very painful recession, small businesses in the communities I serve need me to customize financial tools to answer their needs. I know you want me to do that; but the thousands and thousands of pages of regulation we labor through crush our ability to respond effectively, efficiently and quickly. Looking to the future, Dodd Frank will add more thousands of pages of new regulations.

This last statement should not be interpreted as opposition to effective regulatory modernization. The country needs effective, efficient financial regulation. We all will suffer if we fail to achieve it. Long before the financial crisis, most bankers I know had been calling for a streamlined, modern system which justified public confidence.

Without question our regulatory safety net had developed severe flaws. Dodd-Frank improves parts but it does not do enough. As a community banker, I appreciate the steps taken to try to benefit me. Unfortunately, I fear there are unintended consequences Congress did not consider. Let me provide a few examples.

Deposit Insurance - In Dodd-Frank, Congress changed the basis for deposit insurance premiums from deposits to assets. That change has been touted by some as a great victory for community banks that fund most of their loans from local deposits. Ignored in that analysis are FDIC's subsequent actions to increase its target reserve ratio from 1.25 to 2.0, an increase of 60 per cent. Moreover, the FDIC eliminated the threshold beyond which it would charge no premium because the fund was judged adequately capitalized. Today, I am paying premiums at a historically high rate because an obsolete regulatory structure failed to catch bad guys in time. These changes mean that I will continue to pay more than I have historically paid, not less, for a very long time.

It does make sense to build the insurance fund reserves in good times; but please consider that every dollar I pay in deposit insurance translates into ten dollars I cannot lend. We need to stop the traditional swing of the regulatory pendulum from too lax in good times, to too punitive in the wake of economic troubles. It is the good actors who will pay this greatly inflated bill. The increase is huge despite the many other changes which will limit future risk to the fund. And under it all, the overly complex, inflexible regulatory structure that let the bad guys run rampant is too little changed.

Capital - Capital is a challenge for community banks. Historically, most community bank capital came from the leaders of our communities who wanted a locally focused bank. That source was doubly helpful because investors cared about long term benefit to the community as well as the return on their investment. A troubled economy both increases the need for capital while it reduces the ability of those traditional sources to invest. A further barrier to investment comes from an expensive regulatory regime for traditional banks which artificially constrains the potential return on any investment.

A tool the marketplace had evolved to address this dilemma was the trust preferred security. Some of the early banks closed by regulators proved to have invested in poorly underwritten trust preferred securities. As a result FDIC lost money. In reaction the Senate adopted the Collins amendment to Dodd Frank that will likely kill this source of funding for community banks. Dodd Frank created nothing to replace it. The right response would have been to limit banks' ability to directly invest in these securities. It was counterproductive to cripple the use of trust preferred securities as a tool for healthy community banks looking to raise funds from investors outside the banking industry.

Too-Big-to-Fail - Community banks and the nation were grievously harmed by financial institutions grown too-big-to-fail. The risks from a Fannie or AIG were not new, yet nothing substantive was done to control them. We heard there was no government guarantee of the very big against failure. Of course there was.

For years I faced funding costs higher than the largest financial institutions because the marketplace knew they were guaranteed against failure. Proportionally I also paid far higher regulatory costs than my large competitors.

The marketplace does not believe Dodd Frank has ended too-big-to-fail. The Wall Street Journal recently reported that the funding costs for the biggest institutions are still 78 basis points lower than mine. While we all supported ending too-big-to-fail, the market suggests we have not done so. And we continue to aggressively, if unintentionally, to forge what is in affect "too small to survive".

Debit card transaction fees - I know the intent of Dodd – Frank was to exempt community banks from the rule that set a ceiling on debit interchange fees at roughly a fourth of my cost. However, my understanding is the choice of the transaction processor is the retailer's. Processors competing for business from the big box stores will drive down the price I am paid. In the real world, the exemption will prove fiction.

The campaign by retailers focused on the big and only told part of the story. When my customers use debit cards I provide them, it saves a merchant on each transaction over their acceptance of checks or cash. Additionally, it is the bank that faces the risk of fraud. Only the merchant will have the contact when it can check to see that the card is not stolen. Few check. In 2009, a case of fraud involving a single merchant cost me more than our entire interchange income for the year.

Banking is very competitive. Competition has driven banks to spend interchange income on benefits we hope will attract customers – free checking accounts, convenient branches, more ATMs. Now my debit account income will be far less than my expense. Home Depot tells financial analysts my loss will translate into $35 million in an annual, windfall profit to its shareholders. Where is the consumer benefit?

A focus on trees ignoring the forest - In the lead-up to the global financial meltdown, a significant portion of the financial services market evaded governmental oversight. People motivated by greed flowed into the enforcement vacuum. Some were criminals. Many newer market entrants evaded governmentally imposed costs of doing business.

Banks must meet significant capital requirements. We must pay the full cost of regular, onsite, extensive examination. We pay for deposit insurance. We pay material sums for personnel and paperwork required by voluminous, too often poorly crafted regulation. Government says banks are the most important financial service provider. It sets up an extensive system to prevent failure and protect consumers if it does happen. Then policy and practice perversely tilt the competitive playing field steeply against traditional banks. And community banks suffer the greatest harm because scale provides compliance efficiency.

Consumer Financial Protection Bureau - To right consumer wrongs Congress created the CFPB. It promises clearer, simpler disclosures and universal coverage. The goal is right, but Congress chose to exempt a substantial percentage of financial service providers. Many exempted companies offer direct or functional substitutes for what I sell. Inevitably that very artificial wall will spawn more providers operating outside it.

I do have a community bank exemption from direct examination by CFPB. Congress determined that my primary regulator will continue to enforce compliance rules, now written by the new bureau. CFPB will handle the big guys. That exemption sounds like it should be helpful to me; but please understand any time a rule changes, whether for good or bad, traditional banks face a significant burden in replacing forms, systems, and then re-training. The smaller the bank, the harder it will prove to absorb these costs without losing competitiveness.

Today and tomorrow my regulator will regularly come into my bank with a large examination team to probe every aspect of my operations. That is effective but it is also a huge disruption to business. In contrast, no government compliance examiners visited my non-bank competitor's office. There is little reason to believe they will tomorrow either. And to the extent the new bureau does examine my non bank competitor; the cost of that exam will be paid for by the Federal Reserve System. I get a bill.

I want to emphasize this point. The consumer's safety net failed to keep pace with the marketplace. It failed to recognize and oversee new providers of functionally equivalent products and services. As a result costs were imposed on banks but not on new non bank competitors. That meant banks continually struggled to be price competitive. Government regulation often had the perverse impact of motivating consumers to use a company where they would have little or no protection. One reason many of these problematic new financial companies escaped attention was that they were individually small; but they became very large in number and even larger in damaging impact. CFPB is not being developed to catch or prevent abuse in small companies where history suggests it will likely occur.

There had long been warning voices within Congress; but for a variety of reasons Congress as a whole rarely acted. One relevant example - if you read transcripts from Senate banking committee hearings four decades ago, you will find then Chairman William Proxmire repeatedly pointing to risks to the public in Freddie and Fannie that arguably led both to fail.

Did we fail to act because an existing agency was perceived as too politically powerful, or even if inefficient, that its purpose was too worthy? Did inconsistent Congressional oversight mean we failed to detect a foundation built on sand? Did divided committee jurisdiction cost Congress important perspective?

Over the years we have responded to crises by adding agency after agency. I cannot detect grand design. I would argue we mistook actions for progress.

Predictably the multiplicity of inward looking financial regulators resulted in glaring holes in our safety net. One good example - AIG told state insurance departments that debt swaps weren't insurance. The SEC apparently thought they were insurance. Ultimately no one looked to see if AIG had the money to make good on its commitments.

Theoretically, to prevent conflict of interest U.S. policy separates finance from commerce. We haven't always adhered to that separation in practice. An example - we allowed Detroit automobile companies to form captive finance companies that subsidized rates from the price of the cars. It was hard for a bank that wasn't selling the car, to compete with a 0% loan. Even though it was a shell game, no government agency intervened. Unfair competition largely drove banks out of the auto finance business. The new auto lenders got bigger, began mortgage lending, and soon grew so big they became "too big to fail". To add to the injury, we then pretended they had been banks all along. We bailed the failed companies out in part by using the deposit insurance fund which traditional banks had capitalized.

We failed to address other conflicts of interest. Unless a mortgage broker closed a loan it didn't get paid. In some cases the broker received a bonus if it convinced the consumer to buy unneeded extra features. As a result the broker's needs fundamentally differed from the borrower's. Yet no one in government checked for misrepresentation or fraud.

A car salesmen closing an auto loan faces the same conflict. Dodd Frank attempted to address the problem of the mortgage broker. However, it specifically exempts the car salesman. We lack a comprehensive theoretical regulatory concept. As a result we get very different answers to very similar questions over time.

I have heard some observers conclude that the financial melt down was the result of deregulation. Specifically, some have cited the Gramm, Leach, Bliley Act. Whether you liked GLBA or not, there was little de-regulation in that bill. It simply acknowledged what had already happened in the marketplace. What was completely absent from the bill was any modernization of financial regulation to cope with that new marketplace reality.

The OBL shared our concern about the shortcomings of Gramm Leach Bliley with the then chairman of the House Financial Services Committee. He acknowledged the shortcoming; but observed regulatory turf had grown so entrenched in Washington, that it would take a crisis to trigger modernization. Well, we have now suffered that crisis. And we have gotten a 2,300 page bill. Some of its provisions do represent progress. But I believe it missed fundamental flaws that continue to plague our regulatory system.

The news last week brought an example of obsolete design when six federal agencies jointly issued a rule on mortgage risk retention in response to the Dodd Frank mandate. My point is not the rule – but six agencies? That is the post Dodd Frank world. Can so many be nimble, efficient, effective, or timely? Can they detect the new marketplace abuse? Or will the traditional agencies assume, as was the case consistently on our path to financial meltdown, that the abuse was somebody else's responsibility. In practice complexity seldom supports effective or efficient.

As this country began to be victimized by predatory lending mortgage securitization had allowed the invention of the mortgage broker – tens of thousands of them. My understanding is the FTC had jurisdiction over non bank consumer lending. Yet the FTC's structure was not well suited to overseeing mortgage closings in this new, very decentralized environment. Congress hadn't given FTC examiners so it didn't systematically examine.

This new form of consumer loan broker wasn't paid unless the loan closed. It wasn't penalized if the borrower couldn't repay. That structure created powerful incentive to the broker to falsify and lie. No government agency looked to find the ones who were doing so.

In Ohio alone we estimate there were twelve thousand mortgage brokers at the high point. Theoretically their lending was covered by the many federal consumer protection laws dealing with mortgages. Mortgage documents arriving on Wall Street appeared correctly filled out; but no one checked for fraud or that consumers had been told the truth. Consumers labored to protect themselves. Federally required mortgage closing forms were so lengthy and complex that few read, let alone understood, them. Where the lender was honest, there was no harm. When it was not, we got predatory lending. Ohio became a national scandal of predatory lending. When my state belatedly got around to licensing those brokers, it discovered a very high percentage had criminal records.

Dodd Frank does address those mortgage brokers. I hope that will result in better consumer protection. But I fear we have missed the lesson. Will we quickly detect and effectively respond to the next marketplace invention which seeks to avoid governmental imposed costs of consumer protection? History suggests that is unlikely.

Why did dishonest mortgage brokers escape detection for so long? They were small.

Individually they were inconsequential. Collectively they collapsed the global financial world. No federal regulator saw them as their responsibility. States pled poverty even when they saw the problem.

Historically, our laws have tended to address specific types of companies. Dodd Frank attempted to refocus on the product; but my understanding is that is the model the new Financial Consumer Protection Bureau is using to organize itself focused on provider not product or service. If that is correct I think that is the wrong model.

Would it not make more sense to make rules consumer centric?

Should not all functionally equivalent products be regulated equally?

Should not government imposed costs of business fall on all competitors evenly? Should the consumer have some assurance of honest treatment regardless of provider?

If compliance costs do not favor one competitor over another, then competition works to the consumer's advantage. We need to end regulatory gaps driven either by regulatory or Congressional committee jurisdiction at the expense of the consumer.

No one ever would have designed the regulatory structure we have today on purpose. It is the product of historic accident, not grand design. That it has worked as well as it has is amazing. It speaks to the many good people that work for the agencies. That it has not worked as well as the American public deserves, is testimony to the fact many successive Congresses have failed to systematically address evolution of the marketplace. We have an alphabet soup of moving pieces in this protective engine. Many of the pieces were machined to fit engines in a different century. And today's engine, using those parts, gets very bad mileage and breaks down frequently.

Before Dodd-Frank we had too many regulators, and too many holes between them. Dodd Frank gave us more regulators. We still have the gaping holes. I am asked to believe that's progress.

Let me close with a few suggestions.

Community Bank Regulator - The Dodd Frank Act did eliminate an agency. In July the Office of Thrift Supervision disappears, giving the OCC jurisdiction over federally chartered savings & loan institutions and the FDIC that authority over state charters.

Nevertheless, community banks will wind up with more regulators. We have already discussed CFPB. There are other examples.

Today OTS examines both savings & loan companies and their holding companies. That makes sense to me. Corporate veils shouldn't frustrate public protection. Transactions in either the parent or the bank can affect the safety of the other. Dodd Frank transfers thrift holding company jurisdiction to the Federal Reserve. It transfers regulation of the bank to one of two other agencies. Two different regulators with overlapping turf create opportunity for inefficiency and ineffectiveness.

I would submit that Congress might have served the consumer and country better by creating a community bank regulator, merging the current oversight of smaller, healthy banks and their holding companies conducted by either OCC, FDIC, OTS or Federal Reserve. Freed of small bank exam responsibility, the agencies could concentrate on areas of greatest national risk. The new community bank regulator could focus on rules and examinations that work for small banks and their customers.

Community Bank Examinations - I want to briefly address the bank examination process itself. Its current form can drive focus on form over substance. I understand it is easier to check to see if there is a policy in a file, than it is to determine whether practice works. It is easier to check to see that collateral protects against any loss, rather than to evaluate lender judgment in trying to help a small business navigate through the land mines of a serious recession. I do understand the risk Washington would take when it tells examiners that if a bank's management team in both ethical and competent that their job is to help the bank navigate the mine field with advice and counsel. Some judgments will be wrong. Nevertheless, the question should always be what approach leads to the greatest success not that which best shields the regulator from blame.

I have great respect for the individuals that make up the teams that examine my bank. They are bright and well intentioned. But too little in exams really deals with what is most important to my community. During my last exam, a few weeks ago, there was little discussion over the regulator's decision to downgrade a loan to a small business which had been a long time customer of the bank. The business was troubled but we were paying close attention and working closely with the business to try to help it survive. We had already taken steps to fully protect the bank, and the customer was making payments. The regulator's decision cut the funds I had available to lend and hampered my flexibility in working with my customer. In contrast there was extensive discussion on issues like depreciation schedules of minor amounts which had little to do with my bank's safety and nothing to do with the well being of its customers.

We have evolved a system that is safest for regulators. The goal must be one that is safer for the communities I serve. I believe one reason for the system we have is that Congress flails regulators when they are wrong. It rarely commends them for taking risks that result in benefit for the economy.

More Rigorous Oversight - I can claim no expertise in politics, but I suspect a Senator would not be rewarded were he to go back home and campaign on the slogan "I didn't introduce a single new bill; but I worked hard to make sure that existing law and the rules worked well." However it is exactly that rigorous, unrelenting, painstaking, unglamorous oversight we will need if we are to reinvigorate the American economy and avoid a recurrence of the financial meltdown that began in 2008.

I do recognize that we, as constituents, literally expect you to be expert on everything in the universe. Demands on your time are unrelenting. You individually cannot spend as much time looking and listening as I want. However, you can systematically get your aides out of the artificial environment defined by the beltway. Get them back home talking with consumers, small businesses, farmer and community bankers, so they understand the financial world your constituents live in. And please dramatically expand systematic, rigorous oversight. Be vigilant. Study carefully. Act only when the case to do so is compelling. When you act, do so with comprehensive vision that considers unintended consequence.

If you want to protect the consumer you must simplify the structures that serve that end. Consumers must know how they are protected and who protects them. Forge a modern regulatory system that:

- looks through their eyes;
- treats all functional competitors equally;
- is designed to stop the bad guy from causing harm; but in ways that do not keep good guys from innovation in response to legitimate customer needs.

Thank you for the important step you take today.

In: The State of Community Banks …
Editor: Jeffrey R. Holman
ISBN: 978-1-62417-227-4

Chapter 8

TESTIMONY OF TOMMY G. WHITTAKER, CEO, THE FARMERS BANK. HEARING ON "THE STATE OF COMMUNITY BANKING: OPPORTUNITIES AND CHALLENGES"*

Chairman Brown, Ranking Member Corker, and members of the Subcommittee, my name is Tommy Whittaker, President and Chief Executive Officer, The Farmers Bank, Portland, Tennessee. The Farmers Bank was chartered in 1912 and is a $560 million institution with 11 offices and 152 employees. We serve Robertson and Sumner Counties in northern middle Tennessee, with a population of approximately 130,000 people. I appreciate the opportunity to present the views of the ABA on the state of community banking and the challenges and opportunities that we face. The ABA represents banks of all sizes and charters and is the voice of the nation's $13 trillion banking industry and its two million employees.

At my bank, as is true of my banker colleagues around the country, we are intensely focused on building and maintaining long-term relationships with our customers. It is because of these relationships The Farmers Bank will be celebrating a century of service to our customers and community in 2012. We cannot be successful without such a long-term philosophy and without treating our customers fairly.

---

* This is an edited, reformatted and augmented version of a Testimony Presented April 6, 2011 before the Senate Committee on Banking, Housing, and Urban Affairs, Subcommittee on Financial Institutions and Consumer Protection.

We are proud to say we have been in business for almost 100 years, but our long tradition of service is not unique among banks. In fact, there are 2,735 banks – 35 percent of the banking industry – that have been in business for more than a century; 4,937 banks – 64 percent – have served their local communities for more than half a century. These numbers tell a dramatic story about the staying power of banks and their commitment to the communities they serve.

The success of The Farmers Bank is inextricably linked to the success of the communities we serve, and we are very proud of our relationships with them. They are, after all, our friends and neighbors.

Let me give you just a glimpse of The Farmers Bank's close ties with our communities. We have $348 million in loans on our books. Included in that number are approximately 175 loans, totaling $3.8 million to our farmers for agricultural operations, 750 loans, totaling $29.2 million to our local businesses for their commercial and business needs, 633 loans, totaling $191.2 million to developers for commercial construction projects and farmers for purchase of farm land, and 1,765 loan, totaling $116 million for the construction and financing of 1 to 4 family homes. In addition, we have $4 million in loans to our local municipalities that help them fund improvements to services to their cities.

Not only do we provide the funding to meet the credit needs for our communities, our people are truly a part of these communities. For example, each year our bank participates in the ABA's National Teach Children to Save Day. In 2010, we had 26 employees volunteer their time in fifteen area schools. We had another 22 employees involved in community organizations, such as The Chamber of Commerce, Lions Club, Rotary Club, and numerous other Civic Clubs. Moreover, in the last two years, our bank has donated over $112,000 for scholarships, community events, and other local projects.

When a bank sets down roots, communities thrive. A bank's presence is a symbol of hope, a vote of confidence in a town's future. The health of the banking industry and the economic strength of the nation's communities are closely interwoven. We strongly believe that our communities cannot reach their full potential without the local presence of a bank – a bank that understands the financial and credit needs of its citizens, businesses, and government. I am deeply concerned that this model will collapse under the massive weight of new rules and regulations. The vast majority of banks never made an exotic mortgage loan or took on excessive risks. They had nothing to do with the events that led to the financial crisis and are as much victims of the devastation as the rest of the economy. We are the survivors of the problems, yet we are the ones that pay the price for the mess that others created.

Banks are working every day to make credit and financial services available.

Those efforts, however, are made more difficult by regulatory costs and second-guessing by bank examiners. Combined with hundreds of new regulations expected from the Dodd-Frank Act, these pressures are slowly but surely strangling traditional community banks, handicapping our ability to meet the credit needs of our communities.

Managing this mountain of regulation will be a significant challenge for a bank of any size. The median-sized bank has only 37 employees – for them, and for banks like mine, this burden will be overwhelming. Historically, the cost of regulatory compliance as a share of operating expenses is two and a half times greater for small banks than for large banks. Moreover, it creates more pressure to hire additional compliance staff, not customer-facing staff. It means more money spent on outside lawyers to manage the risk of compliance errors and greater risk of litigation.

It means more money to hire consulting firms to assist with the implementation of all of the changes, and more money hiring outside auditors to make sure there are no compliance errors. It means more risk of regulatory scrutiny, which can include penalties and fines. All of these expenditures take away precious resources that could be better used serving the bank's community.

The consequences are real. Costs are rising, access to capital is limited, and revenue sources have been severely cut. It means that fewer loans get made. It means a weaker economy. It means slower job growth. With the regulatory over-reaction, piles of new laws, and uncertainty about government's role in the day-to-day business of banking, meeting local community needs is difficult at best.

Without quick and bold action to relieve regulatory burden we will witness an appalling contraction of the banking industry, with a thousand banks or more disappearing from communities all across the nation over the next few years.

These are good banks that for decades have been contributing to the economic growth and vitality of their towns, cities, and counties but whose financial condition is being undermined by excessive regulation and government micro-management.

Each bank that disappears from the community makes that community poorer.

Congress Must Be Vigilant in Overseeing Regulatory Actions That Unnecessarily Restrict Loans to Creditworthy Borrowers

Holding oversight hearings like this one is critical to ensure that banks are allowed to do what they do best – namely, meet the credit needs of their communities.

In my testimony today, I'd like to focus on three key themes:

- New Rules Substitute Washington Bureaucratic Judgment for That of Local Bankers

Increasingly, the government has inserted itself in the day-to-day business of banking. The government should not be in the business of micro-managing private industry. Traditional banks tailor products to borrowers' needs in local communities, and prescriptive rules inevitably translate into less access to credit and banking services.

The most egregious example is the price-controls on interchange fees resulting from the Federal Reserve's implementation of the Durbin Amendment in the Dodd-Frank Act. Such actions will have significant unintended consequences. The legislation introduced by Senators Tester and Corker – S. 575 – rightly recognizes that the Federal Reserve's rule will cause significant and immediate harm to community banks, consumers and the broader economy. The ABA strongly supports S. 575 and urges fast action to adopt this important legislation.

- New Laws End up Punishing Community Banks That Had Nothing to Do with the Crisis

Each change in law adds another layer of complexity and cost of doing business. Dodd-Frank rules threaten to drive community banks out of lines of business altogether, particularly mortgage lending and services to municipalities. It has also stimulated an environment of uncertainty and added new risks that will inevitably translate into fewer community financial services.

- The Consequences for Consumers and the Economy Are Severe

The Dodd-Frank Act will raise costs, reduce income, and limit potential growth, all of which drives capital away from banking, restricts access to credit for individuals and business, reduces financial resources that create new jobs, and retards growth in the economy.

I will discuss each of these in detail in the remainder of my testimony.

I. Individual Rules Substitute Washington Bureaucratic Judgment for That of Bankers in Local Communities

Increasingly, the government has inserted itself in the day-to-day business of banking. Micro-managing private industry should not be the role of government. Inevitably it leads to negative unintended consequences.

The most egregious example is the price-controls for interchange fees being promulgated by the Federal Reserve under the Durbin Amendment. The result devastates retail bank profitability, stifles innovation, lowers productivity in our economy and forces a number of individuals out of the protection of the banking system.

The price-controls proposed by the Federal Reserve in the implementing rule will reduce interchange income by as much as 85 percent. Some will say that the so-called "carve-out" from the Federal Reserve's rule under Dodd-Frank for community banks (under $10 billion in assets) will protect community bank earnings. Nothing could be further from the truth. *Having two different prices for the exact same product is not sustainable.* The price cap proposed by the Federal Reserve is so severe that it creates enormous economic incentives for retailers to adopt strategies to favor the cards with lower interchange rates. Market share will always flow to the lowest priced product, even if those lower prices are mandated only for some. The result for small banks is either a loss of market share, loss of revenue that supports free checking and other valuable services, or both.

Revenue from interchange in many cases does not cover the cost of providing debit card services. With the Federal Reserve's proposal, debit cards would be completely unprofitable. In fact, the proposed rule dictates that banks *must* lose money on every debit card transaction we process *unless* we charge consumers more. It makes no sense to force any provider of any service to offer products below the cost of producing them. I cannot offer financial services if I cannot cover the costs of doing so and provide a reasonable return to my shareholders.

Consumers have embraced debit cards for obvious reasons – they are fast, safe, and accepted around the world. It is consumers who will be severely affected by the government-mandated price control in the Federal Reserve's proposed rule. It will cause new consumer fees, probably including checking account fees, and likely push low-income customers out of the banking system.

Such an important change did not receive the thoughtful and thorough consideration in Congress it deserved. The process, in fact, was deeply flawed. *It should be revisited and Congress should take immediate action to stop the proposed Federal Reserve interchange rule from being implemented.*

The ABA is grateful for the willingness of Senators Tester and Corker, and the many other cosponsors of S. 575 to reconsider the harmful, unintended consequences that will result from the Federal Reserve's proposal to implement the Durbin Amendment.

S. 575 rightly recognizes that the Federal Reserve's rule will cause significant and immediate harm to community banks, consumers and the broader economy. Various concerns over the proposed rule have been raised in recent weeks by bank regulators, including Federal Reserve Chairman Ben Bernanke and Sheila Bair, chairman of the Federal Deposit Insurance Corporation, and by numerous lawmakers from both sides of the political aisle. The clear implication is that more time to study the impact of this provision is definitely warranted, especially considering that the Durbin Amendment was adopted at the 11th hour, without hearings, committee action or informed debate. It is for these and other reasons that we strongly support S. 575 and are thankful that the Senate has taken the first step toward stopping the Fed's rule and thereby protecting consumers, banks and the broader economy. We urge quick action to enact this important piece of legislation.

II. The Cumulative Burden of Hundreds of New or Revised Regulations Will Lead to a Massive Consolidation of the Banking Industry

Banks have to be profitable and provide a reasonable return to investors. If they do not, capital quickly flows to other industries that have higher returns. The Dodd-Frank Act, in combination with intense regulatory over-reaction, has increased expenses, decreased potential revenue, and limited community bank access to capital. Added to greater uncertainty about new regulatory and legal risks, these pressures directly take resources away from the true business of banking – making loans in local communities.

The impact of Dodd-Frank and bank supervision on community banks can be broken down into four categories: (1) higher operating costs to comply with scores of new rules; (2) pressures on capital; (3) restraints that may drive community banks out of lines of business; and (4) greater uncertainty and risk. As I will discuss in the next section, all of these will have severe consequences for consumers and communities that banks serve.

1. Dodd-Frank Rules Increase Costs of Doing Business

The Dodd-Frank Act will have an enormous and negative impact on all community banks. Already there are nearly *2,000* pages of new proposed rules and there will be many thousands more as the 200+ rules under the Act are promulgated. This is on top of the 50 new or expanded regulations affecting banks over the two years leading up to the enactment of the Dodd-Frank Act. This flood of new regulations is so large that regulators are urging banks to add new compliance officers to handle it.

The Farmers Bank is typical of many community banks in the U.S., and I know how demanding the crush of paperwork is for my staff. It is hard enough to deal with one new regulation or a change in an old one, but with reams of new proposals and reams of final regulations, it is overwhelming. We used to close many of our loans internally with our loan officers assuring compliance with all the requirements. This model simply will not work now with all the new requirements and we are very likely to seek outside compliance help to assure that we are in compliance.

Managing compliance with these new requirements adds time and costs – all of which makes it more difficult and costly to make loans to our customers. It is a sad commentary when our investment dollars this year and next – and probably longer – will be spent on compliance with the Dodd-Frank Act rather than making new loans, products and services available. There are many community banks smaller than mine, and I cannot imagine the pressure they face with fewer employees. The cumulative burden of hundreds of new or revised regulations may be a weight too great for many smaller banks to bear.

Of particular concern is the additional regulatory and compliance burden expected once the Bureau of Consumer Financial Protection (CFPB) becomes fully operational. This new bureaucracy – expected to hire over 1,200 new staff – will certainly impose new obligations on community banks – banks that had nothing to do with the financial crisis and already have a long history of serving consumers fairly in a competitive environment.

One of the claims was that small banks would be exempt from the new CFPB. *But small banks are not exempt.* All banks – *large and small* – will be required to comply with rules and regulations set by the CFPB, including rules that identify what the CFPB considers to be "unfair, deceptive, or abusive." Moreover, the CFPB can require community banks to submit whatever information it decides it "needs." There are also many other new regulatory burdens flowing from the Dodd-Frank Act empowerment of the CFPB which will add considerable compliance costs to every bank's bottom line.

It is true that although the CFPB will not *regularly* examine community banks for compliance with its rules, it can join the prudential regulator by doubling up during any such exam at the CFPB's sole discretion. It is also true that bank regulators will examine for compliance at least as aggressively as the CFPB would do independently. In fact, the FDIC has created a whole new division to implement the rules promulgated by the new CFPB, as well as its own prescriptive supervisory expectations for laws beyond FDIC's rule-making powers. Thus, the new legislation will result in new compliance burdens for community banks and a new regulator looking over their shoulders.

Dodd-Frank also adds to the compliance burden by unleashing a fragmented enforcement mechanism that empowers Attorneys General to invent their own interpretations of federal standards and bring actions without regard for the exam conclusions of the CFPB or the prudential regulators. This generates increased regulatory uncertainty and litigation risk that will chill innovation and raise barriers to market competition, especially for banks without an army of lawyers to navigate the enforcement minefield.

Where the CFPB should focus its energies is on *supervision* and *examination* of *non-bank* financial providers. Many of the problems that led to the financial crisis began outside the regulated banking industry and creation of the CFPB was largely a result of this enormous gap in the system that ultimately led to problems. *We urge Congress to ensure that this focus on non-banks is a priority of the CFPB.*

My bank's philosophy – shared by community banks everywhere – has always been to treat our customers right and do whatever we can to make sure that they understand the terms of the loans they are taking on and their obligations to us. We will continue to do this, but now there will be many new hurdles that we will have to jump to serve our customers' most basic needs that will inevitably add cost, time, and hassle for my customers.

The bottom line is the more time bank personnel devote to parsing regulatory requirements, the less time they can devote to the financial and credit needs of bank customers. Adding such a burden on banks that had nothing to do with the financial crisis constitutes massive overkill. In the end, this cumulative burden will only impede fair competition among trusted providers seeking to serve responsible customers.

Much needs to be done to reverse the burdens Dodd-Frank threatens to impose through the CFPB. We recommend the following steps as only a beginning:

- Eliminate the expansive definition of "abusive" practices since appropriate use of existing unfair and deceptive practices authority is more than adequate;
- Prohibit Attorneys General from enforcing federal standards subject to federal supervision, or at least limit such actions to remedy only conduct occurring after the last CFPB or prudential regulator examination; and 3/4Prevent States and prudential regulators from augmenting or interfering with consumer protections otherwise covered by CFPB rules.

2. Access to New Capital for Community Banks is Problematic

Capital is the foundation upon which all lending is built. Having sufficient capital is critical to support lending and to aborb losses when loans are not repaid. In fact, $1 worth of capital supports up to $10 in loans. Most banks entered this economic downturn with a great deal of capital, but the downward spiral of the economy has created losses and stressed capital levels. Not surprisingly, when the economy is weak, new sources of capital are scarce.

The timing of the Dodd-Frank limitations on sources of capital could not have been worse, as banks struggle to replace capital used to absorb losses brought on by the recession. While the market for trust preferred securities (which had been an important source of capital for many community banks) is moribund at the moment, the industry needs the flexibility to raise capital through various means in order to meet increasing demands for capital. Moreover, the lack of readily available capital comes at a time when restrictions on interchange and higher operating expenses from Dodd-Frank have already made building capital through retained earnings more difficult.

These limitations are bad enough on their own, but the consequences are exacerbated by bank regulators piling on new requests for even greater levels of capital. As I travel the country, I often hear how regulators are pressing many banks to increase capital-to-assets ratios by as much as 4 to 6 percentage points – 50 to 75 percent – above minimum standards. For many banks, it seems like whatever level of capital they have, it is not enough to satisfy the regulators. This is excess capital not able to be redeployed into the market for economic growth.

Thus, to maintain or increase capital-to-assets levels demanded by the regulators, these *banks have been forced to limit, or even reduce, their lending.* The result: the banking industry becomes smaller while loans become more expensive and harder to get.

Ever-increasing demands for more capital puts a drag on the economy at the worst possible time for our nation's recovery. Moreover, it works at cross purposes with banks' need for the strong and sustainable earnings that will be the key to addressing asset quality challenges. *Therefore, anything that relieves the increasing regulatory demands for more capital will help banks make the loans that are needed for our nation's recovery.*

3. Dodd-Frank Rules May Drive Community Banks Out of Lines of Business

Congress must be vigilant in its oversight of the efforts to implement the Dodd-Frank Act to ensure that rules are adopted only if they result in a benefit that clearly outweighs the burden. Already we are seeing proposals – such as those implementing the rules regarding interchange, municipal advisors, and swaps transactions – that fail that simple test. Some rules under Dodd-Frank, if done improperly, *will literally drive banks out of lines of business.* New rules on registration as municipal advisors and on mortgage lending are two particularly problematic provisions.

New SEC rules on municipal advisors – if done improperly – will drive community banks out of providing basic banking products to local and state governments.

ABA believes that Dodd-Frank intended to establish a regulatory scheme for *unregulated* persons providing advice to municipalities with respect to municipal derivatives, guaranteed investment contracts, investment strategies or the issuance of municipal securities. Most community banks, like The Farmers Bank, do not deal in bonds or securities. But community banks do offer public sector customers banking services and we are regulated closely by several government agencies.

The Securities and Exchange Commission has proposed a very broad definition of "investment strategies" that would cover traditional bank products and services such as deposit accounts, cash management products and loans to municipalities. This means that community banks would have to register as municipal advisors and be subject to a whole new layer of regulation on bank products for no meaningful public purpose. The result of this duplicative and costly regulation: community banks like mine may decide not to provide banking services to their local muncipalities, forcing these local and state entities to look *outside* of their community for the services they need. This proposal flies in the face of the President's initiative to streamline federal oversight and avoid new regulations that impede innovation, diminish U.S. competitiveness, and restrain job creation and economic expansion.

We urge Congress to oversee this implementation and ensure that the rule addresses *unregulated* parties and that *neither* Section 975 of Dodd-Frank nor its implementing regulation reaches through to traditional bank products and services.

New proposed mortgage rules likely to drive many community banks out of mortgage lending.

The housing and mortgage markets have been battered in recent years and are still struggling to recover. Addressing the systemic problems which led to the crisis is critical, but care must be taken to avoid unnecessary actions that do not address systemic issues and which could further destabilize the fragile recovery. *We have grave concerns that the risk retention proposal issued by the regulators last week will drive community banks from mortgage lending and shut many borrowers out of the credit market entirely.* It is true that the proposal's immediate impact is muted by the fact that loans sold to Fannie Mae and Freddie Mac while they are in conservatorship escape risk retention. However, once the rule's requirements are imposed broadly on the market (should they be adopted) they would likely shut out many borrowers entirely and act to destabilize an already fragile market. Since it is also the stated goal of both the Congress and the Administration to end the conservatorship of Fannie and Freddie, it is important that risk retention requirements be rational and non disruptive when they are applied broadly to the market. The rule as proposed does not meet those tests.

Therefore, ABA urges Congress to ensure that the regulators revise the risk retention regulation before it is imposed on the mortgage market broadly. Specifically we recommend:

3/4*Exemption from risk retention provisions must reflect changes in the market already imposed through other legislative and regulatory change.*

In the Dodd-Frank Act, Congress determined that some form of risk retention was desirable to ensure that participants in a mortgage securitization transaction had so-called “skin in the game.” The goal was to create incentives for originators to assure proper underwriting (e.g., ability to repay) and incentives to control default risk for participants beyond the origination stage. There have already been dramatic changes to the regulations governing mortgages.[1]

The result is that mortgage loans with lower risk characteristics – *which include most mortgage loans being made by community banks today* – should be exempted from the risk retention requirements – regardless of whether sold to Fannie Mae and Freddie Mac or to private securitizers. Exempting such “qualified residential mortgage” loans (QRM) is important to ensure the stability and recovery of the mortgage market and also to avoid capital requirements not necessary to address systemic issues. However, *the QRM as proposed is very narrow and many high-quality loans posing little risk will end up being excluded. This will inevitably mean that fewer borrowers will qualify for loans to purchase or refinance a home.*

For example, for the loan to qualify, borrowers must make at least a 20 percent down payment – and at least 25 percent if the mortgage is to be a refinance (and 30 percent if it is a cash-out refinance).

Certainly loans with lower loan-to-value (LTV) ratios are likely to have lower default rates, and we agree that this is *one* of a *number* of characteristics to be considered. However, the LTV should not be the *only* characteristic for eligibility as a “Qualified Residential Mortgage,” and it should not be considered in isolation.

Setting the QRM cutoff at a specific LTV without regard to other loan characteristics or features, including credit enhancements such as private mortgage insurance, will lead to an unnecessary restriction of credit. To illustrate the severity of the proposal, even with *private mortgage insurance,* loans with less than 20 percent down will *not* qualify for the QRM.

ABA strongly believes that creating a narrow definition of QRM is an inappropriate method for achieving the desired underwriting reforms intended by Dodd-Frank.

- The Risk Retention Requirements as proposed will inhibit the return of private capital to the marketplace and will make ending the conservatorship of Fannie Mae and Freddie Mac more difficult.

The proposal presented by the regulators will make it *vastly more difficult to end the conservatorship of Fannie and Freddie* and to *shrink FHA* back to a more rational portion of the mortgage market. As we observed earlier, under the proposed rule, loans with a federal guarantee are exempt from risk retention – including loans sold to Fannie Mae and Freddie Mac while they are in conservatorship.

Because of their conservatorship status, the GSEs have the backing of the federal government. FHA loans (as well as other federally insured and guaranteed loan programs) are also exempt. Since almost 100 percent of new loans today being sold are bought by Fannie and Freddie or insured by FHA – and as long as these GSEs can buy loans without risk retention – it will be dramatically more difficult for private securitizers to compete. In fact, the economic incentives of the proposed risk retention strongly favor sales of mortgages to the GSEs in conservatorship and not to private securitizers. Thus, this proposal does not foster the growth of private label securitizations that would reduce the role of government in backing loans.

Equally important is the fact that the conservatorship situation is unsustainable over the long term.

That means that eventually, these highly narrow and restrictive rules would apply to a much, much larger segment of the mortgage market. That means that fewer borrowers will qualify for these QRM mortgage loans and the risk retention rules make it less likely that community banks will underwrite non-QRM – *but prudent and safe* – loans. Some community banks may stop providing mortgages altogether as the requirements and compliance costs make such a service unreasonable without considerable volume. Driving community banks from the mortgage marketplace would be counterproductive as they have proven to be responsible underwriters that have served their borrowers and communities well.

The imposition of risk retention requirements to improve underwriting of mortgage loans is a significant change to the operation of the mortgage markets and must not be undertaken lightly. *ABA urges Congress to exercise its oversight authority to assure that rules adopted are consistent with the intent of the statute and will not have adverse consequences for the housing market and mortgage credit availability.*

There are other related concerns affecting housing that need to be addressed by Congress as well.

In particular, Congress needs to make the "Qualified Mortgage" in Title XIV a true safe harbor and ensure that it does not unnecessarily constrict credit. Title XIV of Dodd-Frank sets out new consumer protections for mortgage loans. As defined in Title XIV, a Qualified Mortgage (QM) is one which has specific features and is underwritten in such a way that it is presumed to meet these consumer protection standards. That presumption, however, can be rebutted – subjecting the lender to significant potential liability.

The Qualified Mortgage definition (as set in statute and as refined through regulation) also serves as a limitation on the Qualified Residential Mortgage (QRM) standard discussed above because the QRM cannot be broader than the QM. As the law stands now, the Federal Reserve Board (and eventually the CFPB after the transfer of powers) can unilaterally narrow both the QM and QRM.

To avoid inadvertent and unintended impacts on safety and soundness as well as credit availability, ABA strongly urges Congress to require that any changes which could narrow the eligibility requirements for the QM be undertaken jointly with the regulators responsible for determining eligibility under the QRM.

4. Regulatory Risk and Uncertainty Are Rising, Reducing Incentive to Lend

Businesses – including banks – cannot operate in an environment of uncertainty. Unfortunately, Dodd-Frank increases uncertainty for banks, and as a consequence, raises credit risks, raises litigation risks and costs (for even minor compliance issues), leads to less hiring or even a reduction in staff, makes hedging risks more difficult and costly, and restricts new business outreach.

All of this translates into less willingness to make loans. In fact, banks' biggest risk has become regulatory risk. Let me illustrate the regulatory risk and uncertainty with four examples: (1) the unknown burden that will arise from the Bureau of Consumer Financial Protection; (2) the potential lawsuits that may arise on preemption; (3) the potential risk of future price controls following the precedent set by the Durbin Amendment; and (4) the potential loss of effective methods to hedge risk from rules on use of swap contracts.

The Nature and Extent of Rules from CFPB are Unknown

As discussed above, the CFPB has significant authority to create new rules for consumer lending. What will happen is unknown, but it does create potential litigation risk for actions taken now that may conflict with the ultimate rules devised. The expectation of significant new disclosures will translate into less willingness to lend (and therefore less credit extended overall), greater costs for any loans that are made, and higher costs to borrowers that still have access to credit to cover the added risks undertaken by banks.

Preemption Uncertainty and State Attorneys General Given More Power

One important example of uncertainty and unease created by Dodd-Frank arises from the provisions regarding preemption. Congress *explicitly* preserved in the Dodd-Frank Act the test for preemption articulated by the United States Supreme Court for deciding when a state law is preempted by the federal laws that govern national banks' activities.

Nevertheless, any mention of the preemption standard in a statute is likely to generate lawsuits from those who argue that the standard somehow has changed.

The standard for federal thrifts has changed, from an "occupation of the field" test to the same "conflicts" test that has applied, and continues to apply, to national banks.

This creates uncertainty, will lead to years of litigation, and places savings associations at greater risk of suits over whether a patchwork of state laws applies.

The Dodd-Frank Act preemption provisions will affect *all* banks, including state-chartered banks and thrifts that benefit from wild-card statutes. State attorneys general will have greater authority to enforce rules and regulations, specifically including those promulgated by the CFPB.

Moreover, in the case of state-chartered institutions, the state AGs may enforce the Dodd-Frank Act even in the absence of implementing regulations. This means that state AGs soon may be in the business of deciding what is an unfair, deceptive, or abusive act or practice for state banks.

Price Control Precedent Poses Future Risks

As discussed above, government involvement in price controls related to interchange fees will create many negative unintended consequences. But the concern about the Durbin Amendment goes far beyond the impact on my bank, my customers, and the economy. It sets a dangerous precedent, suggesting that financial institutions may be subject to future, unknowable price controls on other financial products and services, undermining important free-market principles.

We have always accepted the operational, reputational, and financial risk associated with developing new products and services and making them available to millions of consumers. Now financial institutions risk losing their investments of billions of dollars into improvements of existing products and services, and the creation of new ones, through government price controls. Why would any business invest in an innovative product knowing the government ex post facto will interfere and completely dismantle its free-market business model by imposing price controls? The Durbin Amendment serves as a strong disincentive for innovation and investment by financial institutions in other emerging payment systems and financial products and services. In the end, it is the American public who suffers.

Banks Face Uncertainty and Higher Risk as Regulators Implement Swaps Rules

It is difficult, if not impossible right now, for banks to determine how the new swaps regulatory framework mandated by Dodd-Frank will affect the way banks do business. We do not know yet how the swaps exchanges will operate, what impact the clearing requirements will have on banks' ability to customize swaps, or even which banks and transactions will be subject to each of the new rules. For example, while other end users will be exempt from complex and costly clearing requirements, we are waiting to find out if our community banks will receive the same treatment. If not, then these banks might not be able to use swaps and the end result would be reduced lending, increased risk for banks, and higher costs for customers if banks cannot hedge the risk.

Beyond the uncertainty of the current situation, it is critical to ensure that banks have sufficient time to consider the implications that the proposed swaps regulations will have on their ability to manage business risks.

Considering the number of new rules that are needed and the way they are interconnected, doing them hastily could cause serious economic harm.

We urge Congress to actively oversee the Commodity Futures Trading Commission (CFTC) and SEC as they implement the new swaps requirements to be sure there are no adverse affects on lending or competition for U.S. banks. We also encourage Congress to enact legislation explicitly granting small banks the same exemption from swaps clearing requirements that is available to other end users.

III. Consequences for Banks, Consumers, and the Economy are Severe

Certainly, I want my bank to be successful, as do all of my fellow bankers throughout the country. Every day, we are facing new challenges that threaten our very existence. But for community banks, it goes beyond just our parochial interests to be successful. We are very much a part of our community. It is why every bank in this country volunteers time and resources to make their communities better. If the relentless pressures on our small banks are not relieved, the loss will be felt far beyond the impact on any bank and its employees. It will mean something significant has been lost in the community once served by that bank.

Ultimately, it is consumers that bear the consequences of government imposed restrictions. The loss of interchange income will certainly mean higher costs of using debit cards for consumers. Greater mortgage restrictions and the lack of certainty on safe harbors for qualified mortgages means that community banks may no longer make mortgage loans or certainly not as many. Higher compliance costs mean more time and effort devoted to government regulations and less time for our communities. Increased expenses often translate into layoffs within the bank.

Thus, jobs and local economic growth will slow as these impediments inevitably reduce the credit that can be provided and the cost of credit that is supplied. Fewer loans means fewer jobs. Access to credit will be limited, leaving many promising ideas from entrepreneurs without funding. Capital moves to other industries, further limiting the ability of banks to grow. Since banks and communities grow together, the restrictions that limit one necessarily limit the other.

Lack of earning potential, regulatory fatigue, lack of access to capital, limited resources to compete, inability to enhance shareholder value and return on investment, all push community banks to sell. The Dodd-Frank Act drives all of these in the wrong direction and is leading to consolidations. The consequences for local communities are real. As the FDIC noted: "The conversion of a once-main-office to a branch is sometimes accompanied by reductions in customer services, customer service hours, and managerial authority and decision-making discretion."

The Farmers Bank will survive these changes. I fear that many other community banks may not. I have spoken to many bankers throughout the country who describe themselves as simply miserable. Some have already sold their banks; others plan to do so once the economic environment improves. The Dodd-Frank Act was intended to stop the problem of too-big-to-fail, yet now we have even bigger institutions; ironically, the result may be that some banks will be toosmall-to-survive the onslaught of the Dodd-Frank rules.

CONCLUSION

An individual regulation may not seem oppressive, but the cumulative impact of all the new rules plus the revisions of existing regulations is oppressive. The regulatory burden from Dodd-Frank and the excessive regulatory second-guessing must be addressed in order to give all banks a fighting chance to maintain long-term viability and meet the needs of local communities everywhere. It is important to understand that our bank, indeed, any small business, can only bear so much. Most small banks do not have the resources to easily manage the flood of new rules. Higher costs, restrictions on sources of income, limits on new sources of capital, regulatory pressure to limit or reduce lending in certain sectors, all make it harder to meet the needs of our communities. Ultimately, it is the customers and community that suffer along with the fabric of our free market system.

End Note

[1] For example, changes have been made under the Real Estate Settlement Procedures Act (RESPA), the Truth in Lending Act (TILA), and the Secure and Fair Enforcement for Mortgage Licensing (SAFE) Act. In addition, the federal bank agencies have just announced significant changes to appraisal standards.

INDEX

C

D

E

F

G

H

I

J

K

L

M

R

S

T

U

V

W

Economists and financial journalists rarely contemplate the processes by which theoretical ideas shape and inform the public discussions that, ultimately, render certain ideas or policies acceptable, unacceptable, or simply beyond the pale. Those who have considered such matters are aware that over the past several decades the language of conventional economic discourse has shifted dramatically to the right. In this book, Professor David George has checked the validity of this supposition by gathering and presenting an analysis of the language deployed in reporting on the economy, and how it has evolved over time. Stated simply, the evidence he uncovers overwhelmingly confirms the existence of a pronounced rightward shift in the way that stories about the economy are framed and presented. Anyone interested in economic policy, American politics, current affairs, and public administration will want to read this book.

Robert E. Prasch, *Professor of Economics, Middlebury College, Middlebury, Vermont, USA*

David George's new book makes a significant contribution to our understanding of shifts in public discourse on the economy in the past 50 years. His fascinating analysis of newspaper coverage documents how things that used to be discussed favorably (like government policies to offset abuse of corporate power or collective actions by unions) came to be portrayed negatively – while things that used to be portrayed negatively (like concentration of wealth and income) came to be represented as inevitable corollaries of social gains from market-driven growth. The book's long-term perspective helps illuminate how prevailing views of economic questions and problems tend to be shaped by prevailing economic structures and institutions, and in turn dynamically change with them. By denaturalizing our economic understandings, then, George's book can help clear the way for better-grounded, less ideological thinking about how economies and societies should best be structured and coordinated to sustainably meet human needs.

Martha Starr, *Associate Professor, Department of Economics, American University, USA*

The Rhetoric of the Right

This study seeks to demonstrate the subtle ways in which changes in the language associated with economic issues are reflective of a gradual but quantifiable conservative ideological shift.

In this rigorous analysis, David George uses as his data a century of word usage within the *New York Times*, starting in 1900. It is not always obvious how the changes identified necessarily reflect a stronger prejudice toward laissez-faire free market capitalism, and so much of the book seeks to demonstrate the subtle ways in which the changing language indeed carries with it a political message. This analysis is made through exploration of five major areas of focus: the broader "economics rhetoric" scholarship and the growing "behavioral economics" school of thought; the increasingly negative flavor of the discourse associated with government and taxation; the changing meaning of "competition" and "competitive," and the increasing favorable contexts in which these words appear; changing attitudes toward labor; and the increasing celebration of growth at the same time that economic justice and social equality decline in the attention they are given.

This is a fascinating and uniquely detailed study, which will be of great interest to all economists and students of economic thought, political economics and political science.

David George is Professor of Economics at La Salle University, USA.

Routledge studies in the history of economics

1 **Economics as Literature**
Willie Henderson

2 **Socialism and Marginalism in Economics 1870–1930**
Edited by Ian Steedman

3 **Hayek's Political Economy**
The socio-economics of order
Steve Fleetwood

4 **On the Origins of Classical Economics**
Distribution and value from William Petty to Adam Smith
Tony Aspromourgos

5 **The Economics of Joan Robinson**
Edited by Maria Cristina Marcuzzo, Luigi Pasinetti and Alesandro Roncaglia

6 **The Evolutionist Economics of Léon Walras**
Albert Jolink

7 **Keynes and the 'Classics'**
A study in language, epistemology and mistaken identities
Michel Verdon

8 **The History of Game Theory, Vol 1**
From the beginnings to 1945
Robert W. Dimand and Mary Ann Dimand

9 **The Economics of W. S. Jevons**
Sandra Peart

10 **Gandhi's Economic Thought**
Ajit K. Dasgupta

11 **Equilibrium and Economic Theory**
Edited by Giovanni Caravale

12 **Austrian Economics in Debate**
Edited by Willem Keizer, Bert Tieben and Rudy van Zijp

13 **Ancient Economic Thought**
Edited by B. B. Price

14 **The Political Economy of Social Credit and Guild Socialism**
Frances Hutchinson and Brian Burkitt

15 **Economic Careers**
Economics and economists in Britain 1930–1970
Keith Tribe

16 **Understanding 'Classical' Economics**
Studies in the long-period theory
Heinz Kurz and Neri Salvadori

17 **History of Environmental Economic Thought**
E. Kula

18 **Economic Thought in Communist and Post-Communist Europe**
Edited by Hans-Jürgen Wagener

19 **Studies in the History of French Political Economy**
From Bodin to Walras
Edited by Gilbert Faccarello

20 **The Economics of John Rae**
Edited by O. F. Hamouda, C. Lee and D. Mair

21 **Keynes and the Neoclassical Synthesis**
Einsteinian versus Newtonian macroeconomics
Teodoro Dario Togati

22 **Historical Perspectives on Macroeconomics**
Sixty years after the 'General Theory'
Edited by Philippe Fontaine and Albert Jolink

23 **The Founding of Institutional Economics**
The leisure class and sovereignty
Edited by Warren J. Samuels

24 **Evolution of Austrian Economics**
From Menger to Lachmann
Sandye Gloria

25 **Marx's Concept of Money**
The God of Commodities
Anitra Nelson

26 **The Economics of James Steuart**
Edited by Ramón Tortajada

27 **The Development of Economics in Europe since 1945**
Edited by A. W. Bob Coats

28 **The Canon in the History of Economics**
Critical essays
Edited by Michalis Psalidopoulos

29 **Money and Growth**
Selected papers of Allyn Abbott Young
Edited by Perry G. Mehrling and Roger J. Sandilands

30 **The Social Economics of Jean-Baptiste Say**
Markets and virtue
Evelyn L. Forget

31 **The Foundations of Laissez-Faire**
The economics of Pierre de Boisguilbert
Gilbert Faccarello

32 **John Ruskin's Political Economy**
Willie Henderson

33 **Contributions to the History of Economic Thought**
Essays in honour of R. D. C. Black
Edited by Antoin E. Murphy and Renee Prendergast

34 **Towards an Unknown Marx**
A commentary on the manuscripts of 1861–63
Enrique Dussel

35 **Economics and Interdisciplinary Exchange**
Edited by Guido Erreygers

36 **Economics as the Art of Thought**
Essays in memory of G. L. S. Shackle
Edited by Stephen F. Frowen and Peter Earl

37 **The Decline of Ricardian Economics**
Politics and economics in post-Ricardian theory
Susan Pashkoff

38 **Piero Sraffa**
His life, thought and cultural heritage
Alessandro Roncaglia

39 **Equilibrium and Disequilibrium in Economic Theory**
The Marshall–Walras divide
Michel de Vroey

40 **The German Historical School**
The historical and ethical approach to economics
Edited by Yuichi Shionoya

41 **Reflections on the Classical Canon in Economics**
Essays in honour of Samuel Hollander
Edited by Sandra Peart and Evelyn Forget

42 **Piero Sraffa's Political Economy**
A centenary estimate
Edited by Terenzio Cozzi and Roberto Marchionatti

43 **The Contribution of Joseph Schumpeter to Economics**
Economic development and institutional change
Richard Arena and Cecile Dangel

44 **On the Development of Long-run Neo-Classical Theory**
Tom Kompas

45 **F. A. Hayek as a Political Economist**
Economic analysis and values
Edited by Jack Birner, Pierre Garrouste and Thierry Aimar

46 **Pareto, Economics and Society**
The mechanical analogy
Michael McLure

47 **The Cambridge Controversies in Capital Theory**
A study in the logic of theory development
Jack Birner

48 **Economics Broadly Considered**
Essays in honour of Warren J. Samuels
Edited by Steven G. Medema, Jeff Biddle and John B. Davis

49 **Physicians and Political Economy**
Six studies of the work of doctor-economists
Edited by Peter Groenewegen

50 **The Spread of Political Economy and the Professionalisation of Economists**
Economic societies in Europe, America and Japan in the nineteenth century
Massimo Augello and Marco Guidi

51 **Historians of Economics and Economic Thought**
The construction of disciplinary memory
Steven G. Medema and Warren J. Samuels

52 **Competing Economic Theories**
Essays in memory of Giovanni Caravale
Sergio Nisticò and Domenico Tosato

53 **Economic Thought and Policy in Less Developed Europe**
The nineteenth century
Edited by Michalis Psalidopoulos and Maria-Eugenia Almedia Mata

54 **Family Fictions and Family Facts**
Harriet Martineau, Adolphe Quetelet and the population question in England 1798–1859
Brian Cooper

55 **Eighteenth-Century Economics**
Peter Groenewegen

56 **The Rise of Political Economy in the Scottish Enlightenment**
Edited by Tatsuya Sakamoto and Hideo Tanaka

57 **Classics and Moderns in Economics, Volume I**
Essays on nineteenth and twentieth century economic thought
Peter Groenewegen

58 **Classics and Moderns in Economics, Volume II**
Essays on nineteenth and twentieth century economic thought
Peter Groenewegen

59 **Marshall's Evolutionary Economics**
Tiziano Raffaelli

60 **Money, Time and Rationality in Max Weber**
Austrian connections
Stephen D. Parsons

61 **Classical Macroeconomics**
Some modern variations and distortions
James C. W. Ahiakpor

62 **The Historical School of Economics in England and Japan**
Tamotsu Nishizawa

63 **Classical Economics and Modern Theory**
Studies in long-period analysis
Heinz D. Kurz and Neri Salvadori

64 **A Bibliography of Female Economic Thought to 1940**
Kirsten K. Madden, Janet A. Sietz and Michele Pujol

65 **Economics, Economists and Expectations**
From microfoundations to macroeconomics
Warren Young, Robert Leeson and William Darity Jnr.

66 **The Political Economy of Public Finance in Britain, 1767–1873**
Takuo Dome

67 **Essays in the History of Economics**
Warren J. Samuels, Willie Henderson, Kirk D. Johnson and Marianne Johnson

68 **History and Political Economy**
Essays in honour of P. D. Groenewegen
Edited by Tony Aspromourgos and John Lodewijks

69 **The Tradition of Free Trade**
Lars Magnusson

70 **Evolution of the Market Process**
Austrian and Swedish economics
Edited by Michel Bellet, Sandye Gloria-Palermo and Abdallah Zouache

71 **Consumption as an Investment**
The fear of goods from Hesiod to Adam Smith
Cosimo Perrotta

72 **Jean-Baptiste Say and the Classical Canon in Economics**
The British connection in French classicism
Samuel Hollander

73 **Knut Wicksell on Poverty**
No place is too exalted
Knut Wicksell

74 **Economists in Cambridge**
A study through their correspondence 1907–1946
Edited by M. C. Marcuzzo and A. Rosselli

75 **The Experiment in the History of Economics**
Edited by Philippe Fontaine and Robert Leonard

76 **At the Origins of Mathematical Economics**
The Economics of A. N. Isnard (1748–1803)
Richard van den Berg

77 **Money and Exchange**
Folktales and reality
Sasan Fayazmanesh

78 **Economic Development and Social Change**
Historical roots and modern perspectives
George Stathakis and Gianni Vaggi

79 **Ethical Codes and Income Distribution**
A study of John Bates Clark and Thorstein Veblen
Guglielmo Forges Davanzati

80 **Evaluating Adam Smith**
Creating the wealth of nations
Willie Henderson

81 **Civil Happiness**
Economics and human flourishing in historical perspective
Luigino Bruni

82 **New Voices on Adam Smith**
Edited by Leonidas Montes and Eric Schliesser

83 **Making Chicago Price Theory**
Milton Friedman–George Stigler correspondence, 1945–1957
Edited by J. Daniel Hammond and Claire H. Hammond

84 **William Stanley Jevons and the Cutting Edge of Economics**
Bert Mosselmans

85 **A History of Econometrics in France**
From nature to models
Philippe Le Gall

86 **Money and Markets**
A doctrinal approach
Edited by Alberto Giacomin and Maria Cristina Marcuzzo

87 **Considerations on the Fundamental Principles of Pure Political Economy**
Vilfredo Pareto (Edited by Roberto Marchionatti and Fiorenzo Mornati)

88 **The Years of High Econometrics**
A short history of the generation that reinvented economics
Francisco Louçã

89 **David Hume's Political Economy**
Edited by Carl Wennerlind and Margaret Schabas

90 **Interpreting Classical Economics**
Studies in long-period analysis
Heinz D. Kurz and Neri Salvadori

91 **Keynes's Vision**
Why the great depression did not return
John Philip Jones

92 **Monetary Theory in Retrospect**
The selected essays of Filippo Cesarano
Filippo Cesarano

93 **Keynes's Theoretical Development**
From the tract to the general theory
Toshiaki Hirai

94 **Leading Contemporary Economists**
Economics at the cutting edge
Edited by Steven Pressman

95 **The Science of Wealth**
Adam Smith and the framing of political economy
Tony Aspromourgos

96 **Capital, Time and Transitional Dynamics**
Edited by Harald Hagemann and Roberto Scazzieri

97 **New Essays on Pareto's Economic Theory**
Edited by Luigino Bruni and Aldo Montesano

98 **Frank Knight and the Chicago School in American Economics**
Ross B. Emmett

99 **A History of Economic Theory**
Essays in honour of Takashi Negishi
Edited by Aiko Ikeo and Heinz D. Kurz

100 **Open Economics**
Economics in relation to other disciplines
Edited by Richard Arena, Sheila Dow and Matthias Klaes

101 **Rosa Luxemburg and the Critique of Political Economy**
Edited by Riccardo Bellofiore

102 **Problems and Methods of Econometrics**
The Poincaré lectures of Ragnar Frisch 1933
Edited by Olav Bjerkholt and Ariane Dupont-Keiffer

103 **Criticisms of Classical Political Economy**
Menger, Austrian economics and the German historical school
Gilles Campagnolo

104 **A History of Entrepreneurship**
Robert F. Hébert and Albert N. Link

105 **Keynes on Monetary Policy, Finance and Uncertainty**
Liquidity preference theory and the global financial crisis
Jorg Bibow

106 **Kalecki's Principle of Increasing Risk and Keynesian Economics**
Tracy Mott

107 **Economic Theory and Economic Thought**
Essays in honour of Ian Steedman
John Vint, J. Stanley Metcalfe, Heinz D. Kurz, Neri Salvadori and Paul Samuelson

108 **Political Economy, Public Policy and Monetary Economics**
Ludwig von Mises and the Austrian tradition
Richard M. Ebeling

109 **Keynes and the British Humanist Tradition**
The moral purpose of the market
David R. Andrews

110 **Political Economy and Industrialism**
Banks in Saint-Simonian economic thought
Gilles Jacoud

111 **Studies in Social Economics**
Leon Walras
Translated by Jan van Daal and Donald Walker

112 **The Making of the Classical Theory of Economic Growth**
Anthony Brewer

113 **The Origins of David Hume's Economics**
Willie Henderson

114 **Production, Distribution and Trade**
Edited by Adriano Birolo, Duncan Foley, Heinz D. Kurz, Bertram Schefold and Ian Steedman

115 **The Essential Writings of Thorstein Veblen**
Edited by Charles Camic and Geoffrey Hodgson

116 **Adam Smith and the Economy of the Passions**
Jan Horst Keppler

117 **The Analysis of Linear Economic Systems**
Father Maurice Potron's pioneering works
Translated by Christian Bidard and Guido Erreygers

118 **A Dynamic Approach to Economic Theory: Frisch**
Edited by Olav Bjerkholt and Duo Qin

119 **Henry A. Abbati: Keynes' Forgotten Precursor**
Serena Di Gaspare

120 **Generations of Economists**
David Collard

121 **Hayek, Mill and the Liberal Tradition**
Edited by Andrew Farrant

122 **Marshall, Marshallians and Industrial Economics**
Edited by Tiziano Raffaelli

123 **Austrian and German Economic Thought**
Kiichiro Yagi

124 **The Evolution of Economic Theory**
Edited by Volker Caspari

125 **Thomas Tooke and the Monetary Thought of Classical Economics**
Matthew Smith

126 **Political Economy and Liberalism in France**
The contributions of Frédéric Bastiat
Robert Leroux

127 **Stalin's Economist**
The economic contributions of Jenö Varga
André Mommen

128 **E.E. Slutsky as Economist and Mathematician**
Crossing the limits of knowledge
Vincent Barnett

129 **Keynes, Sraffa, and the Criticism of Neoclassical Theory**
Essays in honour of Heinz Kurz
Neri Salvadori and Christian Gehrke

130 **Crises and Cycles in Economic Dictionaries and Encyclopaedias**
Edited by Daniele Bensomi

131 **General Equilibrium Analysis**
A century after walras
Edited by Pascal Bridel

132 **Sraffa and Modern Economics, Volume I**
Edited by Roberto Ciccone, Christian Gehrke and Gary Mongiovi

133 **Sraffa and Modern Economics, Volume II**
Edited by Roberto Ciccone, Christian Gehrke and Gary Mongiovi

134 **The Minor Marshallians and Alfred Marshall**
An evaluation
Peter Groenewegen

135 **Fighting Market Failure**
Collected essays in the Cambridge tradition of economics
Maria Cristina Marcuzzo

136 **The Economic Reader**
Edited by Massimo M. Augello and Marco E. L. Guido

137 **Classical Political Economy and Modern Theory**
Essays in honour of Heinz Kurz
Neri Salvadori and Christian Gehrke

138 **The Ideas of Ronald H. Coase**
Lawrence W. C. Lai

139 **Anticipating the Wealth of Nations**
Edited by Maren Jonasson and Petri Hyttinen, with an Introduction by Lars Magnusson

140 Innovation, Knowledge and Growth
Edited by Heinz D. Kurz

141 A History of Homo Economicus
The nature of the moral in economic theory
William Dixon and David Wilson

142 The Division of Labour in Economics
A history
Guang-Zhen Sun

143 Keynes and Modern Economics
Edited by Ryuzo Kuroki

144 Macroeconomics and the History of Economic Thought
Festschrift in honour of Harald Hagemann
Edited by Hagen M. Krämer, Heinz D. Kurz and Hans-Michael Trautwein

145 French Liberalism in the 19th Century
An anthology
Edited by Robert Leroux

146 Subjectivisim and Objectivism in the History of Economic Thought
Edited by Yukihiro Ikeda and Kiichiro Yagi

147 The Rhetoric of the Right
Language change and the spread of the market
David George

The Rhetoric of the Right

Language change and the spread of the market

David George

Routledge
Taylor & Francis Group
LONDON AND NEW YORK

First published 2013
by Routledge
2 Park Square, Milton Park, Abingdon, Oxon OX14 4RN

Simultaneously published in the USA and Canada by Routledge
711 Third Avenue, New York, NY 10017

Routledge is an imprint of the Taylor & Francis Group, an informa business

British Library Cataloguing in Publication Data
A catalogue record for this book is available from the British Library

Library of Congress Cataloging in Publication Data
George, David (David L.)
The rhetoric of the right: language change and the spread of the market/by David George.
p. cm.
1. Economics–Authorship. 2. Economics literature. 3. Rhetoric–Social aspects. 4. Economics–Psychological aspects. I. Title.
HB74.2.G46 2012
330.12'2014–dc23

2012005132

ISBN: 978-0-415-67997-8 (hbk)
ISBN: 978-0-203-10352-4 (ebk)

Typeset in Times New Roman
by Wearset Ltd, Boldon, Tyne and Wear

Printed and bound in the United States of America by Publishers Graphics, LLC on sustainably sourced paper.

Contents

Tables

Acknowledgments

I have been fortunate to have research interests that are relatively low cost. Grants for the funding of materials, travel, and personnel were unnecessary. It is that precious resource, time, that I needed, and time that I was able to get for the project that comes to completion with this book. My thanks to La Salle University for providing a research leave in the Spring of 2009. When combined with a Sabbatical the following semester, I was able to devote a solid year to data collection and the writing of the greater part of this book. I also thank La Salle for providing a teaching and research environment ideally suited for the sort of writing that I do. Being at a teaching-focused institution has been an advantage to me over the years when it comes to the directions of research that I've been inspired to follow. As every economist knows, ours is not an easy subject, and confusion is more the rule than the exception. Leading text writers and researchers tend to have little contact with the beginning student, and when they do, it is more often than not top-tier students most able to navigate the strange language of economics that they encounter. In contrast, the non-majoring, less elite students who I so often teach are more comfortable admitting that the words we use are, more often than they wish, unclear. Exposed to this over the years, I have gravitated away from interest in the mathematical and toward a fascination with the language of economics.

When it comes to the research environment at La Salle, our small size, and approach to research that is, shall I say, more laid-back than what prevails at the leading Ph.D. institutions is ideal for the heterodox economist. Cross-disciplinary contacts, while praised by all, are considerably easier when distances, both geographical and psychological, are kept to a minimum. While members of the economics department have provided great support for my efforts, so too have colleagues outside the department. Within the department, I would like to thank Richard Mshomba who carefully read and commented on an early draft, David Robison, who contributed with useful suggestions, Beth Paulin, whose econometric background provided suggestions on the data-driven aspects of the project, and department secretary Elizabeth McDonald who was always there when help was needed. Outside of the department, Gary Clabaugh of education, Marc Moreau of philosophy, and English department members John Beatty, Marjorie Allen, and Vincent Kling. Each provided moral support as well as aid in the prevention of any slide into a sort of writing understandable only to economists. Thanks as well to reference librarian Steven Breedlove who provided great assistance at the earliest stages of the project. And a special thanks to Paul Roden, of our Office of Human Resources. As one very adept at the public relations side of getting out a message and as one who has shown the most intense interest of anyone yet exposed to the book, he has gone well beyond his professional responsibilities here at La Salle to provide a wealth of advice on ways of bringing attention to the book.

Since this project represented a new direction for me, I cannot claim to have built up over the years a long list of scholars outside of my institution engaged in similar projects. There have been, nonetheless, a number of colleagues at other institutions who have made useful suggestions. Thanks, in particular, to John Davis, Martha Starr, Rojhat Avsar, Tim Brennan, Daniel Akst, Will Richan, William White, Rita Mall, and Tucker Taylor. Their comments on papers that I presented and answers to questions that I asked helped shape the final product. Thanks as well to Simon Holt, senior editorial assistant at Routledge, as well as to Claire Toal and Allie Waite of Wearset. Though the ocean-wide distance between us prevented me from meeting them, their care and thoughtfulness in answering my countless questions went far in relieving any anxieties I had about the state of the project.

As part of the learning experience here at La Salle, our students work with professors on their research. As one less than comfortable with information technology (the heavy use of word search in this work to the contrary notwithstanding), it was a facility with the technology that Sarah Tereniak, Kevin Prendergast, Claire Fisher, Steve Kernytsky, and Emily Schmitt displayed that made my project that much easier.

Parts of Chapters 2 and 3 draw on articles published elsewhere. Some slightly altered parts of Chapter 2 appeared in "The Rhetoric of Economics Texts," *Journal of Economic Issues* 24(3), (1990): 861–878, and Chapter 3 is an extensive rewrite and expansion of "On Being 'Competitive': The Evolution of a Word," *Real-World Economics Review* 8(6), (2008): 319–334. Thanks to the publishers of these articles for permission to use them here. And my thanks as well to the *New York Times* for the excellent database from which so much of the data appearing in the tables was drawn and for the many quotes from a number of articles that appeared in the *Times* over the last century.

Solo writing can be a lonely process, and many of us feel the need to "share" the findings of a day's work. Most of my time working on this project occurred at home. Thanks to my wife Patty, and to Alex and Rebecca for providing the occasional sounding board when being alone with new findings was too much to bear. And thanks to all three, Patty in particular, for coming to my aid when computer-related problems occurred, a too frequent event for the technology-challenged such as myself.

1 Introduction

In this project, I will be taking two directions that differ from what is usually called *behavioral economics*. This now flourishing field has managed to reduce in status the armchair theorists who have been in charge of economics – continual challenges notwithstanding – since at least the time of Adam Smith. Armchair theorists like to talk, setting forth assumptions and deriving conclusions very much in the deductive tradition. Behaviors are assumed rather than observed, at least in the simplified characterization of such theorists.

Behavioral economics constitutes one more step in a long history of challenging this and introducing a more scientific, inductive tradition to economics. "Observe how people actually behave and only then put together theories," runs the message. Facts must be gathered before theories are formulated, not merely assumed in a way that makes theorizing tractable.

I will not be contesting the overall importance of this very skeletal description of behavioral economics, but the starting point of my work will be two weaknesses that limit what its overall project has been taken to be. As a first weakness, *talk* should not be an activity exclusively associated with the armchair theorists. Yes, these theorists too often simply create a reality through words ("assume that people are perfectly rational"). But talk is also a behavior and as such must be more a part of behavioral economics. In what follows it will be words that receive attention and the change in word usage over time.

As a second weakness, to argue that armchair theorists have fallen short in their understanding and portrayal of reality should not be treated as evidence that they have failed to influence that reality. People may behave differently than theory assumes, but what if with the passage of time their behaviors are influenced by that theory?[1]

Focus on rhetoric

An interest in how economists communicate with each other is usually assumed to have taken off with the publication in 1985 of Donald McCloskey's book, *The Rhetoric of Economics.* While this project has taken a good number of twists and turns, its usual focus has remained internal to economics. The starting point was dissatisfaction with the modernist vision of economics as a social science, and a desire to demonstrate that the sheer art of persuasion exerts influence far more often than the advocates of mathematical models and statistical analyses are willing to admit.

The importance of this project should not be underestimated. The heterodox movement to break free of the neoclassical methodology and focus is deeply engrained with many of the post-modern ways of thinking that began with McCloskey and whether they succeed or not in upsetting the still dominant orthodoxy, there is no doubt that their influence has been and will continue to be significant.[2]

I start with this appreciation of a vital movement to give credit where credit is due but to also announce that my motive for writing this book and the sort of questions I raise will represent a break from the rhetorical movement as it is generally understood. Only on a few occasions in the chapters that follow will I be studying the language of economists, and even when I do, it will be economists writing for the introductory student, not economists writing for each other, that will be the focus. What inspired this project was a long-festering, hard to pinpoint irritation with the economic language of the non-economist. During the long-running move to the right economically that just happens to coincide with my professional career as an economics teacher, I have frequently found myself paying attention to words and phrases that bothered me, often not quite sure as to why they did so, and often unable to imagine what used to be said in place of these words and phrases.

To give some examples of the questions that arose, what was the cause and the path by which *competitive* came to be encountered so frequently and came to be an unequivocally good thing? Has it always been true, as it currently appears to be, that the act of politicizing is disreputable? Has the act of commercializing changed in its acceptability? It was not hard to recall when one would never give someone advice to *sell yourself* or *market yourself* and yet just such advice seemed to be increasingly common. Was this so? And what about earnings? On tax forms in the United States, earnings signify returns to labor, not returns to property. Yet unless I was imagining things, it seemed to be increasingly associated with profits. As recently as the 1970s, *entrepreneur* was a pretentious name for a business owner and was used mainly in the writings of economists. Has there been an increased usage of this word in the general society? And as a final example, I felt certain that saying one would *create jobs* was an expression rising in popularity. If this were so, what might have been said previously instead of this?

The main source for data to try to answer questions such as these will be the *New York Times Historical Newspapers* data base. Data for the *Times* itself extends back to 1850, but, except for a few exceptions, my focus will be limited to years since 1900. Sometimes word counts will appear by decade, but more often I will divide data into three periods: pre-Great Depression (1900–1929), pre-Ronald Reagan (1930–1979), and post-Ronald Reagan (1980–present). When trends are uncovered, corroboration will be sought by comparing similar early 20th century word usage (1900–1922) as revealed by the *America's*

Historical Newspapers database (hereafter abbreviated AHN) with more recent word usage (since 1980) as revealed by the newspapers included in the *ProQuest Historical Newspapers: The New York Times (1851–2008)* database (hereafter ProQuest).[3] The data sources describe populations rather than samples and for this reason no traditional significance tests will be applied. My general *modus operandi* will be to simply show the trends in relative usage over time by noting the ratio changes of one particular word or phrase to another.

The trends that I will uncover will, I believe, be surprising inasmuch as the *New York Times* has been, and continues to be, the bastion of liberal economic perspectives, though great care must be taken in drawing conclusions. These trends will with few exceptions reflect the general rightward shift of the nation over at least the last forty years. But to the extent that the language change is accounted for by changes in the languages of others being quoted or paraphrased, these changes may not reflect any shifts in the thinking of *Times* reporters themselves.

And this raises the question of what the change in language can tell us about the intentions of those who adopt these changes. There is one tradition, well represented by the work of Geoffrey Nunberg (2006), that approaches changes as deliberate strategies. Self-awareness of the words one chooses has spread over the last century from being the special preserve of the literary set to being something which advertisers can ignore only at their own peril. That conservatives have very deliberately introduced words and phrases with very specific intents is undeniable.

But as surely as an injection of spending into a depressed economy can have ripple effects that add to the initial deliberate stimulative action, deliberate change in language, while having its own immediate effects, can change the language of those not sharing the views of those who precipitated the changes. To take just one example that will receive more attention in a later chapter, nearly everyone today uses *politicize* in a negative sense not originally intended by those who appear to have first used the word during the activist 1960s. In short, a change in the language exerts an impact by affecting what we all hear (as spoken by the originators of the change) but can exert at least an equal effect by changing the language of those sharing none of the beliefs of the originators of the change.

Added to this, there is a type of language change that will be explored that is likely to be no one's conscious intent. The clearest example of this in the chapters ahead is the propensity to use *our* instead of *the* when something begins to hold greater appeal and to do the reverse when something falls out of favor. Here, far more often than not, the speakers are wholly unaware of their changes. While not a deliberate action of anyone, it can serve as a useful indicator of attitudinal change.

The chapters ahead

We know instinctively that the old saying "it's impossible to be too thin or too rich" is deliberately simplistic and not quite true. This comes through poignantly with the rising incidence of eating disorders in recent years that glorify thinness to the point of near starvation. It may be less obvious when it comes to wealth, but at least from an economist's standpoint, it is possible to have too much of everything, with wealth being no exception. In the chapter that follows it is the language associated with government's role in the economy that will receive attention. The United States has since its inception been more suspicious of government than most other advanced capitalist nations of the world. But even acknowledging the near inborn disposition of Americans to question anything that government touches, the fact does remain that the cynicism and distrust continue to grow. In this chapter, century long rhetorical trends will be studied. Why is our government ever less likely to be called *ours*? Since when is it always seen as wrong to *politicize*? Why does a quarter-century shrinkage of government not translate into a fading away of references to *big government*?

As government fades in status, the market's reputation rises. Chapter 3 examines the spreading love affair with *competition*. Why does it appear ever more frequently compared with *monopoly* even while industrial concentration increases? And why does *competition* grow in usage relative to *cooperation*, when most would agree that the latter of these is not as plentiful as it ought to be.

At the level of the individual, the market's replacement of government is paralleled by the consumer's replacement of the voter-citizen. In Chapter 4 it is the steadily ascendant consumer that will be the focus of analysis. Most of us are aware that the consumer has snuck in to conversations where *clients* or *students* or *citizens* once prevailed. The greater acceptance of advertising and marketing has, not surprisingly, coincided with the embrace of the *consumer*. While advertising to *clients* or *students* may raise ethical red flags, advertising to consumers is as natural as tending to the sick. The different ways in which consumerism has affected the language will be the focus of this chapter.

While consumers need spending power, it is no secret that that the source of most spending power, salaries and wages, have fared poorly for many years now, at least for the lower earning 80 percent of wage earners. In Chapter 5, it is the language associated with labor that will be investigated. That a loss in power and influence might lie behind the wage trends is fairly clear, but we should not underestimate the role that language has played in diminishing the status of workers, and not just reflecting but contributing to this ongoing event. Why are wages more frequently referred to as *costs* and less frequently referred to as *earnings* than they used to be? Why is it that employers *create jobs* instead of *providing employment*, as they once did? And why do we treat firms that demand labor as the ones creating or providing jobs instead of describing the suppliers of labor this way. Don't we, after all, treat the suppliers of goods, not demanders, as the *creators* of these goods?

Chapter 6 examines *economic growth*, the dynamic process that stands today as the *sine qua non* for anything worth calling "good times." What has happened to *progress*, *equality*, *justice*, and *fairness*? And is there significance to be found in the habit of speaking of academics and scientists as *achievers* while reserving the word *successful* for one doing well in the world of business? Also rather unconsidered has been the habit of making steadily more references to the virtues *more equal opportunity* while ever less references to *more equal results.* Might the much used metaphor of the *level playing field* have led us to assume that all participants – small proprietor and mega-corporation alike – can be expected to play the very same game rather than each having its own separate field on which to compete?

What nearly all of the trends in word usage seem to share is an increasingly relaxed reliance on that old bad guy – government – to *intervene* on the *level playing field.* To this we turn in the chapter that follows.

2 Markets over governments

The Libertarian juggernaut

When it comes to economic affairs the label *conservative* represents a libertarian (or *classically liberal*) position. Such a position is simple to describe and stands as testimony to the simplistic ideology that underlies it. In two words, the recommendation is *less government*. That this has been the recommendation of choice for Republican candidates in the United States is obvious. That it is a position that Democrats feel the need to reflexively support as well speaks volumes about the attractiveness of its simplicity. No matter how it is measured, the economic role of government has not been growing in the United States for a very long time. Federal government outlays as a percentage of GDP have varied little for an entire half-century. In 1962, they comprised 18.8 percent of all outlays, rose to a high of 23.5 percent during President Reagan's third year in office – 1983 – and generally fell through 2007, when they comprised 20.0 percent of all outlays.[1] While state and local spending has risen slightly in response to the lack of relative growth in government spending, the fact remains that by almost any way of looking at the matter, government outlays have been steady, proportionally speaking, for a very long time. Sometimes even the simple facts are not allowed to speak for themselves. So, for example, Garrett and Rhine conclude their article "On the Size and Growth of Government" with the claim that "[t]he past 90 years has seen a dramatic rise in the size and growth of the government in the United States" (2006, 27), despite presenting earlier in the same article extremely clear evidence that all of the gain in relative size occurred between1930 and 1952.

One may argue that the dislike that the libertarian has for government has less to do with taxing and spending than with control, regulation, and intrusiveness. But here too, by most any way of looking at the matter, government was lessening rather than increasing (at least through the middle of 2008). All but the most recalcitrant libertarian has been forced to acknowledge that it was the absence of government brought about by the deregulatory movement going all the way back to the 1970s that set in motion the financial collapse of 2008. In short, whether one chooses to measure the size of government by its level of spending or by its degree of control, prior to 2008 it had not been growing for quite a while. Despite this, the felt need to shrink government more continues to be expressed.[2] Despite U.S. government expenditures ranking near the bottom of advanced Western nations as a percentage of GDP, the general position that government is too large continues to dominate public discussions.[3]

That the rightward shift is limited to economic affairs, and that a culturally liberal position has carried the day politically for some time, remains an often heard claim. Steady de-regulation of corporations, the weakening of unions, the adoption of a less progressive tax system, the weakening of anti-trust laws and the penetration of the business model into the non-profit realm are all trends that economic conservatives have strongly supported. But there has also been occurring the strengthening of equal opportunities for women, for African-Americans, for Hispanics, and for gays and the greater general acceptance of behaviors outside of the mainstream, trends these same conservatives are likely to regret.

For some commentators, these simultaneous social drifts, to the right economically but the left socially, suggest something of a draw in the wider struggle between conservatives and liberals. Near the end of his book – *The Right Talk* – that investigates how conservatives won followers with their economic ideas, political economist Mark A. Smith notes that:

> [C]onservatives achieved the least success on their social and cultural agenda – the very agenda that attracted so much attention in popular and scholarly discourse. Religious conservatives, in particular, repeatedly failed in recent decades to restrict pornography, outlaw abortion, reinstate school prayer, or restore traditional gender relations, and they fought rearguard battles against the American public's growing tolerance of homosexuality and demands for stem-cell research.
>
> (2007, 198)

What goes unremarked is the possibility that the very success of their economic platform carried with it the seeds of destruction of social conservatism. Linguist George Lakoff points out that "[a] focus on unimpeded pursuit of self-interest – and with it, extreme limits on state power over the individual – defines the libertarian strain of right-wing thought" (2004, 81), without choosing to even mention that it is exactly such libertarianism that has formed the backdrop for opposition to conservative efforts to restrict in any way, the free choice of individuals regarding their sexual behaviors, job choices, decisions to indulge in pornography, and decisions to have abortions. In short the overall social drift to the right economically and to the left socially is really no paradox at all. Nearly all is consistent with a growth in libertarianism. The paradox is to be found in the constellation of beliefs uniting traditional conservatives and the constellation of beliefs uniting liberals. Each group is libertarian on some of the issues, and decidedly unlibertarian on the others, not inherently contradictory but odd nonetheless.

Ever less *ours*?

A major claim of "The Rhetoric of Economics Texts" (D. George, 1990) was that the principles textbooks represented government in a way that ignored the fact that the United States is a democracy. Rather than reflecting the will of the people, government was portrayed more as an outsider, an *intrusive alien*. Rather than speaking of governments *acting*, governments were more often said to *intervene*, a practice suggested to likely follow from the market purists imagining a state of nature when market behavior prevailed but government in any meaningful sense simply did not exist. This view of government came through especially clearly in the claim of one text that "[g]overnment purchases measure the percentage of GNP that is 'used up' by government" (Dolan and Lindsey, 1988, 105). That the people being served by their government might actually benefit from these redirected resources was not even suggested. When these biases were studied two decades ago, data that might strengthen (or weaken) the points made was not available.

As a first step in exploring the long-term trend of treating the government as an *intrusive alien*, it will be useful to compare the past with the present in the frequency with which *our* precedes *government*. Consider the following sentence from one of the 1980s texts that I surveyed: "[T]remendous increases in federal employment and spending have [given] *the* government an increasing share of *our* total resources" (Schiller, 1989, 64) [emphases mine]. While it is perfectly common for someone feeling a close attachment to, for example, their city to use *the* ("the city needs our help"), it seems reasonable to assume (and later facts will support) that the closer the attachment the more likely is *our* to appear. Thus we might expect to be more likely to see *our* preceding *wounded soldiers* than, say, *lawyers*.[4]

Column 1 in Table 2.1 shows the number of times that *government* appeared each decade (irrespective of what words preceded or followed). Column 2 shows

Table 2.1 Decreasing frequency of *government* described as *our*

Years	*1*	*2*	*3*
2000–2009	90,999	658	138.3
1990–1999	131,571	784	167.8
1980–1989	167,152	1,155	144.7
1970–1979	176,293	1,185	148.8
1960–1969	177,589	1,224	145.1
1950–1959	196,725	2,218	88.7
1940–1949	213,000	3,071	69.4
1930–1939	219,955	3,200	68.7
1920–1929	153,826	2,924	52.6
1910–1919	106,860	2,357	45.3
1900–1909	67,362	1,415	47.6

Notes
Column 1: *government.*
Column 2: *our government.*
Column 3: column 1/column 2.

the number of times that *our government* appeared, and column 3 shows the ratio of column 1 divided by column 2. What stands out? Trends in the raw numbers are not very useful since the overall size of the newspaper was expanding over some periods and contracting over others. Trends in the ratio are more promising, but here too, caution is needed. The ratio declined gradually through 1960 as *our* went from preceding *government* once every forty-eight times early in the century to once every eighty-nine times by the 1950s. There also appears to have been a big plunge in the use of *our* in the 1960s, with little change since that time.[5]

Could it simply be that changing professional standards discouraged the too cozy use of *our* and that the trend signals nothing about how close the writers felt to the government, but instead reflects how they viewed their responsibilities as reporters? To test this possibility, a similar time series was constructed for the private sector. Column 1 in Table 2.2 shows the number of times that *companies* and related terms appeared. Column 2 shows the number of times that *our* preceded any of these words. And as with the preceding table the third column simply shows the ratio of column 1 to column 2 for each decade.

Here too a pattern emerges, but a pattern unlike the other one. From 1900 through 1960, *companies* and related terms became steadily less likely to be referred to as *ours*. But beginning in the 1960s, a clear turnaround occurred, as the frequency of *our* rose four-fold, from once every 298 times in the 1950s to once every seventy-six times in the 2000s, despite there being more companies mentioned that were not *ours*. Could this change have been due to an expanding business section in the *Times*? This seems unlikely given the lack of any sudden rise in the column 1 numbers.[6] Was worker's capitalism at work, as more and more people (including *Times* writers) held stocks in their 401(k)s and thus regarded companies as *ours*? Perhaps, but the shift toward *our* well preceded the

Table 2.2 Increasing frequency of *corporations* (and related words) described as *our*

Years	*1*	*2*	*3*
2000–2009	238,057	3,138	75.9
1990–1999	330,690	3,823	86.5
1980–1989	376,346	4,469	84.2
1970–1979	368,706	3,074	119.9
1960–1969	392,197	1,923	204.0
1950–1959	445,029	1,490	298.7
1940–1949	431,780	1,563	276.3
1930–1939	533,046	2,114	252.2
1920–1929	428,228	1,757	243.7
1910–1919	223,853	1,751	127.8
1900–1909	200,203	1,476	135.6

Notes
Column 1: *companies, corporations, businesses, enterprises*, and *firms*.
Column 2: *our companies, our corporations, our businesses, our enterprises*, and *our firms*.
Column 3: column 1/column 2.

shift into 401(k)s.[7] What we appear to have is a perception of the public sector as less *ours* at the same time that the private sector was being perceived as ever more so. Table 2.3 summarizes just how strong the shift was. Prior to 1960 *government* was more than twice as likely as *company* to be preceded by *our*. Since 1980 it has been just over half as likely. And somewhat surprisingly, in the 1960s, well before the Reagan revolution, a strong shift was already underway. The "*push*" away from identifying with government is in part explained by opposition to the Vietnam War. A simultaneous "pull" factor toward private firms, however, is something of a surprise, not fitting well with the perceived leftward shift that is usually associated with this decade.

While my other data sources do not allow corroboration with these strong mid-century shifts, contrasting the early source with the more recent does reinforce the suggested trend revealed by the *Times.* AHN show *our* preceding *business* around once every 500 prior to 1923, while ProQuest shows the number falling more than two-fold, to close to once every 200 times since 1980. And these same sources reveal more than a three-fold drop in *our* modifying *government*, from once every sixty times to once every 219 times over the same period.

But this raises another question. Is the use of the adjective *our* always a positive thing, a sign of closeness between speaker and object? We might be more eager to refer to children of the world as *ours* precisely because of their vulnerability. For more independent, respected middle-age individuals the personal pronoun might be used far less (as a generation goes from being "*our children*" to "*the middle-age population*") not because of any dislike of them but because of strength. Might it not similarly be possible that the rising power of government has led us to take away the personal pronoun while the increasing vulnerability of the private sector has made us more prone to use it?

Once again this is a question worth further investigation. Here, however, I want to offer what I think is a far more likely explanation for the century long shift. The *New York Times* writers reflect a general human tendency to be far

Table 2.3 Ratio of column 3 in Table 2.2 to column 3 in Table 2.1

Years	*Ratio*
2000–2009	0.55
1990–1999	0.52
1980–1989	0.58
1970–1979	0.81
1960–1969	1.45
1950–1959	2.23
1940–1949	2.45
1930–1939	2.25
1920–1929	2.67
1910–1919	1.79
1900–1909	1.62

more likely to refer to something that is viewed positively as *ours* than something that is viewed negatively. To provide evidence for this, I compiled the frequency of *our* for twelve clearly positive adjectives (dedicated, loyal, talented, skilled, beautiful, creative, imaginative, victorious, winning, honest, law-abiding, and healthy) and the frequency of their negative opposites (undedicated, disloyal, untalented, unskilled, ugly, uncreative, unimaginative, defeated, losing, dishonest, law-breaking, and unhealthy). Table 2.4 summarizes the data.

Because some of the numbers were quite low when using just *Times* articles, I elected to include everything else appearing in the *Times* with the exception of ads. In both the first half of the 20th century and over the last thirty years, *our* described negative adjectives approximately one-sixth as often as it did positive adjectives. This is captured by the data appearing in columns 3 and 6, summarized in column 7. A positive adjective was referred to as *our* once every 397 times in the early period, and once every 372 times since 1980, as shown in column 3. A negative adjective was only about one-sixth as likely to be so described in each period, as the numbers in column 6 reveal. Column 7 divides the column 6 numbers by the column 3 numbers for each period and shows no significant change. In both periods, a negative adjective was roughly one-sixth times as likely to be preceded by *ours* as was a positive adjective.

Table 2.5 has the same general set-up as Table 2.4 for *government* and *business*. To make comparisons with Table 2.4 consistent, the raw data is again for appearance anywhere in the *Times* except for the ads. A comparison of columns 3 and 6 in Table 2.4 with columns 3 and 6 in Table 2.5 is revealing. Whereas through both time periods *our* was one-sixth as likely to precede a negative as a positive adjective, the pattern flips when government and business are being compared. Though the frequency of *our government* was more than cut in half (from every fifty-three times to every 117 times as shown in column 3) the frequency of *our companies*, etc. more than doubled (from once every 215 to once every eighty-nine times as shown in column 6). As column 7 summarizes,

Table 2.4 Frequency of favorable adjectives described as *ours* relative to unfavorable adjectives described as *ours*

Years	*1*	*2*	*3*	*4*	*5*	*6*	*7*
1980–2009	587,383	1,577	372.5	165,518	75	2,206.90	0.169
1900–1949	664,902	1,673	397.4	289,150	116	2,492.70	0.159

Notes

Column 1: *dedicated, loyal, talented, skilled, beautiful, creative, imaginative, winning, honest, law-abiding*, and *healthy*.

Column 2: column 1 adjectives with *our* preceding.

Column 3: column 1/column 2.

Column 4: *undedicated, disloyal, untalented, unskilled, ugly, uncreative, unimaginative, losing, dishonest, law-breaking*, and *unhealthy*.

Column 5: column 4 adjectives with *our* preceding.

Column 6: column 4/column 5.

Column 7: column 3/column 6.

Table 2.5 Frequency of *government* described as *our* relative to *corporations* (and related words) described as *our*

Years	*1*	*2*	*3*	*4*	*5*	*6*	*7*
1980–2009	500,648	4,298	116.5	1,360,249	15,367	88.5	1.32
1900–1949	941,644	17,940	52.5	2,504,877	11,632	215.3	0.24

Notes
Column 1: *government.*
Column 2: *our government.*
Column 3: column 1/column 2.
Column 4: *companies, corporations, businesses, enterprises,* and *firms.*
Column 5: *our companies, our corporations, our businesses, our enterprises,* and *our firms.*
Column 6: column 4/column 5.
Column 7: column 3/column 6.

government went from being four times more likely to be modified by *our* in the first period to slightly less likely after 1980, as the relative frequency of *our business* exceeded that of *our government* by 30 percent.

While a distancing from *government* was occurring, a similar distancing from *nation* was not. The government related columns 1 through 3 in Table 2.6 are the same as columns 1 through 3 in Table 2.5. Columns 4 through 6 show *nation* where *business* appeared in Table 2.4. Note that prior to 1950, *government* and *nation* were nearly equally likely to be preceded by *our*, government once every fifty-three times and nation once every fifty-one times. Since 1980, however, a strong difference emerged. While *nation* was preceded by *our* about once every fifty-four times (little change from the earlier period), *government* was less than half as likely to be similarly described, being preceded by *our* only once every 117 times since 1980.[8] The military often reminds us that its function is to protect *the nation* or *our nation* but is far less likely to speak of protecting *the government* or *our government. Nation* tends to conjure up an image of everything to be found within the boundaries of a country while *government* is usually taken to represent a particular component of the nation and one that often stands

Table 2.6 Frequency of *government* described as *our* relative to *nation* described as *our*

Years	*1*	*2*	*3*	*4*	*5*	*6*	*7*
1980–2009	500,648	4,298	116.5	1,135,071	21,045	53.9	2.16
1900–1949	941,644	17,940	52.5	2,061,122	40,466	50.9	1.03

Notes
Column 1: *government.*
Column 2: *our government.*
Column 3: column 1/column 2.
Column 4: *nation.*
Column 5: *our nation.*
Column 6: column 4/column 5.
Column 7: column 3/column 6.

in opposition to the private sector. What makes the trend away from *our government* especially odd is that it was occurring over the same period of time when the right to vote was being extended to women and minorities. It would seem that in strong democracies, of all places, *our government* would be as frequently heard as *our nation*. Those living in unpopular dictatorships might nonetheless feel comfortable using the personal pronoun to describe the nation. Thus, citizens of Egypt were far less likely to call the recently deposed Mubarek regime *our government* than they were to call Egypt *our nation*. In short, dictator notwithstanding, a citizen might see the nation as hers while seeing the government as belonging to someone else.

Yet while the right to vote has widened over the last century and as the actions of government thus reflect the desires of an ever wider segment of the population, newspapers in the United States have become less likely to call this government *ours*. Could it be that the white males who still form a large majority of newspaper writers are less inclined, consciously or not, to view the government as *theirs*? While a possibility, a more likely cause of the decreased use of the personal pronoun is that that which is admired (or successful) is more likely to be embraced than anything that is not. If government has fallen in status, it should be no surprise that we are less inclined to call it *ours*.

A final point remains before leaving the *our* theme. The *New York Times* represents a rich source, but if the changes that I uncover can be explained by a conscious movement of the *Times* from the economic left to the economic right, then this will remain little more than a very limited history. While a possibility, what I think more probable is that the dominance of conservative ideology has managed to change the dialogue for all parties, and that the *Times* leans as much toward the left as ever, at least as *the left* is defined in the United States. The data in Table 2.7 tend to support this.

Table 2.7 Comparative frequency of *conservative*, *liberal*, and *progressive* being described as *our*

Years	*1*	*2*	*3*	*4*	*5*	*6*	*7*	*8*	*9*	*10*
1980–2009	60,720	54	45,934	78	12,864	48	1,124.4	588.9	268.0	466.7
1930–1979	80,694	56	121,304	230	36,557	110	1,441.0	527.4	332.3	464.3
1900–1929	22,558	28	44,568	81	20,480	62	805.6	550.2	330.3	454.9

Notes
Column 1: *conservative*.
Column 2: *our conservative*.
Column 3: *liberal*.
Column 4: *our liberal*.
Column 5: *progressive*.
Column 6: *our progressive*.
Column 7: column 1/column 2.
Column 8: column 3/column 4.
Column 9: column 5/column 6.
Column 10: [column 3 + column 5]/[column 4 + column 6].

Columns 1 through 6 present the raw data, and columns 7 through 9 the rates of occurrence of *our*. What is most interesting about these figures is their relative consistency through time. While columns 7 and 8 reveal that *our conservative* has become slightly more common and *our liberal* slightly less common over the last thirty years, the latter still appears at about twice the rate as the former, as it has throughout the century. The *Times*, in short, has become no less inclined to see itself as a liberal source of news. Also to be considered is that the word that has in recent years begun to replace liberal – *progressive* – has throughout the century been considerably more likely than *conservative* or *liberal* to be described as *our*. And as column 10 shows, if *liberal* and *progressive* are combined there is virtually no change in how frequently *our* appears. The drop in *our liberal* has been exactly matched by the rise in *our progressive* over the same time that the latter has become the term of choice for many, with *liberal* becoming a term of attack over the thirty years of conservative strength. It is thus possible to conclude that the *New York Times* has not consciously and deliberately moved to the right. The drift of its rhetoric mainly mirrors the overall shift within the United States.

This conclusion is further supported by the data in Table 2.8. In the first column appear the number of times that a favorable adjective (constructive, valuable, thoughtful, reflective, productive, creative, enlightened or outstanding) preceded *progressive* or *progressivism* in each of the three periods shown (ignore the bottom row for now). Column 3 shows a similar count of the favorable adjectives for *liberal* and *liberalism* and column 5 the count for *conservative* and *conservativism*. The even number columns show the

Table 2.8 Comparative frequency of favorable adjectives and unfavorable adjectives preceding *progressive*, *liberal*, and *conservative*

Years	*1*	*2*	*3*	*4*	*5*	*6*	*7*	*8*
1980–2009	33	3	219	142	40	131	1.74	0.31
1930–1949	116	12	591	157	100	248	4.18	0.40
1900–1929	53	6	133	32	27	155	4.89	0.17
ProQuest 1980–2009	126	6	325	811	280	494	0.55	0.57

Notes

Column 1: *constructive progressive, constructive progressivism, valuable progressive, valuable progressivism, thoughtful progressive, thoughtful progressivism, reflective progressive, reflective progressivism, productive progressive, productive progressivism, creative progressive, creative progressivism, enlightened progressive, enlightened progressivism, outstanding progressive*, and *outstanding progressivism*.

Column 2: *extreme progressive, extreme progressivism, thoughtless progressive, thoughtless progressivism, unreflective progressive, unreflective progressivism, unproductive progressive, unproductive progressivism, knee-jerk progressive*, and *knee-jerk progressivism*.

Column 3: same adjectives as column 1 for *liberal* and *liberalism*.

Column 4: same adjectives as column 2 for *liberal* and *liberalism*.

Column 5: same adjectives as column 1 for *conservative* and *conservativism*.

Column 6: same adjectives as column 2 for *conservative* and *conservativism*.

Column 7: [column 1 + column 3]/[column 2 + column 4].

Column 8: column 5/column 6.

number of times that unfavorable adjectives were used (extreme, thoughtless, unreflective, unproductive, and knee-jerk) to describe each of the three groups.

Column 7 combines the data for liberals and progressives and shows the ratio of favorable to unfavorable for the three periods. Column 8 does the same with the data for conservatives. The column 7 figures show that for all three periods, favorable descriptions outpaced the unfavorable, by a factor of more than four prior to 1980 and by a factor slightly less than two since 1980. Column 8 figures show a much less favorable description of conservatives for all three periods, with the negative descriptions outpacing the positives by considerably more than a two to one margin throughout. Thus while the degree to which favorable descriptions surpass unfavorable descriptions has fallen since 1980, a strongly positive attitude toward liberals and progressives relative to conservatives continues in the *Times*, much as the stereotype suggests. And this conclusion is strengthened by the ProQuest data shown in the bottom row. Going back just to 1980, these figures, drawn from a considerably larger sample of newspapers, give support to the idea that the *Times* is indeed more liberal leaning than other national newspapers are on average. Column 7 indicates that unlike the *Times*, where liberals and progressives were described favorably close to twice as often as unfavorably, ProQuest newspapers described them favorably just over half as often. And while the *Times* described conservatives favorably only one-third as often as liberals and progressives, the ProQuest newspapers did so slightly over half as often. The wider selection of papers was clearly more neutral in describing political leanings, while the *Times*, true to popular opinion, was decidedly liberal. This makes the overall rhetorical turn to the right in the *Times* that has already been seen in this chapter and the last, and which will be seen in much of what is to the follow, all the more curious. Even liberals seem to be sounding more like conservatives.

In one area at least the *Times* seems to be going along with the larger cultural shift against liberalism. Increasingly, to refer to something as *elitist* is unflattering. In ProQuest newspapers unfavorable adjectives (privileged, unworthy, undeserving, ruthless, out-of-touch) preceding *elitist* and *elites* have been used far more frequently than favorable adjectives (worthy, humble, conscientious, deserving, needed, admirable). Since 1980, the unfavorables have appeared thirty-five times as often as the favorable (2,872 to eighty-two).

Columns 1 through 4 of Table 2.9 show the frequency of occurrences of *liberal*, *liberal elites*, *conservative*, and *conservative elites*, respectively. The first three rows show figures from the *Times* for the last three decades ("elites" was infrequently used prior to this). The numbers in columns 2 and 4 are quite small, and for this reason the much larger set of data from ProQuest data appear in rows 4 through 6. Columns 5, 6, and 7 are informative both for the habit of linking *liberal* with *elites* far more frequently than *conservative* and for showing a deepening trend. Focusing first on the *Times* (with the reminder again that the raw data numbers are small), *elites* became twice as likely to describe *liberal* from the 1990s to the 2000s while becoming just half as likely to describe *conservative* over the same period. And as column 6 shows, *liberal elites* went from being 1.7 times as frequent as *conservative elites* to 7.4 times as frequent.

The ProQuest data for the same period is more revealing since the raw numbers are so much greater. Focusing again on the ratios shown in columns 5 and 6, there was an increase in the frequency with which liberals were called *elitist* and a corresponding decrease in the frequency with which conservatives were so labeled. Column 7 provides a summary, showing that in ProQuest newspapers *elitist* went from being 4.5 times as likely to describe *liberal* than to describe *conservative* to being 8.7 times as common.

Summing up, the *New York Times* appears to more self-identify with liberalism than do other U.S. newspapers. In addition, the *Times* has not moved away from such self-identification, while newspapers more generally have. Finally, all the newspapers have been more likely to refer to liberals than conservatives as *elitist* – a generally unflattering description – with the difference widening since 2000.

And this brings up a final point. According to Geoffrey Nunberg:

> [T]he whole idea of liberalism as a political doctrine sometimes seems to be beside the point these days. The word itself isn't used nearly as much as it used to be – today, the media talk about liberals a great deal more than they talk about liberalism.
>
> (2006, 44)

A look at the data sources supports part of what Nunberg appears to be saying. Consistent with the passage, *liberalism* is indeed encountered considerably less often relative to *liberal* than *conservatism* is encountered relative to

Table 2.9 Frequency of *liberals* described as *elites* relative to *conservatives* described as *elites*

Years	*1*	*2*	*3*	*4*	*5*	*6*	*7*
2000–2009	11,448	37	15,686	5	309.4	3,137	7.40
1990–1999	16,026	24	21,851	14	667.8	1,561	1.71
1980–1989	20,328	8	25,870	6	2,541.0	4,312	1.33
2000–2009	1,554,003	3,685	1,556,828	423	421.7	3,680.4	8.71
1990–1999	881,749	1,578	1,047,490	351	558.8	2,984.3	4.50
1980–1989	271,729	181	289,921	47	1,501.3	6,168.5	3.85

Source: data in first three rows from the *New York Times*; Data in next three rows from ProQuest.

Notes
Column 1: "liberal."
Column 2: "liberal elites," "liberal elitism."
Column 3: "conservative."
Column 4: "conservative elites," "conservative elitism."
Column 5: column 1/column 2.
Column 6: column 3/column 4.
Column 7: column 2/column 4.

conservative.[9] This is not, however, a recent phenomenon. The data all the way back to 1900 show that the relative frequency of *conservatism* has been somewhere between 50 percent and 100 percent greater than the relative frequency of *liberalism.* Why this might be is something of a mystery, but it fits uncomfortably with Nunberg's position that "These days, it's as if being a liberal has less to do with a commitment to a particular -ism than with … a political fashion" (2006, 44). For even before the "latte loving" view of liberals gained traction, for some reason mention of the belief system called *liberalism* could not keep up with mention of the belief system called *conservatism*. If, however, we compare the frequency of the *-isms* not relative to the respective root words but standing by themselves, Nunberg's point gains greater support. Between 1930 and 1979, *liberalism* was just about as frequent as *conservatism.* Since then it's appeared less than two-thirds as often.[10]

Why not *politicize*?

As another indication of government's fall in status, consider the trend to treat *politicize* as something negative. The 1982 edition of *The American Heritage Dictionary* provides a definition that is not in any way negative ("to engage in or discuss politics" and "to make political"). Yet it is difficult to imagine the word currently being used in any way that is not negative. As Table 2.10 indicates, the likelihood that this word will be used negatively has risen sharply. In the 1980s, *politicize* was preceded by advice to avoid doing it once every 122 times. The frequency rose to once every forty-one times by the 2000s, a three-fold rise.[11]

In the private domain, there has been an opposite trend at work when it comes to *commercializing*. As columns 4 through 6 in Table 2.10 reveal, the frequency with which this word is preceded by a negative recommendation ("must not

Table 2.10 Frequency of *do not politicize* (and related expressions) relative to frequency of *do not commercialize* (and related expressions)

Years	*1*	*2*	*3*	*4*	*5*	*6*
2000–2009	81,289	1,968	41.3	204,839	217	944.0
1990–1999	38,473	501	76.8	38,832	104	373.4
1980–1989	8,697	71	122.5	4,911	2[illegible]	233.9

Notes
Column 1: *politicize, politicized,* and *politicizing.*
Column 2: *avoid politicizing, do not politicize, don't politicize, must not be politicized, must not politicize, should not politicize, should not be politicized, shouldn't politicize,* and *stop politicizing.*
Column 3: column 1/column 2.
Column 4: *commercialize, commercialized,* and *commercializing.*
Column 5: *avoid commercializing, do not commercialize, don't commercialize, must not be commercialized, must not commercialize, should not commercialize, should not be commercialized, shouldn't commercialize,* and *stop commercializing.*
Column 6: column 4/column 5.

commercialize," etc.) has fallen four-fold, from once every 234 times to once every 944 times. Consistent with what the last section's data suggested, government, and the activities associated with it have fallen in favor while markets and the activities associated with them, have been rising.

There has not been a dramatic difference in the frequency of use of *commercialize* prior to 1970 and since. In addition, its meaning has not changed in any obvious ways. *Politicize*, in contrast, is a relatively recent word, appearing in *Times* articles only 27 times prior to 1970 but 992 times since. More significantly, its meaning has undergone some important shifts. Its usage began to pick up in the late 1960s. At that time to *politicize* or to *be politicized* was not always viewed unfavorably. As an example, the head of a protest demonstration at meetings of the American Medical Association announced that "the purpose of the planned demonstration had been to 'politicize the health consciousness of the American people'" ("Policemen," 1969, 18). As another example, in reporting on an anti-war demonstration, the *Times* reported that "Many blacks … said they had been 'politicized' to the need for alliances" ("Few Blacks," 1969, 61). And in reporting that "public school and scholarship students came to predominate [at Princeton], and the silent generation of the nineteen-fifties gave way to today's more politicized students" ("Changing," 1969, 60), the writer's high opinion of what it means to be *politicized* seems clear. Opposition to *politicizing* appears to have first been based on the belief that some things were simply outside the realm of political influence. Thus a writer to the *Times* says that "Pressures to politicize the universities … are pernicious because they imply that the institution henceforth will be held responsible for what is said and thought in its classrooms and lecture halls" ("Free," 1969, 46).

A peculiar change occurred at some point regarding what it meant to *politicize*. Looking at recent articles, one headline reads "Don't politicize history" (2009, B1), while another reads "Don't politicize county procurement process" ("Don't politicize county," 2009). It is evident that *politicizing* is treated as an act that undermines purer motivations. And this practice appears to stretch far beyond just the United States. So, for example, a Canadian letter writer says that "efforts to improve the lives of B.C.'s children must not be politicized" (Polak, 2009, 6), while the president of Taiwan announces that "We consider this assistance humanitarian and we don't politicize the assistance" ("Taiwan," 2009), and the agriculture minister of Kenya "reiterate[s] that the Mau issue was about conservation, relocation, and resettlement and should not be politicized" ("Kenyan," 2009).

Politicization, it seems, has gone from signifying "becoming active in politics" to "bringing political considerations to bear where they don't belong." And curiously enough, even the linguist Geoffrey Nunberg, in his otherwise insightful book on the conservative dominance of language, seems to adopt the new meaning when he writes that "The politicization of 'values' began in the late 1960s, when Republicans seized on the word to contrast the mores of Middle Americans with the antics of the hippies and anti-war protestors" (2006, 106). While keenly aware of the changing meaning of *values* he apparently manages to miss the similar transformation of *politicization*.

What makes this changed meaning of *politicization* especially bizarre is that it is in the realm of politics itself that *politicization* is viewed as most often occurring and most regrettable. It is comparable to regretting *economizing* in the economic realm. And I would suggest that it might be the influence of a cynical brand of public choice theory that is responsible for this change in meaning. Public choice theory rests on the assumption that people are narrowly self-interested and that the behaviors of elected officials can therefore be analyzed in much the same way that the behavior of the most narrowly defined *homo economicus* is analyzed.[12] Thus, *being political* or *politicizing* is treated as doing whatever will get one re-elected rather than doing what is right. The implication that democratic systems fail seems to follow, though is rarely acknowledged explicitly. At the same time that it becomes more acceptable to carry market thinking further by *commercializing* what was previously off limits, *politicizing* in the political realm, of all places, comes under increasing attack.

The degree to which it has become more acceptable to *commercialize* becomes especially clear when considering changes in attitudes toward the selling of oneself. In column 3 of Table 2.11 appear the number of times, by decade, that *sell yourself* (and *sell myself*, etc.) appeared. Column 1 shows the number of times that the pronouns appeared and column 2 the number of times that *sell* or *market* appeared.

The critical columns are 4 and 5. Focusing first on column 4, it can be seen that the frequency with which the pronouns were preceded by *sell* or *market* increased markedly, from between once every 1,000 to 2,000 times prior to 1970

Table 2.11 Increasing frequency of *myself* (and related words) being preceded by *sell* or *market*

Years	*1*	*2*	*3*	*4*	*5*
2000–2009	102,326	98,875	260	393.6	380.3
1990–1999	140,642	127,174	352	399.6	361.3
1980–1989	136,863	130,233	273	501.3	477.0
1970–1979	129,315	106,013	169	765.2	627.3
1960–1969	93,500	94,866	91	1,027.5	1,042.5
1950–1959	90,897	93,676	71	1,280.2	1,319.4
1940–1949	96,814	96,671	80	1,210.2	1,208.4
1930–1939	130,162	136,254	79	1,647.6	1,724.7
1920–1929	118,916	109,141	85	1,399.0	1,284.0
1910–1919	89,384	55,871	48	1,862.2	1,164.0
1900–1909	84,038	47,345	42	2,000.9	1,127.3

Notes
Column 1: *myself, yourself, himself, herself,* and *themselves.*
Column 2: *sell* and *market.*
Column 3: *sell myself, sell yourself, sell himself, sell herself, sell themselves, market myself, market yourself, market himself, market herself,* and *market themselves.*
Column 4: column 1/column 3.
Column 5: column 2/column 3.

to once every 394 times since 2000. Column 5 was included to see if the increased likelihood of having *myself* as well as the pronouns preceded by *sell* or *market* was simply due to selling and marketing being more pervasive for all imaginable things. To the extent beans, shirts, entertainment, and furniture, are increasingly unlikely to be produced for self and correspondingly more likely to be bought, we might expect to see their column 4 equivalent number to be rising as well. If this were true, occurrences of *sell myself, market myself*, etc. would be expected to rise at the same rate as *sell* and *market* and the column 5 numbers would not have changed much over time. As column 5 makes clear, however, this is not the case as the numbers shown parallel closely the numbers in column 4.[13] The increasing reference to selling living people, therefore, represents an apparently greater acceptance of this way of describing what one does when seeking employment.

A closer look at contexts in which *selling himself*, etc. appeared shows quite a shift in the acceptability of this practice over time. At the very turn of the last century, the Omaha World Herald reported on someone who "refused to accept the money [because] he could not afford to sell himself" ("Too High," 1900, 7), the implication being that there would be an unacceptable cost of lost integrity. Ten years later, a *Times* article about the merchant marines emphasizes their bad condition by saying that one joining "sells himself body and soul" ("Shanghaing," 1910, SM13). Images of slavery and prostitution were often evoked by mention of "selling oneself." So a 1915 *Times* article is given the title "Arrest three men as white slavers: Police accuse Newark youths of 'selling' and delivering three girls" ("Arrest," 1915, 22). With hard times came ads by people willing to sell themselves, and the plight of such people was always portrayed as pitiful. Thus appears a story about someone "alleged to have inserted an advertisement in a New York morning newspaper offering to sell himself into slavery" ("Fleets," 1916, 7). And so another article title reads "To sell himself at auction: Nashville man takes this means to get bread for his family" ("To sell," 1911, 7). Another article reports on a destitute person with the article title "Offers body and life for medical tests: fifty-year-old man would sell himself for $50 a week" ("Offers," 1927). Still another quotes Secretary of the AFL Frank Morrison from a 1927 Labor Day event reasoning that "to say that he can sell his labor power is to say he can sell himself" ("Defends," 1927, 27). Apparently for him a rhetorically effective way to demonstrate that *selling* labor power was unjust was found by equating it with what was at that time the obviously immoral act of selling oneself.

For politicians, too, there prevailed a taboo against the selling of the self. The shame of such an act comes through in a 1923 column entitled "The Voice of the People." It is reasoned that though "There is no implication a poor successful candidate sells himself, but he can hardly help being under obligations to his 'angels'" ("The Voice," 1923, E4). Certainly within the realm of politics, the expression has taken on an entirely different meaning, along the lines of *differentiating yourself* or *promoting your unique qualifications*. Thus on the Democratic side an advisor to Hillary Clinton speaks of "a very, very strong indicator of how Hillary can sell herself to voters" (Healy, 2006, B1) while on the Republican side the argument is made that defeat of a Democrat up for reelection would be made more likely if the Republican candidate "could credibly sell himself as the candidate of change." (Kocieniewski, 2005, NJ1). And of course the accepting view of *selling yourself* is not limited to the political realm. As a consultant for high school students seeking good colleges to attend put it, "You're your own unique brand. You have to sell yourself" (Zezima, 2006, D39) From originally being something to be avoided at all costs, *selling yourself* had become, according to this consultant a requirement for economic success.

Government as a constraint on freedom

There are solid reasons for economists' hesitance to speak of a good being *free*. Consider Milton Friedman's often repeated claim that "there's no such thing as a free lunch." He made this claim in the context of school *free lunch* programs and the main point that he was trying to make was that there is an opportunity cost to virtually anything. Making a lunch available to low-income students precluded using the resources that went into the production and serving of the lunch available for some other activity. In short, while the student was indeed getting the lunch without having to hand over money, this student might be said to have borne the cost of not receiving some other sort of assistance from the government.

Ironically, this very same Milton Friedman who is known for reminding us that *free lunch* is something of a misnomer gained much greater recognition outside the economics profession with his book (co-authored with Rose Friedman) *Free to Choose* (1980) that played a not insignificant role in lending intellectual credibility to the Reagan revolution. Is it possible to reconcile these two sides of Milton Friedman? It appears that the conservatives who so celebrate *free choice* are primarily drawing this expression from the fact that there is no government standing in the way of one's actions. A choice is not free in the broadest sense since to choose X must preclude one's choosing some alternative. But for government to get out of the way is for government to expand one's choice set, allowing previously forbidden options to now be possible. In that sense, the decision maker has become *free* of government constraint and in that sense certainly has a *freer choice* if not an outright *free choice.*

The conservative revolution of the last 30 years appears to have wrapped itself more around the *free to choose* adage than the pessimistic reminder that "there's no such thing as a free lunch." For as a look at the data in Tables 2.12 and 2.13 will show, a rather remarkable shift has occurred during this period from associating the word *free* with political institutions to associating it with the economic institution so very much revered by conservatives – the market.

Columns 3, 6, 9, and 12 of Table 2.12 summarize what has been occurring. Since 1980, *free* has preceded *nation* only about one-fourth as often as prior to 1980 (from about once every 250 times prior to 1980 to about once every 1,250 times post-1980). For *government*, it similarly occurs only about one-fourth as often, while for *democracy* it appears only one-fifth as often. In contrast to this, *free* precedes *markets* approximately twice as frequently post-1980 as from 1930 to 1979 and more than ten times as frequently as prior to 1930. Strangely enough, while economists are the ones who like to emphasize the reality of cost, it is their most revered institution – the market – that has, so to speak, cornered the market on the use of *free*.

Lest there be any lack of clarity in understanding this trend, Table 2.13 expresses it slightly differently. The first three rows in column 1 indicate the likelihood that *free* will precede *market* relative to the likelihood that *free* will precede *government*. Thus, *market* has gone from being 1.1 times as likely as *government* to be described as *free* prior to 1930, to 75.8 times as likely since 1980. Similarly, *free* has gone from being only 0.3 times as likely to precede *market* as to precede *nation* before 1930 to 16.7 times as likely since 1980. And much the same remarkable shift appears in column 3 for *democracy* as well. To once again make certain that the trend uncovered here is not a trend unique to the *Times*, the bottom two rows contrast similar figures for ProQuest post-1980 with AHN pre-1922. Though the shift toward *free markets* is somewhat less dramatic, it remains striking nonetheless.

One trend that might be expected to accompany the trend of associating *free* with *markets* is an increasing focus on what Isaiah Berlin (1969) refers to as

Table 2.12 Comparative frequency of *nation*, *government*, *democracy*, and *markets*, being described as *free*

Years	*1*	*2*	*3*	*4*	*5*	*6*
1980–2009	847,970	1,285	659.9	403,930	137	2,984.8
1930–1979	1,997,891	11,726	170.4	984,135	1,427	689.6
1900–1929	711,815	5,058	140.7	328,075	633	518.3
Years	*7*	*8*	*9*	*10*	*11*	*12*
1980–2009	34,978	28	1,249.2	279,579	7,094	39.4
1930–1979	63,830	296	215.6	425,485	6,330	67.2
1900–1929	16,858	63	267.6	170,763	363	470.4

Notes
Column 1: *nation*.
Column 2: *free nation*.
Column 3: column 1/column 2.
Column 4: *government*.
Column 5: *free government*.
Column 6: column 4/column 5.
Column 7: *democracy*.
Column 8: *free democracy*.
Column 9: column 7/column 8.
Column 10: *markets*.
Column 11: *free markets*.
Column 12: column 10/column 11.

Table 2.13 Summarization of Table 2.12 data

Years	*1*	*2*	*3*
1980–2009	75.8	16.7	31.7
1930–1979	10.3	2.5	3.2
1900–1929	1.1	0.3	0.6
ProQuest (post-1979)	46.9	10.1	12.2
AHN (pre-1922)	0.2	0.3	0.4

Notes
Column 1: multiple by which *market* likely to be called *free* relative to *government* likely to be called *free*.
Column 2: multiple by which *market* likely to be called *free* relative to *nation* likely to be called *free*.
Column 3: multiple by which *market* likely to be called *free* relative to *democracy* likely to be called *free*.

negative freedom relative to focus on what he calls *positive freedom*. While these expressions are almost never found in the *Times*, the expressions *freedom to* and *freedom from* are and in Table 2.14 appear the century long occurrences of each.

The relative decline in *freedom from* thorough the century is unmistakable. Though we associate *freedom from want* with Franklin Roosevelt, it is apparent that the movement toward *freedom to* was well underway even before his first term in office. Exactly what this trend tells us is not at all apparent. Might the *freedom froms* (hunger, danger, poverty) simply be of more importance when a nation is poorer and might economic growth lead to a natural shift toward the more expressive *freedoms tos*? To some extent this may explain the trend but also relevant is the proclivity to increasingly associate freedom with

Table 2.14 Frequency of *freedom from* relative to *freedom to*

Years	*1*	*2*	*3*
2000–2009	1,366	5,404	0.253
1990–1999	1,874	7,714	0.243
1980–1989	2,406	8,904	0.270
1970–1979	2,563	8,117	0.316
1960–1969	2,936	6,756	0.435
1950–1959	3,478	6,544	0.531
1940–1949	4,235	6,592	0.642
1930–1939	6,255	5,833	1.072
1920–1929	5,156	4,615	1.117
1910–1919	4,275	3,641	1.174
1900–1909	3,683	2,372	1.553

Notes
Column 1: *free from* and *freedom from*.
Column 2: *free to* and *freedom to*.
Column 3: column 1/column 2.

the market rather than the government. It is, after all, typically a collective act that guarantees freedom from. There must be institutions in place to protect against hunger and the like and these institutions are more often than not governmental in nature. In contrast, *freedom to* is most exemplified in the marketplace where government gets out of the way and allows market forces to dominate. It is also worth noting that while *freedoms from* are typically equality enhancing, *freedoms to* are not, at least if income and wealth is taken to serve as the measure of equality. *Freedoms from* are unconditional in nature. To guarantee freedom from hunger is to guarantee that no one will be hungry. *Freedoms to*, in contrast, depending on how they are specified, can be conditional. To say that everyone is free to buy a BMW or that everyone is free to sleep on the sidewalk obviously does not mean that everyone will do these things. For many, the BMW is simply outside their choice set. For at least as many, sleeping on the sidewalk is possible but simply something they would rather not do.

The rise of *big government*

While it is not always inevitable that *big business* and *big government* come with, as Deirdre McCloskey would put it, a "sneer" attached, the word has more often than not been negative in what it suggests.[14] *Major corporations* sounds nicer than *big business* as surely as *strong, effective government* sounds better than *big government*. From a public relations standpoint, being a *big* anything is to institutions probably comparable to what being a *strongman* is to political leaders, a positive sounding word suggesting something far from positive. As Geoffrey Nunberg has noted:

> [B]ig government is … laced with ideological undertones.… The phrase always implies either that the government is trying to do something that the market could do better, that it's coercing people into doing what they ought to choose freely, or that it's doing something for people that they'd be morally better off doing for themselves.
>
> (2006, 127)

As Table 2.15 shows, the probability that *business* will be preceded by *big* has long exceeded the probability that *government* will be. Since 1930 *big* has been used to describe *business* slightly more than once every 100 times that *business* has appeared. With *government*, in contrast, there has been a three-fold rise in the chances that it will be referred to as *big*, from approximately once every 900 times prior to 1980 to once every 300 times since. The bottom two rows provide complete equivalent data for AHN and for ProQuest. Summarizing columns 3 and 6, over the same period that *business* was becoming less than half as likely to be referred to as *big* (120 to 279 frequency) there was a near tripling in the likelihood that government would be (1,775 to 614).

While it may seem that *big* is usually negative when applied to businesses and governments, is there any way to test whether this is indeed so? Two stories emerge from Table 2.16. Consider first columns 3 and 6. Column 3 indicates that one of the negative adjectives indicated in the table preceded *government* once every 899 times. Column 6 indicates that one of these adjectives occurred just once every 8,135 times that *business* appears. As column 7 summarizes, it

Table 2.15 Frequency of *business* described as *big* relative to *government* described as *big*

Years	*1*	*2*	*3*	*4*	*5*	*6*
1980–2009	447,440	4,802	93.2	389,722	1,248	312.3
1930–1979	754,302	9,120	82.7	983,562	1,090	902.4
1900–1929	303,488	2,991	101.5	328,048	86	3814.5
ProQuest (post-1979)	15,678,906	56,287	278.5	8,445,536	13,764	613.6
AHN (pre-1922)	2,703,331	22,480	120.3	1,436,051	809	1775.1

Notes
Column 1: *business*.
Column 2: *big business*.
Column 3: column 1/column 2.
Column 4: *government*.
Column 5: *big government*.
Column 6: column 4/column 5.

Table 2.16 Frequency of negative descriptions of "government" relative to negative descriptions of *big government* and frequency of negative descriptions of *business* relative to negative descriptions of *big business* (ProQuest, 1980–2009)

1	*2*	*3*	*4*	*5*	*6*	*7*
25,184,491	27,996	899.6	33,767,064	4,175	8,087.9	8.99
8	*9*	*10*	*11*	*12*	*13*	*14*
68,282	150	455.2	281,989	56	5,035.5	11.06

Notes
Column 1: *government*.
Column 2: negatively defined *government*.
Column 3: column 1/column 2.
Column 4: *business*.
Column 5: negatively defined *business*.
Column 6: column 4/column 5.
Column 7: column 6/ column3.
Column 8: *big government*.
Column 9: negatively defined *big government*.
Column 10: column 8/column 9.
Column 11: *big business*.
Column 12: negatively defined *big business*.
Column 13: column 11/column 12.
Column 14: column 13/column 10.

appears that *government* was nine times more likely than *business* to be described negatively. Columns 8 through 14 follow the same pattern as the first seven columns. All that differs here is that *big government* and *big business* replaced *government* and *business*. What emerges? The greater likelihood of *government* being described negatively is reflected here as well. As columns 10 and 13 show, one of the negative descriptions precedes *big government* once every 455 times that *big government* appears and once every 5,033 times that *big business* appears. Once again, government is roughly ten times more likely to be described negatively than business (as reflected by the 11.06 figure in column 14).

More significantly for present purposes, it seems clear that "big" carries negative connotations with it. This follows from the fact that *big government* is twice as likely to be described negatively as is *government* (once every 455 times as shown in column 10 versus once every 899 times as shown in column 3) and from the fact that *big business* is roughly 60 percent more likely to be described negatively than is just *business* (once every 5,053 times, as shown in column 13, compared with once every 8,135 times, as shown in 6).[15]

Prior to the 1930s both *big* and *government*, when appearing together, typically were used to describe a program, project, or something else and it was thus not government that was being characterized as *big* but this *something else*. Thus to take an example from a century ago, the reader is cautioned that "a big government loan by no means implies," the implication being that it is the loan, not government, that is *big* ("Our," 1900, 1). To take another example, the *Times* reader is told that "contractors, who have several big Government contracts on hand, have failed" ("Unable," 1906, 12), with the *big* this time modifying *contracts*. And as a third example, the *Times* reports that the death of a member of the Supreme Court "will make necessary the postponement of the big Government cases" ("Big Suits," 1910, 8). The clear meaning here is "government cases that are big," rather than "cases about big Government." Yet so accustomed have we become to hearing *big government* used as a mantra consisting of adjective and noun rather than adjective and adjective that the intent is blurred.

In the entire pre-1930 sample of twenty cases that I investigated not once was government itself the thing being referred to as *big*. It was apparently a reaction to Roosevelt's New Deal that brought with it reference to *big government* as we have come to use the expression today. The first clearly pejorative use of *big government* that I located appeared alongside an expression of equal dislike for *big business*. Thus Wyoming Senator Joseph C. O'Mahoney offered the following to a graduating class at Catholic University:

> For half a century the people of America have been resisting direction of their economic life and of their government by "big business." But when, to resist the evil effects of the monopolistic corporation, we increase the discretionary regulatory power of the central government over the activities of both corporations and citizens, we are moving inevitably in an anti-democratic direction and toward a collectivist State.
>
> (Quoted in "Big Labor," 1937, 16)

And as another example, 1940 presidential candidate Wendell L. Willkie stated that in his youth he had opposed the "'domination of the people by big business, and while I still hold to that, I now oppose the domination of the people by big government'" (Willkie, 1940, 7)[16]

Burdensome taxes

The unpopularity of taxes runs deep. There is the old saying, "Only two things in life are certain: death and taxes." But aren't *prices* more certain than *taxes*? Isn't it true that at least as great a percentage of the population has to pay prices for things as has to pay taxes? The anti-tax sentiment must long pre-date democracy. In the most authoritarian regimes, taxes were likely regarded as essentially "shake-downs" that had little to do with the desires of the ruled. And the reliance on this pre-democratic image has served the era of conservatism well. Kiewe and Houck note that when mentioning the federal government Ronald Reagan "used the metaphor of the 'tax collector' as his referent" and go on to point out that "[s]uch a referent has fairly obvious religious connotations, typically portraying the tax collector as the godless Pharisee, the villain of the citizens of the state" (1991, 25). As will be shown later in this section, more than one textbook still speaks of the tax collector and seldom in a favorable light.

There is also the often used expression, "tax relief," that reveals something about our attitude toward taxes. As George Lakoff points out:

> For there to be relief there must be an affliction, an afflicted party, and a reliever who removes the affliction and is therefore a hero ... When the word *tax* is added to *relief*, the result is a metaphor: Taxation is an affliction. And the person who takes it away is a hero, and anyone who tries to stop him is a bad guy.[17]

But as Nunberg notes, "The phrase *tax relief* wasn't invented by the Bush White House; it has been used by every major Democratic figure from Al Smith to Bill Clinton" (2006, 104). And a look at the *Times* data through the years indeed demonstrates that the phrase has a long history. With little change in relative frequency over the last century, *tax relief* has appeared an incredible 140 times more often than *cost relief*.

As private goods have become easier to produce we have for the last half-century reacted not by increasing leisure time but by increasing considerably our production and consumption of private goods, but as public goods become easier to produce we generally appear to react in a way that doesn't change the production of these public goods much at all. A little history may shed some light on this. The mercantilist economists who dominated economic thinking prior to Adam Smith argued for low wages as a way to keep production levels high. As Bernard Mandeville reasoned, "[l]ow wages ... ensure an adequate supply of labor" while "[h]igher wages reduce labor supply" (Landreth and Colander, 2002, 53). By this version of things, the average person labored just for the time needed to fill his needs. To double the wage would cut by half the time needed to meet this goal. The worker might feel better off with more leisure time, but overall output per person would fall, as the surplus going to resource owners would plummet.

While this view was not held by many economists who followed in the centuries since, a recurrent concern was that workers would have to be taught to want more things rather than more leisure as their wages rose. And they were supported in this view by those outside the field. As one example, turn of the 20th century sociologist and advertising pioneer Emily Fogg Mead spoke of "the necessity to apply new stimuli to convert the individual to the use of goods" and the need to "break up fixed habits, to allow new wants to develop" (quoted in Leach, 1993, 160). The fear that productivity gains would lead to voluntary decisions to leave production unchanged but gain increased leisure has seemed quaint and even bizarre to many since the rise of "the consumer culture" after World War II. We are always bombarded with advertisements whetting our appetites for private goods. And while Coke ads may raise the overall demand for Coke at the expense of demand for Pepsi, when Coke, Pepsi, and every other private good producer raises advertising, it must come at the expense of public spending and leisure.[18] Persuasive advertising does enter the political scene when it comes to getting elected but not when it comes to deciding how much public spending to do. Being less sexy than food, clothing, and entertainment, the urgency of our demand for roads, schools, and public health are less likely to be suggested by advertisements. These goods remain much closer in spirit to the necessities that drove 17th century workers to cut their work hours as their wages rose.

In addition to the widespread mention of *tax relief* it is common to hear mention of the *tax burden*, an expression that has done nothing to help the goods that taxes buy be viewed as positively as the goods that private dollars buy. The phrase was used as far back as the late 19th century by Alfred Marshall in his classic textbook. His interest focused on the question of how much of a tax on one party could be passed on to another. So, for example, Marshall asked why it was that the introduction of a sales tax on sellers would cause some goods to rise in price while others would not. In the first, case, the *burden* would be shared by buyers and sellers, while in the second case, the full burden would be borne by sellers. Marshall was asking how the burden was distributed, and was not showing any particular prejudice against taxes by his word choice. He in fact used *effect* and *burden* as synonyms, speaking of the "shifting of the effects of some tax 'forwards' " (1920, 412) at one point, while just sentences later describing an action that "tends to shift a large part of the burden of the tax forwards" (1920, 412–413). In the century since Marshall wrote, *tax incidence* has become the expression most favored by economists, but burden seems like a perfectly fine alternative, particularly when it is considered how familiar non-economists are with the expression *sharing the burden*.[19]

The causes of differences in *tax burden* uncovered by Marshall were elasticity of demand and supply. Though this will not be taken up here, I bring it up because it turns out that the work of Marshall can be easily generalized to the private sector and that the same terminology can follow as well. When sellers face a higher cost, how much do they ultimately bear, and how much is passed on to consumers? In other words, how is the *cost burden* distributed? Oddly, one encounters this expression far less frequently. Since 1900, *tax burden* has appeared 8,512 times in the *Times* while *cost burden* has appeared just 204 times. Considering that *cost* appears much more frequently than tax, the difference is even more impressive. *Tax* is fully fifty-five times as likely as *cost* to be followed by *burden*.[20]

Consider now the adjective *burdensome*. This carries with it a more negative connotation than *burden*. In attempting to defend taxes, Lakoff points out that "[h]omework in school is burdensome too, but you have to do it if you're going to learn anything. Exercise is burdensome, but you have to do it if you're going to be in good physical shape" (2004, 108). This is a reasonable reminder as far as it goes but it doesn't go far enough. Keeping his examples closer to the traditionally economic realm, Lakoff might have reminded the reader that *cost* is surely a burden. It's something you have to be prepared for if you want to own something that is offered in the marketplace. Yet, for some reason, talk of *cost burden* is rare relative to talk of *tax burden*. Over the century, *burdensome* has been 7.3 times more likely to precede "tax" than "cost."

A look at specific uses of *burdensome tax* suggests it is always something that is believed to be in some sense wrong. Thus a turn-of-the-last-century U.S. representative remarks that "members of both parties … should take immediate steps to relieve the … people of the burdensome tax" ("To repeal," 1900, 5) and thus, writing twenty years later, the chairman of the National Publishers Association can speak of "the discriminatory burden of taxation that this industry has suffered during the past four years" ("Object," 1922, 10). And the beneficiary of getting rid of such taxes can be more than just the one being taxed, goes the message at times. Thus in the 1950s, the governor of New Jersey can claim that "'every step which frees [his constituents] from burdensome taxes … will result in more jobs for more people at better wages'" (Article 3, 1958, 40). Even the possibility of being painted with a much reviled label is not enough to deter the tax cutting efforts of one Connecticut state senator when he announces that "'If cutting their most burdensome tax is social engineering, then I think most people … will be happy to get that kind of socially engineered tax cut" ("Rowland," 1997, B5).

Notice that in each of these instances, a *burdensome tax* is a tax that should not exist. The same is true for the less frequently used *burdensome price*. So, for example, an early trade commissioner can claim that certain "unreasonable and burdensome prices are usually for sales [which] in some instances, appear to [result in] excess profits" ("Publishers," 1916, 1). Note the implications of all this. As long as *tax burden* is equivalent to *tax incidence* and that *cost burden* is equivalent to *cost incidence* it is a strictly descriptive expression. But the use of *burden* as an adjective (burdensome) carries with it the message that the burden is unfair.

Why it is that prices and costs are so much less likely than taxes to be described as *burdensome* has much to do with the ideology of free markets but there are two other more subtle forces at work that put public spending at a psychological disadvantage. First, taxes must be paid whether one does or does not support the specific spending that the taxes are intended to fund. That is, after all, the nature of majoritarian democracy. While the requirement of unanimity may hold some intuitive appeal, even the pioneers of public choice theory – never known as blind supporters of democracy – recognized in their pioneering work (Buchanan and Tullock, 1962) that pre-constitutionally something other than unanimity as a criterion would be acceptable to all reasonable people. But to agree to a system that allows the majority to decide is to at the same time agree to a system in which one is certain to find instances of spending that one regards as simply not worth it and in which one thus regards the taxes raised to fund such spending as *burdensome*.[21] In the realm of private goods, in contrast, one need not usually bear a cost that one regards as unfair. Going to a different seller or simply doing without the product are other possibilities. In the language suggested by Albert Hirschman (1970), private buyers can express dissatisfaction by *exit* while dissatisfied taxpayers have no option but to raise their *voice*.

Added to this is the difference between private and public goods in precisely matching a cost with a benefit. A prospective buyer knows that she must bear a cost in order to claim ownership. While cost is a *bad*, this is a *bad* only when considered in complete isolation. Having a new car while not paying anything for it is superior to having a car while paying for it but is not a possibility. In contrast, while the taxes paid to help fund, say, the national highway system, are *bad*, the counterfactual world of not paying these taxes is not a world in which taxes are lower and highways fewer and less well maintained, but a world in which taxes are lower while the highway system is just as it would have been had the taxes been paid. Either by shifting the tax to another or by cleaning up waste the decline in what the eliminated taxes paid for is, by this way of analyzing the counterfactual world, avoided. This may account at least in part for why taxes are viewed as *burdensome* while the prices paid for private goods are not.

And along with the burdensomeness of taxes goes a more often voiced opinion that they are unfair. Column 1 of Table 2.17 shows the number of times that *fair price* and related expressions appeared in the *Times* during each period shown, column 2 the number of occurrences of *unfair price*, and related expressions and column 3 the ratio of column 1 to column 2.[22] The column 3 numbers show that *fair price* outpaced *unfair price*, by a factor of 20 early in the century, by a factor of 15 in mid-century, and back again to nearly a factor of 20 since 1980.

Columns 4 and 5 show the number of occurrences of *fair tax* and *unfair tax*, respectively, with column 6 showing the ratio of the two figures. In comparing the column 6 figures with column 3 figures, two facts stands out. First, and most obviously, *fair tax* appears more often than *unfair tax* by only a factor of

Table 2.17 Frequency of *fair price* relative to *unfair price* compared with frequency of *fair tax* relative to *unfair tax*

Years	*1*	*2*	*3*	*4*	*5*	*6*
1980–2009	2,993	153	19.6	275	170	1.62
1930–1979	5,591	372	15.0	378	313	1.21
1900–1929	3,338	165	20.2	179	146	1.23

Notes
Column 1: *fair price, fair prices, fair pricing, reasonable price, reasonable prices,* and *reasonable pricing.*
Column 2: *unfair price, unfair prices, unfair pricing, unreasonable price, unreasonable prices, unreasonable pricing, excessively high price, excessively high prices,* and *excessively high pricing.*
Column 3: column 1/column 2.
Column 4: *fair tax, fair taxes, fair taxation, reasonable tax, reasonable taxes* and *reasonable taxation.*
Column 5: *unfair tax, unfair taxes, unfair taxation, unreasonable tax, unreasonable taxes, unreasonable taxation, excessively high tax, excessively high taxes,* and *excessively high taxation.*
Column 6: column 4/column 5.

between one and two for each period shown, far less than the double-digit factor by which *fair price* outstrips *unfair price*.[23] And second, there has been little change in the numbers over the periods shown, with tax phobia by no means being a recent phenomenon.

Looking at a grimmer description than *unfair* – *oppressive* – shows the same strong tilt toward taxes relative to costs. Searching the huge data base provided by ProQuest reveals 285 mentions of *oppressive taxes* since 1980 and fifty-one mentions of *oppressive costs* or *oppressive prices*. Considering that *costs* and *prices* appear three times as frequently as *taxes*, it further follows that *taxes* are seventeen times as likely to be labeled *oppressive* than their private sector equivalents. Perhaps the most extreme characterization of taxes was provided by Ronald Reagan when running for President in 1980, as the following passage from Kiewe and Houck reveals:

> Reagan's word choice … is also noteworthy. He stated, "When the individual is penalized a half [or] three-fourths or nine-tenths of the dollar he earns by his own effort and ability, it is imperative that some relationship exist between the individual's sacrifice and the Government's fiscal needs." … Reagan's use of the word "penalized" is of particular interest. To be penalized one typically must do something in opposition to a perceived authority. Taxes, Reagan implied, were a direct penalty for work.
>
> (1991, 16)

The huge gap in the perceived fairness of prices and taxes can be attributed to at least three causes. First, and most obviously, while the individual has input into how the tax money is spent, the control is not even close to the control exercised over private spending. Second, and related to the first, one has considerably less discretion whether or not to pay a tax than whether or not to pay a price. An unfair price can lead a person to simply take her business elsewhere. While a tax that is perceived to be unfair can lead to an alteration of activities so as not to pay the tax, it is typically hard to avoid, such as in the case of a property tax. And third, while a *price* usually applies to all potential buyers, the tax one is obligated to pay differs across people. This may be a cause of the belief of the more heavily taxed that their tax obligations are unfair since people paying less have identical access to the roads, parks, and government services that the tax dollars make possible. Perhaps we have an instance here of the market's dominance even when it comes to thinking about what is fair. Charging the same price to all is commonly seen as *fair* today but charging the same price to all does entail charging differently in terms of the value of what is given up. The well-being gained from going to a movie priced at, say, nine dollars, need not differ between rich and poor. But the value of the money likely does given the differences in how much the two parties possess. Thus common sense (but not official economic theory) might tell us that the rich pay a lower price for the identical experience than do the poor, the rich handing over money that they will hardly miss, the poor handing over money whose absence will definitely be felt.

Differential taxation was based at least in part on the recognition that equal sacrifices require different tax levels for rich and poor. While a progressive tax does not necessarily follow from this, differential taxation does, with tax responsibilities rising with income levels. And contrary to popular thinking, efficiency concerns (what economists are best at) serve as a justification for this at least as much as equity concerns. A first principle of economic efficiency is that a good should be purchased only as long as the satisfaction that it provides exceeds its price. More formally, consumption should be expanded (and, given rationality assumptions, will be) just as long as the marginal benefit exceeds the marginal cost. At least half of tax dollars go for the purchase of public goods, those goods that simultaneously provide benefit to all and which are not *used up* in the process of being *consumed.* Since all, rich and poor alike, must consume the same level of, say, national defense, it follows that the rich taxpayer values the last unit of defense provided by a much greater monetary amount than a poor taxpayer, for the simple reason that each dollar is less valuable to the wealthy person. Efficiency therefore requires that the contribution to any good that is shared by all differs, with higher income and wealth leading to higher contributions.

How well understood is this? Does the fact that the *Times* writers are several times more likely to label taxes as unfair than to label prices as unfair tell us much? Or does calling a tax *unfair* usually occur when the particular differences in what each taxpayer is required to pay simply cannot be justified? The more that people are encouraged to think of the taxes that they pay being similar, in nature, to the prices they pay for private goods, the more we might expect to see complaints occurring. To refer to the money held by government as *your tax money* likely adds to the drift toward treating as private what is in fact public.[24]

It is no secret that a drift toward self-centeredness has been underway for a long time, in some ways causing the shift toward Reaganomics as well as being fed by it. The historian Christopher Lasch wrote his classic *The Culture of Narcissism* in 1979 and since then other books have looked at the same phenomenon from a variety of angles.[25] Table 2.18 shows the increase in the singular pronouns *your* and *my* relative to *our* in articles appearing in the *Times* from 1900 to the present. As the third column reveals, *your* appeared about one-third as often as *our* prior to 1980. Since then, however, a clear shift occurred, as *your* appears just over half as often.

I have included these numbers for two reasons. First, they are consistent with the individualism that is generally recognized to have occurred. Second, and more importantly, they provide a point of comparison for the drift away from *our taxes* toward *your taxes*. Column 4 presents the number of times that *your taxes* appeared and column 5 shows the same for *our taxes*. Column 6 shows the ratio of column 4 to column 5. Note that prior to 1980 *our taxes* appeared just about as often, relative to *your taxes* as *our* appeared relative to *your*. But since 1980, the shift toward *your taxes* has been considerable, both on its own terms, and in relation to the more general shift toward *your*. Not only has the column 6 number tripled from 0.36 to 1.07, but this movement away from the collective and toward the individual outstrips significantly the more general shift in that direction that is indicated in column 3. Since 1980, in fact the propensity to speak of taxes with respect to the individual outstrips the propensity to focus in general on the individual. While *your taxes* are 1.07 times more common that *our taxes*, *your* is only 1.26 more common than *our*.[26]

Think of the rhetorical effect this has likely had. *Your taxes* would seem best spent as you see fit, as surely as your private spending dollars are. To speak of *our taxes*, in contrast, at least carries the collectivist implication that how these dollars are spent will have to be collectively decided through democratic processes. To what extent the shift toward *your taxes* has been a cause and to what extent an effect of the rhetorical attack on government is nothing that can be said

Table 2.18 (1) Frequency of *your* and *my* relative to *our* and (2) frequency of *your taxes* and *my taxes* relative to *our taxes*

Years	*1*	*2*	*3*	*4*	*5*	*6*
1980–2009	479,596	379,937	1.26	1,801	1,079	1.67
1930–1979	449,537	605,747	0.74	907	1,444	0.63
1900–1929	204,163	257,522	0.79	204	381	0.54

Notes
Column 1: *yours* and *my*.
Column 2: *our*.
Column 3: column 1/column 2.
Column 4: *your taxes* and *my taxes*.
Column 5: *our taxes*.
Column 6: column 4/column 5.

based on this very limited data. But it is noteworthy that the newspaper so often said to be written by and for liberals, if the conservative message of the past three decades is to be believed, would be carrying forth the language changes that further the message of these very conservatives.

There is another point worth considering. In a democratic system, the taxes one must pay are partly determined by oneself. The prices that the individual faces are partly determined by the individual to the extent that she supported politically the institutions that allowed the seller the freedom to set their price. At the same time, isn't it true that the same individual has less say in the price that she pays than in the taxes she pays? Wouldn't it appear to follow that one would be more inclined to call these prices "unfair"? Regardless, this has certainly not been the trend.

As goes the trend in the *New York Times*, so too goes the trend in economics textbooks. In the pre-1960 texts, it was not unheard of to remind the reader that tax revenues might be spent in order to advance the well-being of all. So, for example, one early text notes that, "It is the absence of a *quid pro quo* or distinct equivalent value which most sharply distinguishes taxes from other sources of public revenue. Taxes flow into the public treasury and are spent for the common good" (Kiekhofer, 1946, 753).

One can find plenty of mention of *public goods* in the modern texts but the stronger expression connoting an element of social solidarity and the transcendence of narrow self-interest is not to be found. Writing twenty-seven years earlier, Frank Taussig more strongly suggests that the acceptance of taxes signals a certain sort of social advance when he writes that "the essential nature of taxation [is] no *quid pro quo*" and that "taxes [are] a sign of wider consciousness of common interest" (1915, 5).

Also considered was democracy's effect. As Garver and Hansen state, "in democratic countries public-welfare projects, including social security, education, health, low-cost housing, and recreational facilities, are more and more demanded by the citizens" (1947, 404). At another point they say:

> [T]here are many services, such as education, social security, sanitation, police protection, and the public highways, which *we* [my emphasis] believe should be available to everyone regardless of ability to pay; hence *we* [my emphasis] turn these services over to governments.
>
> (1947, 393)

Had this passage stopped at the semi-colon, the modern reader would be inclined to interpret the first use of *we* as referring to the authors. The second *we* makes apparent, however, that *we* is being used in a truly collective sense, as *we* signal to our government what it ought to do. As late as 1967, the Samuelson text included such an implicit respect for democratic outcomes, reasoning in a set-aside highlighted section of his text that "In deciding how to tax themselves ... the people are really deciding how resources needed for social wants shall be taken from all the various families and from the enterprises they own and be made available for governmental goods and services" (1967, 154).

Such a positive treatment of democratic outcomes is not to be found in the modern text. For beginning with their 1962 classic, *The Calculus of Consent*, James Buchanan and Gordon Tullock spread the narrow view that self-interest in the selfish sense is the norm. As just one example, Gwartney, Stroup, Sobel, and Macpherson have the voter asking, "[W]hat can you do for me and my goals, and how much will it cost me?" and conclude that "voters will tend to support those candidates whom they believe will provide the most government services and transfer benefits to them and *their favorite causes* [emphasis again added]" (2009, 128). Here we see a prime example of the vacillation between defining consumer maximization as motivated by narrow self-interest (a testable proposition) and defining it more broadly to include anything the consumer might choose freely. "One's favorite cause" may improve one's personal well-being not one iota. There is the *warm glow* from giving and all of that but the point remains the same: once we allow for agents to be other than narrowly self-interested, there is no need to believe that the predictions of public choice theory will be good predictions. Citizens may actually be moved to vote for candidates that will not improve their life yet by doing so will undermine the predictions.

The cynical view of government spending and taxing was furthered by the public choice theorists but didn't begin with them. Writing twenty years before Buchanan and Tullock, Kiekhoffer reasons as follows:

> While taxation may not have started as a class struggle ... modern taxation ... in its most characteristic aspect is a group contest in which powerful interests vigorously endeavor to rid themselves of present or proposed tax burdens. It is, first of all, a hard game in which he who trusts wholly to economics, reason, and justice, will in the end retire beaten and disillusioned. Class politics is of the essence of taxation.
>
> (1946, 755)

Two things stand out in comparing this passage with the public choice thinking of today. First, it is not self-interested people that undermine the democratic ideal, but self-interested groups. Social solidarity still exists in the world described above, albeit a solidarity that leads to public spending inefficiencies. Second, the focus is not on too much spending that results from these inefficiencies, but too little taxation! Those projects justified by reasonable cost benefit analyses are underfunded as selfish groups manage to lower their tax liabilities, a phenomenon better suited to explain today's situation in the U.S. than the models focusing on inefficient spending that came out of the public choice theorists and that appears to dominate the conversation today. Declarations of foolish and wasteful spending play far better on the campaign trail than declarations of unfair tax cuts.

In examining the current texts what I frequently encountered was a nearly schizophrenic sort of treatment, as text authors in the role of good scholar-scientist report facts inconsistent with popular anti-tax beliefs yet feel the need to adopt the language of the very anti-tax crowd likely to spout such beliefs.

Thus, Baumol and Blinder note that "Many Americans believe that taxes have been gobbling up an ever-increasing share of the U.S. economy," and go on to warn "that this supposition is not true" (2006, 376). The implied truth is that they have been *gobbling up* the same share. This is reminiscent of defending someone accused of eating live cat sandwiches by insisting he doesn't like bread. The supposed escape from an accusation deflects the attention from the more serious accusation. In the case of eating live cats, the absurdity is obvious. In the case of Baumol and Blinder's choice of words it is less so, but still very real. To *gobble up* any of the U.S. economy sounds pretty bad. While it may be true, as Baumol and Blinder demonstrate, that the act hasn't escalated, it still sounds like something worth stopping altogether. Spending on cars, entertainment, or food are not said to *gobble up* some of the American economy but are part of that economy. So why is public spending presented as different?

Baumol and Blinder further manage to play on the whine that signals strong dislike of taxes with the following:

> Sometimes it seems that the tax collector is everywhere. We have income and payroll taxes deducted from our paychecks, sales taxes added to our purchases, property taxes levied on our homes. We pay gasoline taxes, liquor taxes, cigarette taxes, and telephone taxes. Not surprisingly, tax cuts are more popular politically than are tax increases.... Yet ... by international standards, Americans are among the most lightly taxed people in the world.
>
> (2006, 377)

Why do they indulge the claim that "the tax collector is everywhere"? That is little more than an unsophisticated claim of someone disliking taxes, of someone still not able to recognize the connection between taxes and common interests.

The anti-tax prejudices are similarly found in Lipsey, Ragan, and Storer (2008). They begin their section on taxation by announcing that "There is a bewildering array of taxes in the United States" (bewildering in what way? Isn't the production of any product bewildering? Isn't the workings of the market bewildering?), and go on state that "[a]lthough 30 percent of national income may seem like a great deal to pay in taxes, it actually puts the United States near the bottom of the list of industrialized counties" (2008, 438). Is this again the good scholar-teacher side of the authors in conflict with their desire to connect with modern prejudices? They manage to state that U.S. taxes, in relative terms, are the lowest while fully acknowledging that they may *seem* awfully high. To whom? To a thoughtful person? On what grounds?

The same pattern of reconciling tax phobia with facts appears in Irvin B. Tucker's text. For him:

> [W]e must ask how burdensome overall taxation in the United States is. It may surprise you to learn that by international standards U.S. citizens are among the most lightly taxed people in the industrialized world.... [I]n

> 2005 the tax collector was clearly much more heavy-handed in most other advanced industrial countries based on the fraction of GDP paid in taxes. (2008, 556)

We see here the earlier discussed rhetorical mistake of moving from *tax burden* to taxes being *burdensome*. The *burden* was used to specify tax incidence or how much of the tax was borne by different parties. *Burdensome* is considerably more judgmental, carrying a clear sense of unfairness. We are told to ask how burdensome taxes are, not whether or not they are indeed burdensome. In addition, after noting that the U.S. is lightly taxed relative to other countries, we are told the "tax collector was clearly much more heavy-handed" elsewhere. Not only does this suggest that the tax collector was indeed heavy-handed in these other nations, it manages to suggest that he was heavy-handed in the U.S. as well.

Interfere, *intervene*, or just *act*?

There is no normative bias associated with *acting*. One acts when taking a bite of food, taking out the garbage, giving a generous donation, or engaging in mass murder. To *act*, in short, says nothing about the moral status of the action itself. To *intervene* can also be neutral. A concerned citizen might intervene in an argument to help prevent it from escalating into something worse. A busybody, in contrast, might intervene where he is unwanted.

What appears to most separate *acting* from *intervening* is the assumption in the latter case of a pre-existing status quo. *Acting* does not similarly require a pre-existing something is being interfered with. Religions speak of the *act* of creating the universe but would never say that their deity *intervened* in the universe. No universe existed prior. Similarly, those who *act* on the stage and screen do not *intervene* in any meaningful sense. To say that government intervenes in the market presupposes a chronological priority for markets. We do not hear it said that markets *intervene* in the public sphere, but the construction of a business on land that was held in common for millennia might be characterized as precisely this. By not even suggesting that markets sometimes *intervene* we imply that they were always there.

Since 1900 in the *Times*, *act* has, less than surprisingly, been far more common than *intervene* or *interfere*. Summing the number of occurrences of these words (and their noun forms, *action*, *intervention*, and *interference*) *act* comprises 85.8 percent, *intervention* 4.8 percent and *interference* 9.4 percent of the total. In Table 2.19 appear the raw figures for the occurrence of each in columns 1 through 3, the sum of the three in column 4, and the fraction that each of the three words comprised each decade in columns 5 through 7. There has clearly been no strong overall trend at work. *Act* has comprised between 82.5 percent and 88.1 percent with no overall secular trend apparent. *Intervene* has fluctuated between 3.1 and 7.1 percent with a slight upward trend discernible. And *interference* has comprised between 7.2 and 12.2 percent of the whole with a very slight downward trend, if any.

Table 2.19 Frequency of *acts* relative to *intervenes* and *interferes*

Years	*1*	*2*	*3*	*4*	*5*	*6*	*7*
2000–2009	74,937	4,489	6,232	85,658	0.875	0.052	0.072
1990–1999	91,199	7,271	10,326	108,796	0.838	0.067	0.095
1980–1989	113,265	9,787	14,159	137,211	0.825	0.071	0.103
1970–1979	136,545	8,355	13,065	157,965	0.864	0.053	0.083
1960–1969	124,222	7,988	13,188	145,328	0.855	0.055	0.090
1950–1959	131,104	6,886	12,720	150,710	0.870	0.046	0.084
1940–1949	150,752	6,338	13,948	171,038	0.881	0.037	0.082
1930–1939	174,790	8,927	18,976	202,693	0.862	0.044	0.094
1920–1929	126,845	5,449	15,627	147,921	0.858	0.037	0.106
1910–1919	89,719	4,297	11,740	105,756	0.848	0.041	0.111
1900–1909	68,433	2,521	9,977	80,831	0.847	0.031	0.122

Notes
Column 1: *act*, *acts*, and *actions*.
Column 2: *intervene*, *intervenes*, and *intervention*.
Column 3: *interfere*, *interferes*, and *interference*.
Column 4: sum of columns 1–3.
Column 5: column 1/column 4.
Column 6: column 2/column 4.
Column 7: column 3/column 4.

When *government* is allowed to precede *act*, *intervene*, and *interfere*, it is no longer true that *act* is so dominant over the other two. Since 1900 *government act* has comprised 54.3 percent of the whole, *government intervention* 18.0 percent, and *government interference* 27.5 percent. And less than surprisingly, the tendency to speak of government *intervening* and *interfering* does not hold true for *nations*. Given the three possibilities, nations have been said to *act* 90.8 percent of the time, to *intervene* just 6.1 percent of the time and to *interfere* a mere 3.0 percent of the time. Just as we saw in the earlier section that the tendency to refer to the nation as *ours* has remained strong at the same time that the tendency to speak of the government as *ours* has fallen noticeably, here we see that nations are much more likely than government to be described as *acting* while *government* is much more likely to be described as *intervening* or *interfering*.

Table 2.20 is organized like Table 2.19, the only difference being that the counts in columns 1 through 4 are limited to instances where *government* also appears. Thus, while the first number in Table 2.19 indicates that the words *act*, *acts*, and *actions* appeared 74,937 since 2000, Table 2.20 shows that *government act*, *governments act*, and *government action* appeared 355 times. Table 2.20 reveals that when it comes to government there has been a slight trend away from *act* and toward *intervention* and *interference*. Only since 1980 has *government acts* comprised less than half the total, has *government intervention* pushed above 20 percent and *government interference* above 30 percent.[27]

Summarizing this point, *intervention* and *interference* are more common than *action* when these words are preceded by *government* than when they are not. In

Table 2.20 Frequency of *government acts* relative to *government intervenes* and *government interferes*

Years	*1*	*2*	*3*	*4*	*5*	*6*	*7*
2000–2009	355	145	225	725	0.490	0.200	0.310
1990–1999	561	288	423	1,272	0.441	0.226	0.333
1980–1989	1,084	469	661	2,214	0.490	0.212	0.299
1970–1979	1,024	364	547	1,935	0.529	0.188	0.283
1960–1969	840	287	413	1,540	0.545	0.186	0.268
1950–1959	934	250	403	1,587	0.589	0.158	0.254
1940–1949	978	270	430	1,678	0.583	0.161	0.256
1930–1939	892	234	446	1,572	0.567	0.149	0.284
1920–1929	528	125	207	860	0.614	0.145	0.241
1910–1919	358	49	78	485	0.738	0.101	0.161
1900–1909	148	20	51	219	0.676	0.091	0.233

Notes
Column 1: *governments act, government acts*, and *government actions.*
Column 2: *governments intervene, government intervenes, government interventions.*
Column 3: *governments interfere, government interferes, government interference.*
Column 4: sum of columns 1–3.
Column 5: column 1/column 4.
Column 6: column 2/column 4.
Column 7: column 3/column 4.

addition, while there is no general trend toward an increase in *intervention* and *interference* relative to *action* there is such a long-term trend toward the use of *government intervention* and *government interference* relative to *government action.*

It was earlier noted that both *action* and *intervention* can be viewed favorably. The data presented in Table 2.21 leaves little doubt, however, that *intervention* is used unfavorably far more than *action* is. Looking at the top row that shows *Times* data from its very inception, *action* was preceded by *necessary* or *appropriate* forty-five times as often as it was preceded by *unnecessary* or *inappropriate* as indicated in column 3, while the positive adjectives were barely over twice as common for *intervention* and just one-third as common for *interference,* as indicated in columns 6 and 9, respectively. Drawing on the larger sample provided by ProQuest corroborates these results, though less dramatically, with the favorable adjectives being 16.7 times as frequent for *action*, 2.6 times as frequent for *intervention* and 0.78 times as frequent for *interference.* Clearly the habit of speaking of government actions as interventions or interferences carries with it a less than favorable attitude toward these actions.

As one more bit of evidence that *action* is relatively favored over *intervention* when the activity is favored by the writer, Table 2.22 shows the relative use of the two words in the *Times* and ProQuest when the subject is the U.S. military or foreign military. Not too surprisingly (in light of the Table 2.21 data), action is the term of choice when talking about the U.S. military, but intervention becomes much more popular when it is a foreign military that is the topic of discussion. Looking just at the ProQuest data (the *Times* data is consistent with this but the numbers are again quite small), with *U.S. military action* appearing ninety times as frequently as *foreign military action*, while *U.S. military intervention* is just 3.5 times as frequently observed as *foreign military intervention*. Quite clearly, the bad guys are presented more as the interveners than are the good guys.[28]

Table 2.23 provides a sense of the relative frequency with which other groups and institutions are said to *act*, relative to *intervening* or *interfering*. What stands out is that businesses, corporations, and firms are reported as *acting* forty-eight times for every single time that they are said to *intervene* or *interfere*. A partial explanation for this might be that businesses are seen as prime actors in the marketplace making it hard to characterize their behaviors as *intervention*. Just like a cast member *acts* in the process of performing a play but doesn't in any

Table 2.21 Frequency of favorable relative to unfavorable descriptions of *action* compared with frequency of favorable relative to unfavorable descriptions of *intervention* and *interference*

Source	*1*	*2*	*3*	*4*	*5*	*6*	*7*	*8*	*9*
New York Times	3,584	80	44.8	31	15	2.07	45	148	0.31
ProQuest	81,276	4,855	16.7	2,002	768	2.61	1,251	1,601	0.78

Notes
Column 1: *necessary action*, and *appropriate action*.
Column 2: *unnecessary action*, and *inappropriate action*.
Column 3: column 1/column 2.
Column 4: *necessary intervention*, and *appropriate intervention*.
Column 5: *unnecessary intervention*, and *inappropriate intervention*.
Column 6: column 4/column 5.
Column 7: *necessary interference*, and *appropriate interference*.
Column 8: *unnecessary interference*, and *inappropriate interference*.
Column 9: column 7/column 8.

Table 2.22 Frequency of *U.S. military action* relative to *foreign military action* compared with frequency of *U.S. military intervention* relative to *foreign military intervention*

Source	*1*	*2*	*3*	*4*	*5*	*6*
New York Times	73	4	18.3	53	89	0.60
ProQuest	13,441	167	80.5	5,251	1,486	3.53

Notes
Column 1: *U.S. military action*.
Column 2: *foreign military action*.
Column 3: column 1/column 2.
Column 4: *U.S. military intervention*.
Column 5: *foreign military intervention*.
Column 6: column 4/column 5.

Table 2.23 Ratio of frequency of *acts* to frequency of *intervenes* and *interferes* for different actors, arranged from highest to lowest

Actor	*Ratio*
Business	48.7
Managers	29.1
Teachers	20.8
Nations	17.0
Cities	13.0
Executives	12.3
Police	3.8
President	2.7
States	1.4
Government	1.2

meaningful sense *intervene* in the play itself, so too the primary actors in the market can act without intervening (or interfering).

More curious is the high number associated with managers. While very much a participant in an enterprise, a manager specifically stands apart as an overseer and guide, similar in certain respects to what government's role is in the economy. And yet while government is said to *intervene* or *interfere* almost as often it is said to *act*, managers are described as *acting* twenty-nine times as frequently as they *interfere* or *intervene*. Perspective clearly matters and from the firm's standpoint, managers act in the interest of the firm even though they may be *intervening* or *interfering* from the standpoint of those being managed. So accustomed is the United States to seeing government as an outsider that this narrow perspective has much greater currency in the *Times* when it is acts of government being considered.

Two other features of the table are worth mentioning. First, we see here again how *nations* are viewed differently than *governments*, the former being far less likely to be referred to as *interveners* or *interferers*. Second, the high propensity to refer to police behaviors as interventions or interferences draws attention to the fact that any evaluation of the behaviors can be tricky. The actions that police officers take are very often interventions in matters that from a social standpoint are very much in the public interest. To intervene in a robbery or a kidnapping is obviously a good thing. And even to say that *interference* in the act has occurred is not to cast any doubts on the wisdom of the act. Here we have a case in which the police are very much outsiders to the action going on but from a social standpoint are welcomed in their action.

When it comes to government, however, it is readily apparent that the *interventions* and *interferences* are not always welcomed. Writing in the 1920s, the famed Austrian economist Ludwig von Mises offered the following definition: "Intervention is a limited order by a social authority forcing the owners of the means of production and entrepreneurs to employ their means in a different manner than they otherwise would" (1977, 20).

On the same page he turns attention to a particular type of government action and tells his reader that "price controls [are] 'interference with the structure of prices'" (1977, 20). That he is using *intervention* and *interference* interchangeably becomes clear four pages later when he titles a new section "Interference with prices" and proceeds to announce in the very first sentence that "price *intervention* [emphasis added] aims at setting goods prices that differ from those the unhampered market would set" (1977, 24). That *intervention* (and the more negative *interference*) are, according to von Mises, worth avoiding becomes as clear as can be two pages after this with the following claim: "There is no … choice: government either abstains from limited interference with the market forces, or it assumes total control over production and distribution. Either capitalism or socialism; there is no middle of the road" (1977, 26). The data in Tables 2.21 and 2.22 showed that neither *intervene* nor *interfere* are used as favorably as the simple word *act*, and also showed that *interfere* was less favorable than *intervene*. For von Mises to use the words interchangeably was to cast doubt on virtually any actions that the government might take that would have an impact on the economy.

Turning now to the use of these expressions in the popular press, the first five instances of *government interference* that I surveyed in the *Times* and in ProQuest displayed, less than surprisingly, an extremely negative assessment of what it meant to *interfere*. In five of these cases, *interference* involved acting outside of any legal jurisdiction or of flouting the law. Thus one article announces that the appropriate authorities had "suspended the Guatemalan federation from all international competitions … because of 'government interference'" ("Corner Kicks," 2004, D6). Another describes an action by the Thai government that "has renewed criticism by journalists and the opposition of government interference in Thailand's press" (Perlez, 2004, A10). A spokesperson for a Muslim organization announces support of Christians by standing "with them against government interference … in their faith" (Mink, 2004, 1). A BBC wire feed announces "Portuguese government 'interference' in the media" ("Portuguese," 2009). And a Florida newspaper editorial says "[w]e must insist that Ukraine be allowed to work out its future without U.S. government interference" ("Editorial," 2004, A6).

Note again that all of these instances involve the defiance of either national or international authority, or of exercising power where no official authority exists. *Government interference* has nonetheless also appeared where simple *government intervention* would have sufficed and where nothing remotely illegal was the object of criticism. So a *London Times* letter writer can describe the requirement that two mothers who swap babysitting services register as "childminders" as the victims of nitpicking government and characterize this as "the final straw in government interference in responsible people's daily lives" ("Childminder," 2009, 21) and so Sarah Palin can assess the 2009 economic crisis by announcing that "'[w]e got into this mess because of government interference in the first place'" (Cheng and Frangos, 2009, 11).

While complaints about interference suggest a strong, over-reaching government, there is an equally common complaint that suggests an incompetent and ineffective government. *Waste* and *inefficiency* are the mantras to characterize such incompetence, suggesting a government that might be driven to interfere while simply being unable to do so at all effectively.

Waste and *inefficiency*

Efficiency is one of those words that economics has foisted upon the world without needed provisos and warnings attached. Just as it's possible to be "too thin" and, at least from a social perspective, "too rich," so it is possible to be too efficient. The failure to recognize this led to an uproar when noted economic historians wrote about the efficiency of slavery. Critics took this description as a defense of slavery, despite the fact that *efficiency* does not imply moral approval.[29]

When it comes to comparisons of the efficiency of the public and private sectors, there is no similar question of moral injustice to confront. In a democracy people may, after all, simply decide that certain economic functions will be carried out in the public domain while others will remain in the private domain. But to speak of the former being inefficient may well suggest a problem to be settled via a reshuffling of activities out of the public into the private sphere.

In the absence of careful warnings, the introductory economics student is likely to be left with the impression that markets lead to maximal efficiency in both the production of goods and in their distribution. Every introductory text's chapter on perfect competition precedes the chapters on monopoly, monopolistic competition, and oligopoly and likely manages to leave an imprint on the student's mind that it basically summarizes the world as it is while the more real-world models simply raise some non-threatening challenges to the main points reached. In fact, of course, none of the efficiencies associated with perfect competition carry over to the world of competition that actually exists. Despite this, *efficiency* has become one of those conversation stopping words in countless settings. To declare A more efficient than B provides A with a comparative advantage difficult for B to overcome.

There are three main types of efficiency. *Allocative* efficiency consists of devoting the optimal quantity of resources to the production of a good, this optimal quantity being determined by the costs of production and the tastes of consumers. *Productive* efficiency has to do with producing at a rate of output that minimizes average cost.[30] And *X-efficiency* means that any sloppiness in production is avoided. All three types are achieved in the mythical world of perfect competition. None are fully achieved in the world of markets as we know them.

There nonetheless persists a view that activities channeled through markets will allow an attainment of efficiency simply not achievable through the plodding and cumbersome actions (and interventions) of government. Moreover, this belief that the market can easily outstrip the government in efficiently delivering its goods has grown over the same period of time when all pretensions of the text-book ideal of efficiency has virtually disappeared.

Table 2.24 provides some indication of the trend. The numbers in column 1 show the number of times that certain positive descriptions of government (efficient, competent, and creative) appeared and the numbers in column 2 the number of times that certain negative descriptions (inefficient, incompetent, uncreative, wasteful) appeared. Column 3 shows the ratio of column 1 to column 2. Columns 4, 5, and 6 repeat the same procedure for the private side of the economy (corporations, companies, firms, businesses, and private sector). While there has been a rise in the relative occurrence of negative descriptions for both government and business over the 110-year period, it is, not too surprisingly, government that has seen the more rapid shift toward the negative descriptions, particularly when comparing the 1930–1979 period with the period since 1980. For the private sector, the positive descriptions went from being about five times as common as the negative to about four times as common. But for government, the corresponding change was from nearly seven (slightly more tilted to the positive description than business) to just 1.3 (considerably less so).

The talk of wasteful and inefficient government often has specific government spending in mind, be it the purchasing of military equipment from private firms or the hiring of personnel which then provide public services directly. There is, however, another sort of activity that is often singled out as inefficient – the much maligned government act of *regulating*.[31]

Table 2.24 Frequency of favorable relative to unfavorable descriptions of *government* compared with frequency of favorable to unfavorable descriptions of *companies*

Years	*1*	*2*	*3*	*4*	*5*	*6*
1980–2009	162	127	1.3	312	75	4.2
1930–1979	946	138	6.9	309	60	5.2
1900–1929	506	46	11.0	205	11	18.6

Notes

Column 1: *efficient government, competent government, creative government, efficient public sector, competent public sector*, and *creative public sector*.

Column 2: *inefficient government, incompetent government, uncreative government, wasteful government, inefficient public sector, incompetent public sector, uncreative public sector*, and *wasteful public sector*.

Column 3: column 1/column 2.

Column 4: *efficient companies, competent companies, creative companies, efficient corporations, competent corporations, creative corporations, efficient private sector, competent private sector, creative private sector, efficient firms, competent firms, creative firms, efficient businesses, competent businesses*, and *creative businesses*.

Column 5: *inefficient companies, incompetent companies, uncreative companies, wasteful companies, inefficient corporations, incompetent corporations, uncreative corporations, wasteful corporations, inefficient private sector, incompetent private sector, uncreative private sector, wasteful private sector, inefficient firms, incompetent firms, uncreative firms, wasteful firms, inefficient businesses, incompetent businesses, uncreative businesses*, and *wasteful businesses*.

Column 6: column 4/column 5.

The heavy hand of *regulation*

Government regulation was a response to markets that were no longer recognizable as the 18th century ideals of Adam Smith. As concentration grew, perfectly competition slowly faded as an attainable ideal. Antitrust legislation was one way that the United States countered this rise of the giants. And beginning with the publication of Arthur Pigou's classic work (1929), it became increasingly accepted that people might take actions through their governments that would improve upon market outcomes. The growing complexity of the world and specialization of knowledge meant that buyers were less likely to be aware of what they were buying.[32] Hence arose one branch of regulation that required the provision of information. The growing tendency for both production and consumption to give rise to environmental damage (as well as purely aesthetic pollution) cast increasing doubt on the market's efficiency in determining what would be produced. Hence was born the case for actions to control negative spillover effects. And perhaps most significantly, the financial disasters of the 1930s resulted in extensive financial regulation that went largely unchallenged until the 1970s.

Prior to the 1980s, *deregulation* rarely appeared in the *Times*. For this reason, the data in Table 2.25 only goes back to 1960. Only sixteen times prior to 1970 did the word appear, while appearing about once every other day since then, with the peak occurring, unsurprisingly, during the 1980s. Column 4 reveals just how frequent *deregulation* became relative to *regulation*. In the 1960s, *regulation* appeared 1,500 times as often. During the 1980s, this number had plummeted to 6.7, before rising to 12.5 in the 2000s. Considering that *regulation* is a rather general word, column 2 shows just the number of occurrences of *federal regulation* and *government regulation* and column 5 the ratio of this figure to the

Table 2.25 Frequency of *regulation* relative to *government regulation* and frequency of *regulation* relative to *deregulation* (data in top five rows from *New York Times* and bottom three rows from ProQuest)

Years	*1*	*2*	*3*	*4*	*5*
2000–2009	11,807	827	943	12.52	0.877
1990–1999	19,014	2,029	2,007	9.47	1.011
1980–1989	23,601	2,872	3,533	6.68	0.813
1970–1979	25,364	2,858	1,027	24.70	2.782
1960–1969	16,467	1,032	11	1,497.00	93.820
2000–2009	2,319,001	156,572	103,835	22.33	1.508
1990–1999	1,330,104	104,887	108,824	12.22	0.964
1980–1989	327,966	24,797	33,280	9.85	0.745

Notes
Column 1: *regulation*.
Column 2: *federal regulation* and *government regulation*.
Column 3: *deregulation*.
Column 4: column 1/column 3.
Column 5: column 2/column 3.

number of occurrences of *deregulation*. As the numbers in this column show, *deregulation* has actually occurred more often than *federal* or *government* regulation over this period. The data from ProQuest that appear in the bottom three lines of the table corroborate the finding that *deregulation* popularity reached a clear peak of relative usage in the 1980s, as the numbers in both columns 4 and 5 have risen in the two decades since.

The data in Table 2.25 do not indicate attitudes toward regulation. In Table 2.26 are shown the numbers of favorable descriptions of *regulation* and unfavorable descriptions by decade since 1900 in articles appearing in the *Times*.[33] While we tend to associate *regulation* with Roosevelt's New Deal, the dominance of favorable over unfavorable extends clear back to 1900. To be sure, when criticism was voiced, it was typically business interests doing the complaining and the language sounded much like today. For instance, U.S. and European companies that heavily invested in Cuba following the Spanish American War were said to "dread the complete restoration of home rule, [foreseeing] excessive taxation, and burdensome regulations placed upon their enterprises" ("Mr. Taft," 1908, 6). But as the table shows, from the Progressive Era right through the laissez-faire 1920s, favorable descriptions held a wide margin over unfavorable. The heavily regulated war economy of the 1940s saw unfavorable descriptions rise into the double digits, but the dominance of negative descriptions clearly began in the 1970s and took off in the twenty years that followed.

Table 2.27 gives a more general summary of the trend, and the ratio of favorable to unfavorable by periods longer than a decade. Again, while the raw numbers are not large prior to 1980, the magnitude of the difference suggests a different attitude toward regulation.[34] From favorable descriptions appearing more than twice as frequently as unfavorable prior to 1980, they appeared only half as often since then. What might lie behind the switch that appeared to begin (as the preceding Table 2.26 suggests) in the 1970s? While occurring at the same

Table 2.26 Frequency of favorable descriptions of *regulation* relative to unfavorable descriptions

Years	*Favorable* regulation	*Unfavorable* regulation
2000–2009	22	11
1990–1999	47	75
1980–1989	54	66
1970–1979	42	27
1960–1969	29	5
1950–1959	18	7
1940–1949	38	17
1939–1939	74	6
1920–1929	38	8
1910–1919	26	5
1900–1909	22	0

time as the tax revolution of the 1970s, regulation is, for the most part, not expensive in the monetary sense, and thus deregulation did not have much to do with attempts at budget cutting as a response to decreasing tax revenue. Instead, regulation is about control, and rebellion against outside control of any sort may have had the most to do with the anti-regulatory movement. To be sure, the reasons for advocating deregulation made a different case.

Typical was the following sort of quick and short argument that appeared just two months into Reagan's first term as president: "The banks propose the elimination of costly regulation, to make them more competitive" ("Consumer," 1981, A26). This argument, repeated countless times since, clings to the worship of *competitiveness* but even on those terms is problematic. Professional football requires all players to wear protective gear that meets certain standards and hockey requires all goalies to wear facemasks. It appears to be easily recognized that making this optional would lead to a "race to the bottom" and competitive pressures would lead teams to scale down or even eliminate such protective equipment and gain an advantage by doing so. To achieve the ideal of *fair competition* by deregulating the currently regulated instead of regulating the currently unregulated likely spells higher profits but at the same time points in the direction of an overall drop in social well-being, a generalization supported by the outsized gain in banking profits and CEO salaries in the thirty years since the banks began to be heavily deregulated while social well-being, at least as far as financial security is concerned, plummeted.[35]

And complaints about being overly regulated managed, amazingly enough, to be made by governments themselves. So in downplaying the case that New York City would benefit from becoming the 51st state, a *Times* writer asks, "[w]ho needs statehood when one has the vows of Congress and the Governor to … free local officials from costly regulation?" ("A City," 1995, E3).

The changing textbook treatment of *regulation*

Probably the largest leap from laissez-faire into government regulation began with the Sherman Antitrust act of 1890 and the Clayton Antitrust act of 1913 and continued clear through Roosevelt's New Deal and the 1960s. The shift in

Table 2.27 Frequency of favorable descriptions of *regulation* relative to unfavorable descriptions with greater aggregation of data than in Table 2.26

Years	*1*	*2*	*3*
1980–2009	123	243	0.51
1930–1979	201	88	2.28
1900–1929	86	20	4.30

Notes
Column 1: favorable *regulation*.
Column 2: unfavorable *regulation*.
Column 3: column 1/column 2.

textbook support for antitrust legislation has been rather remarkable. Richard T. Ely, founder of the American Economic Association, had the following to say about the need for antitrust in the 1937 edition of his textbook:

> We must admit that unregulated monopolies in private hands have always been odious and are opposed to the principles of the laws of civilized nations. They are opposed to that endeavor to secure equality of opportunity which is fundamental in modern democracy and which manifests itself as a red thread running through American history.
>
> (1937, 634)

What did Ely propose in the way of regulation? Strict enforcement of the antitrust laws. Ely is worth quoting at length here:

> Our anti-trust laws express what is undoubtedly the dominant public sentiment in the United States with respect to large industrial combinations formed with the purpose of obtaining a monopoly. Our policy has been one of repression, of compulsory dissolution, of monopolistic organizations. Undoubtedly we have made many blunders in the ways in which we have formulated and enforced this policy. We have, in some cases, attempted to force competition into the field of the natural monopolies; we have often attributed too large a significance to the mere fact of combination; we have in particular attempted to cure, by a sweeping prohibition of "restraint of trade" and "monopolizing," many evils that are, in their more important aspects, matters of corporation finance rooted in the laxity of our statutes with respect to the organization and management of corporations.
>
> (1937, 645)

He further goes on to note that:

> There are differences between monopoly and competition in their effects upon the distribution of wealth, upon the equality of economic opportunity, and upon a host of economic and social relations; and in most of these particulars, it is generally believed, the advantage rests with competition.
>
> (1937, 645)

These passages are remarkably out of tune with what the textbooks have to say today. Note in the second passage that there is mention of *our* anti-trust laws and *our* policy. Note as well that Ely chooses to say *we* have made blunders, forced competition where it doesn't belong, and done other unwise things. In no modern texts is it possible to speak so glowingly of anti-trust or to use personal pronouns when discussing it. The transition, however, was not overnight.

In the seventh edition of his classic textbook, Paul Samuelson critically assesses the Sherman and Clayton Acts and is by no means thrilled with all that he finds. He does nonetheless manage to conclude that:

> The Sherman and Clayton Acts, and most of the antitrust laws, have contributed enormously toward improving the degree of competition in our system. All who value the capitalistic way of life should applaud this kind of public intervention which helps to lessen the imperfections of competition.
>
> (1967, 500)

Yet forty-three years later, in his 19th edition (co-authored now with William D. Nordhaus) we find a far less glowing overall assessment:

> Economic and legal views toward ... antitrust have changed dramatically over the last three decades. Increasingly ... antitrust laws are aimed toward the goal of improving economic efficiency rather than combating businesses simply because they are big or profitable.
>
> (2010, 206)

The perspective here suggests that of one who feels himself a victim of antitrust. Bigness, per se, has never been a sufficient (or necessary) condition for antitrust action, nor has profitability. The perspective taken in this passage brings to mind the complaint of one who sees himself as a victim of such action, not an economist carefully assessing the patterns of antitrust enforcement.

Baumol and Blinder manage to not only shed doubt on the wisdom of antitrust, but manage to simultaneously recast one person's *monopolist* as another's *vigorously competitive* firm. As they put it:

> One problem that haunts most antitrust litigation is that vigourous competition may look very similar to acts that *undermine* competition and support monopoly power. The resulting danger is that the courts will prohibit, or the antitrust authorities will prosecute, acts that *appear* to be anticompetitive but are really the opposite.
>
> The difficulty occurs because effective competition by a firm is always tough on its rivals.
>
> (2006, 275)

Here again we have an instance where firms that are neither perfectly competitive nor monopolistically competitive (the only two types of competitive industries) are said to be vigorously competitive! And as the final sentence shows competition is said to *always* be tough on rivals, in spite of this being simply not true in the case of perfectly or monopolistically competitive industries. In both cases, any one seller is too small to be noticed by rivals and can hence act with virtual anonymity and without having an impact on others.

That an easing of restraints on mergers has been occurring comes through rather clearly in the textbooks. In their 2008 edition, Lipsey *et al.* make the following claim that is likely to be conveniently missing from their next edition.

> Since 1999 "financial holding companies" have also been allowed to own banks, insurance companies, and securities firms. The resulting mergers have led to financial institutions like JPMorgan Chase that offer "one stop shopping" for financial services at bank branches and on the Internet. It is likely that the financial services industry will continue to see this type of merger activity.
>
> (2008, 297–298)

The legislation being referred to is a major embarrassment today and almost impossible to defend unless higher profits for those pushing the legislation are allowed as a sufficient rationale. That a leading text could take such a cavalier attitude to the long tradition of preventing monopoly is disturbing.

Also to be noticed in this quote is the stress on the way in which the consumer might be well served by the giant corporation. The tendency to call upon the political dangers of such mergers receives no similar attention. Calls to the *citizen* in each of us fade while calls to the *consumer* gain importance. And it is this development that will be the focus of Chapter 4. First, however, a closer look at competition is necessary.

3 Competition over cooperation and monopoly

In Chapter 2 the alternative to government was, of course, the market. In this chapter, the focus will be on *competition*, the condition that at least since the time Adam Smith, is seen as ensuring that the market excels at delivering the goods.

As the chapter title is meant to suggest, competition is a more complex word than is usually realized. In some contexts, its opposite is "monopoly," and in other contexts its opposite is *cooperation*. The one most familiar to economists – *monopoly* – will be the focus of the two sections that follow. Following this, it will be changes in the frequency of *cooperation* relative to *competition* that will receive attention. The chapter's final section will seek to solve some of the puzzles uncovered in the first three sections by noting the gradual expansion in the meaning of *competitive*.[1]

More *competition* and less *monopoly*

Ask an economist to name the opposite of *competition*, and the most likely response will be *monopoly*. While the general public is less likely to give this answer (about which more later), to those shaped by nearly any economics tradition, *competition* implies industries with many firms and *monopoly* an industry with just one firm.[2]

Table 3.1 shows the number of times that these two words have appeared in the *New York Times* articles, by decade, over the last century and the ratio of the one (*competition*) to the other (*monopoly*). As column 3 indicates, before 1960 *competition* appeared between four and six times more frequently per decade, a fairly constrained spread. While the relative frequency of *competition* rose markedly between 1960 and 1989, it has fallen back since 1990 to just slightly more than the earlier average.[3]

In Table 3.2, occurrences of the related *adjectives* have been added to the Table 3.1 data. Occurrences of *competition* have been combined with *competitive* in column 1 and occurrences of *monopoly* have been combined with *monopolistic* in column 2.[4] The ratios of column 1 to column 2 now yield a more pronounced pattern. From 1900 through 1959 there occurred a gradual rise in the relative frequency of *competition* and *competitive*, from four times as frequent as

Table 3.1 Frequency of *competition* relative to *monopoly*

Years	*1*	*2*	*3*
2000–2009	18,637	2,450	7.61
1990–1999	31,099	4,163	7.47
1980–1989	33,872	3,680	9.20
1970–1979	28,555	3,568	8.00
1960–1969	28,881	3,457	8.35
1950–1959	28,236	4,802	5.88
1940–1949	24,579	5,266	4.67
1930–1939	43,460	6,754	6.43
1920–1929	28,033	4,752	5.90
1910–1919	17,430	3,452	5.05
1900–1909	13,988	3,342	4.19

Notes
Column 1: *competition*.
Column 2: *monopoly*.
Column 3: column 1/column 2.

monopoly and *monopolistic*, to close to seven times as frequent. From 1960 through 1989, its relative growth accelerated before falling back since 1990, yet even after this decline it can be seen that *competition* and *competitive* remain roughly twice as common relative to *monopoly* and *monopolistic* as they were before 1960.[5]

Netting out the nouns – *competition* and *monopoly* – from Table 3.2 yields more striking results. In Table 3.3, left with just the adjectives, *competitive* in column 1 and *monopolistic* in column 2, a clear increase towards *competitive*

Table 3.2 Frequency of *competition* and *competitive* relative to *monopoly* and *monopolistic*

Years	*1*	*2*	*3*
2000–2009	28,467	2,642	10.77
1990–1999	47,916	4,585	10.45
1980–1989	50,844	4,133	12.30
1970–1979	41,269	4,330	9.53
1960–1969	40,599	3,958	10.26
1950–1959	39,189	5,709	6.86
1940–1949	34,878	6,633	5.26
1930–1939	52,506	8,111	6.47
1920–1929	32,631	5,574	5.85
1910–1919	20,163	3,992	5.05
1900–1909	15,688	3,882	4.04

Notes
Column 1: *competition* and *competitive*.
Column 2: *monopoly* and *monopolistic*.
Column 3: column 1/column 2.

throughout the 110 year period emerges. From appearing between three and eight times as often during the pre-1950 decades, *competitive* has ballooned and now appears fifty-one times as frequently.[6]

Whether or not the adjectives of *competition* and *monopoly* are appearing more or less often relative to their nouns requires a different breakdown of the data, and this is done in Tables 3.4 and 3.5. As Table 3.4 reveals, there was a steady, if gradual rise in the use of *competitive* relative to *competition* as the latter went from being more than four times as common before 1940, to between two and three times as common between 1940 and 1979, to slightly less than twice as common since 1980.[7] Strangely, Table 2.5 shows an *opposite* pattern at work for *monopoly*. From the 1940s through the present there has been an increase in the ratio of occurrences of *monopoly* to occurrences of *monopolistic*, indicating a relative *decline* in the use of the adjective. In the 1940s, the noun appeared about four times as frequently as the adjective. By the 2000s, the noun was appearing nearly thirteen times as frequently. Looking all the way back to 1900 makes the trend more evident still. Over the same time that (as Table 3.4 shows) *competition fell* from occurring eight times as frequently as *competitive* to less than two times as frequent, *monopoly rose* from being six times as frequent as *monopolistic* to over twelve times as frequent.[8] That *competitive* grew in popularity while *monopolistic* was waning in popularity raises the possibility that a new meaning was coming to be associated with *competitive* that led to the much greater use of this word, a new meaning that will receive more consideration at the chapter's end.

Government as ever less *competitive*?

In the last chapter it was shown that government has been referred to as *big* with increasing frequency, while for business, the label of *big* has, if anything,

Table 3.3 Frequency of *competitive* relative to *monopolistic* and *monopolized*

Years	*1*	*2*	*3*
2000–2009	9,830	192	51.20
1990–1999	16,817	422	39.85
1980–1989	16,972	453	37.47
1970–1979	12,714	762	16.69
1960–1969	11,718	501	23.39
1950–1959	10,953	907	12.08
1940–1949	10,299	1,367	7.53
1930–1939	9,046	1,357	6.67
1920–1929	4,598	762	6.03
1910–1919	2,733	540	5.06
1900–1909	1,700	540	3.15

Notes
Column 1: *competitive*.
Column 2: *monopolistic* and *monopolized*.
Column 3: column 1/column 2.

declined slightly. We would also be likely to see a rising tendency to associate *monopoly* with government, and the data shown in Table 3.6 provide evidence that this is indeed so. Columns 1, 2, 4, and 5 provide the raw figures for the occurrence of certain phrases but it is the other three columns (3, 6, and 7) that tell an interesting story.

It comes as no surprise that throughout the 110 year period *competitive* was more common than *monopoly* for the private sector (with column 3 figures thus greater than one) but not for government (with column 6 figures less than one). Government, after all, enjoys a monopoly of power that actors in the private

Table 3.4 Frequency of *competition* relative to *competitive*

Years	*1*	*2*	*3*
2000–2009	18,637	9,830	1.90
1990–1999	31,099	16,817	1.85
1980–1989	33,872	16,972	2.00
1970–1979	28,555	12,714	2.25
1960–1969	28,881	11,718	2.46
1950–1959	28,236	10,953	2.58
1940–1949	24,579	10,299	2.39
1930–1939	43,460	9,046	4.80
1920–1929	28,033	4,598	6.10
1910–1919	17,430	2,733	6.38
1900–1909	13,988	1,700	8.23

Notes
Column 1: *competition*.
Column 2: *competitive*.
Column 3: column 1/column 2.

Table 3.5 Frequency of *monopoly* relative to *monopolistic* and *monopolized*

Years	*1*	*2*	*3*
2000–2009	2,450	192	12.76
1990–1999	4,163	422	9.86
1980–1989	3,680	453	8.12
1970–1979	3,568	762	4.68
1960–1969	3,457	501	6.90
1950–1959	4,802	907	5.29
1940–1949	5,266	1,367	3.85
1930–1939	6,754	1,357	4.98
1920–1929	4,752	762	6.24
1910–1919	3,452	540	6.39
1900–1909	3,342	540	6.19

Notes
Column 1: *monopoly*.
Column 2: *monopolistic* and *monopolized*.
Column 3: column 1/column 2.

sector do not have. But what is of interest here is the pattern of change in these numbers over time.

Column 3 shows that prior to 1980, *competitive industry* (and related expressions) were five times as common as *monopolized industry* (and related expressions) but that since 1980 this difference has risen three-fold with the former now fifteen times as common as the latter. Column 6 shows no similar pattern for government. Prior to 1930, *government monopoly* was about five times as frequent (reflected in the 0.212 figure) as *government competition*. Over the next fifty years *government competition* pulled nearly even, but since then monopoly has again become roughly five times more frequent (reflected in the 0.198 figure).[9]

Column 7 provides a summary. The numbers in this column indicate the amount by which the relative frequency of using *competitive* rather than monopoly to describe the private sector exceeds the same relative frequency in the public sector. Thus the private sector was twenty-four times more likely to be described as *competitive* rather than *monopolized* than was the public sector in the first period. While this number fell to 4.9 in mid-century it has ballooned to 73.7 since 1980.[10]

Does such a change make any sense? The claim that firms having near monopoly power prior to globalization now face considerable competition is often heard but is quite inconsistent with the increasing rates of return enjoyed by these major corporations over the last quarter-century. By some measures of industry concentration, there has been a consolidation and less competition, not more. As Barry C. Lynn argues:

Table 3.6 Frequency of *competitive industry* (and related expressions) relative to *monopolized industry* (and related expressions) and frequency of *government competition* (and related expressions) relative to *government monopoly* (and related expressions)

Years	*1*	*2*	*3*	*4*	*5*	*6*	*7*
1980–2009	849	58	14.6	44	222	0.198	73.7
1930–1979	954	209	4.6	646	682	0.947	4.8
1900–1929	211	41	5.1	73	344	0.212	24.1

Notes

Column 1: *competitive industry, competitive corporation, competitive firm, corporate competition, competition between firms, competition among firms, competition between corporations, competition among corporations, competitive business, business competition, competition between businesses, competition among businesses,* and *business competition.*

Column 2: *monopolized industry, monopoly industry, monopoly corporation, monopoly firm, monopoly business, corporate monopoly,* and *business monopoly.*

Column 3: column 1/column 2.

Column 4: *government competition, competition in government, governments competing, competitive government,* and *competing governments.*

Column 5: *government monopoly, monopoly in government, government monopolizing,* and *monopolizing government.*

Column 6: column 4/column 5.

Column 7: column 3/column 6.

> One of the more pronounced patterns after [the] last wave of monopolization was that it was the countries that boasted of having the most "free-market" policies – the United States, Britain, Australia, and Mexico – that ended up with the greatest concentrations of private governance.
>
> (2010, 14)

At the same time, where governments might have previously acted as monopolists, the trend since the 1970s has been to introduce more active competition, not less. It is thus strange indeed to see *monopoly* ever more associated with government and ever less associated with private businesses. The explanation most likely is to be found in some of the data presented in the last chapter. That data revealed a steady increase in the degree to which *competition* was viewed favorably. It is thus less than a surprise to discover that the *big* bad government has *competitive* withdrawn as a descriptive label and *monopolistic* increased.

To help gain some sense of what might explain the shift toward associating government ever more with monopoly, I inspected a random sample of eighteen *Times* articles from the 1990s in which *monopoly* appeared. Four of these eighteen used *monopoly* metaphorically, and three of these four were clearly negative. William Safire reports on a public library in California "refusing to be pushed around by scholastic monopolists at Harvard, Notre Dame and Hebrew University" (Safire, 1991, A27). Economist Alice H. Amsden advises "welcome[ing] competition for the mainstream's monopoly of advice" ("From," 1993, A21). And after acknowledging that "[b]oys do the greater share of physical bullying," Christina Hoff Sommers adds that "they have no monopoly on hurtful behavior" ("The Preteen," 1999, A15).

Six of the eighteen articles mention government monopoly, none in a remotely favorable way. One *Times* writer praises Mikhail Gorbachev, who "ended the Communist Party's historic monopoly of political power" (Lewis, 1992, A21). Another suggests that in making the transition to capitalism, "the solution" for the then young Russian government, was "to break up the Government's monopoly and privatize the food outlets" ("What," 1992, A21).

The dislike of government monopoly spreads across political ideologies. With a distinctly left-wing view, a *Times* article on conditions in Central America acknowledges that "the Indians were reclaiming some dignity," while also asserting that it was evident that "most lived in appalling destitution while the state oil monopoly and landholders drained the riches of their land" ("The Bishop," 1994, A21). An editorial notes that a Mexican official "did not overcome internal opposition to selling key parts of the state-owned oil monopoly" ("A Plausible," 1995, A26). An article dealing with the O.J. Simpson trial tells us that "the state has no monopoly on carelessness" ("Trails," 1995, A26), a textbook case of damning with faint praise. And advocates of the privatization movement in education managed the following claim:

> Without competition, monopolies are free to impose high prices and shabby products on consumers. Our government employs thousands of bureaucrats

> to bust monopolies in the marketplace. Yet the same government is intent on protecting its own monopoly in education.
>
> ("How to," 1998, A11)

This passage manages to portray the efforts of antitrust enforcers as wasteful (*thousands of bureaucrats*) while simultaneously portraying the *education monopoly* as worth destroying.

Of the remaining articles in my sample, three dealt with traditional instances of unregulated situations that were interpreted as private monopolies – patented drugs, major league baseball, and the meat packing industry. The remaining five articles dealt either with long-ago monopolies, irrelevant in the 1990s, or with government created and regulated monopolies judged to be no longer worth having. Thus one article describes the just retired Interstate Commerce Commission as "[i]nitially created to protect farmers and communities from the monopoly power of railroad barons" ("The I.C.C.," 1996, A14). Another reports that "[i]n 1982, with the breakup of the AT&T monopoly, we were permitted to choose long-distance companies" ("New," 1991, A15). There is the fear expressed that a proposed action "would scare others out of entering the local market, entrenching a monopoly, Nynex, which has a dismal customer-service record" ("Challenging," 1997). Still another welcomes deregulation of utilities, with the reminder that "to introduce competition to the monopoly-ridden electric power industry may eventually give consumers a wider range of choices" ("Environmental" 1998, A16).

More *competition* and less *cooperation*

Though it may not be obvious, the two noted opposites of *competition* – *monopoly* and *cooperation* – really share much in common. Within a competitive industry, a firm is not motivated to act for the benefit of other firms. Rather than *cooperate*, they *compete*. For the firms in an industry to join forces and become one is for the many firms that might otherwise be competing with each other to abandon this stance and agree to contribute to the production of a product and to act in ways that are in the interest of all.[illegible] Thus, *monopoly* might be said to require lots of *cooperation* between agents and might be understood as just a special case of cooperation that emerges from *competition*. More often than not, however, the use of *cooperation* has nothing at all to do with monopoly.

Table 3.7 shows the number of occurrences of *competition* and *cooperation* in the *New York Times*, by decade, since the turn of the last century. Analysis of the change through time in the relative use of these two words again provides a curious story. *Competition* fell in relative usage over the first half-century from being 3.3 times as frequent as *cooperation* in the 1920s, to just 0.7 times as frequent in the 1940s. Since the 1950s, however, there has been a consistent movement in favor of *competition*, from being just about as frequent as *cooperation* in the 1950s to being three times as common in the 2000s.

Table 3.7 Frequency of *competition* relative to *cooperation*

Years	*1*	*2*	*3*
2000–2009	18,637	6,089	3.06
1990–1999	31,099	9,980	3.12
1980–1989	33,872	13,076	2.59
1970–1979	28,555	15,606	1.83
1960–1969	28,881	17,571	1.64
1950–1959	28,236	26,076	1.08
1940–1949	24,579	34,331	0.72
1930–1939	43,460	32,905	1.32
1920–1929	28,033	20,632	1.36
1910–1919	17,430	10,701	1.63
1900–1909	13,988	4,221	3.31

Notes
Column 1: *competition*.
Column 2: *cooperation*.
Column 3: column 1/column 2.

Table 3.8 represents an attempt to account for the possibility that a substitution of teamwork for cooperation may account for some of the change in the relative frequency of *competition* and *cooperation*. *Teamwork* has certainly grown in usage relative to *cooperation*. But including this word in the column 2 count and including *rivalry* in the column 1 count makes little difference in the century long trend. With *rivalry* being much more frequently used than *teamwork*, the ratios are larger in every decade shown, but the overall pattern of change remains basically what it was in Table 3.7.[12] Once again the movement was away from

Table 3.8 Frequency of *competition* and *rivalry* relative to *cooperation* and *teamwork*

Years	*1*	*2*	*3*
2000–2009	24,595	6,474	3.80
1990–1999	39,256	10,779	3.64
1980–1989	42,766	13,651	3.13
1970–1979	38,838	16,073	2.42
1960–1969	38,140	18,032	2.12
1950–1959	37,143	26,711	1.39
1940–1949	32,731	35,085	0.93
1930–1939	54,930	33,400	1.64
1920–1929	37,874	21,063	1.80
1910–1919	24,510	10,893	2.25
1900–1909	19,859	4,254	4.67

Notes
Column 1: *competition* and *rivalry*.
Column 2: *cooperation* and *teamwork*.
Column 3: column 1/column 2.

competition from the 1900s through the 1940s, and ever more in the direction of *competition* ever since.

Table 3.9 shows trends in the specifically economic meanings of *competition* and *cooperation*. As indicated below the table, only competition between firms and cooperation and agreements across firms are being counted. While no clear pattern emerges through the 1960s, a strong shift in the direction of competition again emerges in the years since. From being just 1.2 times as common as cooperation in the 1960s, competition became twice as common in the 1970s and fully four times as common in the 2000s. Table 3.10 adds *rivalry* and *teamwork* to the analysis without affecting to any extent the pattern already described. We can conclude that a long-term trend is at work that makes *competition* ever more common than *cooperation*.

To this point nouns have been the focus of concern. Table 3.11 analyzes the century long trends in the use of the related adjectives *competitive* and *cooperative*. The trend here is similar to what the earlier tables revealed. While *cooperative* rose in relative significance through the 1920s, it has fallen ever since. From being just 0.6 as common as *cooperative* in the 1920s, *competitive* caught up to *cooperative* in the 1940s and has been on a steady rise ever since. During the 2000s, *competitive* has appeared three times as often as *cooperative* a magnitude of difference more than twice than anything that appeared in any decade before 1980.

Comparing now the growth in the relative use of *competition* with the growth in the relative use of *competitive* reveals something of a mystery. The relative use of *competition* was 2.6 times greater in the 2000s than in the 1930s, the

Table 3.9 Frequency of *competition among firms* (and related expressions) relative to *cooperation among firms* (and related expressions)

Years	*1*	*2*	*3*
2000–2009	130	32	4.06
1990–1999	235	71	3.31
1980–1989	182	72	2.53
1970–1979	121	61	1.98
1960–1969	88	72	1.22
1950–1959	101	59	1.71
1940–1949	80	39	2.05
1930–1939	87	69	1.26
1920–1929	68	55	1.24
1910–1919	39	27	1.44
1900–1909	32	18	1.78

Notes

Column 1: *competition among firms*, *competition across firms*, *inter-firm competition*, and *business competition*.

Column 2: *cooperation among firms*, *cooperation across firms*, *inter-firm cooperation*, *business cooperation*, *agreements across firms*, *agreements among firms*, *inter-firm agreements*, and *business agreements*.

Column 3: column 1/column 2.

relative use of *competitive* fully 8.5 times as great. Comparison of the 2000s with the 1940s tells a similar story, though less pronounced, with the relative frequency of *competition* growing by a factor of 4.6, while the relative frequency of *competitive* grew by a factor of 6.7. The ProQuest database shows a rate of growth nearly as impressive, with Table 3.12 pointing to *competitive* steadily gaining on *cooperative* over the thirty-year period shown.[13]

Table 3.10 Frequency of *competition among firms* and *rivalry among firms* (and related expressions) relative to *cooperation among firms* and *teamwork among firms* (and related expressions)

Years	*1*	2	3
2000–2009	170	32	5.31
1990–1999	302	72	4.19
1980–1989	246	73	3.37
1970–1979	175	61	2.87
1960–1969	136	73	1.86
1950–1959	170	60	2.83
1940–1949	134	41	3.27
1930–1939	180	71	2.54
1920–1929	136	55	2.47
1910–1919	87	27	3.22
1900–1909	90	18	5.00

Notes
Column 1: *competition among firms, competition across firms, inter-firm competition, business competition, rivalry among firms, rivalry across firms, inter-firm rivalry,* and *business rivalry.*
Column 2: *cooperation among firms, cooperation across firms, inter-firm cooperation, business cooperation, agreements across firms, agreements among firms, inter-firm agreements, business agreements, teamwork among firms, teamwork across firms, inter-firm teamwork,* and *business teamwork.*
Column 3: column 1/column 2.

Table 3.11 Frequency of *competitive* relative to *cooperative*

Years	*1*	2	3
2000–2009	9,830	2,880	3.41
1990–1999	16,817	5,489	3.06
1980–1989	16,972	8,345	2.03
1970–1979	12,714	8,172	1.56
1960–1969	11,718	8,042	1.46
1950–1959	10,953	9,332	1.17
1940–1949	10,299	9,687	1.06
1930–1939	9,046	11,740	0.77
1920–1929	4,598	7,441	0.62
1910–1919	2,733	2,132	1.28
1900–1909	1,700	953	1.78

Notes
Column 1: *competitive.*
Column 2: *cooperative.*
Column 3: column 1/column 2.

Table 3.12 Frequency of *competitive* relative to *cooperative* since 1980 (data from ProQuest)

Years	*1*	*2*	*3*
2000–2009	2,144,988	485,499	4.42
1990–1999	1,032,167	311,589	3.31
1980–1989	197,530	76,928	2.57

Notes
Column 1: *competitive*.
Column 2: *cooperative*.
Column 3: column 1/column 2.

A rise in the popularity of a word is not sufficient evidence that it is regarded with favor. As scholars (particularly those lacking citations to their work) sometimes like to point out, there is a problem with using citations as a measure of the worth of scholarship. It is possible for an article or book that becomes notorious for its poor methodology, logic, writing style, or whatever else, to be cited precisely because of these shortcomings. Similarly, a word's popularity does not assure that the word is favorably regarded.

Table 3.13 offers some strong evidence that the rising popularity of *competition* and *competitive* has coincided with a more favorable attitude toward these words. Column 1 in the table tallies the number of times that *competition* was described as *needed, healthy, desirable, necessary, good, constructive, productive*, or *perfect*. Column 2 shows the number of times it was preceded

Table 3.13 Frequency of positive descriptions of *competition* relative to negative descriptions of *competition*

Years	*1*	*2*	*3*
2000–2009	62	9	6.89
1990–1999	91	34	2.68
1980–1989	112	94	1.19
1970–1979	78	84	0.93
1960–1969	70	111	0.63
1950–1959	66	79	0.84
1940–1949	81	77	1.05
1930–1939	87	311	0.28
1920–1929	59	111	0.53
1910–1919	70	76	0.92
1900–1909	48	46	1.04

Notes
Column 1: *needed competition, healthy competition, desirable competition, necessary competition, good competition*, and *construction competition*.
Column 2: *unneeded competition, unnecessary competition, destructive competition, damaging competition, imperfect competition, unhealthy competition, excessive competition*, and *harmful competition*.
Column 3: column 1/column 2.

by *unneeded*, *unhealthy*, *undesirable*, *unnecessary*, *bad*, *destructive*, *damaging*, *imperfect*, *excessive*, or *harmful*. As might be expected, the tendency toward a negative description was strongest during the depression-plagued 1930s, with the positive descriptions occurring only 0.29 as often as the negative. But for five of the first eight decades of the 20th century, negative descriptions were more common than positive and in the other three decades (1900s, 1940s, and 1970s) were nearly equal. Combining all decades prior to 1980, positive descriptions occurred just 65 percent as often as negative descriptions. Since 1980, in contrast, the positive descriptions have been twice as frequent as the negative. And the trend has been steadily upward during these years, as the numbers in column 3 of the table show.[14] Because these results were so strong while the raw numbers were smaller than in any of the previous tables, I again went to the broader data databases, ProQuest and AHN, for some corroboration of these results. Table 3.14 draws from the other sources, and besides having larger raw numbers shows an even greater trend than reflected in the *Times*.

Substituting *competitive* for *competition* yields numbers that support the trends shown in both Tables 3.13 and 3.14 and also supports the claim that *competitive* tends to be even more positively regarded than *competition* in the *Times*, favorable descriptions went from being four times more frequent than unfavorable prior to 1980 to fully sixty-six times as frequent since. And the other sources corroborate this trend. In AHN there were twenty-two favorable and fourteen unfavorable descriptions (a 1.57 ratio) while in ProQuest newspapers since 1980 the favorable descriptions have been thirty times as frequent as the unfavorable. As still another bit of evidence, not only is *competitive* a generally flattering description, it is, unsurprisingly, more likely to be described as *ours*. While *the* precedes *monopolistic* sixty-two times as frequently as *our* does and precedes *non-competitive* sixty-six times as often, it precedes *competitive* only 10 times as often.

Table 3.14 Frequency of positive descriptions of *competition* relative to negative descriptions of *competition* (data since 1980 from ProQuest and pre-1980 from AHN)

Years	*1*	*2*	*3*
2000–2009	26,951	2,609	10.33
1990–1999	12,134	1,671	7.26
1980–1989	2,353	426	5.52
1900–1923	362	387	0.94

Notes

Column 1: *needed competition*, *healthy competition*, *desirable competition*, *necessary competition*, *good competition*, and *constructive competition*.

Column 2: *unneeded competition*, *unnecessary competition*, *destructive competition*, *damaging competition*, *imperfect competition*, *unhealthy competition*, *excessive competition*, and *harmful competition*.

Column 3: column 1/column 2.

To provide some insights into what may have occurred over the years to change the attitude toward *competition*, I took a much closer look at the occurrences of *destructive competition* that appeared in the 1920s and compared these with what appeared in the 2000s. *Destructive competition* appeared fifty-seven times in the 1920s. A random selection of ten of these revealed a quite different meaning of the expression then than now.[15]

One article argues against anti-trust while still acknowledging that it had at one time been useful: "The destructive competition of the eighties led to trusts and combinations which the Sherman Anti-Trust Law of 1890 was intended to regulate. Destructive competition has given way very largely to constructive competition" ("Call," 1922, 34). In another article, the Interstate Commerce Commission is offered as one way in which to counter harmful competition: "'Destructive competition may afford a temporary benefit ... but this does not compensate for its far-reaching and serious adverse effect upon the interests of the carrier and of the shipping public as a whole'" ("Can't," 1923, 27). And a 1924 article states that "Motor-truck operating companies are compelled to operate largely under the contract system on account of the destructive competition of competing motor-truck companies" ("Motor," 1924, xxii).

New technology is identified as the culprit in an article appearing a year later when the future of live theater is pessimistically assessed and the conclusion reached that "radio is only the latest element in this destructive competition" ("Saharas," 1925, 16). And lack of proper foresight appears responsible when mention is made of "waste due to destructive competition of people who exhaust their capital through lack of understanding of the fundamentals of their business" ("A Top-Heavy," 1925, E6).

As the decade proceeded, there remained no shortage of the belief that unregulated markets could result in destructive competition. The American Bankers' Association saw a need for regulation of the trucking industry modeled after railroad regulation, arguing that "[i]n States where there is little or no regulation, soundly operated trucking companies are forced to compete with irresponsible operators who cut rates" and that "[l]imitation of motor transportation companies would reduce vehicles on highways, reduce wear on the roads, and, by eliminating destructive competition, put commercial motor transportation on a firmer basis" ("Advocates," 1926, 27). And two years after this the Chamber of Commerce called for the "[p]rotection for American agriculture products subject to destructive competition from abroad" ("Merchants," 1928, 30).

Compared with the fifty-seven times that *destructive competition* appeared in the 1920s, the expression was used only nine times in the 2000s. The deregulation that began thirty years ago has naturally lessened the number of agencies whose job might have been to seek out such competition, but one would think that individual actors in the marketplace might be even more prone to draw attention to actions that they regarded as destructive of their own position in the economy, irrespective of whether they regarded these actions as legitimate or not. But curiously, the few instances of *destructive competition* that have appeared have not been examples of what is usually meant by market failure.

In an article describing tax changes planned by Russian president Vladimir Putin, it is alleged that "[a] destructive competition to raise revenue rages among Russia's local, regional, and federal authorities" ("Russia's," 2000, WK10). Four years later there is mention of "destructive competition between police officers and firefighters" (Purnick, 2004, B8). And in a lawsuit against the State of New Jersey we are told that the plaintiff "claims that New Jersey Transit has violated its 1979 charter by engaging in 'destructive competition' with a private bus line" (Bruder, 2004, NJ6).

What stands out is that in all three of these instances it was government that was *competing destructively*! As still another example, in a 2006 article appears the following: "American concerns about runaway arms races are very likely to be overshadowed by American concerns about the need to prevent a destructive competition for scarce fossil-fuel resources with India and China." ("Globalization," 2006, E13).

Only once over the last decade has a use of *destructive competition* in the 1920s sense appeared, when an airline industry consultant stated that, "'When you become a commodity industry, as steel and autos and airlines have done, then you have a lot of destructive competition'" ("Maynard," 2004, C1). While all nine of the fifty-seven instances of *destructive competition* from the 1920s that were quoted involved the private sector, it is remarkable that just one from the 2000s did, especially so since the possibility of truly dangerous spillover costs has only risen to awareness since the 1920s.

The contemporary amnesia about the possibility of competition being destructive is especially puzzling when it is considered that the prisoner's dilemma game has had such an impact over the last sixty years. Starting with the classic game theory work of Von Neumann and Morgenstern (1953) and John Nash (1950, 1951) there was for the first time a formalization of the hunch of countless thinkers over the centuries that competition could, given certain circumstances, be unfavorable to all. Let there be a situation in which two players must each choose one of two possibilities. Further suppose that the payoff to each player depends not only upon his own choice but also upon what the other player has chosen. When a prisoner's dilemma prevails, the action that is rational for each player, regardless of what the other player might do, leads to an outcome that leaves each player worse off than he or she would be had each chosen the other possible action.

Students are generally introduced to the prisoner's dilemma in their introductory microeconomics course. Yet strangely enough, the context in which it is introduced is typically the study of oligopolistic behavior. That two firms would have trouble colluding is neatly demonstrated by showing that a less than monopolistic price is in each firm's interest regardless of whether its rival firm charges the monopoly price or a lower price. With each firm thus charging the lower price, profits for each are lower than what they would be had each firm charged the monopoly price.

Note how this differs from most prisoner's dilemma games. Typically, only the players themselves are affected by the game and from a broader social standpoint self-interested competition is thus destructive, since there are losers but no winners. But in this particular prisoner's dilemma involving oligopolists, it is to the advantage of the broader society that the players fall into the trap. The oligopolists will suffer but the broader society benefits as powerful firms price in a way that is closer to the competitive ideal than is the case for a monopolist. Students are not sufficiently reminded that this is a very special case indeed and that the world is filled with instances where competitive behaviors leave everyone worse off.

Becoming more *competitive*: good by definition?

We are now in a position to draw some interpretations from three trends up to this point: (1) the rise of *competitive* relative to *competition*, (2) the fall of *monopolistic* relative to *monopoly*, and (3) the earlier noted rise in the positive description of *competitive*. Why has *competitive* become so often heard and so favorable? What elements of society are served by this rhetorical development?

Among economists, extending at least back to the writings of Adam Smith, *competition* has been the defining feature of effectively functioning markets. And whether one is speaking of perfect competition or the later introduced *monopolistic competition*, competitive industries are necessarily comprised of many firms. Thus at least among economists, *competitive* was originally nothing more than a way of describing such industries and the firms comprising them. Describing a firm as *competitive*, it should be noted, was to say nothing about the firm considered in isolation. A firm that was *competitive* one day could become a monopolist the next if all its fellow firms were to disappear. To speak about a competitive firm was to thus draw on the context in which the firm found itself, not the firm's internal attributes.

When *competitive* appeared in the *Times* in the 1850s, it carried with it a negative rather than positive connotation. *Competitive*, it appears, was not a description that a person, firm, or nation would seek, but was rather something to be avoided or overcome. An article from 1852 speaks of a place "where the icthyological apothegm of eat or be eaten maintains in the depths of competitive strife" ("France," 1852, 2), a colorful reference to the not always pleasant outcome for fish engaged in competitive struggles. In a letter appearing in 1852, the following appears: "it is possible enough that the competitive principle may be brought into play in a fashion that even the undersellers may not approve" ("England," 1852, 4). The implication is that the competitive principle will *obviously* meet with the disapproval of those who lose out by charging a higher price and *may even* not be favored by the underseller. Clearly, being *competitive* was seen as *destructive* to at least some of the market participants.

Writing in the same year, another *Times* writer found the fact that labor in Europe was *competitive* and took this to be harmful to labor, claiming that: "[C]ompetitive labor, conjoined with the illimitable power of machinery … [has]

so deranged the stability of prices. With such a state of things, the laborer cannot contend, and … he is left to the alternative of revolution or emigration" ("The Homestead," 1852, 2). And five years later the troubles faced by the railroads in the U.S. were said to arise "partly from neglect on the part of the financial authorities, and partly from an unduly competitive spirit" ("The Great," 1857, 4).

By the 1920s, outright negative meanings of *competitive* were rare but the positive meanings we have grown so familiar with today were also uncommon. Exactly what *competitive* meant when it appeared in the *Times* in this period can be initially quite confusing. A 1920 ad states that three salesmen "[w]ould like to represent a few high-grade non-competitive firms" ("Display Ad 135," 1920, 26). Another ad, this one from 1930, announces the availability of a "floor in exclusive women's specialty shop; excellent opportunity for non-competitive firm to benefit by marvelous clientele" ("Display Ad 204," 1930, W12). In these instances (and there are many more like these) *competitive* appears to define a relationship between the parties. If we substitute *competing* for *competitive*, the writer's intent is more understandable to the modern reader. The salesmen are expressing the desire to represent only one firm per industry. This sort of use of *competitive* appeared as late as 1963 when mention was made of employment contracts that specified "employees will not work for competitive firms for a given period" ("Who Owns," 1963, 11).

If nothing more were at work here than the replacement of *competing* by *competitive*, this would be nothing more than a curiosity. But something more is at work. Using *competing* today in contexts where *competitive* was previously used would naturally suggest that the use of *competing* would have grown in usage relative to *competitive*. But the facts say otherwise. In the 1920s, *competitive* was used 1.3 times as much as *competing*. By the 1990s, this number hadn't fallen but instead had risen to 3.1. The fact that the relatively slow-growing *competing* was substituting for *competitive* can be best explained by the increasing reliance on the latter to mean *successful* or *capable of winning*. In short, the widening definition (and use) of *competitive* required that it give up some of the contexts in which it was previously used.

Around the very time that competitive was used to mean *successful*, faith in free market capitalism was plummeting. By stating that "Competitive wage reductions, competitive tariffs, competitive liquidation of foreign assets, competitive currency deflation, competitive economy campaigns, competitive contractions of new development – all are beggar-my-neighbor description" (Merz, 1932, BR10), Keynes illustrates how the normative shading of *competitive* was certainly capable of going in a negative direction.

By the end of the 1930s and through the 1940s, increasing use of *competitive* tended not to denote *destructive*, as in the above passage, but *successful*. Department store chain Montgomery Ward announces its opposition to a recently recommended closed shop rule for its employees via a full page ad in the *Times* that announces, "Wards desires … to maintain management by ownership, to remain competitive, and to leave its employees free to belong or not to belong to a union as they wish" ("Display Ad 15," 1943, 13). Around the same time, the U.S.

Gypsum Company took out an ad opposing a ruling of the War Labor Board that gave strength to the union by announcing that "The company desires ... to remain competitive, and to leave its employees the freedom preserved for them by the Constitutions and the Bill of Rights" ("Display Ad 31," 1943, 15). Even a head of the Communist Party in Hungary was employing the new use of *competitive* to defend the Soviet system. As quoted in the *Times*, he reasons that " '[w]e must remain competitive. We can only do this when we accept the new form of agriculture,' " this new form being the "Sovietization of agriculture" ("Hungary," 1948, 32).

Table 3.15 shows the 110 year trend in the use of *stay competitive* and *remain competitive* relative to the use of *competitive*. (Occurrences of the phrases prior to 1940 were so few that they have been allowed to comprise a single category.) As the data indicates, these phrases have gone from occurring just once every 2,259 times that *competitive* appeared to once every thirty times.[16] And as some reflection should indicate, the use of these phrases almost always has a normative component. Seriously questioning whether one should *remain competitive* has come to seem as odd as questioning whether one's business should continue to exist.

I was able to find a few instances prior to 1950 in which *stay competitive* was not automatically in the interest of those remaining competitive. An article titled "Financial dailies negotiate merger" (1930: 45) discusses ongoing merger talks between the *Wall Street Journal* and *The Wall Street News*. The merger of the two newspapers was clearly seen as something that the papers' owners desired to do. In the articles second paragraph the reader is informed that "[t]he news ticker services of Dow, Jones & Co. and of the New York News Bureau will remain competitive." When the context of this sentence is considered it becomes clear that we are being told that "they will continue to compete with one other rather than merge." We are not being told that they will each *remain successful*.

Table 3.15 Frequency of *competitive* relative to *stay competitive* and *remain competitive*

Years	*1*	*2*	*3*
2000–2009	9,830	320	30.7
1990–1999	16,817	636	26.4
1980–1989	16,972	551	30.8
1970–1979	12,714	177	71.8
1960–1969	11,718	195	60.1
1950–1959	10,953	51	214.8
1940–1949	10,209	13	785.3
1900–1939	18,077	8	2,259.6

Notes
Column 1: *competitive*.
Column 2: *stay competitive* and *remain competitive*.
Column 3: column 1/column 2.

Dictionaries differ in their definitions of *competitive*. Some make no mention of *successful* and *able*. In its second edition, *The Oxford English Dictionary* defines it as "Of, pertaining to, or characterized by competition; organized by competition" (1989). The second edition of *Webster's New International Dictionary of the English Language* offers much the same, namely "Of, or pertaining to competition; based on, used in, or resulting from competition" (1956). There is no mention of being *successful* or *capable of succeeding*. And it is not just those dictionaries based outside the United States that omit this more recent meaning. The fourth edition of *The American Heritage Dictionary of the English Language* (2000) mentions "liking competition or inclined to compete" without mentioning a successful outcome of the competition in its definition.

The earliest dictionary that I found that included *successful* among its definitions was the first edition of *The Random House Dictionary of the English Language* (1966, 300). According to it, *competitive* can mean "able to attain the desired response or results in a competitive situation, as the prices, services or quality of products of a business organization." That Random House was the apparent first may be in part explained by the inertia of the earlier dictionaries, since issuing a new edition did not necessarily mean a thorough rethinking of all previous definitions. Interestingly, it was *The New Oxford American Dictionary* that, unlike its British counterpart, defined *competitive* in the new way, namely, "as good as or better than others of a comparable nature" (2001, 350). Some dictionaries were less categorical in their introduction of the new definition. While for Random House, "competitive" could mean "able to attain the desired response," others cast a wider net. The *Chambers Concise Dictionary* defined competitive "(of e.g. price) such as to give a chance of successful results" (1991, 210). No guarantee of success, just a chance. The 11th edition of *Merriam-Webster's Collegiate Dictionary* (2003, 253) defines *competitive* as "inclined, desiring, or suited to compete." To be *suited* can, of course, be subject to a range of interpretations, but usually does not mean the competitor necessarily sees much chance of coming out on top. In short, *Merriam-Webster* would be prepared to offer its definition of *competitive* to a sports team that is universally regarded as incapable of finishing first, whereas *Random House*, for example, would have to withhold the *competitive* description from such a team.[17] An even stronger link between *competitiveness* and success is made by Robert Z. Lawrence. Writing in the conservative *Concise Encyclopedia of Economics*, Lawrence puts to rest any notion that the worthiness of competitiveness might be questioned. In his words,

> "Competitiveness," particularly with reference to an entire economy, is hard to define. Indeed, competitiveness, like love or democracy, actually has several meanings. And the question "Is America competitive" has at least three interpretations: how well is the United States performing compared to other countries? How well has America performed in international trade? Are we doing the best we can?
>
> (Lawrence, 2002)

The nature of the forces behind the expanded definition of *competitive* is complex and more than can be taken up here. We should, however, take very seriously Nunberg's claim that "Most of the words [conservatives have] made central to their narratives involve either blurring two senses of a word or using a word in a new way while pretending that it still has its old meaning" (2006, 152). While it is unlikely that the above quote from Lawrence reflects an awareness on his part of the dual meanings of *competitive*, consider the propaganda effects that these dual meanings have likely had. Prior to the introduction of *competitive* as *successful*, economists generally defined the word one way ("an industry with many firms," "any firm within a multi-firm industry") while the general public tended to define it another way, namely, "trying hard to succeed." While these definitions are quite different, I am unaware of any mischief done by conflating these uses. Trouble begins when the more recent usage becomes prevalent.

Being *competitive* in the sense of *successful*, if conflated with *competitive* in the sense of *trying hard*, can create a habit of thinking that *to try* is *to succeed.* To state that a firm, or an athlete, was very *competitive* would seem odd to many, if accompanied by another statement that the athlete had done poorly. This can have the unfortunate effect (common with many students) of believing that *trying hard* is a sufficient condition for receiving an A. At a broader level, it can create the illusion that creating opportunities for excluded groups to participate "on a level playing field" will result in their success. Since they can now be *competitive* in the sense of *trying hard* they can be *competitive* in the sense of *winning*, can't they?

As ideologically loaded as the above may seem, there is an even more curious effect of the introduction of the new meaning of *competitive*. Paradoxically enough, the firm that manages to become the only seller (an economist's *monopolist*) or the firm that manages to be one of just a few sellers (an economist's *oligopolist*) now qualifies for the title of *very competitive firm* since it is the only one (or one of a few) that managed to survive the competitive struggle. Amazingly, the firm that is least able to be described as *competitive* in the original sense of being a single firm in a sea of many firms is now able to be described as *competitive* in the sense of being *victorious*. This is a coup d'état writ large. The Achilles heel of market advocates – the concern that competitive industries would disappear as concentration and monopolization increase – has been turned on its head. The fiercest advocates of *competition* can now point to the large monopolist and large oligopolist as a clear example of what it means to be *competitive*.

We now have an explanation for the paradoxical trends in Tables 3.4 and 3.5 that were mentioned earlier. To again summarize, *competition* went from being mentioned approximately seven times more often than *competitive* to just above 1.2 times more often a century later. But *monopoly* went from appearing approximately seven times more often than *monopolistic* to *twelve* times more often. As the discussion suggests, two forces explain the relative rise of *competitive*. First, it has taken on a new meaning – *successful* – and is increasingly used to mean this. Second, firms that might have been described as *monopolistic* at one time (and might still fit this definition) can and are also now described as *competitive*. Thus when an adjective is needed to refer to a monopolist, where *monopolistic* may have been selected once, *competitive* is an option now, an option that places the monopolist in a far more flattering light.

And when it comes to government, there appears to be at work a trend to stray from its role as a cooperative solution to social problems to just one more institution through which competition may be carried out. The recent struggle over health care reform reached a stage where the opposing sides fine-tuned their rhetorical strategies and these stories served as one more indication of the high status that competition holds. The single payer option for health insurance stands as one example where a cooperative solution is called upon to provide a solution for the failure of the competitive system. Private health insurance has risen astronomically in price for reasons having to do with market failure. Competitive pressures lead those facing the highest medical bills to be excluded from coverage and lead to unusually high competitive marketing cost, just to name two of these failures.

Yet as sponsors of the *public option* made their case, what did they say? That such an option can be justified on the grounds that it will make the industry more *competitive*. The very possibility of calling upon the language of *cooperation* or of making the case for a public monopoly solution to destructive competition was simply off the table. Even government has, in short, been advertised for its great abilities to provide more competition. And as the next chapter will show, citizens too have increasingly been treated as consumers.

4 Consumers over citizens

From *citizen* to *consumer*

Just when the age of *consumerism* began is debatable. Historian William Leach (1993) focuses on 1880 to 1930 as the transitional period when the rate of emigration from countryside and small town to large city took off and when technological and cultural changes combined to shift the national mindset from the work ethic outlined by Max Weber to the consumer ethic. For Leach,

> This highly individualistic conception of democracy emphasized self-pleasure and self-fulfillment over community or civic well-being. As the older grounds for economic and political freedom were eroding (ownership of property and control of work), newer and "better" grounds were coming into being.
>
> (1993, 6)

From the perspective of consumerism, the 1930s and 1940s were a temporary pause as the Great Depression, World War II, and economic anxieties immediately after brought a return of the more Calvinist dispositions to scrimp, save, and defer short-term gratification. Perhaps for this reason, it is the 1950s which stand today as the decade when consumerism truly took off.[1]

From the time of Bernard Mandeville – writing a half-century before Adam Smith's *Wealth of Nations* – mainstream economists have been invoking the *self-interest* assumption.[2] Just what is meant by *self-interest* has never been successfully resolved. To some, it means little more than "acting in a way that one prefers to act" while to others it is roughly synonymous with *selfishness*.[3] That reference to *self-interest* has spread into the wider culture is clear. In Table 4.1 appear the long-term trends in *New York Times* articles.

Note that *selfish* has gone from being six times more common in the early 20th century to just slightly more common today.[4] Does this represent nothing more than a greater penetration of economic rhetoric into the broader culture? Is it perhaps a trend toward treating more delicately, or euphemistically, the act of being strictly focused on the self? A closer examination of individual cases will help to answer these questions.

The fall in status of the government might be expected to spill over to the general public in their governmental – *civic* – capacity. And this indeed does appear to be the case. It has been hard not to notice in recent years the tendency for government agencies to refer to those they serve as their *customers* or *consumers*. So too in the private realm that previously regarded those it served as something other than *customers*, the language has changed. As just one example, the policy of colleges and universities to speak of student as *customers* appears to be growing.[5]

Column 1 in Table 4.2 shows the number of times that *buyers*, *customers*, or *consumers* appeared in *Times* articles over the three periods shown. Column 2 does the same for *voters* and *citizens*. Column 3 divides the column 1 numbers by the column 2 numbers to show the long-term trend in the relative use of these labels. As the numbers reveal, the words suggestive of the *private self* appeared approximately as often as words describing the *public self* between 1900 and 1929. Between 1930 and 1979 the private self appeared 30 percent more often while over the last forty years *buyers*, *consumers*, and *customers* have been encountered twice as often as *voters* and *citizens*.

Table 4.1 Frequency of *selfish* relative to *self-interested*

Years	*1*	*2*	*3*
1980–2009	4,394	3,269	1.34
1930–1979	10,637	4,495	2.37
1900–1929	7,929	1,333	5.95

Notes
Column 1: *selfish* and *selfishness*.
Column 2: *self-interest* and *self-interested*.
Column 3: column 1/column 2.

Table 4.2 Frequency of positive descriptions of *consumers* relative to positive descriptions of *voters*

Years	*1*	*2*	*3*	*4*	*5*	*6*	*7*	*8*
1980–2009	213,557	110,554	1.93	491	170	2.89	434.9	650.3
1930–1979	304,338	229,949	1.32	205	252	0.81	1,484.6	912.5
1900–1929	101,381	99,704	1.02	12	68	0.18	8,448.4	1,466.2

Notes
Column 1: *buyer*, *consumer* and *customer*.
Column 2: *voter* and *citizen*.
Column 3: column 1/column 2.
Column 4: *informed buyer*, *informed consumer*, *informed customer*, *sophisticated buyer*, *sophisticated consumer*, *sophisticated customer*, *knowledgeable consumer*, *knowledgeable customer*, *demanding buyer*, *demanding consumer*, *demanding customer*, *educated buyer*, *educated consumer*, and *educated customer*.
Column 5: *informed voter*, *informed citizen*, *sophisticated voter*, *sophisticated citizen*, *demanding voter*, *demanding citizen*, *educated voter* and *educated citizen*.
Column 6: column 4/column 5.
Column 7: column 1/column 4.
Column 8: column 2/column 5.

The increasing popularity of the *consumer* has, significantly, been accompanied by an increasing tendency to speak well of her. In the fourth column appears the number of times certain positive adjectives (informed, sophisticated, knowledgeable, demanding, educated) were used to describe her. Column 5 presents the number of times these same descriptions were applied to voters or citizens. Column 6 divides the column 4 figure by the column 5 figures, and reveals that *the positive description of the consumer (or customer or buyer) went from appearing just 18 per cent as often as the positive description of the voter (or citizen) in the first period to appearing nearly three times as often over the last three decades, a fifteen-fold relative increase.*

The last columns show the trends in the likelihood of seeing a positive adjective describe the consumer and a positive adjective describe the voter. To illustrate, the first figure in column 7 reveals that every 435 times that *buyer*, *consumer*, or *customer* appeared, one of the favorable listed adjectives also appeared. The trends revealed through these two columns are extraordinary. Between 1900 and 1929, *voter* or *citizen* was nearly six times more likely to be preceded by a positive adjective than was *buyer*, *customer*, or *consumer*. By mid-century, they were just about 1.6 times more likely. And since 1980, things have flipped, with the *buyer*, *customer*, *consumer* 1.5 more likely to be favorably described than the *voter*, *citizen*. Not only has the private self been steadily more mentioned in the *Times*, he has been steadily more likely to be praised as well.[6] The extent of the decline in regard for the voter has not gone nearly far enough for public-choice theorist Bryan Caplan, who maintains that "democracy … is widely *over*-rated [his emphasis] not only by the public but by most economists too" (2007, 4).

And limiting attention to the public self alone, the more *private* side of this public self has been gaining relative to the more *public* side as well. Though I thought it made sense to look at two words – *voter* and *citizen* – to represent the public self, some further consideration led me to realize that one of these fits more comfortably with the contemporary market sensibility. A voter has much more in common with a customer than does a citizen. A voter, after all, acts privately, going behind a curtain to register her preference. A voter may, it is true, take the broad public good into account when making a decision, but need not. A voter, in short, has no real obligation to behave in any particular way. The drop in voting percentages in the United States reflects gains in the ethos that says "why vote if you can't make any difference." Most significantly, the mantra of the marketplace, *choice*, describes what a voter does. As surely as consumer preferences are registered through the act of *choosing*, so too does the voter choose one candidate rather than another.

Citizenship, in contrast, is an ongoing state. What one does in that capacity is self-determined but to imagine being an acting citizen while having no concerns beyond one's own welfare would make no sense. The individual need not be a strictly self-centered voter, but can be. In contrast, the individual simply cannot act in a strictly self-centered way in her role as a citizen.

Table 4.3 has the same basic layout as Table 4.2. Now, however, the number of occurrences of just *voter(s)* appears in column 1 and the number of just *citizen(s)* in column 2. The similarity to the trends in the earlier table is what we might expect. Column 3 of the earlier Table 4.2 showed an approximate doubling of the *consumer, customer, buyer* relative to the *voter, citizen.* Column 3 of Table 4.3 shows a near tripling in the use of *voter* relative to the use of *citizen,* from 30 percent as often in the first period, to 82 percent as often most recently. Column 6 of the earlier Table 4.2 showed a huge rise in positive descriptions of the *consumer, customer, buyer* relative to the positive descriptions of the *voter, citizen.* And column 6 of Table 4.3 just as surely shows a strong shift in the direction of the *voter* relative to the *citizen* (though it still remains slightly more common to see the *citizen* praised than the *voter*). It thus seems that the rising use of *buyer, customer, consumer* relative to *voter, citizen* has followed a path much like the rise of *voter* relative to *citizen.* Even within the non-market realm, the simulated act of being a *chooser* has crowded out the more old-fashioned act of just being a *citizen.*[7]

Legitimizing advertising

Advertising and marketing stand at the pinnacle of modern commercial society and a consideration of changing attitudes toward these ever increasing practices will be instructive. In Table 4.4 appear data from the *Times* for the three periods shown as well as ProQuest and AHN data. Column 1 shows the number of times that *advertising* or *marketing* were preceded by positive adjectives (creative, clever, informative) and column 2 the number of times they were preceded by negative adjectives (excessive, intrusive, tasteless, offensive) with the third column showing the ratio of positive to negative.

Table 4.3 Frequency of positive descriptions of *voters* relative to positive descriptions of *citizens*

Years	*1*	*2*	*3*	*4*	*5*	*6*	*7*	*8*
1980–2009	52,583	64,427	0.82	78	92	0.85	674	700.3
1930–1979	72,627	169,245	0.43	44	209	0.21	1,650	809.8
1900–1929	24,509	80,523	0.30	9	59	0.15	2,732	1,364.8

Notes
Column 1: *voter.*
Column 2: *citizen.*
Column 3: column 1/column 2.
Column 4: *informed voter, sophisticated voter, knowledgeable voter, demanding voter,* and *educated voter.*
Column 5: *informed citizen, sophisticated citizen, knowledgeable citizen, demanding citizen,* and *educated citizen.*
Column 6: column 4/column 5.
Column 7: column 1/column 4.
Column 8: column 2/column 5.

Table 4.4 Frequency of positive descriptions of *advertising* relative to negative descriptions of *advertising*

Years	*1*	*2*	*3*
1980–2009	393	41	9.59
1930–1979	377	92	4.10
1900–1929	38	23	1.65
ProQuest (post-1979)	20,609	2,231	9.24
AHN (pre-1922)	187	49	3.82

Notes
Column 1: *creative advertising clever advertising, informative advertising, creative marketing, clever marketing,* and *informative marketing.*
Column 2: *excessive advertising, intrusive advertising, tasteless advertising, offensive advertising, excessive marketing, intrusive marketing, tasteless marketing,* and *offensive marketing.*
Column 3: column 1/column 2.

The ratios shown reveal a steady and significant rise in favorable relative to unfavorable descriptions. The *Times* numbers are relatively small and the ProQuest data is included as evidence from a larger data source that supports the near ten to one ratio of favorable to unfavorable since 1980. And while the numbers from AHN are small they suggest, consistent with the *Times* pre-1930 numbers, a much smaller ratio during the early part of the 20th century. The introduction of television advertising in the 1950s certainly made advertising more salient but might have been expected to result in more ads to criticize as well as more to praise.[8] With the expansion of the business section in the *Times* and rise in the number of articles specifically devoted to advertising and marketing, there may have been a rising appreciation of good advertising. But one would have expected to see more harsh critics emerging as well. As a parallel, we can be sure that periodicals with movie reviews have more good *and* bad things to say about the films they review. A more likely explanation for the pattern observed is the remarkable ability of advertisers to go from the status of outsider to insider, as we have grown increasingly comfortable with salesmanship in all its different forms.

A pattern consistent with the *Times* appears when economics textbooks written prior to 1960 are compared with contemporary texts. Looking at nine early textbooks, negative opinions of advertising well outstrip the positive. For Frank Taussig, the problem was one of waste. In his words,

> That competition operates wastefully seems in some cases obvious.... Advertising ... seems to be in large part designed to induce a customer to turn simply from one dealer to another. If there were no competition, – if one great establishment supplanted ten rivals, – the same wants would make themselves felt, the same purchases would be made, the expense of advertising eliminated, the goods sold cheaper.
>
> (1915, 65)

Writing around the same time, John Roscoe Turner likewise stresses the likely wastefulness of advertising when he writes "It is estimated that the annual outlay for advertising amounts to over $1,000,000,000 in the United States. Probably the larger part of this huge sum may be counted as social waste…" (1919, 570–571).

Well into the 1930s, advertising's volume and influence had increased and more positive attributes were being noted. But even while concluding that "the function which advertising fulfills in the modern commercial world is indispensable," and its ethics improving, Richard Ely notes as well that "[a]dvertising awakens some harmful and many trivial wants" and "is costly and frequently … misleading" (1937, 110).

Raymond Bye similarly concedes positive informational roles to advertising but goes on to claim that:

> A vast amount of advertizement (*sic*) … is purely competitive. Its purpose is not to inform consumers where goods can be purchased, nor to educate them to new ways of gratifying their desires, but simply to persuade customers to purchase the wares of one producer instead of the similar goods of a rival. … [T]here is apparent here a great deal of waste and unproductive effort.
>
> (1934, 77)

The themes of waste and creation of regrettable tastes are combined by Bruce Winton Knight.

> If competitive misrepresentation is merely "unsuccessful" – that is, if the efforts of the competitors cancel out … then it simply wastes the resources which are devoted to it. If it draws patronage to one product from another equally good one, the result is much the same. But if it weakens more wholesome wants, including the desire for truthfulness and for sober uses of leisure time, then a decline in the general level of culture must be added to its other costs. On the whole, we are probably treating the great institution of sales promotion fairly if we pronounce it "very unsatisfactory."
>
> (1942, 251–252)

And according to William H. Kiekhofer,

> Advertising is so extensive and marketing is so aggressive that some people are inclined to think that consumers' choice is fictitious or at most nominal, not real.… With ubiquitous advertising by day and by night, with "high-pressure salesmanship," with "fall openings," with special "sales" for every month in the year, with "selling campaigns" for this and for that, what chance has the ordinary consumer to express his own judgment?
>
> (1946, 655)

Frederick B. Garver and Alvin Harvey Hansen (1947, 58) stress the zero-sum nature of much advertising and even into the 1950s, and television's arrival, the text authors remained far from sold on the merits of advertising. As late as the 1955 edition of his text, Paul F. Gemmill included the following:

> Advertising has been, and will probably continue to be one of the chief obstacles to the maximization of utility in consumption. There is no question that advertising may play a socially useful role in the creation of possession utility. But if, at any time, advertising subtracts from the sum total of utility in society, instead of adding to it, those who are responsible are clearly guilty of social waste; and if advertising leads buyers astray and prevents them from maximizing utility, it may properly be condemned on the basis of contributing to waste in consumption.
>
> (1955, 649)

Contemporary texts have, to put it mildly, grown much more comfortable with advertising. One could already see changes occurring by Samuelson's seventh edition. Rather than reaching any judgments about the social role of advertising, he concluded that "we are dealing here with moot issues, on which each citizen must form his own judgment" (1967, 496). Following the strategy of reaching no general conclusion that advertising is, all things considered, a regrettable enterprise, many of the contemporary texts parrot Samuelson. Welch and Welch, for example, present a sidebar "up for debate" with pro and con positions on advertising (2007, 383). As other examples, Tucker (2008, 247) has a "you're the economist" sidebar that presents conflicting positions on whether advertising serves as a barrier to entry, and McConnell, Brue, and Flynn (2009) have sections both pro and con on advertising's effects. While Welch and Welch at least manage to convey a neutral stance, the other books give evidence of leaning toward the favorable view. McConnell, *et al.* (2009), for example, label their sections "Positive effects of advertising" and the other "*Potential* negative effects of advertising" (italics added). And Tucker's sidebar, in addition to devoting twice as much space to the positive view than to the negative, ends with the following sentence to which the student is asked to offer counterarguments: "Advertising is tasteless, offensive, and a waste of resources; therefore, all advertising should be banned" (2008, 247). As worded, even a student strongly doubtful of advertising's benefit would have little trouble fulfilling the assignment. Who, after all, would wish to argue that it is unequivocally true that advertising has these regrettable features? And even if it did, only the most extreme sort would advocate a complete ban. Tucker has managed, in short, to create a straw man critic who a thoughtful student would have no trouble countering.

Baumol and Blinder manage to shift the hidden costs of advertising from being borne by the general society to being borne by the firms themselves. In their words:

> [A] perfectly competitive firm does not advertise; it adopts no sales gimmicks; it does not even know who most of its competitors are. But ...

important. Suppose that an agent, call her Sarah, has just purchased and has the title to a new Toyota Prius that she has just paid for in full and is prepared to drive away from the lot. Were the salesperson to intercept Sarah on the way to her car, take her keys, and give her instead the keys to a ten-year-old Toyota Camry that is also available, we would know intuitively that an injustice has occurred. Sarah apparently preferred the new Prius to the old Camry, and did what was necessary to make it hers. To take from her what she preferred and what she paid for and to replace it with what she does not prefer is welfare reducing and illegal.

But now suppose that Sarah is in a food court at the local mall, and has a preference (not the thing itself, but a *preference* for the thing) to buy a very healthy salad to help her with a weight reduction plan. Were the pleasant aromas coming from a pizza seller next to the salad restaurant to result in her experiencing a changed preference that leads her to buy the pizza instead of the salad, Sarah would have been harmed much as in the Toyota switching just described. In this case, the pizza restaurant would not stand accused of having taken from Sarah something that she values and *owns* but rather would be said to have simply taken something that she *values* (her *taste for salad*) but to which she can claim no ownership rights that are currently recognized in our court systems. Without property rights in the tastes that we experience, market sellers will overproduce tastes that people would rather not have, and underproduce tastes that people would prefer.

My argument is a formal one and is solid on formal grounds. There is market inefficiency in the formation of tastes. There has been a move on the part of conservatives to throw the ball back to critics who isolate market failings by asking for evidence that there are any actions to alter the status quo that would truly be worth the cost. Following a social evolutionist strategy, those arguing in this way reason that the mere existence of a custom, practice, or law, suggests efficiency characteristics relative to any foreseeable alternatives. But as argued in *Preference Pollution*, there was casual historical evidence that the issue of unpreferred preferences has been growing with time. That word *addiction* seems to be growing in usage, and general puzzlement over the logic of restrictions on activities without third-party victims seems also to be spreading. And restraints on consumer credit are regarded as embarrassingly paternalistic by many and not something to be tolerated in a culture of free and autonomous individuals.

The rising attention to *bad habits* supports the argument that this problem has indeed been increasing in severity. And if it be thought that the rise in *bad habits* is largely divorced from the world of buying and selling, consider Table 4.6. The appearance of phrases generally suggesting *bad buying habits* (impulse shopping, impulse buying, impulse purchases, compulsive shopping, buying on impulse purchasing on impulse, shopping addiction, and addicted to shopping) has risen steadily since 1900 (with the exception of a lull and slight reversal from 1950 to 1969). Summing up, between the first quarter of the 1900s and today, there has occurred a fifteen-fold rise in the likelihood that *shopping*, and *buying* would have associated with them adjectives suggesting *out of control purchases*.[12]

While in the earlier considered examples, the changes in textbooks mirror the changes in the *Times*, the opposite appears to be the case when it comes to rational choice. While impulsivity, addictions, and bad habits are more frequently mentioned in the press, they are less considered in the textbooks.

Of the ten pre-1960 texts surveyed, seven mentioned consumption that ran counter to the simplistic assumption that consumers are always rational. Turner notes that "Goods having desirability may be positively harmful, may detract from the well-being of the user. Goods having this quality may or may not serve our needs, but they always serve our desires" (1919, 111). Writing fifteen years later, Raymond Bye makes a clear distinction between consumer choice and producer choice:

> The truth is that consumers are often whimsical, thoughtless and foolish. They spend frequently without plan or consideration of whether they are getting the greatest possible satisfaction from their money. Hence, while we can properly base an analysis of production and distribution on the general assumption that business men will follow the opportunities for greatest returns and lowest costs, we cannot assume that the individual consumer apportions his personal income in a similarly systematic manner.
>
> (1934, 470)

A more judgmental assessment appears in Richard Ely and Ralph H. Hess's text when they remark that "the squandering of immense sums on passing caprices whose satisfaction cannot be justified from the standpoint of sane living must be condemned as must be any type of 'ostentatious expenditure'" (1937, 143). And

Table 4.6 Frequency of *shopping* (and related expressions) relative to *shopping addiction* (and related expressions)

Years	*1*	*2*	*3*
2000–2009	79,045	82	964.0
1990–1999	182,364	137	1,331.1
1980–1989	246,513	126	1,956.5
1970–1979	225,301	81	2,781.5
1960–1969	243,784	77	3,166.0
1950–1959	202,049	76	2,658.5
1940–1949	161,368	30	5,378.9
1930–1939	151,970	18	8,442.8
1920–1929	143,042	11	13,003.8
1910–1919	76,477	5	15,295.4
1900–1909	62,825	3	20,941.7

Notes
Column 1: *shopping, buying,* and *purchasing.*
Column 2: *shopping addiction, buying addiction, purchasing addiction, impulse shopping, impulse buying, impulse purchasing, compulsive shopping, buying on impulse, purchasing on impulse,* and *addicted to shopping.*
Column 3: column 1/column 2.

similar sentiments appeared on into the 1940s. Bruce Winton Knight attributes the maximizing defying behavior to the market itself with his claim that "[t]here are 'bad wants' which are not wholly 'born into us'. They are partly the product of economic and political institutions ... Competition, too, has produced its share of wasteful wants" (1942, 13).

William H. Kiekhofer offers a warning reminiscent of what is coming from the currently thriving field of behavioral economics (but which has still not made a dent in the contemporary textbooks):

> The economic behavior of men is as complex as any other form of human behavior. In any given economic situation, men may be driven by instinctive impulses, may act in accordance with thoroughly established habits, or may be guided by rational calculation of consequences. Any attempt, however to explain economic behavior solely in terms of a single mental element is bound to prove disappointing.
>
> (1946, 4)

And as a reminder to take the emerging analytical device of indifference curves with a grain of caution, Garver and Hansen warn that "indifference analysis has not penetrated the complex obscurity of consumers' behavior commonly implied by such words as 'custom,' 'impulse,' 'fad' [and] 'whim'" (1947, 96).

Even after the appearance of Paul Samuelson's text in 1947, widely regarded to have set the tone for modern textbooks, warnings appeared about the circumscribed nature of rationality. Gemmill, for example, even in rejecting the notion that some goods are entirely bad, still chose to note the following:

> [D]isutility in consumption is more likely to result from the misuse or excess use of goods than from the consumption of goods which do not have any legitimate uses. We believe it is imperative to prohibit the production of so-called consumers' goods which seem certain to injure those who use them, and to regulate strictly ... other commodities and services which ... may lead to extensive or irreparable damage.
>
> (1955, 644)

Of the ten contemporary texts surveyed, only two issued thoughtful qualifiers of the rational choice assumption. Welch and Welch offer this:

> Pure market systems do not protect people who lack the knowledge to make informed decisions about purchases or employment. Few people totally understand the effects of chemicals used in food products or medications, or the design and inner workings of a car or airplane. Market systems have no organized way to ensure that products offered for sale are safe; and the information required to assess every product a person could buy would be expensive, technical, and very time consuming to acquire and evaluate.
>
> (2007, 42)

And for McConnell *et al.*:

> "Purposeful behavior" does not assume that people and institutions are immune from faulty logic and therefore are perfect decision makers. They sometimes make mistakes. Nor does it mean that people's decisions are unaffected by emotion or the decisions of those around them.
>
> (2009, 4)

But for the other texts surveyed, qualifiers on the utility maximizing assumptions were non-existent. With the steady shift toward more formalized presentations, philosophical speculation on the nature of free choice disappeared, as graphical and mathematical summarizations of the simplified consumer flourished. Baumol and Blinder start out fairly gently, announcing that:

> In this book, like most other books on economic theory, we will assume that decision makers … seek to reach decisions that are optimal, in other words, decisions that do better in achieving the decision maker's goals than any other possible choice.
>
> (2006, 40)

Once the conversation turns specifically to the consumer, a bolder "rule" is announced: "consumers will select the most desired combination of goods obtainable for their money. The choice will be that point on the budget line at which the budget line is tangent to an indifference curve" (2006, 99).

It is much the same for Samuelson and Nordhaus, who announce "we assume that people maximize their utility, which means that they choose the bundle of consumption goods that they most prefer" (2010, 84). O'Sullivan *et al.* manage to specify the nature of what the consumer prefers when they assert that "[a] key assumption of most economic analysis is that people act rationally, meaning that they act in their own self-interest" (2008, 10). Mankiw informs the student how he (the student) behaves without even suggesting that this is just a simplifying assumption:

> When you walk into a store, you are confronted with thousands of goods that you might buy. Of course … you cannot buy everything that you want. You therefore consider the prices of the various goods being offered for sale and buy a bundle of goods that, given your resources, best suits your needs and desires.
>
> (2001, 463)

Lipsey *et al.* convey the sense that if the rationality assumption is not a reflection of reality (as in "I assume that I'll pay for the lunches") it will be eventually if students learn to behave the way that theory predicts: "[T]he consumer should consume sodas and burritos to the point where the marginal utility *per dollar spent* on the last soda is just equal to the marginal utility *per dollar spent* on the last burrito" (2008, 121). And Gwartney *et al.* manage to give the oddest presentation of all. Rationality is no longer just a simplifying assumption but a fundamental characteristic of people:

> The idea that people behave rationally to get the greatest benefit at the least possible cost is a powerful tool. It can help us understand their choices. However we need to realize that a rational choice is not the same thing as a "right" choice. If we want to understand people's choices, we need to understand their own subjective evaluations of their options *as they see them*.... If Joan prefers $50 worth of chocolate to $50 worth of vegetables, buying the chocolate would be the rational choice for her, even though some outside observer might say that Joan is making a "bad" decision.
>
> (2009, 10)

Several things stand out about the ways in which these texts, looked at collectively, present rationality. First, they provide an example of the movement toward a model building approach to economics that derives conclusions from assumptions. That *assumptions* are becoming increasingly associated with economics is indicated by a trend in the *New York Times.* Prior to 1930, *assumption* followed *economic* once every 14,000 times that the latter appeared. Over the next fifty years the frequency more than tripled, to once every 3,900 times. And since 1980, there has been a nearly eightfold rise, with *assumption* following *economic* once every 550 times.

The use of *assume* has became so connected with economists that a joke about their tendency to make inappropriate assumptions actually began to make the rounds. It goes like this:

> A plane filled with university professors crash landed on a desert island. Most of the passengers survived, and luckily, they found a few crates of canned food. Unfortunately, they had no way to open the cans.
>
> A chemistry professor said, "I can mix sea water, coconut milk and some of the plane's fuel to create an acid that will eat through the cans."
>
> An engineering professor said, "I can use spare parts from the plane to devise a rudimentary blade to cut through the cans."
>
> The economics professor said "Let's assume there's a can opener."[13]

It is hard to imagine an economist who would not get the message of this joke, namely, that in some settings an assumption may be inappropriate. But it is not hard at all to imagine an economist madly defending the assumption that consumers are rational. And the reasons for a defense are several. First, as many of the books remind the student, simplification is necessary to cut away from the buzzing confusion of reality and isolate the effect that one variable has on another. In the context of teaching international finance the student is asked to assume just two nations and just two goods that the two nations produce and consume. Based on these assumptions and some hypothetical cost data, it is possible to determine which country has a comparative advantage in which good and to show that mutual gains from trade are possible. This simplifying assumption is reasonable as long as the conclusions reached can generalize to a many-nation, many-product economy.

In the case of consumer theory, for pedagogical purposes a common practice has been to assume an economy producing just two goods and to also assume a consumer who is rational. Once a hypothetical income constraint and prices are assumed, the rationality assumption permits a precise specification of the mix of goods the consumer will purchase, and permits major normative conclusions to ultimately be reached about the functioning of markets. While it is fairly obvious that different prices and incomes will have little effect on the normative conclusions, it is far less obvious that the assumption of irrationality or *bounded rationality* would weaken the strong case for free markets.

Before giving examples of how the rationality assumption is presented in the texts, the word choice *assumption* is worth some closer examination. Webster's defines it as "the act of taking for granted; supposition; the thing supposed." Now *taking for granted* can occur in the context of building a model. Within the model of the consumer, it is *taken for granted* that consumers are rational. Rationality is a *given* or *conceded* point that allows the analysis to go forth. As just noted, one doing the granting may not believe it describes reality at all. Rather, she need merely believe, if she is to be regarded as a sound theorist, that *granting* or *assuming* rationality within the context of the model will lead to predictions about reality that are quite close to what is actually observed. As Milton Friedman (1953) has argued, it is not the *realism* of assumptions that matter, but their ability to predict.

Conceding Friedman's claim (a highly arguable claim that I will not try to pursue further here), there still would appear to be a serious problem with basing the introductory student's study of the consumer on the assumption that she is always *rational*. Unless it is carefully explained just why economists make the assumption that consumers are rational, the student is likely to misinterpret what this means. While *taking for granted* is exactly what economists are doing when they *assume* consumer rationality, this is not the sort of *taking for granted* that most people usually have in mind.

If you invite someone for lunch you may *take it for granted* or *assume* that you will be paying for both of you. This does not mean that you are creating an imaginary world which includes this assumption. This means that you really and truly believe it will be the case that you do pay for the lunch. Is there reason to believe that students whose economic education ends with the principles class go away believing that economists believe that consumers truly are always rational? For the economists assume this, don't they? So isn't their belief in the reality of the statement every bit as much like your believing you will pay for lunch?

And the last three of the above text passages show that it is not just a possible misunderstanding of the rationality assumption that students may carry with them, but a complete failure to recognize that rationality is indeed, an assumption at all. For Mankiw, one does buy in a way that best suits one's *needs and desires*, evidence to the contrary notwithstanding. For Lipsey *et al.*, if consumers are not behaving as theory assumes, they should learn to do so. And Gwartney *et al.*, defend the compulsive chocolate eater from the busybodies who think she might be better off spending her money differently. The texts have come a long way from the concerns expressed pre-1960. While irrational or regrettable consumption was recognized by a majority of these earlier text authors, such consumption has been recast as basically impossible. We can only wonder what effect this will have on the over-weight, over-drugged, under-exercised, under-studying students. Will they go away with the belief that behavior they once regretted should now be embraced since people are assumed to be rational? If so, a more favorable view of advertising and marketing becomes all the more understandable. Such activities are little more than the clever spread of information for the all-powerful consumer to use or not as she sees fit.

The demise of *desire*

The introductory student learns very early on that *need* is not something that holds much meaning to economists. Because the word is conditional in nature, the rejection of *need* cannot be automatically dismissed. We have all heard very young children in the supermarket harassing their parents and insisting that they *need* that extra bag of candy or cookies. This is not a misuse of the word but simply an indication that the word has lots of wiggle room as long as the conditional is unstated. The four-year-old likely means "*I need the extra cookies if I am going to be as happy as I deserve to be.*" Such use of need has to be kept separate from the more serious sort that characterizes the destitute. For such a person, to say that "I need food" carries with it the conditional "if I am going to avoid severe pain, illness, and maybe death." A more serious need, indeed. In spite of economists general boycott of the word because of the confusions it can cause, it is far more frequently used than the ones that economists like to use, namely, *want*, *desire*, and *preference*.

Table 4.7 analyzes the occurrences of *prefer* and *desire* by decade since 1900.[14] Prior to 1950, *desire* was the more common, though the trend toward *prefer* appears to have been underway by the 1920s. Since 1960, *preference* has been the more common, reaching a peak of nearly twice as frequent in the 1980s before falling back somewhat in the two decades since. That *desire* has fallen relative to *prefer* and *preference* is no surprise. For it was the decade of the 1930s during which the flourishing logical positivist movement caused mainstream economists to turn their back on utilitarianism and the "mentalist" constructs that went along with it. *Desire* smacked of that utilitarian tradition and gave way to *revealed preference* in the writings of the leading economists of that period.[15]

It is paradoxical that *desire* has diminished in relative usage over the same period that *bad habits* have received greater attention. This point becomes

Table 4.7 Frequency of *my preference* (and related expressions) relative to *my desire* (and related expressions)

Years	*1*	*2*	*3*
2000–2007	3,464	2,346	1.477
1990–1999	3,984	2,538	1.570
1980–1989	4,753	2,413	1.970
1970–1979	4,173	2,311	1.806
1960–1969	2,765	2,217	1.247
1950–1959	2,198	2,548	0.863
1940–1949	1,983	3,355	0.591
1930–1939	2,514	5,604	0.449
1920–1929	2,149	5,647	0.381
1910–1919	1,619	4,940	0.328
1900–1909	1,483	4,354	0.341

Notes
Column 1: *my preference, our preference, your preference, his preference, her preference, their preference, I prefer, we prefer, you prefer, he prefers, she prefers,* and *they prefer.*
Column 2: *My desire, our desire, your desire, his desire, her desire, their desire, I desire, we desire, you desire, he desires, she desires,* and *they desire.*
Column 3: column 1/column 2.

clear when we compare the likelihood that *desire* is preceded by *foolish, uncontrolled, irrational,* or *unwanted* relative to the times that these adjectives precede *preference.* Looking at articles appearing in the *Times* over the last century, *desire* was ten times as likely as *preference* to be given these inner-turmoil descriptions. Apparently once it was introduced to the wider society by economists and decision theorists *preference* managed to better suggest the *ubermensch* known as *rational economic man.* The mathematicians were running the economics show and the mathematicians, in the interest of clarity, *assumed* a fully rational economic agent who would simply choose what he preferred. While inner turmoil has been increasingly recognized by the ascendant behavioral economists, the legacy of earlier rational choice theory has managed to conjure up in the public mind a decision maker moved by preferences and apparently not as likely as the desire-driven to face inner conflict.[16]

Preference is a word that I have seen fit to use in my work on the market's manipulation of our tastes. It has the advantage over *desire* of being relational in nature. To say I prefer a bottle of Sam Adams when other beers are also available implies that I would rather have it than any of the alternatives. To prefer one is to not prefer the others. But to say I *desire* a bottle of Sam Adams does not rule out my desiring others as well. Desire is not relational and makes for more difficult economic explanations compared with *preference.*

The title of my book, that was discussed above, *Preference Pollution: How Markets Create the Desires We Dislike,* does, I hope, communicate this main message, but in retrospect, based on some data to be presented shortly, I believe that *Desire Pollution* may have made for a better title. For the same reason that "A Streetcar Named Desire" conveys a sense of inner struggle that "A Streetcar Named Preference" does not, we seem to be less likely to associate *preference* with internal conflict than *desire*.

Consumer as audience

Saying that markets fail to create preferred preferences is not the same as saying that consumers are neglected. It is only to say that they are being served in a way that often does a type of harm unrecognized by those causing it. Sellers have been increasingly motivated to act in ways that they believe are indeed *consumer sensitive*, the *consumer focused* total quality management movement that has held such power for the last twenty years being just one bit of evidence in support of this claim.[17]

Is it more *consumer focused* to describe the amount of money that must be paid in exchange for a good as a *price* or a *cost*? *Price* is more neutral since it signifies an amount paid but also an amount received. Buyers pay a price but sellers receive the price. A cost, in contrast, is viewpoint specific. It suggests something negative and something which one tries to minimize.[18] Within economics the textbooks never choose to label the vertical axis of a supply and demand diagram with *cost*. The vertical axis shows price and the diagram connects each price with a *quantity*. The price is what it is whether one is a buyer or seller, as is the quantity. It transcends specific position. A *cost* in contrast depends on viewpoint. For the buyer the price is indeed a *cost* but just as surely it represents a *benefit* for the seller.

In teaching economics, cost theory takes a specific perspective. It looks at the relationship between the marginal cost of a good (from the producer's perspective) and the average cost (from the same producer's perspective) and links these connections with the theory of what a producer would do. The price of the good in this case is also seen from the producer's perspective. Price is a *benefit*. The perfect competitor expands output as long as the marginal benefit exceeds the marginal cost and this marginal benefit is equivalent to the price from the standpoint of a competitive firm.

I recite these Economics 101 points just to emphasize that there is nothing inherently wrong with assuming a particular perspective. It is, however, necessary for the reader or listener to be aware of what this perspective is. In the case of our newspapers, writers must always be aware that their audience is comprised of people with very different perspectives. Calling a *price* a *benefit* or a *cost* may be appropriate in certain circumstances, but there can be no doubt that *price* is more neutral than these other possibilities.

Table 4.8 shows, by decade, the occurrences of *rising prices*, *rising costs*, *falling prices*, and *falling costs* (and many synonymous expressions for each, as shown below the table) in columns 1, 2, 4, and 5 respectively. Column 3 shows the ratio of one to two and column 6 the ratio of four to five. As usual, it is the columns showing the ratios that will be the focus of attention here.

Table 4.8 Frequency of *rising prices* (and related expressions) relative to *rising costs* (and related expressions) and frequency of *falling prices* (and related expressions) relative to *falling costs* (and related expressions)

Years	*1*	*2*	*3*	*4*	*5*	*6*
2000–2009	2,476	3,290	0.75	4,095	3,326	1.23
1990–1999	5,358	4,375	1.22	6,500	4,223	1.54
1980–1989	5,855	4,375	1.34	9,054	6,313	1.43
1970–1979	3,926	3,088	1.27	11,899	8,769	1.36
1960–1969	4,552	3,038	1.50	7,645	5,005	1.53
1950–1959	5,590	3,174	1.76	9,181	5,707	1.61
1940–1949	6,127	3,097	1.98	12,252	5,428	2.26
1930–1939	10,159	3,480	2.92	13,159	3,104	4.24
1920–1929	6,715	1,103	6.09	10,718	3,272	3.28
1910–1919	3,388	482	7.03	7,215	3,459	2.09
1900–1909	2,719	247	11.01	4,486	306	14.66
1890–1899	2,556	224	11.41	2,888	106	27.25
1880–1889	1,309	82	15.96	1,430	42	34.05
1870–1879	851	32	26.59	811	42	19.31

Notes
Column 1: *rising prices, prices rising, increasing prices, prices increasing, higher prices*, and *high prices*.
Column 2: *rising costs, costs rising, increasing costs, costs increasing, higher costs*, and *high costs*.
Column 3: column 1/column 2.
Column 4: *falling prices, prices falling, decreasing prices, prices decreasing, lower prices*, and *low prices*.
Column 5: *falling costs, costs falling, decreasing costs, costs decreasing, lower costs*, and *low costs*.
Column 6: column 4/column 5.

Consider first column 3. Prior to 1910, *rising prices* appeared more than ten times as often as *rising costs*. Since then there has been a steady drop in the relative popularity of *rising prices* and this expression remained somewhere between one and two times more common than *rising costs* from 1940 through 1999. In the 2000s, for the first time, *rising costs* became the more common. Looking now at column 6, a similar pattern emerges for *falling prices* relative to *falling costs*, though the trend is not quite so smooth. In short, *cost* has grown significantly in usage relative to *price*.[19]

To provide some evidence that the perspective of the readership has much to do with explaining how often *price* is used and how often *cost*, Table 4.9 presents data for four different categories of marketed items. The top example shows *bananas*, *cherries*, and *apples*. These represent products for which readers are much more likely to be consumers rather than producers. The numbers in column 3 show that for these items *price* has over the years appeared between three and six times more often. Considered in isolation, the relative frequency of *price* and *cost* reveals little, but when compared with the column 3 numbers for the other items shown, an interesting story emerges. First, for stocks and for bonds, the column 3 numbers are much larger over each of the time periods relative to the corresponding numbers in the top table. Consider the reason for this. The *Times* reader is more likely to have a portfolio that includes stocks and bonds than a portfolio that includes bananas, apples, and cherries. As owners of stocks and bonds, any future activity of the reader in these markets may be either as buyer or seller. When in the position of an owner who will eventually sell, it thus is more common to think of the terms of trade as a *price* than a *cost*.

Second, though the numbers in column 2 are small, it appears that it has become significantly more common to take the perspective of stock and bond owners and that the ratio of price to cost has thus risen. Rising inequality of income and wealth aside, there is an ever-greater percentage of the population that owns some assets, particularly with the 401(k)s replacing defined benefit pensions. Hence, for both stocks and bonds, mention of their *costs* drops in significance relative to their *price*, a word appropriate for one who already owns and is considering selling.

The last example in the table shows, as would be predicted, exactly the opposite trend occurring for *credit*, *loans*, and *borrowing*. Over the same period of time that stock and bond ownership has become more common, people in the U.S. were borrowing more. While to speak of the *price of loans* would be perfectly fine, to speak of the *cost of loans* resonates more immediately with the massive borrowing public. Hence column 3 shows that *price* has gone from being twice as common as *cost* in the pre-1930 period to just one-fifth as

Table 4.9 Frequency of *price* relative to *cost* by category

Years	*1*	*2*	*3*
"Bananas," "cherries," and "apples"			
1980–2009	104	23	4.52
1930–1979	155	47	3.30
1900–1929	46	7	6.57
"Stocks"			
1980–2009	17,074	91	187.63
1930–1979	13,535	117	115.68
1900–1929	1,834	69	26.58
"Bonds"			
1980–2009	5,683	25	227.32
1930–1979	6,260	85	73.65
1900–1929	968	30	32.27
"Credit," "loans," and "borrowing"			
1980–2009	462	2,211	0.21
1930–1979	2,036	2,366	0.86
1900–1929	280	127	2.20

Notes
Each column 1 *price of______*.
Each column 2: *cost of______*.
Each column 3: column 1/column 2.

common since 1980. The post-1980 movement toward increasing reference to *stock price* rather than *stock cost* and increasing reference to *borrowing cost* rather than *borrowing price* is consistent with the era of leveraged asset ownership.

And this raises a final consideration. Might there be some connection between the shift from *prices* to *costs* and the intense dislike of inflation? More than a century ago Midwestern farmers were able to recognize that rising prices were not always a bad thing. Heavily indebted, they favored a bimetallic currency fully realizing that inflation would follow. They apparently recognized that inflation, putting aside its effect on the overall social good, would be good for them.[20]

There is no similar recognition of potential benefits from inflation today. Heavily indebted students have to be coaxed into believing that they might derive some benefit from inflation as it causes the real value of their debts to fall. With a narrow perspective more common today than a century ago, at least on this one economic issue, students equate inflation with *rising costs* and view inflation as something that will leave them worse off. Were they to have seen more reference to *rising prices* they might not have drawn such conclusions. A price, after all, is as much a benefit to some as it is a cost to others.

Decreasing price competition?

Advertising and marketing have as their primary purposes the changing of our tastes and shifting of our demand curves. While taste manipulation has without doubt grown over the century, what has been happening to price competition? The motive for price competition is not to try to change demand curves but to increase sales by lowering price and raising the quantity demanded as consumers slide along an unchanging demand curve.

Now in the highly mythical world of perfect competition there is, paradoxically, no active competition between sellers occurring. Each seller seeks to maximize profit through reacting to a given price by deciding how much to offer for sale.[21] Collectively the sellers do indeed influence price through their overall supply decisions, but any single seller has as much influence as a single buyer, that is to say, none. Advertising signals imperfect competition, since in the ever less often observed world of perfect competition no seller has a motive to advertise. Each such seller's product is impossible to differentiate from that of other sellers and thus each could never hope to make a case that its product was in any sense to be preferred to that of its rivals. Joe the farmer's corn is just like Jane the farmer's corn and everyone knows it.

Once we introduce product differentiation, whether manifested in differences in how sellers deal with their customers or manifested in slight changes in the product itself, each seller offers something slightly unique and each seller thus faces a downward sloping demand curve that it would like to see pushed to the right. Hence arises the motive to advertise and market. The dark side of persuasion that was considered above had to do with changing preferences, not with changing prices. Has price competition also been heating up over the years or has non-price competition been a substitute for it?

One way to at least start to address this question is to see what has happened over the years to the tendency of products to be sold at just under an even dollar amount. We're all used to seeing prices of *$9.98* and *$33.97*, but far less accustomed to being confronted with prices of *$10.02* and *$34.03*.

In column 1 of Table 4.10 appear the number of times that a price appeared in the *Times* that was either one, two, or three cents below certain even dollar figures. The dollar anchors used were $1, $2, $10, $20, $30, $50, and $100, and so the prices searched for in column 1 included *$0.97*, *$0.98*, *$.99*, etc. The numbers in column 2 show the number of times that a price one, two, or three cents greater than the anchor price appeared.

Note first that a long-recognized sort of consumer "irrationality" is reflected in these figures. That prices just below an even dollar amount have been more common than prices just above these even amounts for more than a century shows us that the simplistic model of consumer rationality should have been challenged long before it was. A second, and somewhat surprising point is the downward trend over time in the extent to which the slightly lower prices exceed the slightly higher. My initial thought was that with the increasingly competitive stances of sellers (sellers who are as often as not oligopolistic rather than *competitive* in the economist's sense) price competition would be on the rise. The trend, however, especially when the late 19th century is compared with post-1980, suggests a movement away from price competition. Perhaps non-price competition has not just been rising relative to old-fashioned competition but has actually been replacing it.

Table 4.10 Frequency of price slightly less than an even dollar amount relative to frequency of price slightly more than an even dollar amount

Years	*1*	*2*	*3*
1980–2009	869,328	94,158	9.23
1930–1979	1,331,720	118,186	11.27
1900–1929	424,980	28,969	14.67
1870–1899	111,257	6,244	17.82

Notes
Column 1: prices $.01, $.02 or $.03 below $1.00, $2.00, $10.00, $20.00, $30.00, $50.00, and $100.00.
Column 2: prices $.01, $.02, or $.03 above $1.00, $2.00, $10.00, $20.00, $30.00, $50.00, and $100.00.
Column 3: column 1/column 2.

5 Management over labor

Salaries as *costs*

For over three decades there has been a general sense in the United States that wage earners have been making miniscule gains at the same time that profits and the salaries received by top management have soared. The lowest earning 60 percent of families have experienced a drop in their share of total income from 34.5 percent in 1979 to 29.4 percent in 2007, a not insignificant decline of some 15 percent. Less well recognized is that the rising inequality is due not only to greater salary gains at the top than at the bottom but to a relative rise in capital income as well, from 13.9 percent of all income in 1973 to 18.4 percent in 2007.[1] Some reflection of labor's decline and management's gain comes through when we look at changes in certain word choices within the *Times*. Consider the difference between referring to the earnings of someone as *salary* or *wages* and referring to it as a *cost*. Just as it was argued in the last chapter that *price* was less viewpoint specific than *cost*, so it will be argued here that *salary* and *wage* are less viewpoint specific than *cost*. An employer pays a salary or wage and an employee receives it, and it is thus a *cost* to the employer and a *benefit* to the employee. To speak of this salary or wage as a *cost* is to assume the perspective of the employer.

This all seems to be lost on the market conservatives who so often claim to be carrying on the tradition of Adam Smith, but it was Smith himself who issued a warning about the inconsistency of how we value the rise in different prices. In Smith's words,

> Our merchants and master-manufacturers complain much of the bad effects of high wages in raising the price, and thereby lessening the sale of their goods both at home and abroad. They say nothing concerning the bad effects of high profits. They are silent with regard to the pernicious effects of their own gain. They complain only of those of other people.
>
> (Pack, 2010, 73. Quote is from A. Smith 1976, ix.24)

With the above in mind, any changes in the patterns of referring to what is received by workers as *benefits* or as *costs* will be revealing. In Table 5.1 appear the trends over the three periods shown in linking *labor*, *workers*, and *employees* (lumped together) with words that assume a relatively neutral standpoint toward the money they receive (wages, salaries, earnings) and with a word that takes the specific viewpoint of the one paying the wages (costs). Table 5.2 does the same thing for *management*.

Notice first that money going to labor, workers, and employees is more than twice as likely to be called a *cost* than to be called *salary*, *wage*, or *earnings*. Column 6 of the Table 5.1 shows the ratios over the three periods. In the earliest period, *earnings*, etc. were only about one-third as likely to accompany *labor*, etc. as costs were. In short, it was considerably more likely for *labor* to be discussed from the standpoint of one who was not doing the laboring. There has been some movement since 1930 in the direction of *earnings* but labor remains more than twice as likely to be linked with *cost* rather than with *earnings*, *salary*, or *wages*.

In contrast to this, Table 5.2 shows a movement in the other direction, away from *management costs* and toward *management salaries*. Prior to 1930,

Table 5.1 Frequency of *labor salaries* (and related expressions) relative to *labor costs* (and related expressions)

Years	*1*	*2*	*3*	*4*	*5*	*6*
1980–2009	352,599	1,845	4,451	191.11	79.22	0.41
1930–1979	659,272	3,107	8,824	212.19	74.71	0.35
1900–1929	176,481	707	2,205	249.62	80.04	0.32

Notes
Column 1: *labors, workers*, and *employees*.
Column 2: *labor salaries, labor wages, labor earnings, salaries of labor, wages of labor, earnings of labor*, (same six for both *workers* and *employees*).
Column 3: *labor costs, costs of labor* (same two for both *workers* and *employees*).
Column 4: column 1/column 2.
Column 5: column 1/column 3.
Column 6: column 2/column 3.

Table 5.2 Frequency of *management salaries* (and related expressions) relative to *management costs* (and related expressions)

Years	*1*	*2*	*3*	*4*	*5*	*6*
1980–2009	172,873	143	79	1,208.9	2,188.3	1.81
1930–1979	269,846	169	120	1,596.7	2,248.7	1.41
1900–1929	109,326	23	44	4,753.3	2,484.7	0.52

Notes
Column 1: *management*.
Column 2: *management salaries, management wages, management earnings, salaries of management, wages of management*, and *earnings of management*.
Column 3: *management costs* and *costs of management*.
Column 4: column 1/column 2.
Column 5: column 1/column 3.
Column 6: column 2/column 3.

management *costs* were mentioned twice as frequently as management *salaries*, but since 1980, the pattern has reversed, as one is now nearly twice as likely to encounter *management salary*, than *management costs*.[2]

Table 5.3 breaks down Table 5.1 into its three components, *labor*, *workers*, and *employees*. Two facts stand out. First, the ratio of *salaries* (and related terms) to *costs* differ markedly. For both *employees* and for *workers*, *salaries* outnumber *costs*. For *labor*, in contrast, *costs* overwhelm *earnings*.

Second, and paradoxically, while Table 5.1 showed a slight rise over the century in the relative likelihood of connecting *salary* with *workers*, Table 5.3 shows a drop in the ratio over the century for each category considered separately. So *labor earnings* (and related expressions) went from being 16 percent as common as *labor costs* before 1930 to being just one percent as common since 1980. And both *worker earnings* and *employee earnings* similarly fell by large amounts over this period.

The paradoxical rise in the corresponding number in column 6 of Table 5.1 becomes understandable when attention is paid to the column 1 figures in Table 5.3. There was a drop in the relative use of *labor* and a large increase in the relative use of *employees*. As Table 5.4 illustrates, while *labor* and *laborer* were dropping in relative usage over the century, from a high of 68.4 percent between 1900 and 1909 to a low of 37.2 percent in the current decade, *employees* was rising from 1.4 percent to 26.8 percent. *Workers* and *workmen*, shown in the third column, remained practically unchanged as a percentage of the whole.

What might explain the drop in the popularity of *labor* relative to the alternative descriptions, *workers* and *employees*? There are several possibilities. First,

Table 5.3 Frequency of (1) *labor salaries* relative to *labor costs*, (2) *worker salaries* relative to *worker costs*, and (3) *employee salaries* relative to *employee costs*

Years	*1*	*2*	*3*	*4*	*5*	*6*
"Labor"						
1980–2009	92,098	53	4,171	1,689	21	0.01
1930–1979	334,660	676	8,730	495	38	0.08
1900–1929	108,944	358	2,199	304	50	0.16
"Workers"						
1980–2009	147,162	1,051	106	140	1,388	9.92
1930–1979	292,352	2,167	73	135	4,005	29.62
1900–1929	60,841	299	5	204	2,168	60.00
"Employees"						
1980–2009	113,339	741	174	153	740	4.26
1930–1979	32,261	264	21	122	1,536	12.57
1900–1929	6,696	50	1	134	6,696	50.00

Note
See Table 5.2.

Table 5.4 Relative frequency of *laborers*, *employees*, and *workers*

Years	*1*	*2 (%)*	*3 (%)*	*4 (%)*
2000–2009	113,344	37.2	26.8	35.9
1990–1999	149,947	38.5	26.6	34.8
1980–1989	170,658	41.4	25.2	33.4
1970–1979	165,633	53.5	11.9	34.6
1960–1969	146,440	65.4	1.3	33.4
1950–1959	169,581	63.3	1.3	35.4
1940–1949	197,522	59.9	1.5	38.7
1930–1939	195,381	62.6	2.9	34.5
1920–1929	123,787	65.1	2.9	32.0
1910–1919	72,754	64.9	3.3	31.8
1900–1909	46,969	68.4	1.4	30.1

Notes
Column 1: *labor, laborers, employees, workers*, and *workmen*.
Column 2: percentage of total that were *labor* or *laborers*.
Column 3: percentage of total that were *employees*.
Column 4: percentage of total that were *workers* or *workmen*.

there is the steady drop in hard, physical "labor." Do cashiers labor? Do professors? The movement out of blue collar work and into white collar work may serve as part of the explanation, but the influence of the teachings of economics would certainly be a force working in the opposite direction. The well-known factors of production are, of course, land, labor, and capital.[3] Labor is defined as any sort of human effort that contributes to the creation of goods and services. To the extent that economics texts influence the popular language, one would expect to see "labor" becoming more popular, not less.

Another possibility for the relative decline in *labor* is the decline in unions, both in membership and social influence. To the extent that *labor* is increasingly linked with unionization, the demise in the use of this word to describe human effort should come as no surprise. Labor's golden decade of the 1930s was followed by both the Taft–Hartley Act of 1947 that reversed some of its gains and also by the linking of unions with organized crime over the next twenty years. But certainly once Jimmy Hoffa Sr. was out of the picture, the habit of connecting labor with organized crime weakened considerably. Was it the Vietnam War that weakened liberals' connections with labor? Did the Archie Bunker syndrome lead to blue collar folks being associated by former supporters with mindless flag waving and attitudes in every way on the wrong side of justice and progress?

Who are the *earners*?

Before trying to answer questions such as these, one more analytical task remains. Notice that *labor earnings* were included in Table 5.1 as one description of what labor received. But this leads to the question, are there any other kind of earnings?

Anyone familiar with making out their income tax forms may recall that income is broken down into two categories, *earned* and *unearned* and that the former refers strictly to returns to labor, the latter to property income. Is this practice of the IRS consistent with modern dictionary definitions of earnings? The seventh edition of Webster's unabridged *New Twentieth Century Dictionary* gives as a first definition "money gained by labor, services, or performance; wages, salary, etc." and as a second definition "money made by an investment or an enterprise; profit." The second edition of *The American Heritage Dictionary* similarly lists returns to any factor of production as *earnings* (1982, 434). Whether one chooses to follow the IRS practice or the dictionary, one thing is clear: labor is no *less* entitled to refer to what it receives as *earnings*.

Despite this, *corporate earnings*, *business earnings* and *company earnings* appear far more often relative to *profit* than *labor earnings*, etc. appear relative to *salaries* and *wages*. Summing column 2 figures in Table 5.5 shows that since 1900, *earnings* appeared near or alongside *corporate*, *business*, or *company* 73,150 times. Column 5 figures show that *earnings* appeared near or alongside *labor*, and related words just 1,914 times. And this 38 to 1 tilt in favor of capital occurred despite the fact that *salaries* and *wages* appeared 45 percent more often than *profit* as a summation of column 4 and column 1 figures shows.

Column 7 of the table provides an overall summary. From 1920 through 1929, *corporate*, etc. were fifty-two times more likely than *labor*, etc. to be preceded or followed by *earnings*. Since 1980 this number has crept slightly higher but not enough to detect any obvious trend. What should stand out is the paradox that the very resources that receive *unearned income* (if the IRS is definition is to be believed) are so much more likely to have *earnings* connected with them throughout this 110 year sweep of time.

Table 5.5 Frequency of *profits* relative to *corporate earnings* (and related expressions) and frequency of *wages* (and related expressions) relative to *labor earnings* (and related expressions)

Years	*1*	*2*	*3*	*4*	*5*	*6*	*7*
1980–2009	175,811	12,572	14.0	307,610	346	889.0	63.5
1930–1979	395,368	43,594	9.1	554,006	1,152	480.9	52.8
1900–1929	172,746	16,984	10.2	221,709	416	533.0	52.3

Notes

Column 1: *profit* and *profits*.

Column 2: *corporate earnings, business earnings, company earnings, earnings of corporations, earnings of businesses, earnings of companies, profit earned* and *earned profit*.

Column 3: column 1/column 2.

Column 4: *salaries, salary, wages*, and *wage*.

Column 5: *labor earnings, worker earnings, employee earnings, earnings of labor, earnings of workers, earnings of employees, wages earned*, and *salaries earned*.

Column 6: column 4/column 5.

Column 7: column 6/column 3.

Table 5.6 contrasts the data since 1980 found through ProQuest newspapers with the data prior to 1923 found in AHN. Column 2 shows a remarkably different pattern than the *New York Times*, and column 7 best summarizes the consequences of this. In the earlier period, *earnings* were six times more likely to be associated with capital than with labor. Since 1980 it has become 158 times more likely. Both of these sources contain the data from the whole newspapers rather than just the articles, and this may contribute to the huge disparity with the *Times* but is remarkable nonetheless, especially when it is considered that over this same period of time that the share of profits earned by working single proprietors were falling as a percentage of all profits. Single proprietors indeed *earn* their income in the old laboring sense even though they report this income as profit. Stockholders and absentee owners in general do not.

Assuming the Table 5.6 data reflects a broader streak of the United States than the *Times* data, what is going on? Could the McCarthyism of the early 1950s have unconsciously lowered the propensity of writers to focus on what labor deserved, while raising the propensity to remind their readers that profits were *earned*? Or might there have been a tendency to attach a more normative tone to *earnings* that in turn caused the owners of capital and those writing about them to be more inclined to lay claim to the word.

As an analogy, consider the history of distinguishing between *productive* and *unproductive* labor. It is likely that when originally used by Adam Smith and the classical economists who followed, to be *unproductive* simply meant that a tangible product did not follow from one's work efforts. If this is so, to be *unproductive* was not to be less important than one who was, but was to be one who delivered a service. Such services did appear to rank below products in the Smithian worldview, not because they failed to produce well-being for their recipients, but because they couldn't be stored up and hence could not add to "the wealth of a nation."

Table 5.6 Same categories as Table 5.5, with data from AHN before 1930, and data from ProQuest since 1980

Years	*1*	*2*	*3*	*4*	*5*	*6*	*7*
1980–2009	684,831	57,093	12.0	1,036,230	546	1,897.9	158.2
1900–1929	526,059	574	916.5	572,223	135	4,238.7	4.6

Notes

Column 1: *profit* and *profits*.

Column 2: *corporate earnings, business earnings, company earnings, earnings of corporations, earnings of businesses, earnings of companies, profit earned*, and *earned profit*.

Column 3: column 1/column 2.

Column 4: *salaries, salary, wages*, and *wage*.

Column 5: *labor earnings, worker earnings, employee earnings, earnings of labor, earnings of workers, earnings of employees, wages earned*, and *salaries*.

Column 6: column 4/column 5.

Column 7: column 6/column 3.

With the passage of time *unproductive* came to be often treated as synonymous with *barren* or *of little use*. To the extent that this was so, it is easy to see why later economists departed from the *productive–unproductive* distinction. Might it also be that *earnings* came to be so associated with *what was deserved* or *what one should receive* and that the very notion of income being unearned implied that it was *undeserved*? Perhaps, and if so this can at least explain the habit of speaking of *corporate earnings* and the like. This cannot, however, in any way justify the forty-two-fold greater propensity to attach *earnings* to profits rather than to wages.

Fading *big business* and rising *big labor*?

An earlier chapter presented data indicating that over the years when by any reasonable account businesses were expanding in power and influence, *business* became less likely to be called *big* while "government" became much more so. It is now time to explore what the trends have been for *big labor*.

While not necessarily negative in connotation, *big labor* is certainly often used that way, and *big* is clearly a code word for workers who are represented by a union or are, in other words, *organized*. In Table 5.7 appear the number of times that *labor*, *organized labor*, and *big labor* appeared, once again divided into the three main historical periods – pre-New Deal, New Deal to Reagan, and post-Reagan. As shown in columns 4 and 5, there has been a slightly decreasing likelihood of *labor* being preceded by *organized*, and a considerable rise in the probability of it being preceded by *big*. The decline in *organized labor* is most understandable since union membership has been in decline for over forty years. But with *big* usually connoting *unionized*, the rapid rise in its rate of use makes little sense. The decline in the relative popularity of *organized* over *big* has been precipitous. The final column provides a summary. In the first period, *labor* was preceded by *organized* forty-three times as often as it was preceded by *big*. For the last thirty years, that number fell to ten. The number for the middle period falls clearly in between, but the

Table 5.7 Frequency of *organized labor* relative to *big labor*

Years	*1*	*2*	*3*	*4*	*5*	*6*
1980–2009	89,505	2,422	250	37.0	358.0	9.7
1930–1979	334,660	11,247	655	29.8	510.9	17.2
1900–1929	108,944	4,063	95	26.8	1,146.8	42.8

Notes
Column 1: *labor*.
Column 2: *organized labor*.
Column 3: *big labor*.
Column 4: column 1/column 2.
Column 5: column 1/column 3.
Column 6: column 2/column 3.

five decades included in that period were not by any means similar. In the 1930s and 1940s *organized* remained just about as frequent as it had in the decades preceding. But between the 1940s and 1950s it fell from being used thirty-five times as often to thirteen times as often. Just as it was earlier shown that *earnings* became disattached from labor in the 1950s, so too did *organized*. And as earlier suggested, the fervent anti-communism of the period goes at least part of the way in helping us understand the trend.[4]

As significant as the rise in the use of *big labor* is, a closer look at examples shows that the shift in mood is greater than the numbers might suggest. Prior to 1950, *big labor* was not a stand-alone phrase but instead each word was an adjective modifying some other word. So, for example, a 1900 article of the *Times* mentions a "big Labor Day mass meeting" ("Cheaper," 1900, 1), and an article three years later announces that "the President will review a big labor parade" ("President's," 1903, 2). Through mid-century, far more often than not *big* continued to modify something other than *labor*. Thus a 1930 article describes the British Prime Minister's address to "a big labor audience at Crystal Palace" ("Macdonald," 1930, 14) and a decade later speaks of the International Labor Office "deserting the big Labor Palace near the League of Nations Building" ("Winant," 1940, 2).

The first specific instance of the use of *big labor* as an adjective followed by a noun was at mid-century when the *Times* labor reporter addressed an audience of school teachers and warned that " 'The plain fact is that we are putting our trust in a jerry-built structure that is inadequate to protect the public in an economy ruled by Big Business and Big Labor' " ("Labor," 1950, 21). And there is an interesting parallel between those who first spoke of "Big Labor" and those who introduced *Big Government*. The latter, as mentioned in Chapter 2, were concerned with *Big Business* as well. So too, here, an early expressed concern about *Big Labor* must be understood in the context of criticizing another big institution.

The use of *Big Labor* by the steadily strengthening conservative movement in the United States can be usually found in contexts where big business is not also mentioned. In a single short article of 685 words *Big Labor* appears fully seven times. After stating that "Mr. Obama hasn't been shy about using his executive power to give Big Labor all the goodies he can," the writer goes on to criticize Obama nominees as "longtime Big Labor lobbyists and compulsory unionism hard-liners." A paragraph later an NLRB nominee is described as "a radical, even by Big Labor's standards" and the NLRB as "one of Big Labor's most treacherous accomplices in increasing its radical forced-dues power" (Mix, 2009, A23). *Big Labor* (always capitalized) has come to represent the conservative description of unions, this at a time when the percentage of the labor force in unions has fallen to its lowest level in over sixty years.

In Table 5.8 appear a similar set of data for business. As with labor, *big* is seldom an adjective of flattery. And much as *organized* is more flattering than *big* in describing labor, *major business* or *major corporation* is more flattering than *big business*. And still again, the trends run precisely in the opposite direction as labor.[5] *Major corporation* and *major business* were rarely used prior to

Table 5.8 Frequency *major corporation* relative to *big corporation*

Years	*1*	*2*	*3*	*4*	*5*	*6*
1980–2009	541,551	4,634	5,828	116.9	92.9	0.80
1930–1979	1,131,386	3,882	10,118	291.4	111.8	0.38
1900–1929	388,171	47	3,611	8,259.0	107.5	0.01

Notes
Column 1: *business* and *corporation*.
Column 2: *major business* and *major corporation*.
Column 3: *big business* and *big corporation*.
Column 4: column 1/column 2.
Column 5: column 1/column 3.
Column 6: column 2/column 3.

1930, but expanded greatly after that. Looking at the last column, the relative frequency of *major* relative to *big* rose almost forty-fold from the early period to the middle, and then doubled since 1980, with the polite expression showing signs of eventually passing the blunter *big*. To say *big business* conjures up anti-trust and basic departures from the ideal world of capitalism But to say *major business* focuses on the firm's *importance*, indicating that it's a real player in the economy. Describing a firm as a *major corporation* is less likely to draw attention to the possibility of antitrust and also weakens the position of those advocating any such action. Thoughts of breaking up a *major corporation* seem more questionable than thoughts of breaking up a *big business*. Its very *competitiveness* (despite not being in a competitive industry) can effectively shame into silence those who might entertain the notion that markets have in some sense failed us.

Summing up, the numbers in Table 5.9 show the ratio for each decade in the ratios of the relative frequency of *organized labor* (rather than *big labor*) to the relative frequency of *major corporation* and *major business* (relative to *big corporation* and *big business*). The figure for the most recent decade indicates that

Table 5.9 Ratio of column 6 from Table 5.7 divided by column 6 from Table 5.8 (by decade rather than longer periods shown in earlier previous tables)

Years	*Ratio*
2000–2009	18
1990–1999	13
1980–1989	10
1970–1979	12
1960–1969	21
1950–1959	62
1940–1949	218
1930–1939	531
1920–1929	2,465

labor is 18 times more likely to be modified by *organized* rather than *big* than business is likely to be modified by *major* rather than *big*.[6] *Organized labor* has always been more relatively frequent than *major business* but there was a precipitous drop in this advantage through the 1980s. In the reputedly pro-business 1920s *labor* was 2,465 times more likely to be referred to as *organized* instead of *big* as *business* was likely to be referred to as *major* instead of *big*. By the 1950s this number had fallen to sixty-two and by the 1980s was below ten. Once again there is some indication that labor's slide extends farther back than we generally realize. Contrary to the claim that everything moves in cycles, no meaningful cycle is discernible here. One might wish to argue that the cycle is 200 years and the last 100 has just been the downward phase. Were there to be any truth to this suggestion, attention should be paid to John Maynard Keynes's famous insistence that though things may improve in the long run, in the long run we'll also be dead.

Shifting identities

In Chapter 2 the decline in referring to government as *ours* and the increase in referring to business as *ours* received attention. In the process of carrying out that analysis, it was shown that the more favorable a word the more likely was it to be described as *ours*. In Table 5.10 appear data for the two extreme ends of the broadly defined labor market. The first three columns focus on the bottom end (unemployed, jobless) while the next three focus on the top end (entrepreneurs, capitalists, financiers).

Columns 1 through 3 reveal a pronounced decline since 1980 in the probability that *our* would appear before *unemployed*. Prior to 1980 *our* appeared close

Table 5.10 Frequency of *unemployed* (and related expressions) relative to *our unemployed* (and related expressions) and frequency of *entrepreneur* (and related expressions) relative to *our entrepreneurs* (and related expressions)

Years	*1*	*2*	*3*	*4*	*5*	*6*	*7*
1980–2009	23,350	34	686.8	69,252	245	282.7	2.43
1930–1979	47,442	191	248.4	141,491	722	196.0	1.27
1900–1929	6,477	25	259.1	73,752	905	81.5	3.18
Post-1979 (ProQuest)	1,209,992	1,320	916.7	3,460,106	8,269	418.4	2.19
Pre-1923 (AHN)	33,899	105	322.8	219,394	1,066	205.8	1.57

Notes
Column 1: *unemployed, jobless, underemployed,* and *laid off*.
Column 2: each of the above with *our* preceding.
Column 3: column 1/column 2.
Column 4: *entrepreneurs, industrialists, capitalists, financiers, bankers, corporate leaders, business leaders, financial leaders,* and *corporate heads*.
Column 5: each of the above with *our* preceding.
Column 6: column 4/column 5.
Column 7: column 3/column 6.

to three times as often as it did after 1980 (from once every 250 times to once every 687 times). A look at the other sources in the table's bottom two lines supports this pattern of change.

Somewhat surprisingly, a similar general trend has been at work for those at the top end, as the data in columns 4 through 6 show. A comparison of column 6 with column 3 reveals that over all three periods those at the top were more likely to be called *ours* than those at the bottom, much as previous findings would have predicted. But the column 6 numbers have risen too, indicating a decline in the likelihood that this economically successful group is referred to as *ours*. It is the column 7 figures that best allow some conclusions to be reached. Each of these entries, arrived at by dividing column 3 by column 6, shows the degree to which *entrepreneurs* are more likely to be called *ours* than are the *unemployed*. While comparisons of the pre-1930 period with the post-1980 show little change, the change from mid-century to the present is significant and revealing. The entrepreneurs went from being just 1.26 times as likely as the unemployed to be called *ours* between 1930 and 1980, to 2.42 times as likely since then.

An equally significant historical shift emerges when we compare the use of *our* when describing the unemployed with its use when describing the employed. Columns 1 through 3 of Table 5.11 are the same as columns 1 through 3 of Table 5.10. Columns 4 through 6, however, now provide data for the *employed* rather than for *entrepreneurs*. It is once again column 7 that well summarizes the data. As the fractional numbers in rows 2 and 3 indicate, before 1980 the *unemployed* were the more likely to be referred to as *ours*. Since 1980, however, a strong turnaround has occurred, and *our* is now used to describe the employed 1.57 times as often as the unemployed. The bottom two rows confirm this shift. AHN show *our* as being slightly less than half as

Table 5.11 Frequency of *unemployed* (and related expressions) relative to *our unemployed* (and related expressions) and frequency of *employed* (and related expressions) relative to *our employed* (and related expressions)

Years	*1*	*2*	*3*	*4*	*5*	*6*	*7*
1980–2009	23,350	34	686.8	161,928	369	438.8	1.57
1930–1979	47,442	191	248.4	361,605	876	412.8	0.60
1900–1929	6,477	25	259.1	111,197	325	342.1	0.76
ProQuest (post-1979)	1,209,992	1,320	916.7	10,125,847	22,152	457.1	2.01
AHN (pre-1923)	33,899	105	322.8	759,628	1,064	713.9	0.45

Notes
Column 1: *unemployed, jobless, underemployed* and *laid off*.
Column 2: each of the above with *our* preceding.
Column 3: column 1/column 2.
Column 4: *employed, workers* and *working population*.
Column 5: each of the above with *our* preceding.
Column 6: column 4/column 5.
Column 7: column 3/column 6.

common for the employed compared with the unemployed, while the post-1980 ProQuest newspapers show *our* to have become twice as common for the employed.

Another way to assess attitudes toward the unemployed is to track trends in the use of adjectives that suggest positive feelings and those that suggest the reverse. Table 5.12 shows, by decade, the frequency, both relative and absolute, of favorable adjectives. The decision to show the data by decade rather than the usual multi-decade periods was made because of how extremely the 1930s stand out from decades both before and following. As the numbers in column 3 show, there has been a steady decrease in the likelihood of a favorable adjective in the seventy year period since the 1930s. Though the raw numbers are small, the trend is too consistent to ignore. After occurring once every sixty-three times that *unemployed* or *jobless* appeared in the 1930s, the relative occurrence rapidly fell to once every 163 times in the 1940s, and once every 344 times in the 1950s. In the half-century since, the trend continued, with the 2000s showing the lowest likelihood of all that the use of *unemployed* would call out the use of a description reflecting clear solidarity. The general century long trend that appears in 5.12 is corroborated by data from the two larger sources. The phrases appeared once every 425 times that *jobless* or *unemployed* in AHN prior to 1922 and at half that rate, once every 825 times since 1980 in ProQuest newspapers.

Negative descriptions of the unemployed were not included in Table 5.12 because there were simply too few such descriptions. The number of times that four such descriptions of *unemployed*, and *jobless* (lazy, undeserving,

Table 5.12 Frequency of *unemployed* and *jobless* relative to sympathetic descriptions of *unemployed* or *jobless*

Years	*1*	*2*	*3*
2000–2009	3,918	5	783.6
1990–1999	5,746	9	638.4
1980–1989	6,426	12	535.5
1970–1979	7,348	15	489.9
1960–1969	5,163	13	397.2
1950–1959	4,472	13	344.0
1940–1949	4,565	28	163.0
1930–1939	19,199	303	63.4
1920–1929	3,431	9	381.2
1910–1919	1,231	3	410.3
1900–1909	779	0	–

Notes

Column 1: *jobless* and *unemployed.*

Column 2: *suffering unemployed, suffering from unemployment, suffering jobless, suffering from joblessness, victims of unemployment, unemployment's victims, victims of joblessness, unfortunate unemployed, unfortunately unemployed, unfortunately jobless, struggling unemployed, struggling jobless, struggling with joblessness, needy unemployed,* and *needy jobless.*

Column 3: column 1/column 2.

unmotivated, and shiftless) appeared were low indeed, occurring just once prior to 1980 and three times since. Now if credibility could be given to the ratio of favorable to unfavorable ratios pre- and post-1980, quite a stunning shift could be concluded to have occurred, the favorable outnumbering the unfavorable by a factor of 360 before 1980 but by a factor of just nine after that year. But the natural doubt about drawing any conclusions based on such small numbers is eased when ProQuest is brought into the picture. Since 1980 the sympathetic descriptions of the unemployed occurred 948 times while the definitely unsympathetic descriptions appeared 107 times. With these larger numbers, the ratio of favorable to unfavorable of around nine is indeed now supported.

So what will a closer look at the rise of negative descriptions of the unemployed reveal? Before looking at the examples of *lazy unemployed* listed below, consider the technical definition of unemployment. One is unemployed only if one is of a certain age and is either seeking work or waiting to be called back to work. One is not counted as unemployed if one simply does not want to work. Such a person is "not a member of the labor force" and is classified neither as employed nor unemployed. This being so, the examples of the *lazy unemployed* that appear above suggest one of two possible misunderstandings. First, it is possible to wrongly assume that if one is laid off or never hired in the first place it is simply because of lack of sufficient effort. By this way of understanding unemployment, those not working are those who fairly lost in the competition for jobs. But, as anyone who studies the subject with any care knows, unemployment is often the result of entire firms or entire plants shutting down. In these instances, all workers, from the most to least motivated, are without work. Moreover, even when a decision must be made to lay off just some of the work staff, it is usually seniority, not laziness, that determines who shall be the one to go. A second and more likely possibility is that the implicit definition of unemployment in the above cases is different than the economist's definition, namely, "without a job." The sense is that the *lazy unemployed* didn't become unemployed because their laziness led to their firing but were unemployed by direct virtue of their laziness. They come across as not trying to find a job. Officially, such people might be called discouraged workers but would not be called unemployed.[7]

Examples of how the *lazy unemployed* are referred to in the sample include:

1 "**Lazy jobless** fella drove me to cheat with boss"

2 "like your mother, who dotes on your **lazy unemployed** brother while you bust your rear working two jobs."

3 "... is about to embark on unholy matrimony with Malcolm ... an uncouth, **lazy**, **unemployed** loser."

4 "Willie Dobbs is overweight, unattractive in appearance and grooming, **lazy**, **unemployed**, a useless husband and not really good at anything."

5 "explore what would happen if a **lazy**, **unemployed** pot and vido-game freak accidentally impregnated a smart, sophisticated career woman."

6 "Hard-working Raimunda has to suffer her **lazy**, **jobless** husband, Paco, but not for long."

7 "Mr. Sanderson is a **lazy**, **unemployed** slob who loafs around the house all day."

8 "...starts out crooning a woman's romantic advice to her man and turns into an all-out indictment of a **lazy**, **unemployed**, club-hopping sponge."

9 "They live with their **lazy**, **unemployed** father ... who is preoccupied with drinking and gambling, and a caring mother with infinite resources of patience."

10 "When Ruth meets and marries a **lazy**, **unemployed** man named Ruby, she feels too guilt-ridden to leave her mother."

11 "First ad: The man looking for a 'petite' non-smoking, non-English speaking slave/housewife described himself over the phone to me as **'lazy**, **unemployed**, and pudgy.' What a catch."

12 "Her sister, Donna ... is coping with a **lazy**, **unemployed** but hyperactive boyfriend..."

13 "Next comes a joke, the one about the woman wanting to divorce her **lazy**, **unemployed** husband."

14 "as we observe Janie, overweight, **lazy**, **unemployed**, endearing and Jewish, and her WASP best friend Harriet, statuesque, ambitious, ambitious and acerbic."

15 " a fun-loving and also irresponsible child, a clever but naive man, a lover of women but a shameless gigolo, an energetic sexual superman and a **lazy** **unemployed** bum."

Particularly striking about these examples is the overwhelming emphasis on lazy unemployed *men.* Of the fifty-four cases that I sampled, twenty-three made direct reference to a man while only one made direct reference to a woman (included as #14 above). This dominance of men is particularly remarkable when it is considered that women currently comprise half of the labor force in the United States. Of the fifteen cases shown, only the latter two "lazy unemployed" have redeeming characteristics. The woman described in #14 is "endearing" while the man in #15 is "fun-loving," and "clever." In all the other cases, the lazy, unemployed man comes across as quite loathsome.

We have a case here of the economic conservatives joining forces with social liberals to move the thinking of the age in an economically conservative direction. As I have argued elsewhere, the libertarian strain runs deep within American style economic conservatism and American style social liberalism. Individuals are solely responsible for their fate and one's only true social duty is to obey the law. In the case of unemployment, the economic conservative never did accept the Keynesian message that unemployment was an inevitable by-product of insufficient demand. When the Great Depression was in full swing it was, of course, more often men who most symbolized work for wages and thus men who were seen as the prototypically unemployed. A radical message was to stop blaming unemployment on the unemployed. In recent years, however, the fully understandable increase in focus on the exploitation of women by men has led to a new narrative well captured in the above quotes. Returning us to the pre-Keynesian age, the men who are unemployed appear to have only themselves to blame. Women, in contrast, are frequently cast in the Horatio Alger role that suggests from equal opportunity can flow well-being for anyone who simply tries.

Retreating unions

Unsurprisingly, a nation that appears to look more favorably upon management than labor would not be inclined to identify with its labor unions. One form of evidence for this will consist of a simple comparison of how often the unionized are called *ours* as compared with the non-unionized. Searching the *New York Times* articles from the very beginning, every 107 times that *workers* or *workforce* appeared, it was preceded by *our*. But the 908 occurrences of *unionized workers* or *unionized workforce* was not preceded by *our* eight or nine times, as simple extrapolation suggests would be the case if *union* did not inhibit the likelihood of *our*. Instead, *our* appeared not even once in this context.

A look at the much larger ProQuest data source lends support to this pattern. *Workers* or *workforce* occurred nearly thirty million times since 1980, and *our* preceded the nouns once every eighty-six times. In contrast to this, *unionized workers* or *unionized workforce* appeared approximately 46,000 times, but *our unionized workers* or *our unionized workforce* just 102 times, indicating that *our* preceded these descriptions just once every 453 times. Clearly, newspaper writers were less inclined to identify with unionized workers than with workers in general.

While this evidence is revealing in its own way, it tells us nothing about trends, and, because of small numbers, the approach used to reach the above conclusions cannot be used to isolate trends over time. In order to see if there have been changes in attitudes over time, a comparison of favorable and unfavorable ways of referring to unions appears in Table 5.13. While the numbers themselves are modest in size, they do reveal a clear shift in attitudes. Prior to 1930, there were forty-five instances of favorable descriptions of the unions (much needed, dynamic, well run, progressive, efficient) and just two unfavorable descriptions (corrupt, inefficient, undesirable, poorly run, inefficient). Since 1980, the number of favorable descriptions fell to thirty-four but the number of unfavorable exploded to 132.[8] The conclusion seems clear. While unions have always lowered the likelihood that the labor force will be described as *ours*, more recent years have seen negative descriptions of these unions outstripping the positive descriptions.

On *creating jobs*

Beginning at least a decade ago, the expression *job creation* seemed to grow in popularity. This leads to the question, what might it have replaced? Its usage did not appear to be linked with any particular ideological position or vantage point. Businesses liked to announce that they *created jobs*, while liberals were prone to

Table 5.13 Frequency of favorable descriptions of *unions* relative to unfavorable descriptions

Years	*1*	*2*	*3*
1980–2009	34	132	0.26
1930–1979	133	115	1.16
1900–1929	45	2	22.50

Notes
Column 1: *much needed unions*, *dynamic unions*, *progressive unions*, and *efficient unions*.
Column 2: *corrupt unions*, *inefficient unions*, *undesirable unions*, and *poorly-run unions*.
Column 3: column 1/column 2.

Table 5.14 Frequency of *job creation* (and related expressions that include *creations* or *create*) relative to *job provision* (and related expressions that include *provide* or *provision*)

Years	*1*	*2*	*3*
2000–2009	1,085	121	8.97
1990–1999	1,397	236	5.92
1980–1989	934	406	2.30
1970–1979	745	610	1.22
1960–1969	194	440	0.44
1950–1959	50	262	0.19
1940–1949	103	561	0.18
1930–1939	150	844	0.18
1920–1929	2	107	0.02
1910–1919	7	58	0.12
1900–1909	0	28	–

Notes
Column 1: *job creation*, *create jobs*, *employment creation*, and *create employment*.
Column 2: *job provision*, *provide jobs*, *employment provision*, and *provide employment*.
Column 3: column 1/column 2.

announce that *job creation* was a vital function of an active government. How and by whom jobs were created may have been a point of disagreement, but not the concept of *job creation* itself.

Column 1 of Table 5.14 shows, by decade, all occurrences of *job creation*, and *create jobs*, as well as the less common but synonymous *employment creation* and *create employment*.

Column 2 shows all occurrences of *job provision* and *provide jobs* as well as the less common but synonymous *employment provision* and *provide employment*. As column 3 reveals, prior to 1970 it was much more common to speak of providing jobs than creating them, while since the 1970s *create* has become the word of choice, rising steadily and becoming nine times more frequent than *provide* in the 2000s.[9] A comparison of the relative frequency of all occurrences of *create* and *provide* in isolation (not necessarily followed by *job* or *employment*) reveals a trend in the same direction, though not nearly as large. Just as with *creation* relative to *provision* in the context of employment, all occurrences of *provision* exceeded all occurrences of *creation* by a factor of three before 1960, but much less so since.

There are notable differences between *creating* and *providing* something. First, *provision* suggests an interpersonal relation, with someone providing and someone receiving. Unless specifically stated, as with *self-provision*, the usual assumption is that more than one person is involved. *Creation*, in contrast, does not require anything interpersonal. A creator can choose to keep what she has created or can share it with others. What appears to follow from this is a social-connectedness, as well as a paternalistic dimension to the act of *providing jobs* or *providing employment* that is missing from *creating jobs*. The reality of employment follows, not just its possibility.

The linkage of economics with religion has been gaining strength in recent years, and we have here one more instance of that.[10] God the provisioner is the benevolent God. God the creator, while awe-inspiring, may or may not be benevolent. And similarly, the creators of jobs, while they may be benevolent, are not required to be so. They are implied to be moved not by duty but by self-interest.

There is another difference between *creating* as opposed to *providing*. To be a provider of jobs does not imply that there would have been fewer jobs in one's absence. Having a parent serve as a provider does not mean that a child would die of hunger were the parents to die. Rather, a substitute provider would step in. But to speak of a parent as a *creator* of the child connotes a more frightening counterfactual. Complex philosophical and religious considerations aside, it seems safe to say that there is no one else other than a child's parents who could have created her.

Very similarly, the brave new world of *job creators* is a world that might be expected to act more reverentially toward these creators. It is rhetorically easier to see *job providers* being replaced by other providers were the first to disappear. The radical shift rightward in economic thinking has led, in general, to a strong rejection of Keynesian thought and strong re-discovery of Say and his famous law. Conservatives often insist that government stimulation of the economy to prevent unemployment is unnecessary, the assumption being that markets will gravitate toward full employment on their own. The blip in relative frequency in the use of *job creation* in the 1930s may be partly explainable by the fact that the expression was being used to describe government actions to create jobs that would not have been there without government. It is one thing to speak of *job creation* in this sense, where the counterfactual is fewer jobs. It is something else to speak of, say, the high tech industry *creating* millions of jobs. Had the information revolution never occurred, these particular jobs would not have been there, but the employment of capital in other activities would have led to other jobs instead.

A closer look at the use of *create jobs* in the newspapers shows a curious transition in meaning since 1900. Prior to the Great Depression, to create a job usually denoted little more than "padding the payroll." Beginning with the massive unemployment of the 1930s, however, to *create jobs* generally meant to take action to put otherwise unemployed people to work. And in more recent years it has come to suggest nothing more than hiring someone, irrespective of whether another job would have been available had capital not been used in a way that made this particular job possible.

As the first example from the pre-Depression era, when *creating jobs* was a thing (and charge) to be avoided, a Texas lawmaker defended a proposal that members of the legislature be paid per session rather than per hour by remarking that "the charge that we desire to create jobs aside from being a gratuitous insult is foolishness" ("Attack," 1905, 2). Around the same time, a Grand Army of the Republic post issued a resolution and, according to the reporter, "The resolutions point to the bill being unfair to many worthy veterans and as being generally calculated to create jobs for a certain favored few who are always on the alert for something to turn up in their behalf" ("Oppose," 1909, 2).

In another instance, the reader is asked to "[t]hink of how the commissioners who are tucked away in a nice berth for four years could create jobs and reward their friends under the Allen law" ("Think," 1911, 2). As the earliest instance that I found of a positive "putting people to work" message attached to creating jobs, a baseball manager, after proposing a pension plan for players, goes on to say that it would be "[b]etter still, if the owners could create jobs during the playing season [for retired players]. The wages these veterans would earn would help them wonderfully for a time" ("Sporting," 1912, 7).

What most stands out is that the counterfactual of the job creating actions is a world in which veteran players would *not* be working. There has been the creation of a job without the destruction of any other. And it is just this sort of situation that can be most often identified when *job creation* appeared in the *New York Times* during the 1930s. Thus, for example, there appears in a 1934 article a description of a proposed program to use a government guarantee of mortgages to encourage spending which would otherwise not occur. As the article states:

> The program is counted upon to spur the building industry, which has lagged far behind most other key industries; to create jobs in almost every

section of the country and to encourage the flow of private capital as well as improve the general well-being of the public.

("Congress," 1934, 1)

While this passage foreshadows the message of Keynes that was still a year away, other cases of *job creation* amounted to spreading an unchanging number of total hours worked so as to create jobs for some while lowering the hours worked for others. Thus, a committee comprised of railroad management and labor suggested that a "Federal bill setting out the number of men needed to man the trains would make for uniformity in all States, remove some of the travel hazards and create jobs for several thousand persons" ("Railworkers," 1935, 27). And in a different version of *job creation* still, a group of women "by education and breeding and previous experience unsuited to public relief jobs ... decided to band together to create jobs for themselves" ("Bright," 1933, 18).

When union strength reached its peak level in the 1950s, even the C.I.O. associated what it was proposing – a guaranteed annual wage – with expanded employment, reasoning that such a guarantee was "designed to create jobs, not to force employers into bankruptcy." By this reasoning, employers would " 'have an incentive to provide steady jobs and to minimize unemployment' " ("C.I.O.," 1955, 33).

Notice that despite the differences in theoretical underpinnings and credibility of these different examples, they appear to have in common the notion that in the absence of the proposed action, there would simply be fewer jobs in existence. In contrast to this, for most of the 1990s and 2000s, economic activity was brisk and near full employment the rule. Despite this, the talk of *job creation* has been more common than ever, and it has been private firms that have been seen as the ones doing the *creating*, not governments through deficit financing, not the unemployed themselves through creative efforts, and not unions through programs to spread around the work available. To *create jobs* has, in short, gone from being something done to fix a broken free market system, into something that employers within this system always do on their own. Apparently forgotten is the grain of truth still lurking in Say's Law. While "supply creates its own demand" is misleading if taken to mean that unemployment is impossible, it still serves as a reminder that the elimination of one firm usually results in a redirection of spending elsewhere and the increase, therefore, of approximately as many jobs in the now busier firms as were lost in the failing firm.

As noted at the start of this section, to *create employment* is roughly equivalent to creating jobs. While both *jobs* and *employment* were included in the data, I noted that *jobs* is the considerably more popular of the two. Table 5.15 confirms this, and shows as well that this was not always the case. Columns 1 shows the number of times, by decade, that *job creation*, *create jobs*, *job provision*, or *provide jobs* appeared. Column 2 shows the number of times that *employment* appeared instead of *jobs*. The shift here is again dramatic. Before 1960 *jobs* and *employment* were about equally common, with a clear trend toward *jobs*.

Post-1960 *jobs* took off and in the 2000s was over forty-three times as common as *employment*. And just as *provide* is more interpersonal than its replacement – *create* – *employment* is more interpersonal than *jobs*. *Employment* joins two parties, one employing and one employed, while *jobs* has no immediate interpersonal ring. Robinson Crusoe, in the absence of Friday, would still have had a *job* to do. But absent Friday, there would not have been an employer or an employee in the traditional sense.

A possible explanation for the movement away from the use of *employment* in this conservative era is the word's association with Keynesian economics. The Full Employment Act of 1949 may represent the pinnacle of broad support for Keynesian demand-management. It may also have been the period when reliance on a word with dreaded liberal connotations reached its peak, at least in the context of describing what businesses *create* or *provide*. Doing a search of the *Times* for *jobs* and *employment* reveals a far smaller shift in the direction of *jobs* than the shift that is observed when *creation* and *provision* are added. While *creating employment* and *providing employment* constituted between 38 and 62 percent of the total prior to 1960, they constituted just 2 percent since 2000. In contrast, *employment* and *jobs* considered in isolation show the former constituting just over 10 percent of the total before 1950 and falling to 6.5 percent of the total since 2000. Thus, the movement away from *employment* is a general phenomenon, but the movement away from *create employment* and *provide employment* is far greater.

There is still another curiosity about the language of jobs and employment that applies no matter what the favored way of expressing the act of employment. Whether speaking of *job creation* at the one extreme (the expression of

Table 5.15 Frequency of *job creation* (and related expressions that include *job* or *jobs*) relative to *employment creation* (and related expressions that include *employment*)

Years	*1*	*2*	*3*
2000–2009	1,180	27	43.70
1990–1999	1,589	50	31.78
1980–1989	1,241	116	10.70
1970–1979	1,226	130	9.43
1960–1969	497	159	3.13
1950–1959	192	138	1.39
1940–1949	403	307	1.31
1930–1939	426	710	0.60
1920–1929	17	101	0.17
1910–1919	19	47	0.40
1900–1909	3	27	0.11

Notes
Column 1: *job creation, create jobs, job provision* and *provide jobs*.
Column 2: *employment provision* and *provide employment*.
Column 3: column 1/column 2.

choice 76 percent of the time since 1980) or the largest occurring alternative prior to 1930 – *employment provision* – there is a priority given to the one doing the hiring that is unusual, particularly given the normal representation of labor markets. The supplier in the labor market is, of course, the individual making her labor services available. The demander is thus the employer.

Note that the *creator* (or provisioner) in any imaginable product market is the supplier. Auto companies *create* autos which are then demanded by consumers. Surgeons offer to *provide* an operation for those meeting certain conditions. Never would we think to speak of the auto purchaser or surgery purchaser as a *creator* of that which they are purchasing. Their anticipated demand for a car leads the auto company to produce (*create*) the car well in advance of the purchase. The expressed demand of the hair-cut seeker leads the barber to create an improved body of hair ex post of payment. In either case, sellers create and demanders purchase. I can think of only a single instance when the demander in a product market is said to essentially create that which he purchases. Less than surprisingly, such demanders are the very wealthy. Thus a rich person might speak of *building a summer home*. What they typically mean is that they paid someone who in turn built the house (or hired those who would build it). But as surely as paying in advance and giving directions to the barber doesn't signify that the one seeking a haircut in any sense created the haircut, placing an order for a new house doesn't really signify that one *built* it but rather signifies that one took steps to have others build a house.

Might a similar deference to the powerful be going on in the language that describes the employment relationship? *Employment* is only possible if there is both an employer and an employee. A *job opening* might exist without there being any potential employee in sight, but if a *job* indeed exists, it implies employer and employee just as surely. This being so, who should be said to have *created* the job?

While pondering this, recall the tradition that prevailed in many patriarchal societies of referring to the male of the species as the one who *created* children. By many accounts, the man carried his child (which had been created within him) and proceeded to inject the child into the women who would then become the mother. Both were parents, but the man had *created* the child. Advances in the biological sciences made clear that it was simply not true that the male of the species was the creator. Rather, as surely as it took two to tango, it took two to produce a child.

For a second example closer to economics, there is the long-running 19th century dispute about whether prices were determined by the costs of producing a product or by the utility that the product could provide. While in special conditions, costs alone might determine price, and with other special conditions, utility alone might be the determinant, far more frequently it was the mutual interaction of the two forces that determined price. It was thus incorrect to say that costs *created* the price at which the product sold, or that *utility* did so. Rather, there was mutual determination.

Why it is that no similar recognition has changed the way that we think about employment is a mystery. We were perhaps closer to adopting more accurate terminology at the turn of the last century when *providing employment* was far more common than *creating jobs*. For one thing, the latter expression almost reifies the employment relation, neglecting altogether the relational notion of employment. For a second, the latter expression links the existence of the job with the one doing the hiring, while, as noted previously, *providing* is less categorical about who brought the job into being. We thus appear to be left with the odd situation that bears a definite resemblance to the pretentious wealthy who *build* their summer homes. Employers, tending to grow in size over time, have come to have the language shaped in a similar way. A job is not something carried out by a hired employee. Instead, it's *created* by the employer.

Going back a century and a half, it was apparently more seriously considered that the worker should be granted higher status relative to capital. In 1859 a social critic questioned the then-spreading assumption "that labor is available only in connection with capital; that nobody labors unless somebody else, owning capital, somehow by the use of it induces him to labor." He went on to conclude that "[l]abor is prior to and independent of capital. Capital is only the fruit of labor, and could never have existed if labor had not first existed. Labor is the superior of capital, and deserves much the higher consideration" (Nichols, 2011, 63 and 64). Though this statement might sound like something that Karl Marx would say, the speaker was Abraham Lincoln, for whom freeing slaves naturally took priority over raising the status of free labor in the years that followed.

Creative management

And it is not just in the alleged creation of jobs that management has been gaining praise for its creativity. The data in Table 5.16 expresses the numbers and ratios by decade rather than by larger time periods to better capture just when the shifts were occurring. Column 1 shows the number of times *managers* or *management* appeared, column 2 the number of times *creative* preceded, and column 3 the ratio of 1 to 2. Prior to 1950, the likelihood that *managers* would be described as *creative* was less than 1 in 5,000. By the 1990s, this frequency had risen over fifty-fold, all the way to once every eighty-eight times.

The next three columns follow the same procedure for *workers* and *workforce*. Note that prior to 1940, *creative* was more likely to describe workers than *management*. Beginning in the 1950s, there was a strong and steady tilt toward management until by the 1990s, *creative* appeared before *management* once every eighty-eight times while appearing before *workers* just once every 14,189 times, a truly remarkable turnaround.

The degree of this historical shift was so great that I had some second thoughts about describing the rank and file as *workers* and *workforce* exclusively.

Table 5.16 Frequency of *managers* relative to *creative managers* and frequency of *workers* relative to *creative workers*

Years	*1*	*2*	*3*	*4*	*5*	*6*
2000–2009	116,020	1,147	101.2	102,934	8	12,866.8
1990–1999	196,703	2,237	87.9	141,887	87	1,630.9
1980–1989	208,317	1,318	158.1	150,883	19	7,941.2
1970–1979	172,284	770	223.7	178,106	36	4,947.4
1960–1969	161,772	763	212.0	173,915	68	2,557.6
1950–1959	173,119	285	607.4	193,879	56	3,462.1
1940–1949	178,661	31	5,763.3	244,934	31	7,901.1
1930–1939	179,576	5	35,915.2	260,278	47	5,537.8
1920–1929	118,271	3	39,423.7	225,641	15	15,042.7

Notes
Column 1: *managers* and *management*.
Column 2: *creative managers* and *creative management*.
Column 3: column 1/column 2.
Column 4: *workers* and *workforce*.
Column 5: *creative workers* and *creative workforce*.
Column 6: column 4/column 5.

Employees and *personnel* were compared with *managers* and then the three words (workers, employees, and personnel) were included in the first category. Rather than construct the detailed type of table that appears in Table 5.15, a simpler summarization appears in Table 5.17. Column 1 draws from Table 5.16, and simply divides column 6 in that table by column 3. Interpreting the numbers, they show the relative likelihood that *creative* will be combined with *manager* relative to the likelihood that *creative* will be combined with *worker*. Thus, in the 2000s it was 127 times more likely that *creative* would describe *manager* than *worker*. This compares with the pre-1950 decades, when it was actually more likely that *creative* would describe *workers* than *managers*. Column 2 carries out the same operation with *employee* and *personnel* substituting for *worker*. While the overall trend is much more modest, it is still in the same overall direction. While *workers* were becoming dramatically less likely to be referred to as *creative*, the slightly higher-brow *personnel* and *employees* were only becoming somewhat less likely. In column 3 all three descriptions of *workers* were included and the same calculations carried out Once again while the 2000s reveals some reversal, the long-term trend from 1930 to the present remains clear.[11] Despite the steady replacement of the most mindless sort of physical labor, the *creativity* torch was being passed from those who work to those who manage the workplace.

Note that while this trend is consistent with the main thesis of John Kenneth Galbraith's (1978) book, *The New Industrial State* (first published in 1968), historical events since the 1960s are usually understood to have contradicted his thesis. For Galbraith foresaw a synthesis of the bureaucratic socialist economy and the corporate capitalist economy. Following the 1930s work of Berle and

Means (1933), he saw the entrepreneur in retreat as the management class gained ever increasing power and influence. In his words:

> With the rise of the modern corporation, the emergence of the organization required by modern technology and planning and the divorce of the owner of the capital from control of the enterprise, the entrepreneur no longer exists as an individual person in the mature industrial enterprise. Everyday discourse, except in the economics textbooks, recognizes this change. It replaces the entrepreneur, as the directing force of the enterprise, with management.
>
> (1978, 74)

Strangely, the conventional wisdom since at least the 1970s has pointed in exactly an opposite direction. Businesses have, as this narrative runs, been increasingly inclined to act like the entrepreneurial-run enterprises that prevailed in the 19th century and that continue to prevail in Economics textbooks. To survive, the narrative continues, managers must shape the workplace in a way that permits the workers to serve the company most effectively. Just why such strengthened management is increasingly described as *entrepreneurial* is a mystery but the evidence suggests that the use of "entrepreneur" is rising indeed.

Idol of the times: the entrepreneur

It is clear that the purpose of management is to manage. Exactly what the functions of a firm's owners are is less clear. While Karl Marx may have provided a new name for the business owner when he chose to call him a *capitalist*, the

Table 5.17 Ratio of the likelihood that *managers* are described as *creative* to the likelihood that *workers* (and related expressions) are described as *creative*

Years	*1*	*2*	*3*
2000–2009	127.1	7.38	17.58
1990–1999	18.6	10.49	23.29
1980–1989	50.2	5.55	11.33
1970–1979	22.1	4.45	9.13
1960–1969	12.1	4.11	7.47
1950–1959	5.7	1.99	3.56
1940–1949	1.4	0.32	0.69
1930–1929	0.2	0.03	0.09
1920–1929	0.4	0.03	0.12

Notes

Column 1: column 6 of Table 5.16/column 3 of Table 5.16.

Column 2: same as above with column 6 calculated with substitution of *employees* and *personnel* for *workers* and *workforce*.

Column 3: same as column 1 with column 6 calculated by adding *employees* and *personnel* to *workers* and *workforce*.

functions he ascribed to him were basically the same as what was ascribed by Smith, Ricardo, and others writing in this period. To be a capitalist was to be a top manager as well. This all changed over the next century as absentee ownership manifested in stock shares became the norm. By any way of looking at it, stock owners are *capitalists*, albeit absentee and often tiny in their individual share of control over the company.

In the first three columns of Table 5.18 appear the number of times that *capitalist*, *entrepreneur*, and *business owner* appeared in the *Times* by decade since 1900. The following three columns indicate what percent of the whole each of the titles constituted in each decade. As column 4 shows, the demise of *capitalist* has been precipitous. And along with the quantitative drop has gone a practice of attributing its usage to those unfriendly to capitalism. As Nunberg notes, "When you see the noun *capitalist* in a *Wall Street Journal* editorial or op-ed, the odds are about 4-to-1 that it's in the context of a quote from Lenin or a sarcastic comment on the language of the left" (2006, 130). Prior to 1940, *capitalist* was favored over 90 percent of the time. After slight erosion in relative usage over the next twenty years, major drops occurred in the 1960s, 1970s, and 1980s, and since then it has constituted only about one-quarter of the total. The 1980 relative drop in *capitalist* follows in part from the sudden rise in the popularity of *business owner* as both the raw numbers in column 3 and the relative numbers in column 6 indicate.

But it is *entrepreneur* that most surged, becoming the most common of the three after 1980.[12] Recall from the last section that over this same period

Table 5.18 Absolute usage of *capitalists*, *entrepreneurs*, and *business owners*, respectively (columns 1–3) and relative usage of *capitalists*, *entrepreneurs*, and *business owners*, respectively (columns 4–6)

Years	*1*	*2*	*3*	*4* (%)	*5* (%)	*6* (%)
2000–2009	1,443	3,604	1,161	23.2	58.1	18.7
1990–1999	2,367	5,457	1,396	25.7	59.2	15.1
1980–1989	2,331	4,959	420	30.2	64.3	5.4
1970–1979	2,441	2,314	79	50.5	47.9	1.6
1960–1969	1,964	1,069	35	64.0	34.8	1.1
1950–1959	2,300	449	38	82.5	16.1	1.4
1940–1949	1,941	312	80	83.2	13.4	3.4
1930–1939	3,513	272	12	92.5	7.2	0.3
1920–1929	3,238	92	6	97.1	2.8	0.2
1910–1919	2,306	43	3	98.0	1.8	0.1
1900–1909	3,025	14	0	99.5	0.5	–

Notes
Column 1: *capitalists*.
Column 2: *entrepreneurs*.
Column 3: *business owners*.
Column 4: column 1 as a percentage of columns 1–3.
Column 5: column 2 as a percentage of columns 1–3.
Column 6: column 3 as a percentage of columns 1–3.

management was rising in usage and was increasingly likely to be referred to as creative. As Galbraith had predicted, the corporation bore many similarities to similarly large organizational entities found in the socialist economies. Yet at this very moment when management was exercising greater power over the production process, the *Times* was increasingly prone to focus on the nearly mythical *entrepreneur*, a person who, as *The American Heritage Dictionary* puts it, "organizes, operates, and assumes the risk for a business venture" (1982: 457). The entrepreneur is one of the most successful additions of the Austrian School to mainstream economics. In the textbooks, economic profits are ephemeral short-run returns, rapidly disappearing as soon as their existence becomes known and new firms enter the industry. In the textbooks, the firm's owner(s) must rely on the return to capital that will still be there when economic profits are bid away, and the return to investment is just normal. For Joseph Schumpeter (1950), however, this neoclassical view missed the magic of capitalism and relegated the adventurous and insightful risk-taking entrepreneur to a back seat. These entrepreneurs lived for those exciting short-run periods when above normal profits would pour in.

Thus historical reality post-1970 comes into conflict with the *zeitgeist* of this period. Though the ranks of management swell, and though power accrues to managers to creatively shape what they manage, a side story emerges of a radically free and independent *entrepreneur*. By most estimates, the small, owner-run enterprise has shrunk in significance, but the symbolic resonance of such an enterprise is thriving.[13] While the relative usage of the name given by Karl Marx to the owners of capital shrinks, the name given to the mythical independent organizer of the factors of production flourishes. And paradoxically enough, hard economic times are periods when there is a sudden uptick of what Jared Bernstein of the Economic Policy Institute has called *involuntary entrepreneurs*, those dropped from payrolls and forced, at least in the short run, to work as independent contractors.[14] All this while stock-owning capitalists remain very much alive and a managerial bureaucracy very much serves them as masters of the bureaucracy.

And what about the textbooks? What is their treatment of the entrepreneur? For many years there has been a split over whether inputs to the production process can be conveniently divided into three categories – land, labor, and capital – or whether entrepreneurship ought to stand as a fourth. Looking back eighty years, Fairchild, Furniss, and Buck limited their list to the classic three. As they wrote,

> Man … enlists in his service two powerful partners, and these three – man, nature, and capital – work together in production, with results which, when compared with man's first efforts, are almost unbelievable. These three partners are commonly called the *factors of production* under the titles, *land*, *labor*, and *capital*.
>
> (1930, 29)

They later acknowledge that "[s]o important is his function that the entrepreneur is by some writers elevated to the rank of a fourth 'factor of production'" (1930, 40) but go on to reason that "[s]ince whatever the entrepreneur does falls clearly within our definition of labor, there seems no need of thus putting him in a class by himself" (1930, 40).

The modern texts are more willing to segregate the exalted entrepreneur, an especially odd development when it is considered that those who *labor* today are more likely to be highly specialized decision makers than they were in 1930, and thus, on average, resemble the entrepreneur more than they once did. In the 13th edition of their text, McConnell and Brue, after defining land, labor, and capital, announce, "[f]inally, there is the special human resource we label entrepreneurial ability" (1996, 23). Lest the student confuse this with *labor* they amend the statement in the 16th edition to read, "[f]inally, there is the special human resource, *distinct from labor* [emphasis added], that we label entrepreneurial ability" (2005, 23).

Nineteenth century writers in economics did not include entrepreneurship (or semantic equivalents) in their listing of resources. This may have been in part due to a failure to distinguish between returns to wealth (interest) and returns to risk-taking (profit), but it was also possibly due to a care in thinking less subjected to political pressures of its time. For there appears to be something about *entrepreneurship* that puts it into a different category than the other three. Land, labor, and capital are abstractions that apply to all imaginable human societies that have ever existed. Land is whatever nature provides, labor whatever efforts humans exert, and capital anything made by humans that facilitates production, from the most primitive tool to the most sophisticated computer. Entrepreneurship, in contrast, is historically specific, existing only in a certain kind of economic system. Nevertheless, we appear to have still another example of how the conservative dominance of the last half-century has managed to change the taxonomy of economics not by winnowing out what doesn't belong, but, in this case at least, by welcoming it.

6 Growth over progress, justice, and equality

Unlike their immediate successors, the classical economists whose ideas prevailed from the time of Adam Smith were preoccupied with economic growth. Smith's *An Inquiry into the Wealth of Nations* is best understood as an attempt to explain why some economies had grown in the 18th century while others had not, and it served as a guide to ensure growth long into the future. The optimism of Smith was soon followed by the far less sanguine theories of Thomas Malthus and David Ricardo. For Malthus, the natural reproductive habits of humans guaranteed that the masses would remain at a subsistence standard level of living. For Ricardo, the overall economy itself would reach a steady state as rents rose, profits sank, and non-wage income ceased to be directed at increasing the capital stock.

While the growth pessimists of the 19th century helped to cement the label that Thomas Carlyle gave to the spreading field of economics – the *dismal science*[1] – not all agreed that zero growth spelled stagnation. John Stuart Mill went so far as to propose that only when growth ceased would the "trampling, crushing, elbowing, and treading on each other's heels"[2] cease as well and more noble human pursuits finally replace the ever accelerating race to succeed in the marketplace. And while his characterization of the 1860s as a time when those of his class had as many things as they could possibly want may seem odd in light of the economic advances that have been realized in the century and a half since, the theme of zero growth has been a recurrent one.

Writing 60 years after Mill, in the eighth edition of his classic text, Alfred Marshall suggested that "It may make little difference to the fullness of life of a family whether its yearly income is £1,000 or £5,000; but it makes a very great difference whether the income is £30 or £150; for with £150 the family has, with £30 it has not, the material conditions of a complete life" (Marshall 1920, 2). Translating these pound amounts into 2008 dollars leads to the conclusion that Marshall, much like Mill, might be derisively dismissed today as a head-in-the-clouds 1960s "flower child." In terms of purchasing power, the 30 to 150 pounds range translates into between $1,800 and $9,000 in 2008 dollars. Thirty pounds, it turns out, would buy approximately what $1,800 bought in 2008 and £150 approximately $9,000. Anyone earning these amounts would indeed benefit from real growth. But the £1,000 to £5,000 group who Marshall argues would not much benefit from real income increases would translate into (again using the highest estimates) between $60,000 and $300,000 in 2008 dollars. It is impossible to imagine anyone today agreeing that families earning $60,000 would not benefit from growth, and almost as hard to imagine anyone agreeing that more stuff wouldn't improve the condition of the $300,000 earners.[3] Whether drawing on the rebellious Mill or the orthodox Marshall, the conclusion is similar. The desire and need for more would fade in importance for nations that had seen their material standards of living rise significantly over the course of 100 years. But in the growth-oriented culture that has itself grown in influence, any such thoughts today are reserved for the fringes.[4]

There was another factor at work that drew economists' attention away from growth. The marginal revolution that began in the 1870s revolutionized the methodology of economics and the focus of attention as well. Growth being something of a fuzzy subject, it was moved to the back burner for decades as the leading economists concentrated on questions of economic efficiency and the project of investigating what conditions best achieved it. But probably more unfortunate victims of the marginalist period were such previously central themes as justice, fairness, and equality. For as economics self-consciously sought to imitate the natural sciences, such normative concerns gradually faded. The positivist revolution of the 1930s dealt the death blow as interpersonal comparisons of well-being, judged impossible to carry out scientifically, were relegated to the scrap heap. And just over a decade later, economic growth re-emerged, both as a subject of cutting-edge theorists and as a measure by which to judge an economy's success. The *New York Times*, as we will now see, closely reflects these changes in emphasis.

Economic growth over ***personal, social, intellectual,*** and ***spiritual*** growth

When we speak of improvement through time, there are three words that seem to best capture the process of change: *progress*, *growth*, and *development*.[5] When it comes to describing what sort of *growth*, *progress*, and *development* is occurring, the possibilities are many. Roughly synonymous with *economic* is the older *material*, whether *growth*, *progress*, or *development* follows. Different from either of these are *personal*, *social*, *spiritual*, and *intellectual* sorts of *growth*, *progress*, and *development*.

Column 1 of Table 6.1 shows the number of times that *economic* or *material* preceded *growth*, *progress*, or *development* over the three periods shown. Column 2 shows the number of times that *personal*, *social*, *spiritual*, and *intellectual* preceded these words. Strong results, consistent with an increasing focus on the economic and material, can be seen. *Economic* and *material* went from being 1.5 times more likely to precede *growth*, *progress*, and *development* before 1930 to being 3.2 times as likely over the next fifty years, to being over fifteen times as likely since 1980. Consistent with the popular wisdom, a focus on the material has been underway for a long time, at least when it comes to talking of *growth*, *progress*, and *development*.

Table 6.1 Frequency of *economic growth* (and related expressions) relative to *intellectual, spiritual*, and *personal growth* (and related expressions)

Years	*1*	*2*	*3*
1980–2009	27,538	1,759	15.66
1930–1979	16,527	5,095	3.24
1900–1929	1,682	1,094	1.54

Notes

Column 1: *economic growth, material growth, economic development, material development, economic progress*, and *material progress*.

Column 2: *intellectual growth, social growth, spiritual growth, personal growth, intellectual development, social development, spiritual development, personal development, intellectual progress, social progress, spiritual progress*, and *personal progress*.

Column 3: column 1/column 2.

I chose to include *material* in the category with *economic* because the prevalence of *economic* only extends back to Alfred Marshall's writings of the late 19th century. As expected, *material* has fallen in usage at the same time that *economic* has surged. This raises, in turn, the possibility that *economic* is abstract enough to permit a hegemonic spread of its usage that would not have been possible with *material.* It is possible, in other words, that the relative rise in attention given to *economic* growth, development, and progress relative to the other kinds, is at least in part explainable by the ability of *economic* to expand its meanings. *Economic growth*, for example, is liable to include under its umbrella the construction of new churches and new libraries, an inclusion less likely if *material growth* was still the expression of choice. To the extent that this is true, it is less a cultural wide spread of interest in what economists historically have studied that explains the rise in the use of *economic* as it is the ability of the profession to spread its net over a wider range of activities.

Growth over *progress* and *development*

There is a different issue worth exploring at this point. While *progress*, *development*, and *growth* have been treated as essentially synonymous to this point, they are certainly not exactly so. As growth critic Steven Stoll reminds his reader, "progress does not depend on economic growth, and economic growth does not always lead to human progress" (2008, 7).

Table 6.2 shows the trend away from *progress* and *development* and toward *growth* when it is the economy that is being discussed. As column 3 indicates, before 1930 *economic* and *material* were only about one-twelfth as likely to be followed by *growth* as to be followed by *progress* or *development* prior to 1930 while since 1980 *growth* has been over 1.2 times as likely. And as Table 6.3 reveals, this preference for *growth* over the alternatives has also been occurring, though to a lesser extent, in the non-economic realms, with *growth* going from being just over one-tenth as likely as *progress* or *development* to follow the four non-economic descriptions (social, intellectual, personal, and spiritual) to being just over one-third as likely. Clearly, the tilt toward growth is not limited to the economy.

The replacement of *progress* and *development* with *growth* represents a curious development, not obviously connected with the rightward political drift of the country. The steadfast belief in progress was, after all, what defined the modernism that social events of the 1960s and the post-modern era that followed took issue with. And for those of us who recall 1950s television, the word *progress* hardly had a radical tinge to it. Ronald Reagan, serving as host of the Sunday night thirty minute drama G. E. Theater, would remind us each week that at G. E., "progress is our most important product."

There are two very different likely contributing causes to the movement toward *growth*. First, the influence of respect for the measureable likely played no small role. The movement toward precisely reporting growth rates by simply computing GDP certainly contributed to the drift toward *growth*. *Progress* (as well as *development*), in contrast, has remained subtle and subjective and thus less susceptible to measurability. Second, *progress* carried with it immediate associations with *progressives*, a complex political ideology which was hardly something with which the business community felt particularly comfortable.

Table 6.2 Frequency of *economic growth* (and related expressions) relative to *economic development* and *economic progress* (and related expressions)

Years	*1*	*2*	*3*
1980–2009	16,091	14,142	1.138
1930–1979	8,501	22,649	0.375
1900–1929	234	2,577	0.091

Notes

Column 1: *economic growth* and *material growth*.

Column 2: *economic development*, *material development*, *economic progress*, and *material progress*.

Column 3: column 1/column 2.

Table 6.3 Frequency of *intellectual growth* (and *personal*, *social*, and *spiritual* growth) relative to *intellectual development* and *intellectual progress* (and *personal*, *social*, and *spiritual* development and progress)

Years	*1*	*2*	*3*
1980–2009	469	1,305	0.359
1930–1979	603	4,538	0.133
1900–1929	112	990	0.113

Notes

Column 1: *intellectual growth*, *personal growth*, *social growth*, and *spiritual growth*.

Column 2: *intellectual development*, *personal development*, *social development*, *spiritual development*, *intellectual progress*, *personal progress*, *social progress*, and *spiritual progress*.

Column 3: column 1/column 2.

The rise of formal growth models within economics in the 1950s may go part of the way in explaining this leap in popularity of *economic growth* (there were no comparable *economic progress* or *economic development* models). It is ironic, nonetheless, that over precisely the period when doubts about economic growth were first being expressed both within the profession at a more general level – doubts based on ecological considerations and psychological considerations alike – that the *Times* would be moving away from *progress* and *development* and into *growth*.[6]

Growth over *equality*

Not only was *growth* swamping words having similar meanings, it appears that it was swamping a word having a much different meaning as well, namely, *equality*. It was earlier noted that Mill questioned the advantages of continued economic growth within the economically most advanced nations as questionable even in his time. He did not feel the same about greater equality. In his words:

> I know not why it should be matter of congratulation that persons who are already richer than anyone needs to be, should have doubled their means of consuming things which give little or no pleasure except as representative of wealth; or that numbers of individuals should pass over, every year, from the middle classes into a richer class, or from the class of the occupied rich to that of the unoccupied. It is only in the backward countries of the world that increased production is still an important object: in those most advanced, what is economically needed is a better distribution.
>
> (1929, 749)

The data to follow suggests no similar thinking for the last seventy years in the much richer United States. Column 1 in Table 6.4 shows (as previously presented) the number of times *economic growth* appeared. Column 2 shows data for *economic equality*, and column 3 shows the ratio of column 1 to column 2.

The changes over time are significant. Prior to 1930 *economic growth* was seven times as common as *economic equality*. Since 1980, it has become 280 times as common. In checking the other sources to see if perhaps there was something peculiar to the *New York Times* that explains this change, more extreme differences were found. AHN show *economic growth* to have been only 0.6 as common as *economic equality* pre-1923, while ProQuest show it to have been fully 407 times as common since 1980.

In order to better identify when the shift away from *economic equality* was greatest, Table 6.5 shows the ratio of *economic growth* to *economic equality* by decade. A huge shift occurred between the 1930s and 1950s with another large shift since 1980. What might explain the trend away from mention of economic equality? Was it increasingly associated with Stalin-style communism? Was the leap away from *economic equality* in the 1950s another instance of the reach of

Table 6.4 Frequency of *economic growth* relative to *economic equality*

Years	*1*	*2*	*3*
1980–2009	25,980	93	279.4
1930–1979	21,796	278	78.4
1900–1929	845	124	6.8
ProQuest (post-1979)	1,906,796	4,684	407.1
AHN (pre-1923)	109	176	0.6

Notes
Column 1: *economic growth*.
Column 2: *economic equality*.
Column 3: column 1/column 2.

McCarthyism? Did the early days of Maoist style communism lead to *economic equality* being interpreted literally rather than metaphorically, with all comrades receiving identical incomes? Was it perhaps becoming more evident that while political equality was a goal worth seeking (one person, one vote), economic equality would be unjust since those choosing to work hard are certainly deserving of more than those who choose not to?

In discussing competing social goals, Goodwin, Nelson, Ackerman, and Weisskopf (2009, 242) contrast *equal outcomes* with *equal opportunities* and, unsurprisingly, make the stronger case for the latter. After all, *equal opportunities* is a goal that seems fair to all (the often referred to level playing field) but *equal outcomes* are unfair given that some of the causes of inequality are themselves quite fair. But had the text authors inserted *more* before the two options, an answer would have been more difficult. Should increased resources be devoted in contemporary America to seeking *increased equal opportunities* or *increased equal*

Table 6.5 Ratio of frequency of *growth* to frequency of *equality* compared with ratio of frequency of *economic growth* to frequency of *economic equality*

Decade	*1*	*2*
2000–2009	52.9	521.2
1990–1999	52.9	255.3
1980–1989	47.3	230.9
1970–1979	27.5	162.8
1960–1969	16.7	148.5
1950–1959	26.0	116.1
1940–1949	18.1	25.4
1930–1939	17.6	8.0
1920–1929	19.8	6.3
1910–1919	15.7	10.4
1900–1909	17.5	5.5

Notes
Column 1: (occurrences of *growth*)/(occurrences of *equality*).
Column 2: (occurrences of *economic growth*)/(occurrences of *economic equality*).

outcomes (that is, outcomes more equal than what markets create)? By almost any measure there are fewer legal and institutional impediments to equal opportunity now than there were a generation ago, while at the same time outcomes are ever less equal. My vote goes for seeking more equal outcomes, but it of course does not follow that in my ideal world everyone will receive exactly equal outcomes. Who but the most unreconstructed Maoist would want exactly equal outcomes?

Growth over *justice* and *fairness*

Since *economic equality* has lost out to *economic growth* it remains possible that the expression has indeed come to be associated with literal equality of outcomes. If that is so, and explains fully the falling popularity of *economic equality*, we might expect to see two other normatively loaded expressions, *economic justice* and *economic fairness*, not similarly losing out to *economic growth*. After all, nothing in either of these expressions suggests a very particular outcome is pre-ordained. Exactly what is just and what is fair has much to do with underlying moral presuppositions but cannot be rejected as something worth attaining. One can say "your proposal leads to more equality" and yet reject it. One would have a much harder time saying, "your proposal leads to more justice and fairness" while rejecting it as well.

Column 1 in Table 6.6 shows again the raw numbers for *economic growth* as previously presented in column 1 of Table 6.4. Column 2 shows the combined number of occurrences of *economic fairness* and *economic justice*, and column 3 again shows the ratio of column 1 to column 2. For both the *New York Times* data appearing in the top three rows and the other data sources shown in the next two, the trend is unmistakable. In the *Times*, *economic growth* went from being eleven times as common as *economic justice* and *economic fairness* pre-1930 to sixty-seven times as common post-1979. The two bottom rows show still more of a change. Pre-1923, *economic growth* was only 40 percent as common as the combined number of instances of "economic justice" and "economic fairness." Since 1980, *economic growth* has become over ninety times as common.

Table 6.6 Frequency of *economic growth* relative to *economic justice* and *economic fairness*

Years	*1*	*2*	*3*
1980–2009	25,980	389	66.8
1930–1979	21,796	542	40.2
1900–1929	845	77	11.0
ProQuest (post-1979)	1,906,796	19,296	98.8
AHN (pre-1923)	109	278	0.4

Notes
Column 1: *economic growth*.
Column 2: *economic fairness* and *economic justice*.
Column 3: column 1/column 2.

The conclusion seems inescapable. Despite the sense of some leading economists from a century before that economic growth would cease to make much sense for all but the poor, attention to growth didn't slow down but on the contrary speeded up. Thoughts of redistribution to eradicate the economic travails of those at the bottom were effectively squelched by the conservative forces that turned to growth and "trickle down" thinking as the way to allow the haves to continue to have more while allowing the have-lesses to have more as well. It is almost as if the cult of economic growth succeeded in defying the most basic economic insight of trade-offs. The rich having more, approached historically, would carry with it no cost at all.

Equal opportunity over *equal results*

It was earlier noted that *economic equality* declined in the attention it received at the same time that *economic growth* was taking off on a growth spurt of its own. But while it is true that equality of results fell in popularity, *equality of opportunity* has suffered no similar drop in popularity.

The concentration on greater opportunities goes back to overcoming racial- and gender-based discrimination that either by fiat or custom excluded members of less favored groups from full participation in the economy and in the broader society. Doubts about the overall effects of *equal opportunity* most often comes from conservatives. Yet I will be arguing that the framing of equality in terms of opportunity may have contributed to the attainment of the less equal results that have so symbolized the conservative era.

In looking back at the abolition of slavery, imagine what the world would look like today if the attainment of equality for African-Americans had consisted of giving everyone an equal starting position as far as rights are concerned, while permitting all rights to be alienable. For the very poor, the temptation of voluntary slavery would likely have been too much to resist, especially if the aspiring slave owner agreed to provide the incentive of generous pay to be used as the slave-to-be saw fit during his last days of freedom. The most impulsive, live-for-the moment sort of person might decide a month of material prosperity might be worth the distant obligation of giving up one's freedom. A remarkably altruistic sort of person might give the upfront pay to family members so they might succeed in carving out a better life. While I am not prepared to predict what portion of the population would choose such a path of voluntary slavery, I strongly suspect that the number would not be insignificant. And while whites would likely comprise a percentage of slave owners in excess of their share of the population, some African-Americans would likely have become slave owners as well. As long as some discrimination exists, and as long as some citizens have high discount rates, the prospect of selling one's freedom for some reasonable security as an unfree slave would likely have proven hard to resist.

This counterfactual bit of historical reconstruction is bizarre yet might be argued to bear some resemblance to what the concentration on *more equal opportunities* rather than *more equal results* has meant to the population's lower half in recent years. Giving women more opportunities to move out of traditional female occupations did not address whether there was something about those occupations that needed improvement. While many women who would have otherwise been stuck in unpleasant jobs have escaped, plenty remain. Is there currently any more dignity or better working conditions associated with being, say, a cleaning woman? Can they unionize more readily? Are vacations longer than they were thirty years ago? Has relative pay improved? In all cases, the answer appears to be no. Equal opportunity has given many who might have been cleaning women better opportunities, but has had no apparent impact on the working conditions of those still so employed.

Fifty years ago trash collectors were overwhelmingly drawn from the African-American population. Are there African-Americans today who might have been stuck in such occupations, but who now have had the opportunity to advance to better occupations? Of course. But are those who lost the *competitive struggle* and have remained in these less desirable jobs (or replaced those moving out) enjoying better relative working conditions than those who preceded them? Nothing suggests so. In short, more equal opportunities have lessened discrimination based on one's identity, but have not led to more equal economic results for the society as a whole. The trouble with focusing on the meritocratic approach by pushing for more equal opportunities for advancement while ignoring whether more equal results would follow was brilliantly described by the British sociologist Michael Young (1958). Writing over a half-century ago, he delivered his insights in the futuristic fictional form, through the voice of a government official in the year 2033 who is reflecting back on the past century. After asking "why has society been so stable in spite of the widening gulf between the bottom and the top?" this official offers the following explanation:

> The cardinal reason is that stratification has been in accord with a principle of merit, generally accepted at all levels of society. A century ago the lower classes had an ideology of their own … and were able to use it as much to advance themselves as to attack their superiors. They denied the right of the upper classes to their position. But in the new conditions the lower classes no longer have a distinctive ideology in conflict with the ethos of society, any more than the lower orders used to in the heyday of feudalism. Since bottom agrees with top that merit should reign, they can only cavil at the means by which the choice has been made, not at the standard which all alike espouse.
>
> (1958, 99)

Table 6.7 presents some hypothetical data to better capture what has been at work over the last forty or so years as more equal opportunities have coincided with rising income inequalities.[7] While gender discrimination is used in the example, race would have been equally suited to demonstrate the phenomenon. The top two lines simplify the long term trend toward greater income inequality. On the left those in the top half are shown to each be earning \$80,000, those in the bottom half \$40,000. Rising inequality has led to the changes shown in the

Table 6.7 Hypothetical example of rising overall inequality accompanied by greater gender equality

	Before	*After*
Per capita income top half	$80,000	$90,000
Per capita income bottom half	$40,000	$30,000
# Men in top half	4	3
# Women in top half	1	2
# Men in bottom half	1	2
# Women in bottom half	4	1
Per capita income men	$72,000	$66,000
Per capita income women	$48,000	$54,000

corresponding numbers in the *After* column. Those in the top have seen their incomes rise to $90,000 while those in the bottom half have seen their incomes fall to $30,000.

The next four rows summarize the gender earning specifics. The working population consists of five men and five women. At the early stage four men are in the top earning class and one male is in the bottom, while for the five women it is the reverse, with only one in the top and four in the bottom. Focusing now on the *After* column, more equal opportunity has allowed a woman to rise into the top category, replaced in the lower category by a male. The fact that men still outnumber women at the top (three men and two women) may still be the result of gender discrimination. All that is important to note here is that women as a group have gained economically.

The bottom two rows show per capita earnings for men and for women. While men's per capita income has fallen by $6,000 (from $72,000 to $66,000) women's per capita income has risen by $6,000 (from $48,000 to $54,000). Yet as the top two rows show inequality overall has risen. Even though women still comprise a majority in the bottom half, they have as a group gained since the movement of one of their members into the top group has more than made up for the losses of the three remaining in the bottom group. And though men as a group have become worse off, the three still at the top have gained, just not enough to offset the decrease in income of the male who fall into the bottom group. This table, I believe, well summarizes what has been going on over these past forty years. Excluded groups continue to make gains, but the bottom, over-represented by these same groups, continues to fall farther behind.

Nothing better captures the dominance of *equality of opportunity* over *equality of result* than the relatively recent spread of the expression *level playing field*, as summarized in Table 6.8. Prior to 1980, *playing field* appeared in the *Times* a total of 3,324 times and *level playing field* just twice, and both of these times the use was literal, not metaphorical. Since 1980, *playing field* has appeared 4,287 times and *level playing field* 1,022 times, or once every 4.2 times that *playing field* appeared.[8]

Curiously, the initial uses in 1981 had to do with the need for deregulation and arose in the context of political support for those measures that are now seen as having contributed to the financial collapse of 2008. Senator Jake Garn, then chair of the Senate Banking Committee, "citing the 'revolution that is taking place in the financial services industry,' introduced legislation … designed to help banks and thrift institutions compete more effectively against other institutions offering financial services." His justification? "'We should attempt to create as level a playing field as possible'" ("Senate" 1981, 11).[9] In the years that followed, the level playing field – first symbolized by unrestrained competition between large firms – began to be applied to providing opportunity for all. There are two rhetorical problems with this development.

First, a *level playing field* on which all can participate is often not the path to fairness. No one speaks with any seriousness of leveling the playing field between high school athletes and college athletes and simply allowing competition to then proceed. The conscious interference with free choice doesn't seek to make the playing field *fair* but instead erects separate playing fields. Similarly, women's sports and men's sports appear to exist side-by-side without much sense of artificial interference in the competitive struggle. There is not a level playing field that allows the two genders to compete in, say, basketball, but separate fields and courts for each.

Second, even when there is indeed just a single playing field out there, the path to achieving a *level playing field* is very poorly defined. For some, public subsides *tilt* rather than *level* the playing field. Thus after noting the tax breaks given to wind farms far exceed those given to more traditional suppliers of energy, *Times* writer John Tierney argues that "Environmentalists have been promising for more than three decades that wind energy would be competitive if there was a 'level playing field,' but it survives only because the field has been tilted in its favor" (Tierney, 2006, 19).

Yet just a few months later another *Times* contributor reported on a spokesperson for *Airbus* commenting on the possibility of requesting state aid by

Table 6.8 Frequency of *field* relative to *level playing field* and frequency of *playing field* relative to *level playing field*

Decade	*1*	*2*	*3*	*4*	*5*
2000–2009	52,490	1,415	305	172	4.64
1990–1999	66,075	1,868	420	157	4.45
1980–1989	73,367	1,042	170	432	6.13
1900–1979	805,764	3,323	2	402,882	1,661.50

Notes
Column 1: *field.*
Column 2: *playing field.*
Column 3: *level playing field.*
Column 4: column 1/column 3.
Column 5: column 2/column 3.

calling "the money 'indispensable' for establishing what he called a level playing field with Boeing" (Bennhold, 2006, C2). For this spokesperson, subsidies didn't *tilt* the playing field but restored an already tilted field to balance. Clearly, the expression *level playing field* requires no precommitment to either active government or to an extreme laissez-faire view – but it is also apparent that conducting the conversation in terms of a playing field biases the perspective in favor of a free-market perspective.

So familiar has the expression become that it is even appearing in settings having nothing to do with what might be called the economy, which are nonetheless settings in which the achievement of fair outcomes is critical. Thus the president of the Detectives Endowment Association in New York asked for assurance that four detectives facing a grand jury would have a "level playing field," since "'they're entitled to a fair and impartial investigation, and most importantly, they are entitled to due process'" (Baker and Rashbaum, 2006, 1).

To be sure, a *level playing field* is often a fitting metaphor. It was, after all, the developed nations that erected constraints against the less developed, and there can be little doubt that the disadvantages suffered by the latter were the specific creation of governments, and were actions that did nothing to make income and wealth distributions more equal within the rich country (with wealthy growers usually the beneficiaries) or more equal between countries.

But even taking this into account, the language of assuring *level playing fields* has us view government as little more than the tool of the privileged, *à la* pre-Adam Smith, and thus views restraints on *play* as causes of unfair inequality. But the regulation that largely began in the Progressive 1910s and was continued in the 1930s and 1960s was aimed far more often than not at liberating the disadvantaged from the results that followed from competing on a *level playing field* and either deliberately tipped the playing field or completely freed the less advantaged from competition with the more advantaged.

What to call the rich and the poor?

What differences are there in speaking of *success* and speaking of *achievement*? There is clearly lots of overlap in usage. *The American Heritage Dictionary* includes among its definitions of achievement, "[s]omething that has been accomplished *successfully*" (1982, 74 [emphasis added]) and among its definitions of success "[t]he *achievement* of something desired, planned, or attempted" (1982, 1214 [emphasis added]), an interesting sort of circularity.

Yet when it comes to *successful*, a link with economic success leaps out. The same dictionary offers as one of its definitions of successful "having achieved wealth or eminence," but it is clearly wealth, however attained, that most have in mind when they ask if someone is successful.

The data in Table 6.9 offers support for this generalization. As column 3 shows, for each of the periods shown, adjectives strongly related to money (market, business, financial, economic, monetary) are just over four times as likely to be followed by *success* than are adjectives that are less so (artistic,

Table 6.9 (1) Frequency of *business success* (and related expressions) relative to *artistic success, intellectual success, academic success,* and *scientific success,* and (2) frequency of *business achievement* (and related expressions) relative to *artistic achievement, intellectual achievement, academic achievement,* and *scientific achievement*

Years	*1*	*2*	*3*	*4*	*5*	*6*
1980–2009	2,033	474	4.29	196	1,234	0.159
1930–1979	1,938	481	4.03	345	1,790	0.193
1900–1929	1,102	243	4.53	79	306	0.258
ProQuest	130,709	35,149	3.72	14,319	139,416	0.103
AHN	8,416	1,061	7.93	193	795	0.243

Notes
Column 1: *market success, business success, financial success, economic success,* and *monetary success.*
Column 2: *artistic success, intellectual success, academic success,* and *scientific success.*
Column 3: column 1/column 2.
Column 4: *market achievement, business achievement, financial achievement, economic achievement,* and *monetary achievement.*
Column 5: *artistic achievement, intellectual achievement, academic achievement,* and *scientific achievement.*
Column 6: column 4/column 5.

intellectual, academic, scientific). But as the numbers in column 6 reveal, *achievement* is considerably less often linked with money than with non-commercial activity, from 0.26 as often in the first period shown to just 0.16 as often most recently.[10]

With economic achievement so often linked to *success* and with the distribution of income and wealth widening, what might be occurring to the respect conferred on the rich and the poor? Might respect be something of a substitute for the harder times those at the bottom face, more forthcoming even as money is less so? Or might the mystique of money and the spread of the competitive ethic, alternatively, be leading to a lessening of such respect?

Table 6.10 supports the latter of these possibilities. Column 1 shows the number of times that *poor* appeared in the *Times* by decade. Column 2 shows the number of occurrences of more respectful synonyms (indigent, impoverished, destitute). Column 3 shows the ratio of column 1 to column 2. Rather than a clear trend in the popularity of the respectful synonyms, there is a rise in popularity followed by a steady fall. It was in the 1930s and 1940s that the three softer expressions were used most frequently relative to *poor* (reaching a high of once every six times that *poor* appeared in the 1930s). Since the 1950s, however, there has been a steady decline in the relative use of the more respectful alternatives. By the 2000s, they appeared only once every fourteen times that *poor* appeared.

The century long trend is exactly the opposite of what has occurred in describing the “haves”. Instead of a relative rise followed by a fall in the use of the respectful synonyms for *rich* there was a fall followed by a rise. The terms of respect fell steadily for a fifty year period, reaching their relative low in the

Table 6.10 Frequency of *poor* relative to *indigent* and *impoverished* and frequency of *rich* relative to *affluent*, *well-to-do* or *wealthy*

Decade	*1*	*2*	*3*	*4*	*5*	*6*	*7*
2000–2009	31,914	2,283	13.98	24,925	11,331	2.20	6.35
1990–1999	42,491	3,428	12.40	30,302	13,426	2.26	5.49
1980–1989	43,686	3,025	14.44	30,618	13,317	2.30	6.28
1970–1979	40,470	2,865	14.13	30,145	12,508	2.41	5.86
1960–1969	26,073	2,427	10.74	20,020	7,144	2.80	3.84
1950–1959	16,978	1,662	10.22	19,437	3,947	4.92	2.08
1940–1949	15,835	2,022	7.83	15,419	3,165	4.87	1.61
1930–1939	26,785	4,312	6.21	21,179	6,901	3.07	2.02
1920–1929	25,403	2,490	10.20	18,845	8,008	2.35	4.34
1910–1919	20,575	2,133	9.65	13,646	6,946	1.96	4.92
1900–1909	20,013	1,752	11.42	12,090	7,293	1.66	6.88

Notes
Column 1: *poor*.
Column 2: *indigent*, and *impoverished*.
Column 3: column 1/column 2.
Column 4: *rich*.
Column 5: *affluent*, *well-to-do*, and *wealthy*.
Column 6: column 4/column 5.
Column 7: column 3/column 6.

1940s and1950s, with *rich* being close to five times as popular as the alternatives. Since then there has been an increase in these alternatives to *rich*. By the 2000s, *rich* was only about 2.2 times more common than *affluent*, *well-to-do*, or *wealthy*, close to where it had been a century before.

Column 7 summarizes the trends shown in columns 2 and 6 in a single number. The 6.88 number for the 1900–1909 period indicates that polite terms were that many times more common for the rich than they were for the poor. Following a clear fall in the number through the 1940s, the rise began in the 1950s with this ratio back above six in the 2000s.[11]

The *truly needy* vs. the *needy*

Though *poor* has gained in usage relative to the more nuanced terms shown in Table 6.11, there has been frequent mention of the *truly needy* in recent years. What makes someone *truly needy*? The natural place to start in answering this question is with the dictionary definitions of *truly*. The second college edition of *The American Heritage Dictionary* provides the following definitions: (1) sincerely; genuinely; (2) truthfully; accurately. But a simple Google search of synonyms for *truly* suggests a broader usage has become common. The nine synonyms that appear in column 1 of Table 6.11 fit closely with *The American Heritage Dictionary* definitions. But the four synonyms shown in column 2 do not and have, I believe, been spreading in acceptance of what it means to speak of something being *truly* so.

Table 6.11 (Column 1) Synonyms for *truly* that suggest those not *truly needy* may not be *needy* at all, and (column 2) synonyms for *truly* that suggest those not *truly needy* may still be *needy*

Column 1	*Column 2*
Absolutely	Exceptionally
Authentically	Extremely
Certainly	Greatly
Definitely	Very
Factually	
Genuinely	
Honestly	
Really	
Sincerely	

Consider the mixed messages that can arise by referring to the *truly needy*. Such people are those that the speaker strongly believes to be needy (column 1) and/or believes to be very needy. Unresolved is whether the speaker believes those who do not deserve to be described as *truly needy* might still deserve to be described as *needy*. One intending just a column 1 meaning of *truly* might be suggesting that if one is not *truly needy*, one is simply *not* needy. But one intending a column 2 meaning is suggesting something very different, namely, that the *truly needy* are those individuals who experience more neediness than most of the needy.

Someone carrying a column 2 definition of *truly* might be content with the rhetoric of caring for the *truly needy* for much the same reason that medical personnel follow a policy of triage after disasters. Acting where the most good can be done is not to rule out helping others. In much the same way, helping the *truly needy* (i.e., the *very needy*) might be understood as attempting to lift them to the status of being the merely *needy*. Having accomplished this, the project of bettering the condition of the *needy* (a class no longer including any who are *truly so*) can now commence. In short, for those viewing the *truly needy* as just a subset of the *needy*, the message of providing aid to the *truly needy* is likely to be acceptable, as long as provision of help to this group is not the end of the story.

Table 6.12 lists ten words, including *needy*, that are adjectives sometimes preceded by *truly*. The data shown are drawn from ProQuest newspapers rather than from the *Times* and aggregated over the thirty year period from 1980 through 2009. There are two reasons for this. First, occurrences of *truly needy*, *truly deserving*, etc. were too few in the *Times* to allow any conclusions to be drawn from the patterns that emerged. And second, no striking trends emerged over time.

What does emerge is clear differences in the use of *truly* relative to the use of *very*, *greatly*, *exceptionally*, and *extremely*. The numbers in column 7 convey the frequency of *truly* relative to the other adjectives. Thus the top line indicates *ill* was preceded by one of the other adjectives 57.7 times as often it was preceded by *truly* Less than surprisingly, *needy* is by far the most likely of the ten words to be preceded by *truly*. Appearing at the bottom of the table, the figure 0.39 indicates that *very needy*, *greatly needy*, *exceptionally needy*, and *extremely needy* are all together only 0.39 as likely as *truly needy* to appear. What might this tell us?

If only column 2 (from Table 6.11) definitions of *truly* prevailed, no substantive message would emerge from the table. In this scenario, though *truly* is used relatively rarely compared with the sum of usages of *very*, *greatly*, *exceptionally*, and *extremely* in all cases except for *excellent* and *needy*, so what? But if column 1 definitions prevail (the older definitions) then an interesting trick may be going on. When a politician announces his or her intent to help the *truly needy* he or she might be understood to mean that the extremely needy must come first in any aid effort. Yet this politician may be signaling something else, namely, that there may be some people out there worthy of aid but certainly not all of those who refer to themselves or who are referred to by others as *needy*. Only those who are *truly so*, who are not con artists or liars, deserve our help. In short, for a politician following a column 1 definition of *truly*, it is worth helping those who really are needy, but this group is not to be confused with the group whose members may claim to be needy.

A look at instances of *truly needy* in the popular press makes it apparent that both meanings of *truly* are used. Writing in the *Financial Times* Jan Dalley makes mention of "the world's starving peoples, the truly needy" (Dalley 2005, 2). While Table 6.11, column 1 synonyms for "truly" might apply here, all of the column 2 synonyms definitely do as well. Contrast this with the BBC wire feed in which an Indonesian disciplinary council chairman explains the paucity of funds for disaster victims by alleging that "the fund has been stolen in many places, thus leaving little

Table 6.12 Column 6 indicates multiple by which words shown are modified by *very*, *greatly*, *exceptionally*, and *extremely* rather than by *truly*

	1	*2*	*3*	*4*	*5*	*6*
I'll	1,352,380	5,999	104	225.4	13,003.6	68.00
Competent	581,937	2,776	50	209.6	11,638.7	55.52
Healthy	682,469	8,168	247	83.6	2 763.0	33.10
Honest	271,051	3,761	196	72.1	1 382.9	19.19
Sincere	63,676	1,525	106	41.8	600.7	14.39
Sorry	302,937	11,133	2,289	27.2	132.3	4.86
Deserving	47,618	1,653	432	28.8	110.2	3.83
In need	254,764	1,054	296	241.7	860.7	3.56
Excellent	581,937	481	517	1,209.8	1,125.6	0.93
Needy	134,229	359	922	373.9	145.6	0.39

Notes
Column 1: number of occurrences of word shown.
Column 2: number of times word preceded by *very*, *greatly*, *exceptionally*, or *extremely*.
Column 3: number of times word preceded by *truly*.
Column 4: column 1/column 2.
Column 5: column 1/column 3.
Column 6: column 2/column 3.

for the truly needy" ("Indonesian," 2005, 1). And contrast it as well with the claim that "The principle guiding ... efforts to transform state assistance programs seems to be separating the 'truly needy' from those drawing benefits as a cushy way of life" ("Who are," 2011, 8). In the case of the Dalley quote, to not be in the class referred to as "truly needy" does not imply that one is not needy. Rather, it implies that one is not *as* needy as the group referred to (the starving). In the other two cases, those not among the "truly needed" are worthy of contempt, those taking money aimed at the "truly needed," by outright theft in one case and by pushing the eligibility envelope in the other.

Prior to 1980, *truly* preceded *needy* a total of thirty-one times in the *Times*, or once every 712 times that *needy* appeared. Since then, *truly* preceded *needy* 289 times, or once every twenty-three times that *needy* appeared, fully thirty times as frequently. The year 1980 does indeed stand as the watershed and the election of Ronald Reagan undoubtedly had much to do with popularizing the expression. Curiously, though the *Times* editorial writers expressed sometimes strong opposition to the proposed reforms, they at the same time chose to include *truly* when mentioning the needy. Thus, in pushing for the maintenance of a strong federal role in the welfare system, they state that "Americans recognized two generations ago that the states alone can't be expected to shield the truly needy from hostile economic and social conditions" ("Dumping," 1981, A18). And in an editorial fourteen years later, at the end of Clinton's first term in office, the *Times* directed strong criticism at House Republicans who, according to them, were seeking "to demolish the core principle that any American who becomes truly needy is entitled to support" (President Clinton's," 1995, A14). Just consider again the peculiarity of including *truly*. Were they column 2 users of *truly* saying that the less needy are not entitled to support? Or were they column 1 users implying that many calling themselves needy (or being called needy by others) were not really so? Neither possibility is at all attractive for a clearly liberal editorial page. Before conservatives hijacked the language all the needy were deserving of support. And in addition, the need to remind your reader that one must actually be needy would seem gratuitous. One never expects, after all, to be told that "you must be truly 21 before you can drink" or that "you must be truly registered before you can vote."

As a final bit of evidence that those most inclined to speak of the *truly needy* are not the greatest fans of the needy, consider this. Since 1980, *the needy* appeared 131 times as often as *our needy* while *the truly needy* appeared fully 276 times as often as *our truly needy*. In other woods the use of "our" was only half as common when speaking of the *truly needy* than when speaking of the merely *needy*. How could that be? Aren't the *truly needy* seen as the more seriously needy? And aren't they at other times seen as the bona fide ones rather than the mere pretenders. Wouldn't you think that they would be referred to as *ours* more often? Not if those who introduced *truly* were inclined to have a less than sterling view of those in need in the first place.

7 Conclusion

The trends uncovered in the preceding chapters were, with only a few exceptions, unidirectional. In making my case I have, in one sense, operated more within the modernist tradition that focuses on unidirectional change, rather than within an older tradition that views history cyclically and not necessarily progressing in some single direction.

Something similar to this difference between long-term unidirectional change and short-term cycles is, of course, a major point of contention among macroeconomists. For John Maynard Keynes, the ebb and flow of economic confidence comprised the starting point. Left uninfluenced by public decisions, Keynes argued, market forces would cause prosperous booms followed by their opposites. And it was these cyclical fluctuations that he saw as most needing the attention of government. Growth was for Keynes a guaranteed long-run feature of the capitalist system, albeit one that would decrease in significance with the continual increase in prosperity. It was the short-run pain brought on by serious downturns that was his focus.

Analogies, as we are all expected to know, can be tempting and less than accurate. But it is at least worth noting that the focus of this work has been strictly on the *long run*. The general tone of the arguments offered has suggested, much more often than not, a one-way movement in the direction of ever freer markets over at least the last half-century and in many cases over the entire century. But in putting together some concluding thoughts, I will be changing hats by bringing political cycles into the story.

Arthur Schlesinger Jr. (1986) offered one explanation for the often observed nature of cyclical change in political and economic ideology. What attracted his attention was a thirty-year ideological cycle in the United States that appeared to be occurring too often to attribute to chance. The progressive 1900s were followed by the less definable 1910s which were in turn followed by the clearly conservative (at least from an economic perspective) 1920s. In turn the progressive 1930s were followed by the less political 1940s which gave way to the conservative 1950s. Still for a third time did the pattern repeat itself, as the rebellious, left leaning 1960s were followed by the less progressive 1970s which in turn evolved into still a third conservative reawakening in the Reagan 1980s.

Whether these nine decades are sufficient to establish that a pattern due to something other than mere chance was occurring is easily debatable, but for Schlesinger, such a pattern was a natural outcome of the handing over of political and economic power from one generation to the next.[1]

By his interpretation, members of a given generation assume power, on average, thirty years after the formative period of life when dominant ideas exert the greatest influence upon them, their college years. If we accept that college students are, on average, in their early 20s and further accept that those assuming top leadership positions are most likely to be in their early 50s, the argument begins to make sense, at least in explaining the repetition of a three generation liberal to conservative cycle. Just looking at the United States since 1930, those who assumed power during the Great Depression received their education during the progressive 1900s while (going to the opposite end of the cycle) those in charge in the 1950s were students in the conservative 1920s. And similarly, the 1960 power elites had been students of the 1930s (on average) while the conservative 1980 leaders were most influenced by the 1950s.

The Schlesinger thirty-year cycle was first brought to my attention in the early 1990s. It provided some hope that the decade ahead would change the country's direction from the path carved out by Reagan and Bush. With the election of a Democrat in 1992, conservatism indeed seemed ready for a retreat. Yet the decade that followed represented perhaps the most extreme period of worshiping at the altar of free markets than any decade, including the 1980s, had ever witnessed. How could that be? Why was it that when it came to income distribution, union strength, control of international trade, or whatever else of an economic nature one might care to name, the steady march to the right continued unabated?

The confusion that *conservative* and *liberal* can create is often noted. At times each is used in a relative sense, with the conservative wishing to preserve the status quo and the liberal being more accepting of change. While perfectly acceptable ways of using these words, this can cause much confusion, as a moment's reflection will show. The former communist leaders of the Soviet Union were, in this relative sense, *conservative* since they didn't wish to change the system then in place. And the conservatives in the U.S. could be described as extremely liberal or even radical in the sense that they felt such a passion for changing the welfare state that confronted them when they took power in the early 1980s.

As important as it is to mention these *relativistic* meanings of conservative and liberal, I will be setting them aside in what follows. *Conservative* will be allowed to have a meaning that does not depend on the institutions of the moment, as will *liberal*. Yet there is still confusion as to how these words are used and it is this confusion that demands attention here. The *liberal* tradition, in the classical sense, is, of course, the tradition championed by Adam Smith and other classical economists. In essence, to be a liberal was to wish maximal freedom in the marketplace and thus minimal *interference* by government. With the passage of time the label of conservative came to be applied to those who wished to conserve (or reintroduce, if it had been eliminated) the classical liberal tradition. Liberal, in contrast, was the name used to describe those who were willing to bend the rules of classical liberalism in the way, for instance, advocated by John Maynard Keynes, and were thus less wedded to classical liberalism. As a more recent twist, *neoconservatism* came into wide usage in the 1970s, and *neoliberal* in the 1990s. Each group is comprised mainly of *conservatives* in the sense that the word is used in the United States, with the *neoconservatives* concentrating on the strong military state and *neoliberals* on maximally free markets.

In the United States there is a distinction often made between being an *economic liberal* and being a *social liberal* and similarly for conservatives. To be an *economic liberal* needs little further explanation. To be a *social liberal* however, requires some clarification. For as typically used, social liberals appear to be most easily characterized as those wishing to see minimal government *interference* in the *private*, non-economic spheres of one's life. A social liberal most opposes laws or restrictions on sexual activity, on public controls over the use of one's free time, on abortion, and so on. For social conservatives, it is the reverse. We are left with what might appear, on the surface at least, to be a contradiction. While economic liberals want more collective action via governmental regulation and government provision, social liberals, who tend to be the same people, want less governmental regulation in the social realm. And for the *full conservative* it is less government in the marketplace, but more in the private, non-economic domain of life.

It might appear that both *standard liberals* and *standard conservatives* are guilty of inconsistent positions. For how, it might be asked, can someone be pushing for more governmental control in one area while at the same time demanding less in the other? Whether or not these positions are contradictory depends on what the status quo happens to be. One can certainly say we need more government in one area than we currently have while at the same time declaring a need for less government in the other area.

During the 1990s, what appears to have happened is that the social dimension of being a liberal took the upper hand and, being in the driver's seat, perhaps even came to define what it meant to be a liberal. To seek freedom from the heavy hand of the government in the bedroom brought forth the progressive libertarian impulse while dampening the collectivist sensibility at the same time. Hence, returning to the Schlesinger thesis, those coming to power in the 1990s may well have been students of the 1960s but it seems to be more the social liberal impulse that took charge, not the economic liberal impulse.[2] And the spread of the internet was continually parlayed into evidence that markets were all, and any opposing institutions outmoded irritations. As Thomas Frank summarized the decade, "whenever a pundit or journalist mentioned the Web, one braced oneself for some windy pontification about flexibility, or the infinite mobility of capital, or the total and unappeasable obsolescence of labor, government, and any other enemy of the free-market enterprise" (2000, 79).[3] There are at least five historical events that can provide some insight as to just how such libertarian forces came together in the 1990s. One of these forces – the focus of identity politics on opportunities more than results – was discussed in the last chapter. Separate consideration of the other four is taken up in the sections that follow.

A planned intellectual offensive

The watershed year for what came to be called *neoliberalism* had to be 1980, when Margaret Thatcher in the U.K. and Ronald Reagan in the U.S. began their ultimately effective efforts to dismantle the welfare state and resurrect a laissez-faire economics. As the preceding chapters were intended to demonstrate, the three decades since stand out as a period when market worship grew fairly steadily and when what began as an extreme set of ideas became part of mainstream thinking.[4]

That the ideological shift predates 1980 is well supported by the many facts presented in previous chapters. Most of the data in these chapters was divided into three periods, pre-1930, 1930 through 1979, and post-1979. My motives for aggregating the data this way were three. First, it allowed economy of presentation; second, the numbers by decade would have often been of insufficient size; and third, the trends were not sufficiently striking when shown by decade. A look at approximately one-quarter of the tables that are organized by decade, however, does show that a trend was underway that began well before 1980. In fact, the percentage shifts from the 1940s to the 1960s were in most cases quite similar to and in the same direction as the shifts from the 1960s to the 1980s.[5]

The earlier shift is consistent with research on the rise of neoliberalism. As British scholars Birch and Mykhnenko explain:

> The origins of neoliberalism as an ideology can be traced back to the late 1930s when a group of liberal intellectuals met in Paris to discuss the threat posed not only by totalitarianism, such as National Socialism in Germany, but also by collectivist planning of the economy as in the British Keynesian state and the New Deal in the USA.
>
> (2010, 2–3)

As they further explain, it was with the formation of the Mont Pelerin Society in 1947 with such participants as the famed Austrians Ludwig von Mises and Friedrich von Hayek and their Chicago fellow traveller Milton Friedman that the neoliberal revolution really began. As David Miller argues, "the ferment of free ideas increased. … At the centre of this intellectual assault was the Hayekian obsession with extending free markets, and by association, corporate power. The political activists involved came directly from the circles nurtured by Mont Pelerin" (2010, 29).

The conservatism that is most associated with the 1950s and 1960s, at least in the U.S., tends not to be as much the conservatism of the *neoliberals* as the conservatism that would later morph into *neoconservatism*. Concerns with national security were in the forefront and thus any notion of truly weakening government was not the message most often evoked. It was only with the shock of oil and other events of the 1970s that a more vigorous rejection of liberal positions began in earnest. And as Naomi Klein (2008) has so exhaustively argued, it is exactly such shocks that the neoliberal has proven particularly adept at parlaying into political change.[6] Commenting on the 1970s, Robert Kuttner notes that

> The period of 'stagflation' discredited economic management and conferred new prestige on laissez-faire. If further confirmation were needed, the erosion and collapse of communism [a decade later] impeached not just state socialism, but European social democracy and American neo-Keynesianism as well.
>
> (1996, 5)

As the choice of title for this section of the chapter makes clear, this first historical event was very much intended. The three additional events to be considered were not similarly planned. They might be described as spontaneous events not usually associated with conservatism. In each case, unfolding history appears to have been successfully used by the growing neoliberal movement to further its ends.

The spread of *globaloney*

A first example of an ostensibly liberal change that ended up being in the service of the rise of market fundamentalism was the fascination with the *global economy*. A rarely questioned assumption was that growth in output and population can always be assumed to result in increasing reliance on international trade. When statistical support is needed, the steady rise in cross-border trading over the last century is typically cited. Unmentioned is that there was a steady drop in exports and imports expressed as a percentage of all output in the U.S. from the time of the American Revolution clear up to 1920. In fact, if one wishes to use "exports as a percentage of all production" as a measure of how global an economy is, it would turn out that the most *global* decade for the United States would be the 1780s (and that is not a typo).

How can this be? Often overlooked is that a rising population exerts downward pressure on cross-border trade and that this serves as a counter to technological change and political openness that works in the other direction. Americans are far more likely to find other Americans producing products that they wish to buy than Luxembourgians are to find Luxembourgians for the simple reason that there are far more Americans. It thus stands to reason that as the population of nations increases the less likely is it that one will have to cross a border before finding the product one is seeking.

The growing significance of increases in international trade since the demise of the Soviet Union does not carry with it any direct implications for whether

Table 7.1 Frequency of *international trade* relative to *world trade* and *global trade*

Decade	*1*	*2*	*3*
2000–2009	792	11,505	0.07
1990–1999	1,703	4,168	0.41
1980–1989	2,799	3,164	0.88
1970–1979	1,934	3,662	0.53
1960–1969	1,735	2,431	0.71
1950–1959	2,623	2,177	1.20
1940–1949	2,745	2,302	1.19
1930–1939	2,329	2,117	1.10
1920–1929	884	589	1.50
1910–1919	391	222	1.76
1900–1909	148	15	9.87

Notes
Column 1: *international trade*.
Column 2: *world trade* or *global trade*.
Column 3: column 1/column 2.

economic power is moving left or moving right. But the language that surrounds the spread of trade provides evidence that this event, too, has taken neoliberal forms by lifting the status of markets relative to governments.[7] As one piece of evidence of the crowding out of government, consider the data appearing in Table 7.1. Column 1 shows, by decade, the number of times that *international trade* appeared in the *Times*. Column 2 shows the number of times that *global trade* or *world trade* appeared, and column 3 shows the ratio of column 1 to column 2. Beginning in the 1960s, *global* and *world* replaced *international* as the more common descriptors. *International* has fallen most dramatically from view since 1990 and the data from ProQuest shows a similar shift for U.S. newspapers in general.

Why should this matter? *International trade* remains the expression of choice in the economics profession and maybe we just have here a healthy case of the profession exerting less, rather than more influence, on everyday language. Notice, however, what is missing from *world trade* and from *global trade*. Neither expression presupposes the existence of nation states or, for that matter, government. And sure enough, the *globalization* movement has been strongly characterized by a sophisticated spread of markets without national governments in any way managing to keep up. For the most extreme free marketers, the very notion of *unfair trade* is something of an oxymoron. More often than not, reference to unfair trade at the global level refers to a difference in the trade laws and trade policy of one country compared with another. Since *international trade* draws our attention to the fact that different countries are involved, while the two other expressions do not, it is less than surprising that *unfair* is three times more likely to precede *international trade* than it is to precede *global trade* or *world trade*. And as political scientist Benjamin Barber has noted:

> The battle between democracy and markets, between public and private, that still persists within states has no international counterpart. There markets are trump, citizens nonexistent, and global sovereignty a dream. In the absence of even a hint of a global citizenry, there is and can be no democratic flywheel to moderate the capitalist whirlwind.
>
> (2007, 163)

Women's movement as *freedom to compete*?

Writing at the outset of the extremist 1990s, the contribution of the influence of identity politics on moving the country rightward was accurately foreseen by Robert Bellah *et al.* As they put it:

> The significant achievements of the civil rights and women's movements should not be underestimated, but their successes were attained largely in terms of the established order whose tenets they originally challenged. Women, blacks, and other minorities were given enforceable legal rights that made it possible for them as individuals to compete in the public sphere as workers and consumers, always provided that they had the competence to take advantage of those rights.... The key was individual competition for property and the private enjoyment of its acquisition.
>
> (1991, 80)

Writing in the 1980s, Albert Hirschman (1982a) described a range of argumentation both in support of and in opposition to the free market When it came to opposition, he noted two diametrically opposed starting points. One tradition sees the market as *going too far*, insinuating itself into spheres where it doesn't belong and adversely affecting the character of people. The other tradition sees the market as *not going far enough* by tolerating preexisting injustices because of its generally amoral perspective.

The claim that market thinking undermines personal intimacy and friendship would serve as an example of markets adversely spreading into non-market spheres of life. To try to tackle such a problem would typically commit one to finding ways to lessen our reliance on markets and to, in general, lessen the range of the market ethos. Those parts of such an effort would be more likely to lose respect for market forces rather than to gain respect.

The overcoming of prejudices and attainment of greater equality can sometimes be interpreted as cases of correcting for markets going too far and sometimes as cases of correcting for markets not going far enough. Consider slavery. By one interpretation, it might be reasoned that the market went too far by treating human beings as commodities and that abolishing slavery was best understandable as putting restraints on markets by outlawing the buying and selling of persons. By a different interpretation, it might be reasoned that slavery was an institution having ancient roots and that the relatively recent adoption of free markets cannot be criticized for creating slavery but for tolerating it. The market would not have gone far enough in admitting that segment of the population into market relations with others. While there is a grain of truth to both interpretations, it is undeniable that abolishing slavery restricted the use of markets. What had previously been treated as property to be bought and sold was ruled to be no longer so. And, something too frequently overlooked, voluntary slavery between consenting adults was made illegal as well. Improving the condition of slaves involved some very important constraints on choice.

When it comes to understanding the women's movement of the last half-century, there is less ambiguity about the nature of the complaint against markets. It's not that they *went too far* by themselves restricting what women were allowed to do, but that they did not go far enough in breaking down pre-market patriarchal institutions. And the liberation of women thus often involved measures to open up choice to women, allowing them to own property and allowing them to compete on the proverbial *level playing field* in the larger public economy.

Over the same thirty-year period when the salary of a firm's CEO went from being, on average, twenty times the average salary received by a worker to 200 times the average, critics claiming to be progressive would lament the "glass ceiling" that prevented women from rising to the top. Mention of any lowering of the glass ceiling at the same time that it was broken was nowhere to be heard. Comparing this with the liberation of former slaves, try to imagine the emancipation of slaves as involving not the elimination of slavery but a system of *competitive slavery*, in which, say, the least productive 20 percent of the population would find it better to be voluntary slaves than starving unemployed workers. Such a system would result in the eventually enslaved being white and black alike, and some of the new more *enlightened* slave owners would themselves be African-American. Simply trying to imagine such an outcome of the Civil War is ludicrous, but isn't it possible to argue that something similar has been going on over the thirty-year period of more equal gender opportunity? Those at the bottom (disproportionally female) have had little economic advance over the past thirty years while those at the top have made outsized gains. And as argued in the previous chapter, equal opportunity has had the likely bizarre side-effect of legitimating inequality.

From hippies to yuppies: the counterculture as an expression of market populism

The spread of the counterculture in the 1960s may well have happened even if there had been no war in Vietnam occurring at the same time. The *beatniks*, after all, arose in the 1950s and going back a half-century prior to this, changes within the art community gave rise to Bohemian culture both in Europe and the U.S., at the end of a century when war was receding from memory.

Nevertheless, the image of the *peace-loving* hippie figured strongly in the picture of anti-war protests that began in the mid-1960s. The war in Vietnam had to play no small role in the distancing of those opposed to the war from their government. As shown in Chapter 2 (see Table 2.1), it was indeed in the 1960s that a strong drop occurred in the likelihood that government would be called *ours*.

While this is not to say that opposition to the war carried it with it an increasing embrace of values associated with those on the right, it does suggest the opening up of a common ground between two otherwise opposed camps. And when it is further considered that a strong libertarian impulse at the social level united those opposed to drug laws, among other things, it becomes more understandable that it was only a matter of time before a rightward drift began.

At least as significant an alienation from government in allowing a certain peace between the incipient neoliberal movement and the remnants of the counterculture was the progressive inward-looking nature of the culture, particularly as manifested in the 1970s. Daniel Bell, in laying out his argument that contradictory forces were at work in contemporary capitalism, drew parallels between the counterculture and its predecessor from a half-century before. As Bell put it, when commenting on the changes that occurred in the 1910s:

> The Young Intellectuals, in their very attack on Puritanism and a crabbed way of life, preached an ethic of hedonism, of pleasure and play – in short, a consumption ethic; yet, ironically … the consumption ethic was to be realized less than a decade later by a capitalism that, without self-consciousness, called itself … the "new capitalism."
>
> (1976, 63)

And from his perspective in 1976, Bell saw something similar going on with the still just decade old counterculture. As he put it:

> The "untrammeled self" … was a product of bourgeois society, with its glorification of rampant individualism. Though bourgeois society approved of rampant individualism in economics, it feared the excesses of self in culture, and sought to inhibit them. For a variety of complex historical reasons, the "cultural self" became anti-bourgeois, and sections of that movement allied themselves with political radicalism. Yet the impulses of the "cultural self" were not really radical, but rebellious. It sought to "express" itself by denying restraint and seeking release.… [T]he search for release has become legitimated in a liberal culture and exploited … by commercial entrepreneurs.
>
> (1976, 144–145)

Through the 1980s changes occurred that in general lent support to the basic thrust of Bell's message. Press coverage of Gary Hart's campaign for the 1984 presidential nomination introduced *yuppie* to the political lexicon. A *Times* editorial declaring it to be "The Year of the Yuppie," laid out rather clearly the drift that a sizable part of the 1960s generation had undergone. Yuppies were said to be "perhaps more than anything, the New Left," and were also described as "the people who created the counterculture." Regarding economics, the editorial claimed that "they tend toward the conservative," being "less concerned about unemployment than other age groups, and more inclined to favor further cuts in Federal spending." In addition, on "social issues, they strongly favor the equal rights amendment and freedom of choice on abortion, and oppose employment discrimination against homosexuals. On social *welfare* issues, color them conservative, less likely than older traditional Democrats to favor income maintenance programs" ("The Year," 1984, E20). While the *Times* editorial did not mention unions, an article that appeared a week prior did. The reader is told that yuppies "respond favorably to [the] suggestion that Democrats can no longer simply take labor's side against management, but must be concerned with long-term economic growth" ("Hart Taps," 1984, 26).

While Bell was prescient in sensing the dampening of politically progressive positions from the ageing 1960s generation, he appears to have been too sanguine about the ability of hedonism and the work ethic to co-exist. Writing a decade after the birth of the yuppie, William M. Sullivan notes that "Contrary to the supposed contradiction between a sturdy work ethic and hedonistic consumerism, once argued by Daniel Bell in *The Cultural Contradictions of Capitalism*, these urban professionals work very ambitiously while also consuming commodities … with equal energy" (1995, 132). The idea that a strong counter culture was simply replaced by a neoliberal crowd clearly can be misleading. It was not as much one group of people displacing another group, but one group of people maintaining its identity while adopting the strongly libertarian line so pleasing to the broader neoliberal culture. Nowhere is this as well captured than by the manifesto in opposition of government regulation of the airways presented by Grateful Dead lyricist John Perry Barlow at the 1996 Davos meetings. Thomas Frank captures the *zeitgeist* of the times in his summary of this event:

> Barlow's proclamation was part of a larger shift in American culture. While the "New Economy" was teaching Americans to heed the words of the Deadhead in Davos, it was also teaching us that those patriotic blue-collar types who had served such a crucial symbolic role in the late sixties were in fact exactly the thick, robotic louts of countercultural legend. Hippies were whispering words of wisdom about deregulation, cyberspace, lower taxes, but the hardhats, American opinion leaders clucked, just didn't get it; they were missing out on the joy, the freedom, the sweet buzz of liberation.
>
> (2000, xii)

Where do we go from here?

Paradoxically, it is the limitations of my own work that make spin-off projects by others all the more likely. Lacking a high comfort level in the realm of information technology, I have not been struck with any urges to take my data gathering in new and unusual directions. This has been, I hope, an advantage to the reader but leaves open to future writers many other directions to follow in building on what has appeared here. At the more traditional end of scholarly expertise – the mastery of other languages – lies another strong possibility for future work. Is it English alone that has changed in the way presented here? The possibilities for future studies here are plentiful indeed.

As optimistic as this sounds, there is a force at work that throws a complication into future studies of rhetorical shifts. Until about twenty years ago it was extremely difficult for a writer to make systematic comparisons between his choice of words and the choices of earlier writers. Moreover, it was difficult if not impossible to easily observe patterns of change in one's own vocabulary. Current technology and likely future technology will make a writer keenly aware of change and thus able to self-consciously magnify, minimize, or fully squelch such change. As George Soros (1998) would express it, the reflexivity of speakers will make any study of them all the more difficult. As surely as economic predictions of a micro nature require agents unaware of the predictions, revealing changes in language patterns will be compromised when those whose language is (or is not) changing are fully aware of the situation.

Turning from issues of method to the substantive issue of political changes in the wind, are there reasons for believing that a greater sensibility will arise in the near future to the right-wing drift in the way that we talk? When I began this project in early 2009, the financial disaster of 2008 was still in the air, and a 180 degree turn away from the worship of laissez-faire seemed likely. Re-thinking was the order of the day as Alan Greenspan admitted his thinking may have been wrong and long-time free-marketer Richard Posner began extolling the virtues of none other than John Maynard Keynes.[8]

Over the next three years, however, a pattern developed that suggested little had been learned from the financial meltdown of 2008. Revisionists increasingly found government failure, not market failure, to be the source of the long recession. As quickly as an appreciation of Keynesian deficits in a weak economy was rejuvenated, it atrophied. By the mid-term elections of 2010, candidates from both parties appeared eager to brag that "my proposed deficit is smaller than yours." The apotheosis of an infatuation with the rhetoric of the right appeared some time over this period when corporations were ever more referred to as *job creators*. The near deification of the remarkable corporations who cannot only give people jobs which they (the corporations) create and to actually pay them money for working on these jobs (rather than charging them for the job) perhaps lifted these corporations on a pedestal to a height not yet foreseen. And we must not forget the suggestion that asking corporations to pay more in taxes (post-recession) would be unseemly since it might discourage them from their job-creating urges.

Lest I end on a pessimistic note, I should mention that I write this final paragraph in December of 2011. *Occupy Wall Street* has only recently pulled up stakes and appears destined to exercise important political influence in the years ahead. It was the Canadian magazine *Adbusters* – originally founded by a disgruntled advertising executive – that must be given credit for instigating the whole affair. We can rest assured that masters of the language will play no small role in exposing change and bias in the way that we talk about the economy in the years ahead.

Notes

1 Introduction

1 The controversy over whether economists may simply be creating the reality that they purported to describe began with the findings of Marwell and Ames (1981) that economics students were more narrowly self-interested than other students. Their argument was lent stronger support by Frank, Gilovich, and Regan (1993), but thrown open to question by Yezer, Goldfarb, and Poppen (1996).

2 While most of the interest in rhetoric has been prompted by methodological rather than political economic concerns, there have been several writings that have attempted to uncover the dominance of neoliberal rhetoric. See, for example, Aune (2001), Starr (2004), and M.A. Smith (2007).

3 Unless otherwise stated, the data presented will be limited to *articles* from the *Times*. Had all categories been included (including birth notices, classified ads, comics, display ads, editorial articles, editorial cartoons, fire loss, front page, legal notice, letters to editor, lottery numbers, marriage, obituaries, photo standalones, real estate transactions, stock quotes, table of contents, and weather) the total occurrences of a word have been between 50 and 70 percent greater. For the other two sources of data (ProQuest and AHN) no similar breakdown by category is possible and the numbers shown reflect the entirety of the newspapers covered.

2 Markets over government

1 Figures are drawn from Table 1.3 in Office of Management and Budget, *Historical Tables, Budget of the United States Government, Fiscal Year 2009*, pp. 26–27.

2 The lack of market incentives on the part of government actors coupled with incentives to grow larger has been the dominant explanation for why governments fail. Among public choice theorists in recent year, the problems with government are also argued to be a direct outgrowth of democracy. See, for example, Caplan (2007), for whom, motives of elected officials aside, democracy is terribly inefficient. For a study of the rhetorical biases of Social Security critics, see Avsar (2011).

3 As data compiled by strong proponents of a smaller government Gwartney, Lawson, and Holcombe (1998, 2) indicate, of the twenty-three OECD countries studied, the United States had the smallest percentage of government outlays expressed as a percentage of GDP, and had by far the smallest increase in this percentage between 1960 and 1996 (6.2 percentage points compared with an average of 21.0 percentage points for the other OECD nations). Note that the overall rise over this period does not contradict the earlier claim that government purchases have been generally flat over this period. It is the maturing of social security, a government transfer rather than "purchase" that accounts for most of the 6.2 percentage point rise.

4 Nunberg argues that the appearance of *government* rather than *the government* is a

conservative strategy for criticizing the public sector. Nunberg points out that by responding to government failure during the Katrina disaster by declaring that "[g]overnment is extremely limited in what it can do," the fact that it was a particular government that failed (*the* government) is obscured and the condemnation becomes general rather than specific (Nunberg, 2006, 144). A search showed no decrease, however, in the likelihood that *government* would be preceded by *the*.

5 The trend in the *Times* appears to generalize to other U.S. newspapers. AHN indicates that between 1900 and 1922, *our* preceded *government* and *public sector* every sixty-three times. ProQuest indicates that since 1980 the frequency fell to once every 108 times.

6 The *Times* was not alone in the trends shown in Table 2.2. The other sources combine to show a doubling of the likelihood that private sector institutions would be called *ours*. AHN reveals an *our* every 487 times pre-1923, while ProQuest reveals a post-1979 likelihood of *205*.

7 T. Frank (2000) argues quite convincingly that the 1990s was an unusual period of increasing concentration of income and wealth occurring concurrent with an odd sort of market populism that characterized market forces as great levelers.

8 The other data sources support this trend. From 1900 to 1922, *government* was slightly more likely than *nation* to be preceded by *our* (once every sixty-three times compared with once every seventy-six times) but since 1985 the ProQuest papers show "government" to be only half as likely (once every 218 times compared with once every 109 times).

9 In gathering the data, *conservativism* – the alternate form of *conservatism* – was also counted.

10 ProQuest data also supports this trend, with *liberalism* going from three-fourths as often as *conservatism* in the 1980s to just over half as often over the last decade.

11 ProQuest data has been used here rather than *New York Times* data because of the small numbers yielded by the *Times*. These small numbers were, nonetheless, consistent with what the ProQuest data shows.

12 For a pioneering works in public choice theory, see Buchanan (1954) and Buchanan and Tullock (1962). *Economic imperialism* – the extension of economic models into new spheres – does not require that narrow self-interest be assumed. For some *imperialists* the maximization assumption is consistent with any rational behavior, with the selfless actions as capable of analysis as selfish actions. For examples of agents who maximize in highly atypical senses see, for example, Becker (1996).

13 The other sources support the trend shown in column 4, but show a considerably smaller change. AHN yields a pre-1923 column 4 equivalent of 962 and ProQuest a post-1979 rate of 613. No trend emerges in the rate at which personal pronouns follow *sell* or *market* (as measured for the *Times* in column 5). AHN shows a pre-1923 rate of once every 1,087 times and ProQuest a nearly equivalent post-1979 rate of once every 1,008 times.

14 *Sneer* is used several times by McCloskey (2000, 55, 61, 138, 157, 222) in the context of advising young economists to avoid the rigidity of the traditional, modernist approach to economics.

15 Negative descriptions of *big government* and *big business* were too few to allow the study of historical trends via the *New York Times* data. However, there was, not too surprisingly, a rise in the likelihood that government would be described negatively since 1980. Prior to 1980, one of the negative descriptions preceded *government* once every 2,520 times and after 1980 three times as often, once every 884 times.

16 According to Nunberg, Willkie's movement away from reference to *big business* and toward *big government* was less nuanced than this quote would suggest. He states that according to Willkie "the New Deal had failed to 'replace this corporate tyranny with a truly liberal faith. Today it is not Big Business that we have to fear. It is big government'" (Nunberg 2006, 123). No citation is provided for the part of this passage attributed to Willkie.

17 Quoted in Nunberg (2006, 103–104).

18 As I argue elsewhere (D. George, 1997), this is an often-overlooked fact when it comes to the question of how advertising and marketing influence desires and indirectly, the time that people choose to work for income. It is true that leisure is a needed as an input to the enjoyment of private goods. This would serve as a dampening effect on the movement out of leisure and into private goods, much as the rise in price that follows from an increase in demand dampens the effect of the increase in quantity demanded. For the work that began the interest in overwork, see Schor (1991). For a series of papers that includes cross-nation comparisons of trends, see Golden and Figart (2000). For studies of advertising's contribution to the rise in work time, see Fraser and Paton (2003), Golden and Altman (2008), Benhabib and Bisin (2010), and Cowling, Poolsombat, and Tomlonson (2011).

19 While Marshall was the one who used *tax burden* with considerable care, I argue elsewhere (D. George, 2012) that he bears much of the responsibility for the questionable claim that taxation of any realistic sort inevitably has *dead-weight* losses associated with it, that taxes are, in other words, always *distorting*.

20 Even Nunberg, the careful critic of conservative economic rhetoric, manages to adopt the common lingo. Contemplating liberal strategies to counter the conservative trends, he says that "It makes both political and rhetorical sense ... for Democrats to call for government that is effective and accountable, and for minimizing the tax *burden* [emphasis added] of the middle class" (2006, 126).

21 This was recognized by Anthony Downs when he noted that "[i]f society is at all complex, the government's gigantic policy mix is bound to contain at least one act which any given voter opposes" (1960, 549). The title of Downs' article ("Why the government budget is too small in a democracy") makes clear that he was no advocate of smaller government. Yet ironically it was a qualification to his basic argument – that when a members of a small group each realize large gains from a piece of legislation while members of the broader society each realize small losses, the legislation passes even when overall losses exceed overall gains – that is the most noted claim of this article.

22 The numbers actually show the number of occurrences of *fair price* and many similar phrases. Likewise, the headings for columns 2, 4, and 5 are simplifications. The full description of what is included in each column appears at the bottom of the table.

23 Despite this much lower tendency to speak of *unfair prices*, it was an article on perceptions of fairness in the private sector (Kahneman, Knetsch, and Thaler, 1986) that may have had the greatest impact in re-introducing fairness to mainstream economics.

24 If the writer did not share citizenship with the reader being addressed, then *your* could function as a collective pronoun. *Your taxes* would in such cases be equivalent to *your nation's taxes*. Typically, however, the writers share common citizenship with their readers and *your taxes* are understood as a singular rather than collective pronoun, with *our taxes* serving in the latter capacity.

25 Ryan, Sweeder, and Bednar (2002) use a spread in narcissism in making their argument for character education in the high schools. Twenge and Campbell (2009) see no let-up in the narcissistic trend fully thirty years after Christopher Lasch first explored the matter.

26 ProQuest newspapers show numbers consistent with this movement toward *my taxes* or *your taxes*. Post-1985 newspapers have spoken of such taxes 1.75 times as often as *our taxes*. However, the historical newspapers show numbers quite inconsistent with the pre-1930s *New York Times.* While *your taxes* and *my taxes* was only 0.535 as common as *our taxes* in the *Times* during this period, it was 1.63 times as common in the historical newspapers.

27 The other sources yield strong support for the trends shown in columns 5 and 7, but less so for the column 6 trend. AHN shows government acts, interventions, and interferences comprising 0.699, 0.168, and 0.133 respectively. ProQuest shows 0.504, 0.209, and 0.287 respectively.

28 *Interference* is not included in Table 2.22 because, for reasons that I was unable to determine, there was a clear tendency for the same number to appear whenever *interference* or *intervention* were keyed in. This omission does not affect the basic conclusions reached.
29 The controversy began with the book by Fogel and Engerman (1975).
30 More formally, allocative efficiency requires that for everything produced, the marginal cost equals the marginal benefit and productive efficiency requires that marginal cost equals average cost.
31 ProQuest newspapers since 1980 match very closely the numbers shown in Table 2.24, and with much larger numbers. For the public sector, there were 1,624 positive and 1,383 negative descriptions for a ratio of 1.2 For the private sector, there were 774 positive and 234 negative for a ratio of 3.3. AHN show a much larger ratio of positive over negative for both private and public sectors, 6.9 and 30.3 respectively.
32 The seminal article on the problems arising from informational asymmetry (Grossman and Stiglitz 1980) appeared, ironically, at the very start of the era that has been ever less inclined to see any shortcomings of the market.
33 The favorable descriptions included were *efficient regulation, needed regulation, needed to regulate, need for regulation, advisable regulation, advisable to regulate, recommended regulation, important regulation, urgent regulation, important to regulate*, and *urgent to regulate*. The negative descriptions were *inefficient regulation, inefficient to regulate, wasteful regulation, wasteful to regulate, cumbersome regulation, cumbersome to regulate, unnecessary regulation, unnecessary to regulate, costly regulation, costly to regulate, foolish regulation, foolish to regulate, burdensome regulation*, and *burdensome to regulate*.
34 The other two sources provide evidence consistent with the *Times*. American's Historical Newspapers show 167 favorable regulation descriptions and ten unfavorable for a 17.7 ratio. ProQuest newspapers show 143 favorable and 173 unfavorable for a 0.83 ratio.
35 See Heinzerling and Ackerman (2002) for a brilliant critique of the anti-regulatory movement. They note, among other things, the literature that traces loss of life to the decrease in incomes allegedly caused by funding environmental programs. As they point out, extending this strange logic to other areas of spending would force us to similarly reason that "this year's budget for national defense … will kill almost 45,000 people" (2002, 669) with these deaths all being domestic and all due to the declining disposable income that the defense spending caused.

3 Competition over cooperation and monopoly

1 For an earlier exploration into the changing meanings of *competitive*, see D. George (1996).
2 *Oligopoly* is another example of a *non-competitive* industry, in the traditional sense. Because occurrences of *oligopoly* were relatively rare in the *New York Times*, I chose to let *monopoly* stand alone.
3 The trends reflected in the other two sources show a stronger trend toward *competition*. AHN reveals *competition* appearing 3.5 times as often as "monopoly" prior to 1923. ProQuest newspapers show the former appearing 13.7 more often than the latter since 1980.
4 As indicated in column 2 of Tables 3.2, 3.3, and 3.5, *monopolized* is included as another adjective of *monopoly*. In the interest of readability, I chose not to mention this in the text, with *monopolistic* alone being mentioned.
5 The trend is again more pronounced when comparing the two other sources. AHN shows "competition" and "competitive" to be 3.9 times more common than "monopoly" and "monopolistic" prior to 1923. ProQuest shows this figure rising to 18.9 since 1980.

6 And still again, the other sources show an even larger shift. AHN, consistent with the *Times*, shows *competitive* to be 3.8 times as frequent as *monopolisitic* prior to 1923. ProQuest shows *competitive* to be 89.5 times as frequent post-1980.
7 AHN reveals *competition* to have been 6.8 times as frequently used as *competitive* prior to 1923. ProQuest corroborates the pattern revealed in the *Times*, as *competition* has appeared 1.9 times as often as *competitive* since 1980.
8 The other data sources reinforce this basic trend. AHN show *monopoly* to be 6.3 times more common than *monopolistic* before 1923, and ProQuest shows *monopoly* to be 15.7 more common than *monopolistic* since 1980.
9 The other two sources reinforce what column 3 shows but diverge considerably from column 6. Starting with column 3, AHN shows a 4.6 ratio and ProQuest a 16.7 ratio. For column 6, the ratios are 0.126 and 0.774, respectively.
10 The direction of change from the early to late periods are also reflected in AHN and ProQuest. The equivalent column 7 number pre-1923 is 12.3 as derived from AHN, and the equivalent number post-1980 as derived from ProQuest is 30.9.
11 Participants in the now monopolized industry will operate in the interest of all fellow participants, not the interest of the wider society.
12 AHN shows relatively greater usage of *cooperation* and *teamwork* prior to 1923 with a column 3 equivalent ratio of just 1.13. ProQuest yields a post-1980 ratio of 3.59, very similar to the *Times.*
13 *Competitive* appeared 33,175 times and *cooperative* appeared 64,286 times in AHN, for a ratio of just 0.52, well below the *Times* figure for this same approximate period.
14 According to Lynn, it was not as much critics of free-market capitalism who were inclined to speak negatively of competition in the late 19th and early 20th centuries but aspiring monopolists. As he argues, "[t]o justify [the] complete elimination of competition, this second generation of post-Civil War monopolists came bearing a new vision, which was that the cutthroat competition in the years after the war was needlessly 'wasteful' and 'inefficient'" (2010, 105). Since Lynn's main focus is the rise of monopoly since the 1970s, it is hard to understand the decreasing tendency to speak negatively of competition unless, as will be argued later in the chapter, these very monopolists have come to describe their behaviors as *competitive*.
15 If the often used expressions *fair competition* and *unfair competition* had been included in the numbers shown in the tables, the same trend would still emerge, though not as pronounced. I elected to not include these because *unfair competition* is less a criticism of competition itself than a criticism of how it is carried out.
16 The other sources once again support this basic trend. Prior to 1923, AHN yield just four instances of *stay competitive* or *remain competitive*, or once every 8,293 times that *competitive* appeared. Since 1980 in the newspapers comprising ProQuest, *stay* or *remain* preceded *competitive* once every thirty-five times.
17 As late as 1964, the practice of using *competitive* to mean something other than *trying hard* was apparently still not common, at least in the *Times*. Speaking of the Notre Dame football team of that year, the quote appears as "Parseghian says we'll have a 'competitive' team" ("Notre Dame," 1964, 18). The quotation marks around *competitive* suggest that the writer of the article was not particularly comfortable with the intended meaning of the word.

4 Consumers over citizens

1 John Kenneth Galbraith's classic (1958) set the tone for this period in suggesting misplaced values. Also see Knox (1960). Goodwin, Ackerman, and Kiron (eds) (1997) provide an excellent source of excerpted articles on the subject of consumerism.
2 See Mandeville (1924) for his "fable of the bees."

3 See Vivian Walsh (1996), particularly Chapter 2 ("Rationality as maximizing utility") and Chapter 5 ("Rationality as the pursuit of self-interest") for a particularly clear analysis of the confusions surrounding self-interest. For a history of shifting understandings of self-interest, see Faulhaber (1977). For a work of fiction that attempts to rescue Adam Smith from simplistic views of his beliefs regarding human motivations, see Wight (2002). And for a history of competing beliefs about the effects of self-interest in the marketplace on the broader society, see Hirschman (1982a).

4 The shift is more impressive when the two other data sets are compared. The historical newspapers used *selfish* 27 times as often as *self-interest* while the ProQuest newspapers since 1980 have used *selfish* just two times as often.

5 See a recent article of mine (D. George 2007) for the problems with thinking of students as customers. The professions in general have been moving in the direction of renaming *clients* and *patients* as *customers*.

6 The data from ProQuest newspapers and AHN provide strong support for these trends. Comparing the bottom and top rows in Table 4.2 with what the recent and historical data shows reveals the following. While the *positive private* to *positive public* ratio went from 0.18 in the first period to 2.89 in the most recent period, as shown in Row 6 of Table 4.2, it went from 0.11 in the pre-1923 historical newspapers to 1.49 in the post-1979 newspapers. This constitutes less of a change but a significant change nonetheless.

7 The other sources show an even greater trend that revealed in Table 4.3. The table shows the ratio of *positive voter* to *positive citizen* going from 0.15 in the first period to 0.85 in the most recent. The other data sources (ProQuest newspapers and AHN) show the earlier ratio to be 0.09 and the later ratio to be 1.25.

8 Since the mid-1950s, *Mad Magazine* has offered spoofs of advertising. But beginning sometime in the 1960s, advertisers managed to adopt an ironic, sometimes self-deprecatory stance. Beginning in the 1990s, *Adbusters* – begun by disgruntled marketing experts – began a more sophisticated attack on the "culture of persuasion." For critical analyses of *Adbusters*, see Rumbo (2002), and Haiven (2007).

9 I examine the fallacies of such evolutionary arguments in an earlier article (D. George 1989). Such simplistic justifications for extant institutions ("because they exist, they must be good") remains widespread but should not be associated with the old school of institutional economics that builds on evolutionary ideas. See Hodgson (1993) and Dugger and Sherman (2000) for strong challenges to the mainstream paradigm.

10 The other sources corroborate this trend. *Good habits* exceeded *bad habits* by a ratio of 1.3 in newspapers prior to 1923 while *bad habits* exceeds *good habits* by a ratio of 7.0 in the ProQuest newspapers since 1980. For purposes of comparison with column 6 of Table 4.5, the early ratio is 1.29, the later one 0.14. And the trend is further corroborated by comparing the number of occurrences of *compulsive impulsive* and *irrational* with the number of occurrences of *deliberate* and *rational*. The former set of descriptions rose from being 1.5 percent as frequent as the latter set prior to 1930 to 2.9 percent as frequent over the next fifty years, to 4.6 percent as frequent since 1980.

11 See Frankfurt (1971), for whom it was the human ability to reflect on one's tastes and thus have meta-preferences (which he chose to call *second-order* preferences) that set humans apart from other animals Also see Jeffrey (1974), and Sen (1974, 1977) for early work on meta-preferences and Altman (2010) and White (2006) for more recent articles. My work in this area (George 1984, 1993, 2001) emphasizes market shortcomings in the shaping of tastes. See Van Tuinen (2011) for more recent work along similar lines. See Akst (2011) for a very readable treatment of self-control as a contemporary problem. As John Davis (2003) argues, the foundations of mainstream economic theory make any recognition of an *interior* conscious agent problematic. If Davis is correct, the very likelihood of the mainstream acknowledging such *unrevealed* preferences becomes all the less likely.

12 AHN and ProQuest newspapers show a considerably larger change. In the pre-1923 newspapers, *shopping addiction* and its many equivalents appeared only once every 193,996 times that *shopping*, etc. appeared (three times out of 581,989). The post-1979 papers show a frequency twice that of the most recent *Times*, with *shopping addiction* and its equivalents appearing once every 454 times.
13 Posting on "Jokes in your profession" of the "Straight Dope Message Board" by Astorian on 1/27/06 http://boards.straightdope.com/sdmb/showthread.php?t=355773&page=2.
14 *Need* and *want* are more commonly used than either *desire* or *prefer*. Since any changes in their relative frequencies bring up different issues than I am trying to focus on here, I have elected to exclude them from the table and from the discussion that follows.
15 Paul Samuelson's dissertation of 1937 was pivotal in moving the discussion toward *revealed preference* (see Samuelson 1947). Another major contributor to the shift was John Hicks (1939) with his introduction of indifference curve analysis that drew upon *preferences* while abandoning any mention of *desire*.
16 It was initially surprising to discover that *want* was the least likely to be described as *foolish*, etc. as *preference* was fully 200 times more likely to be so described. On some reflection, however, I conclude that this is primarily attributable that "want" is used overwhelmingly used as a verb rather than as a noun.
17 See, for example, S. George and Weimerskirch (1994).
18 Another distinction, not of immediate relevance here, is that "cost" is more used to refer to what was required to produce (or acquire) more than just one item, particularly from the production standpoint. Thus producing 100 items costing, on average, $1 each indicates that average cost is $1 while total cost is $100. While *price* is sometimes used to denote a collective expenditure ("What price did you pay for all these clothes?") it more often is used refers to what the buyer pays and seller receives for a single item.
19 The other sources closely parallel this trend. For AHN the column 3 equivalent is 27.4 while for ProQuest it is 1.20.
20 The word *reflation*, defined by Pigou in the 1930s as "inflation undertaken on certain particular occasions, with a specific intention and subject to a predetermined limit" (1935, 91), has pretty much disappeared from usage. This is largely due to deflation, when such "reflation" was called for, having posed no problem since the 1930s but is likely due in part to the modern tendency to treat any rise in prices as nearly by definition a bad thing.
21 All the texts acknowledge that perfect competition is a theoretical ideal that only a very few markets can even approximate. Two books – Keen (2001) and Hill and Myatt (2010, chapters five and six) – offer two particularly compelling critiques of the textbook emphasis on perfect competition that are aimed at the non-specialist.

5 Management over labor

1 The overall income figures are derived from Table 1.7 of Mishel, Bernstein and Shierholz (2009, 61) and the capital income figures from Table 1.18 (2009, 84).
2 These same patterns are found in AHN and in ProQuest. For labor, the ratio was 0.18 in the early source and 0.02 in the recent. For management, the ratio was 8.00 in the early source and 0.59 in the recent.
3 The modern text often includes *entrepreneurship*. This is an error of abstraction. Land, labor, and capital are each defined at such a high level of abstraction that any imaginable economy in history had to make use of all three. Entrepreneurship, in contrast, needs to be kept distinct from labor in just one sort of economy, namely, free-market capitalism. For further examples of such errors of abstraction, see Heilbroner and Milberg (1995).

4 The other sources provide supporting evidence for the overall trend, though the change is not as great. The ratio of *organized labor* to *big labor* went from 14.8 prior to 1923 (AHN) to 6.4 since 1980 (ProQuest newspapers).

5 The post-1980 ProQuest newspapers ratio of *major* to *big* was almost identical to the *Times* figure for this period, 0.82. But the pre-1923 figure a hundred times lower (0.001).

6 The numbers were arrived at by breaking down the data by decades and dividing the equivalent of what appears in column 6 of Table 5.7 (computed by decade rather than the longer periods shown) by what appears in column 6 of Table 5.8 (again computed by decades).

7 A recent *New York Times* article (Rampell, 2011) examines a relatively new practice, namely, limiting job searches to the currently unemployed or only recently unemployed. Long-term unemployment has increasingly been taken as a signal of relative undesirability.

8 The other sources corroborate this trend. There were fifteen favorable and two unfavorable descriptions of unions in AHN, but 1,040 favorable and 1,432 unfavorable in ProQuest since 1980.

9 The other sources mirror the trends shown with *create* and *creation* (of jobs and employment) rising from 10.9 percent pre-1929 to 86.4 percent post-1980. "Job" relative to "employment" (creation and provision of) rose from 26.1 percent to 97.5 percent.

10 The influence of religion on economic thinking is generally regarded to have been in steady decline since the rise of mercantilism in 16th century Europe, though its influence at least through Adam Smith remained significant. The spread of neoliberal thought as something of a secular religion has not gone unnoticed in recent years. See, in particular, Nelson (1991). Writing before the collapse of the Soviet Union, he accurately foresaw the quasi-religious tone that belief in an unhampered market would come to have for many. For a theologian's of how the 1990s brought an increasingly religious attitude toward the market, see Cox (1999).

11 ProQuest yields smaller numbers for the 2000s, namely, 17.08, 2.77, and 5.06 for columns 1, 2, and 3 respectively. These do remain far higher than the pre-1960 *Times* numbers that appear in the table.

12 The other sources support the patterns seen in the table. As with the *Times*, *capitalists* comprised over 99 percent of the three possibilities in the early 20th century. Since 1980, ProQuest has favored *entrepreneur* about the same relative amount as the *Times* (60.1 percent), but *capitalist* considerably less (13.3 percent) and *business owner* considerably more (26.5 percent). According to Nunberg, "*Entrepreneur* was pressed into service in the late 19th century to replace *capitalist*, which had been tainted by its association with silk-hatted predators" (2006, 57). While this may be so in some circles, the data in Table 5.18 show that it would be many decades before the word was widely used in the *Times*.

13 As Rich Morin of the Pew Research Center reports,

> In 1948 the Current Population survey reported that 18.6% of all full-time and part-time workers ages 16 and older were self-employed. Over the ensuing six decades, the percentage of self-employed workers has drifted slowly downward. Today, about 11% of the job force is self-employed and that percentage has been more or less unchanged throughout this decade.
>
> (Morin, 2009, 1)

Based on Bureau of Labor Statistics and their own analysis, Mishel, Bernstein, and Allegretto give lower figures throughout the same period, estimating 12.0 percent of the labor force as self-employed in 1948 and between 6.5 and 7.5 percent since 1967 (2005, 269). Besides the trend over time, the United States stands out in how few are self-employed. Lynn mentions that "[a] new study by the Organization for Economic

Cooperation and Development ranked the United States as the second lowest of twenty-two rich nations in the percentage of workers who are self-employed, above only Luxembourg" (Lynn, 2010: 130–131).

14 Noted in Nunberg (2006, 57).

6 Growth over progress, justice, and equality

1 Referring to how we might best regard "the Social Science … which finds the secret of this universe in 'supply-and-demand'," Carlyle went on to conclude that it was "[n]ot a 'gay science,' I should say, like some we have heard of; no, a dreary, desolate, and indeed quite abject and distressing one; what we might call, by way of eminence, the *dismal science* [his emphasis]" (Carlyle, 1849) quoted in Peart and Levy (2005, 154).

2 Mill (1929, 748), quoted in Landreth and Colander (2002, 172).

3 The conversion from 1920 British pounds to 2008 U.S. dollars is based on the high estimates provided by Officer and Williamson (2009). The low range of their estimates would have the lower earning group earning between $900 and $4,400 dollars and the high earning group between $29,200 and $146,000.

4 See, for example, Hamilton (2004), Czech (2000) and Stoll (2008). For the perspective of a more orthodox economist who questions the wisdom of unlimited growth, see Richard Easterlin (1998).

5 The subtle differences between *progress*, *growth*, and *development* receive the most attention from heterodox economists. See, for example, Hosseini (2003), Starr (2006), and Tiemstra (2008).

6 Soon after ecological warnings first gained wide attention in the 1960s appeared Mishan's *The Cost of Economic Growth* (1967). Hirsch (1976) added to the discussion the self-canceling nature of growth from a psychological perspective. More recently, Hamilton (2004) combines the psychological and ecological.

7 The evidence of increasing inequality is plentiful. For particularly extensive treatment of the thirty-year trends and their consequences, see Lardner and Smith (2005).

8 The ProQuest data strongly corroborates the *Times* data summarized in the table.

9 The two pre-1980 uses of "level playing field" were both literal rather than metaphorical in nature. In defending his qualifications to supervise the construction of a new ballpark, "Frank J. Farrell, President of the New York American League Club Baseball Club," while admitting to no experience in construction, announced that "through his racing interests [he had] known men who could construct grand stands and level playing fields" ("Deny," 1911, 4).

10 The other sources corroborate the pattern for *achievement*, with AHN yielding a ratio figure of 0.24 for the period prior to 1923, and ProQuest a figure of 0.10 since 1980. For *success*, however, the data is counterintuitive. *Market* and related adjectives went from being 7.9 times more often to precede *success* prior to 1923 to 3.7 times more often since 1980.

11 AHN and ProQuest data support this.

7 Conclusion

1 Schlesinger Jr. constructed his argument on the basis of earlier work by his father (Schlesinger Sr. 1939). For an alternative view of political cycles, based on the idea that both a private orientation and a public orientation bear the seeds of their own destruction, see Hirschman (1982b).

2 The co-optation of the liberal intellectual by power elites is well argued by Hedges (2010).

3 That the 1990s stood out more than the 1980s as the decade when the hegemony of markets truly took hold is supported by several books appearing just before and after

the start of the new millennium. See, in particular, Kuttner (1995), Luttwak (1999), Klein (2000), Meeropol (2000) and Stiglitz (2003).

4 The widely shared belief that 1980 is the critical year of the rightward shift is attested to by Cambridge University Press's recent series "The World Since 1980." See D. Baker (2007) for specific focus on the United States.

5 See Tables 2.1, 2.2, 2.10, 2.14, 2.21, 3.1, 3.2, 3.3, 3.5, 3.6, 3.10 3.14, 4.6, 4.8, 5.9, 5.12, 5.19, 5.20, 5.21 6.4, 6.6, and 6.12. For unusual instances where the change from the 1940s to the 1960s was in the opposite direction of the change from the 1960s to the 1980s, see Tables 3.8, 3.12, and 5.20.

6 Events in the summer of 2011 provide still another confirmation of the Klein thesis. Commentators are generally still in shock that the 2008 collapse did not spell the end for neoliberalism. Overlooked is Klein's message that social breakdown paves the way for furthering the neoliberal agenda. The shrinking of government and continued cutting of taxes is being offered as a *cure* to the collapse.

7 Major critics of the globalizing events of the 1990s come from a number of perspectives. For a left-leaning social criticism, see Grieder (1997). For a more traditional economist's critique, see Stiglitz (2002). Gray (1998) brings a traditional British conservative perspective in questioning the spread of global interdependence while Soros (1998) brings the perspective of a global financier.

8 See, in particular, Posner (2010). Well before the economic meltdown began, the noted liberal Keynesian Paul Krugman (2007) saw lots of trouble brewing.

References

"A City Asks for a Return on its Dollar." *New York Times (1923–Current File)*, January 15, 1995. http://search.proquest.com/docview/109436914?accountid=11999.

"A Plausible Mexican Rescue Plan." *New York Times (1923–Current File)*, January 06, 1995. http://search.proquest.com/docview/109420761?accountid=11999.

"A Top-Heavy Society." *New York Times (1923–Current File)*, January 18, 1925. http://search.proquest.com/docview/103680409?accountid=11999.

"Advocates a Curb on Truck Services." *New York Times (1923–Current File)*, May 07, 1926. http://search.proquest.com/docview/103841481?accountid=11999.

Akst, D. (2011) *We Have Met the Enemy: Self-control in an Age of Excess*. New York: The Penguin Press.

Altman, M. (2010) "Freedom to Choose and Choice X-inefficiencies: Human and Consumer Rights, and Positive and Normative Implications of Choice Behavior," *Review of Social Economy* 68(4): 395–411.

"Arrest Three Men as White Slavers." *New York Times (1857–1922)*, Aug 08, 1915. http://search.proquest.com/docview/97655027?accountid=11999.

"Article 3 – no title." *New York Times (1923–Current File*), November 03, 1958, p. 40. http://search.proquest.com/docview/114506552?accountid=11999.

"Attack on News," *Dallas Morning News*, May 14, 1905, p. 2.

Aune, J. A. (2001) *Selling the Free Market: The Rhetoric of Economic Correctness*. New York: The Guilford Press.

Avsar, R. A. (2011) "Mainstream Economic Rhetoric and Institutions," *Journal of Economic Issues*, 45(1): 1–21.

Baker, Al and Rashbaum, William. "Prosecutors Interview Two Shot by Police in Queens." *New York Times (1923–Current File)*, December 05, 2006. http://search.proquest.com/docview/93145953?accountid=11999.

Baker, D. (2007) *The United States Since 1980*. Cambridge, MA: Cambridge University Press.

Barber, B. R. (2007) *Consumed: How Markets Corrupt Children, Infantilize Adults, and Swallow Citizens Whole*. New York: W.W. Norton & Company.

Baumol, W. J. and Blinder, A. S. (2006) *Economics: Principles and Policy*, 10th edn. Mason, OH: Thomson South-Western.

Becker, G. S. (1996) *Accounting for Tastes*. Cambridge, MA: Harvard University Press.

Bell, D. (1976) *The Cultural Contradictions of Capitalism*. New York: Basic Books.

Bellah, R. N., Madsen, R., Sullivan, W. M., Swidler, A., and Tipton, S. M. (1991) *The Good Society*. New York: Alfred A. Knopf.

Benhabib, J., and Bisin, A. (2010) "Social Construction of Preferences: Advertising," in

J. Benhabib, A. Bisin, and M. Jackson (eds.), *Handbook of Social Economics*, 201–220. Amsterdam: Elsevere.

Bennhold, Katrin. "Airbus Considering a Request for State Aid." *New York Times (1923–Current File)*, June 19, 2006. http://search.proquest.com/docview/93247693?accountid=11999.

Berle Jr., A. A. and Means, G. C. (1933) *The Modern Corporation and Private Property.* New York: Macmillan and Co.

Berlin, I. (1969) *Four Essays on Liberty*. New York: Oxford University Press.

"Big Labor a Peril, O'Mahoney Warns." *New York Times (1923–Current File)*, June 17, 1937. http://search.proquest.com/docview/102324597?accountid=11999.

"Big Suits to be Delayed." *New York Times (1857–1922)*, September 27, 1910. http://search.proquest.com/docview/97054977?accountid=11999.

Birch, K. and Mykhnenko, V. (2010) "Introduction: A World Turned Right Way Up," in K. Birch and V. Mykhnenko (eds.), *The Rise and Fall of Neoliberalism: The Collapse of an Economic Order?* New York: Zed Books.

"Bright New Work." *New York Times (1923–Current File)*, May 18 1933. http://search.proquest.com/docview/100688929?accountid=11999.

Bruder, Jessica. "A Bus Company Run Over by a Train." *New York Times (1923–Current File)*, August 08, 2004. http://search.proquest.com/docview/92865420?accountid=11999.

Buchanan, J. M. (1954) "Individual Choice in Voting and the Market," *Journal of Political Economy*, 62: 334–343.

Buchanan, J. M. and Tullock, G. (1962) *The Calculus of Consent: Logical Foundations of Constitutional Democracy*. Ann Arbor: University of Michigan Press.

Budget of the United States Government. *Historical Tables, Fiscal Year 2009.* Washington, D.C.: U.S. Government Printing Office.

Bye, R. T. 1934. *Principles of Economics*, 3rd edn. New York: F.S. Crofts & Co.

"Call Anti-Trust Law Hindrance to Business." *New York Times (1857–1922)*, September 27, 1922. http://search.proquest.com/docview/98676477?accountid=11999.

"Can't Cut Rates on Oils." *New York Times (1923–Current File)*, April 04, 1923. http://search.proquest.com/docview/100226015?accountid=11999.

Caplan, B. D. (2007) *The Myth of the Rational Voter: Why Democracies Choose Bad Policies.* Princeton, NJ: Princeton University Press.

[Carlyle, Thomas]. "Negro Question." 1849. "Occasional Discourse on the Negro Question." *Fraser's Magazine for Town and Country*, 40:670–679.

"Challenging the Telephone Merger." *New York Times (1923–Current File)*, February 13, 1997. http://search.proquest.com/docview/109769154?accountid=11999.

Chamber's Concise Dictionary, (1991) Edinburgh: Chambers.

"Changing Times Beset Princeton Clubs." *New York Times (1923–Current File)*, May 18, 1969. http://search.proquest.com/docview/118746088?accountid=11999.

"Cheaper Powder for Miners." *New York Times (1857–1922)*, September 03, 1900. http://search.proquest.com/docview/96016182?accountid=11999.

Cheng, J. and Frangos, A. "Palin Addresses Asian Conference." *The Wall Street Journal Asia*, September 24, 2009. http://search.proquest.com/docview/315595127?accountid=11999.

"Childminder Mums." *The Times* (London), September 29, 2009. http://search.proquest.com/docview/320239782?accountid=11999.

"C. I. O. Realistic on Pay." *New York Times (1923–Current File)*, May 09, 1955. http://search.proquest.com/docview/113311685?accountid=11999.

"Congress Expects 4 More Messages from Roosevelt." *New York Times (1923–Current File)*, May 14, 1934. http://search.proquest.com/docview/101133637?accountid=11999.

"Consumer Interest and Banking Interests." *New York Times (1923–Current File)*, March 20, 1981. http://search.proquest.com/docview/121537944?accountid=11999.

"Corner Kicks." *New York Times (1923–Current File)*, January 13, 2004. http://search.proquest.com/docview/92783053?accountid=11999.

Cowling, K. R., Poolsombat, R., and Tomlonson, P. R. (2011) "Advertising and Labour Supply: Why do Americans Work Such Long Hours?" *International Review of Applied Economics*, 25(2): 283–301.

Cox, H. (1999) "The Market as God: Living in the New Dispensation," *The Atlantic Monthly*, March.

Czech, B. (2000) *Shoveling Fuel for a Runaway Train.* Berkeley: University of California Press.

Dalley, J. "Failed by Words, so to Speak very Few Proverbs Stand Up to Even Semi-Serious Scrutiny. and then theres the Ones we Need but, Yes, Havent Invented JAN DALLEY." *Financial Times*, September 17, 2005. http://search.proquest.com/docview/249682375?accountid=11999.

Davis, J. (2003) *The Theory of the Individual in Economics: Identity and Value.* London and New York: Routledge.

"Defends Primary and Filibuster." *New York Times (1923–Current File)*, September 06, 1927. http://search.proquest.com/docview/104105057?accountid=11999.

"Deny Gordons Claim to Baseball Stock." *New York Times (1857–1922)*, November 22, 1911. http://search.proquest.com/docview/97112286?accountid=11999.

"Display Ad 15 – no title." *New York Times (1923–Current File)*, June 01, 1943. http://search.proquest.com/docview/106602208?accountid=11999.

"Display Ad 31 – no title." *New York Times (1923–Current File)*, June 15, 1943. http://search.proquest.com/docview/106681305?accountid=11999.

"Display Ad 135 – no title." *New York Times (1857–1922)*, October 15, 1920. http://search.proquest.com/docview/98101064?accountid=11999.

"Display Ad 204 – no title." *New York Times (1923–Current File)*, September 21, 1930. http://search.proquest.com/docview/98910281?accountid=11999.

Dolan, E. G. and Lindsey, D. E. 1988. *Economics*, 5th edn. Chicago: The Dryden Press.

"Don't Politicize County Procurement Process." *McClatchey Tribune Business News*, August 5, 2009.

"Don't Politicize History." *The Windsor Star*, September 10, 2009, B1.

Downs, A. (1960) "Why the Government Budget is Too Small in a Democracy," *World Politics*, 12(4): 541–563.

Dugger, W. M., and Sherman, J. J. (2000) *Reclaiming Evolution: A Dialogue Between Marxism and Institutionalism on Social Change*, London and New York: Routledge.

"Dumping the Poor into State Laps." *New York Times (1923–Current File)*, February 16, 1981. http://search.proquest.com/docview/121579214?accountid=11999.

Easterlin, R. A. (1998) *Growth Triumphant: The Twenty-First Century in Historical Perspective.* Ann Arbor: The University of Michigan Press.

"Editorial." *Northwest Florida Daily News*, December 29, 2004. http://search.proquest.com/docview/379818450?accountid=11999.

Ely, R. T. and Hess, R. H. (1937) *Outlines of Economics*, 6th edn. New York: The Macmillan Company.

"England." *New York Daily Times (1851–1857)*, June 21, 1852. http://search.proquest.com/docview/95778738?accountid=11999.

"Environmental Tasks in 1998." *New York Times (1923–Current File)*, January 02, 1998. http://search.proquest.com/docview/109907082?accountid=11999.

Fairchild, F. R., Furniss, E. S., and Buck, N. S. (1930) *Elementary Economics*, revised edn. New York: The Macmillan Company.

Faulhaber, R. W. (1977) "The Rise and Fall of 'Self-Interest'," *Review of Social Economy*, 35: 311–329.

"Few Blacks among Peace Marchers in the Capital." *New York Times (1923–Current File)*, November 16, 1969. http://search.proquest.com/docview/118441103?accountid=11999.

"Financial Dailies Negotiate Merger." *New York Times (1923–Current File)*, May 06, 1930. http://search.proquest.com/docview/98951868?accountid=11999.

"Fleets War Games Ended." *New York Times (1857–1922)*, July 15, 1916. http://search.proquest.com/docview/97890667?accountid=11999.

Fogel, R. W. and Engerman, S. L. (1975) *Time on the Cross: The Economics of American Negro Slavery.* New York: W.W. Norton and Company.

"France." *New York Daily Times (1851–1857)*, March 18, 1852. http://search.proquest.com/docview/95771513?accountid=11999.

Frank, R. H., Gilovich, T., and Regan, D. (1993) "Does Studying Economics Inhibit Cooperation?" *Journal of Economic Perspectives*, 7: 159–171.

Frank, T. (2000) *One Market Under God: Extreme Capitalism, Market Populism, and the End of Economic Democracy.* New York: Doubleday.

Frankfurt, H. G. (1971) "Freedom of the Will and the Concept of a Person." *Journal of Philosophy*, 68: 5–20.

Fraser, S. and Paton, D. (2003) "Does Advertising Increase Labour Supply? Time Series Evidence from the UK," *Applied Economics*, 35(11): 1357–1368.

"Free Universities – Or Captive?" *New York Times (1923–Current File)*, October 20, 1969. http://search.proquest.com/docview/118525295?accountid=11999.

Friedman, M. (1953) *Essays in Positive Economics.* Chicago: University of Chicago Press.

Friedman, M. and Friedman, R. (1980) *Free to Choose: A Personal Statement*, New York: Harcourt, Brace and Javonovich.

"From P.C. to E.C." *New York Times (1923–Current File)*, January 12, 1993: A21. http://search.proquest.com/docview/109232901?accountid=11999.

Galbraith, J. K. (1958) *The Affluent Society.* Cambridge: The Riverside Press.

Galbraith, J. K. (1978) *The New Industrial State*, 3rd edn, revised. Boston: Houghton Mifflin Company.

Garrett, T. A. and Rhine, R. M. (2006) "On the Size and Growth of Government," *Federal Reserve Bank of St. Louis Review*, January–February: 13–28.

Garver, F. B. and Hansen, A. H. (1947). *Principles of Economics*, 3rd edn. Boston: Ginn and Company.

Gemmill, P. F. (1955) *Current Introductory Economics.* New York Harper & Brothers, Publishers.

George, D. (1984) "Meta-Preferences: Reconsidering Contemporary Notions of Free Choice," *International Journal of Social Economics*, 11(3/4): 92–107.

George, D. (1989) "Social Evolution and the Role of Knowledge," *Review of Social Economy*, 47(1): 55–73.

George, D. (1990) "The Rhetoric of Economics Texts," *Journal of Economic Issues*, 24(3): 861–877.

George, D. (1993). "Does the Market Create Preferred Preferences?" *Review of Social Economy* 51(3): 323–346.

George, D. (1996) "The Rhetoric of Economics Texts Revisited." In A. Aslanbeigui and

M. I. Naples (eds.), *Rethinking Economic Principles: Critical Essays on Introductory Textbooks*, 28–43. Chicago: Irwin.

George, D. (1997) "Working Longer Hours: Pressure from the Boss or Pressure from the Marketers," *Review of Social Economy*, 55: 33–65.

George, D. (2001) *Preference Pollution: How Markets Create the Desires we Dislike.* Ann Arbor: The University of Michigan Press.

George, D. (2007) "Market Overreach: The Student as Customer," *Journal of Socio-Economics*, 36(6): 965–977.

George, D. (2012) "Is it Time to Bury Dead-Weight Loss?" *Review of Political Economy*, 24(1): 1–13.

George, S. and Weimerskirch, A. (1994) *Total Quality Management: Strategies and Techniques Proven at Today's Most Successful Companies.* New York: Wiley.

"Globalization 2.0." *New York Times (1923–Current File)*, March 26, 2006. http://search.proquest.com/docview/93201961?accountid=11999.

Golden, L. and Altman, M. (2008) "Why Do People Overwork? Oversupply of Hours of Labor, Labor Market Forces and Adaptive Preferences," in C. L. Cooper and R. J. Burke (eds.), *The Long Work Hours Culture: Causes, Consequences, and Choices*, London: Emerald Group Publishing Ltd.

Golden, L. and Figart, D. M. (eds.) (2000) *Working Time: International Trends, Theory and Policy Perspectives.* New York: Routledge.

Goodwin, N., Ackerman, F., and Kiron, D. (eds.) (1997) *The Consumer Society.* Washington D.C.: Island Press.

Goodwin, N., Nelson, J. A., Ackerman, F., and Weisskopf, T. (2009) *Microeconomics in Context*, 2nd edn. Armonk NY: M. E. Sharpe.

Gray, J. (1998) *The Delusions of Global Capitalism.* New York: New Press.

Grieder, W. (1997) *One World, Ready or Not: Tthe Manic Logic of Global Capitalism.* New York: Simon & Schuster.

Grossman, S. J. and Stiglitz, J. E. (1980) "On the Impossibility of Informationally Efficient Markets," *American Economic Review*, 70(3): 393–408.

Gwartney, J., Lawson, R., and Holcombe, R. (1998) "The Size and Functions of Government and Economic Growth," Prepared for the Joint Economic Committee.

Gwartney, J. D., Stroup, R. L., Sobel, R. S., and Macpherson, D. A. (2009) *Economics: Private and Public Choice* 12th edn. Mason, OH: South-Western Cengage Learning.

Haiven, M. (2007) "Privatized Resistance: *Adbusters* and the Culture of Neoliberalism," *The Review of Education Pedagogy, and Cultural Studies*, 29: 85–110.

Hamilton, C. (2004) *Growth Fetish.* London: Pluto Press.

"Hart Taps a Generation of Young Professionals." *New York Times (1923–Current File)*, March 18, 1984. http://search.proquest.com/docview/122387734?accountid=11999.

Healy, Patrick. "Re-Election Doesnt Bring End to Clinton Campaign Operation." *New York Times (1923–Current File)*, November 11, 2006. http://search.proquest.com/docview/93030262?accountid=11999.

Hedges, C. (2010) *Death of the Liberal Class.* New York: Nation Books.

Heilbroner, R. and Milberg, W. (1995) *The Crisis of Vision in Modern Economic Thought*. New York: Cambridge University Press.

Heinzerling, L. and Ackerman, F. (2002) "The Humbugs of the Anti-Regulatory Movement," *Cornell Law Review*, 87: 648–670.

Hicks, J. R. (1939) *Value and Capital.* Oxford: Clarendon Press.

Hill, M. and Myatt, T. (2010) *The Economics Anti-Textbook: A Critical Thinker's Guide to Microeconomics.* New York: Zed Books.

Hirsch, F. (1976) *Social Limits to Growth*. Cambridge, MA: Harvard University Press.

Hirschman, A. O. (1970) *Exit, Voice, and Loyalty: Responses to Decline in Firms, Organizations, and States*. Cambridge, MA: Harvard University Press.

Hirschman, A. O. (1982a) "Rival Interpretations of Market Society: Civilizing, Destructive, or Feeble," *Journal of Economic Literature*, 20:1463–1484.

Hirschman, A. O. (1982b) *Shifting Involvements: Private Interest and Public Action*, Princeton: Princeton University Press.

Hodgson, G. M. (1993) *Economics and Evolution: Bringing Life Back into Economics*. Ann Arbor: University of Michigan Press.

Hosseini, H. (2003) "Why Development is More Complex Than Growth: Clarifying Some Confusions," *Review of Social Economy*, 61(1): 91–110.

"How to Energize Education." *New York Times (1923–Current File)*, January 03, 1998. http://search.proquest.com/docview/109898262?accountid=11999.

"Hungary to Push Land Cooperatives." *New York Times (1923–Current File)*, November 28, 1948. http://search.proquest.com/docview/108225962?accountid=11999.

"Indonesian Paper Alleges MPs Involved in Aid Fund Corruption." *BBC Monitoring Asia Pacific*, September 05, 2005. http://search.proquest.com/docview/461011815?accountid=11999.

Jeffrey, R.C. (1974) "Preferences among Preferences," *Journal of Philosophy*, 71: 377–391.

Kahneman, D., Knetsch, J. L. and Thaler, R. (1986) "Fairness as a Constraint on Profit Seeking: Entitlements in the Market," *American Economic Review* 76(4): 728–741.

Keen, S. (2001) *Debunking Economics: The Naked Emperor of the Social Sciences*. London: Zed Books.

"Kenyan Agriculture Minister Downplays Differences with Premier." (2 August). *BBC Monitoring Africa*, 2009, ProQuest Newsstand. (Document ID: 18[illegible]3135321).

Kiekhofer, W. H. (1946) *Economic Principles, Problems, and Policies*, 3rd edn. New York: D. Appleton-Century Company, Inc.

Kiewe, A. and Houck, D. W. (1991) *A Shining City on a Hill*. New York: Praeger.

Klein, N. (2000) *No Logo*. New York: Picador.

Klein, N. (2008) *The Shock Doctrine: The Rise of Disaster Capitalism*. New York: Picador.

Knight, B. W. (1942) *Economic Principles in Practice*, revised edn. New York: Rinehart & Company, Inc.

Knox, F. (1960) "The Doctrine of Consumers' Sovereignty," *Review of Social Economy*, 18: 138–149.

Kocieniewski, D. "Relief, Not Elation, for Republicans." *New York Times (1923–Current File)*, June 12, 2005. http://search.proquest.com/docview/92922145?accountid=11999.

Krugman, P. (2007) *The Conscience of a Liberal*. New York: W.W. Norton & Company.

Kuttner, R. (1996) *Everything for Sale: The Virtues and Limits of Markets*. New York: Alfred A. Knopf.

"Labor Relations Termed Critical." *New York Times (1923–Current File)*, March 15, 1950. http://search.proquest.com/docview/111459927?accountid=11999.

Lakoff, G. (2004) *Don't Think Like an Elephant: Know Your Values and Frame the Debate*. White River Junction, VT: Chelsea Green Publishing.

Landreth, H. and Colander, D. C. (2002) *History of Economic Thought*, 4th edn. Boston: Houghton Mifflin Company.

Lardner, J. and Smith, D. A. (2005) *Inequality Matters: The Growing Economic Divide in America and its Poisonous Consequences*. New York: The New Press.

Lasch, C. (1979) *The Culture of Narcissism.* New York: W. W. Norton and Company, Inc.

Lawrence, R. Z. (2002) "Competitiveness," in *Concise Encyclopedia of Economics*, D. R. Henderson (ed.) Liberty Mutual Fund.

Leach, W. (1993) *Land of Desire: Merchants, Power, and the Rise of a New American Culture.* New York: Pantheon Books.

Lewis, Anthony. "He Let in the Light." *New York Times (1923–Current File)*, January 02, 1992. http://search.proquest.com/docview/108829010?accountid=11999.

Lipsey, R. G., Ragan, C. T. S., and Storer, P. A. (2008) *Economics*, 13th edn. Boston: Pearson Addison-Wesley.

Luttwak, E. (1999) *Turbo-Capitalism: Winners and Losers in the Global Economy*, New York: HarperCollins.

Lynn, B. C. (2010) *Cornered: The New Monopoly Capitalism and the Economics of Destruction.* Hoboken, NJ: John Wiley and Sons, Inc.

McCloskey, D. N. (1985) *The Rhetoric of Economics.* Madison: The University of Wisconsin Press.

McCloskey, D. N. (2000) *How to be Human*: *Though an Economist.* Ann Arbor: University of Michigan Press.

McConnell, C. R. and Brue, S. L. (1996) *Microeconomoics: Principles, Problems, and Policies*,13th edn. New York: McGraw-Hill, Inc.

McConnell, C. R. and Brue, S. L. (2005) *Microeconomcis: Principles, Problems, and Policies*, 16th edn. New York: McGraw-Hill/Irwin.

McConnell, C. R., Brue, S. L., and Flynn, S. M. (2009) *Microeconomics: Principles, Problems, and Policies*, 18th edn. McGraw-Hill, Irwin.

"Macdonald Deplores Situation in India." *New York Times (1923–Current File)*, July 13, 1930. http://search.proquest.com/docview/98633045?accountid=11999.

Mandeville, B. (1924) *The Fable of the Bees*, ed. F. B. Kaye. Cambridge: Oxford University Press.

Mankiw, N. G. (2001) *Principles of Economics*, 2nd edn. Fort Worth, TX: Harcourt College Publishers.

Marshall, A. (1920) *Principles of Economics*, 8th edn (volume 1). London: Macmillan and Co. Limited.

Marwell, G. and Ames, R. (1981) "Economists Free Ride, Does Anyone Else? Experiments on the Provision of Public Goods," *Journal of Public Economics*, 15: 295–310.

Maynard, M. "Coffee, Tea Or Job? for Airline Workers, an Uncertain Future." *New York Times (1923–Current File)*, September 03, 2004. http://search.proquest.com/docview/92682443?accountid=11999.

Meeropol, M. (2000) *Surrender: How the Clinton Administration Completed the Reagan Revolution*, Ann Arbor, MI: University of Michigan Press.

"Merchants Back Farm Aid Projects." *New York Times (1923–Current File)*, Oct 13, 1928. http://search.proquest.com/docview/104429736?accountid=11999.

Merriam-Webster's Collegiate Dictionary 11th edn. (2003). Springfield, MA: Merriam-Webster Inc.

Merz, C. "Consulting at a Sick Worlds Bedside." *New York Times (1923–Current File)*, Jul 31, 1932. http://search.proquest.com/docview/100508438?accountid=11999.

Mill, J. S. (1929) *Principles of Political Economy.* London: Longmans, Green and Co.

Miller, D. (2010) "How Neoliberalism Got Where It Is: Elite Planning, Corporate Lobbying and the Release of the Free Market," in K. Birch and V. Mykhnenko (eds.), *The Rise and Fall of Neoliberalism: The Collapse of an Economic Order?* New York: Zed Books.

Mink, E. "You Don't have to be Christian to Respect Christianity." *McClatchy – Tribune News Service*, December 30, 2004. http://search.proquest.com/docview/456721932?accountid=11999.

Mishan, E. J. (1967) *The Costs of Economic Growth.* London: Staple Press.

Mishel, L., Bernstein, J., and Allegretto, S. (2005) *The State of Working America 2004/2005.* Ithaca: Cornell University Press.

Mishel, L., Bernstein, J., and Shierholz, H. (2009) *The State of Working America 2008/2009.* Ithaca: Cornell University Press.

"Mr. Taft Laughs at Cuban 'Plots'." *New York Times (1857–1922)*, June 16, 1908. http://search.proquest.com/docview/96800186?accountid=11999.

Mix, M. "A Radical by the Board ... HEAD:" *Washington Times*, October 21, 2009. http://search.proquest.com/docview/410046888?accountid=11999.

Morin, R. "Job Satisfaction Highest among the Self-Employed," September 17, 2009. http://pewsocialtrends.org/pubs/743/job-satisfaction-highest-among-self-employed.

"Motor Highway Traffic Studied by Government." *New York Times (1923–Current File)*, March 30, 1924. http://search.proquest.com/docview/103223787?accountid=11999.

Nash Jr., J. (1950) "The Bargaining Problem," *Econometrica*, 18(2): 155–162.

Nash Jr., J. (1951) "Non-Cooperative Games," *Annals of Mathematics*, 54(2): 286–295.

Nelson, R. H. (1991) *Reaching for Heaven on Earth: The Theological Meaning of Economics.* Savage MD: Rowman and Littlefield.

"New Monopolies from Old." *New York Times (1923–Current File)*, November 11, 1991. http://search.proquest.com/docview/108773633?accountid=11999.

Newman, K. S. and Chen, V. T. (2007) *The Missing Class: Portraits of the Near Poor in America.* Boston: Beacon Press.

Nichols, J. (2011) *The "S" Word: A Short History of an American Tradition ... Socialism.* Brooklyn, NY: Verso.

"Notre Dame to Consider Bowl Bid if Title is at Stake." *New York Times (1923–Current File)*, Oct 27, 1964. http://search.proquest.com/docview/115906913?accountid=11999.

Nunberg, G. (2006) *Talking Right: How Conservatives Turned Liberalism into a Tax-Raising, Latte-Drinking, Sushi-Eating, Volvo-Driving, New York Times-Reading, Body-Piercing, Hollywood-Loving, Left-Wing Freak Show.* New York: Public Affairs.

"Object to mail rate rise." Special to the *New York Times (1857–1922)*, February 04, 1922. http://search.proquest.com/docview/99619169?accountid=11999.

"Offers Body and Life for Medical Tests." *New York Times (1923–Current File)*, Dec 11, 1927. http://search.proquest.com/docview/104020848?accountid=11999.

Officer, L. H. and Williamson, S. H. 2009. "Computing 'Real Value' Over Time With a Conversion Between U.K. Pounds and U.S. Dollars, 1830 to Present," Measuring Worth. URL www.measuringworth.com/exchange/.

"Oppose Pension Bill," *The Philadelphia Inquirer*, 160(94), April 4, 1909, p. 2.

O'Sullivan, A., Sheffrin, S. M. and Perez, S. J. (2008) *Economics: principles, applications, and tools*, 5th edn. Upper Saddle River, NJ: Pearson-Prentice Hall.

"Our London Cable." *New York Times (1857–1922)*, 1900. http://search.proquest.com/docview/95941561?accountid=11999.

Pack, S. L. (2010) *Aristotle, Adam Smith and Karl Marx: On Some Fundamental Issues in 21st Century Political Economy.* Northampton, MA: Edward Elgar.

Peart, S. J. and Levy, D. M. (2005) *The "Vanity of the Philosopher": From Equality to Hierarchy in Post-classical Economics."* AnnArbor: University of Michigan Press.

Perlez, J. "Editor Critical of Thai Leader Loses his Job." *New York Times*, February 23, 2004. http://search.proquest.com/docview/432672287?accountid=11999.

Pigou, A. C. (1929) *The Economics of Welfare.* London: Macmillan and Co. Limited.

Pigou, A. C. (1935) *Economics in Practice: Six Lectures on Current Issues.* London: Macmillan and Co., Limited.

Polak, M. "Oh Yes The Premier Cares" (letter to editor). *Prince George Citizen*, July 14, 2009, p. 6.

"Policemen Guard Against Protesters as A.M.A. Installs its New President." *New York Times (1923–Current File)*, July 17, 1969. http://search.proquest.com/docview/118530908?accountid=11999.

"Portuguese Government 'Interference' in the Media – Paper." *BBC Monitoring European*, September 23, 2009. http://search.proquest.com/docview/459268331?accountid=11999.

Posner, R. (2010) *The Crisis of Capitalist Democracy.* Cambridge, MA: Harvard University Press.

Posting on "Jokes in your profession" of the "Straight Dope Message Board" by Astorian on January 27, 2006. http://boards.straightdope.com/sdmb/showthtrea.php?t=355773@page=2.

"President Clinton's Welfare Waffle." *New York Times (1923–Current File)*, January 09, 1995. http://search.proquest.com/docview/109434443?accountid=11999.

"President's Labor Day Journey." *New York Times (1857–1922)*, September 02, 1903. http://search.proquest.com/docview/96404695?accountid=11999.

Pressman, S. and Scott, R. (2009) "Consumer Debt and the Measurement of Poverty and Inequality in the US," *Review of Social Economy*, 67(2): 127–148.

"Publishers Should Unite to Handle Print Paper Situation, Says Federal Trade Commission Chairman," *Miami Herald*, September 17, 1916: 1.

Purnick, J. "Amid Tributes and Blame, a Search for Middle Ground." *New York Times (1923–Current File)*, May 20, 2004. http://search.proquest.com/docview/92805055?accountid=11999.

"Railworkers Open Six-Hour Day Drive." *New York Times (1923–Current File)*, January 11, 1935. http://search.proquest.com/docview/101629128?accountid=11999.

Rampell, C. (2011) "The Help-Wanted Sign Comes With a Frustrating Asterisk," *New York Times*, March 26, http://www.nytimes.com.

Ross, A. (1948) "Hungary to Push Land Cooperatives," *New York Times*, January 21: p. 32.

"Rowland Says G.O.P. Keeps Legislative Power." *New York Times (1923–Current File)*, January 08, 1997. http://search.proquest.com/docview/109741707?accountid=11999.

Rumbo, J. D. (2002) "Consumer Resistance in a World of Advertising Clutter: The Case of *Adbusters*," *Psychology and Marketing*, 19(2): 127–148.

"Russia's Promising Tax Plan." *New York Times (1923–Current File)*, May 28, 2000. http://search.proquest.com/docview/91395182?accountid=11999.

Ryan, F. J., Sweeder, J. J., and Bednar, M. R. (2002) *Drowning in the Clear Pool: Cultural Narcissism, Technology, and Character Education.* New York: Peter Lang Publishing, Inc.

Safire, W. "Breaking the Cartel." *New York Times (1923–Current File)*, September 26, 1991. http://search.proquest.com/docview/108674336?accountid=11999.

"Saharas of the Drama." *New York Times (1923–Current File)*, January 28, 1925. http://search.proquest.com/docview/103649882?accountid=11999.

Samuelson, P. A. (1947) *Foundations of Economic Analysis.* Cambridge, MA: Harvard University Press.

Samuelson, P. A. (1967) *Economics: An Introductory Analysis*, 7th edn. New York: McGraw-Hill Book Company.

Samuelson, P. A. and Nordhaus, W. D. (2010) *Economics*, 19th edn. McGraw-Hill, Irwin.

Schiller, B. R. (1989) *The Economy Today*, 4th edn. New York: Random House.

Schlesinger Jr., A. M. (1986) *The Cycles of American History*, Boston: Houghton Mifflin.

Schlesinger Sr., A. M. (1939) "Tides of American Politics," *Yale Review*, 39: 217–230.

Schor, J. B. (1991) *The Overworked American: The Unexpected Decline of Leisure*, New York: Basic Books.

Schumpeter, J. A. (1950) *Capitalism, Socialism, and Democracy*. New York: Harper.

Sen, A. K. (1974) "Choice, Orderings, and Morality," in S. Korner (ed.), *Practical Reason*, 54–67. Oxford: Blackwell.

Sen, A. K. (1977) "Rational Fools: A Critique of the Behavioural Foundations of Economic Theory." *Philosophy and Public Affairs*, 6: 317–344.

"Senate Bill Asks Bank Decontrol." *New York Times (1923–Current File)*, October 08, 1981. http://search.proquest.com/docview/121758711?accountid=11999.

"Shanghaing, Crimping." *New York Times (1857–1922)*, January 30, 1910. http://search.proquest.com/docview/97071622?accountid=11999.

Smith, A. (1976) *The Theory of Moral Sentiments*, D. D. Raphael and A. L. Macfie (eds.), Oxford (EG): Clarendon Press.

Smith, M. A. (2007) *The Right Talk: How Conservatives Transformed the Great Society into the Economic Society*. Princeton: Princeton University Press.

Soros, G. (1998) *The Crisis of Global Capitalism: Open Society Endangered*. New York: Public Affairs.

"Sporting," *The Daily Herald*, III (94) January 20, 1912, p. 7.

Starr, M. A. (2004) "Reading *The Economist* on Globalisation: Knowledge, Identity, and Power," *Global Society*, 18(4): 373–395.

Starr, M. A. (2006) "Growth and Conflict in the Developing World: Neo-liberal Narratives and Social-Economy Alternatives," *Review of Social Economy*, 64(2): 206–224.

Stiglitz, J. E. (2002) *Globalization and Its Discontents*. New York: W. W. Norton and Company.

Stiglitz, J. E. (2003) *The Roaring Nineties: A New History of the World's Most Dangerous Decade*. New York: W.W. Norton and Company.

Stoll, S. (2008) *The Great Delusion: A Mad Inventor, Death in the Tropics and the Utopian Origins of Economic Growth*, New York: Hill and Wang.

Sullivan, W. M. (1995) *Work and Integrity: The Crisis and Promise of Professionalism in America*. New York: Harper Collins.

"Taiwan President Denies Political Influence in Foreign Aid." *BBC Monitoring Asia Pacific*, August 19, 2009.

Taussig, F. W. (1915) *Principles of Economics, Vol. 1*, 2nd edn, revised. New York: Macmillan.

The American Heritage Dictionary, 2nd College Edition (1982) Boston, MA: Houghton Mifflin Company.

The American Heritage Dictionary of the English Language, 4th edn (2000) Boston, MA: Houghton Mifflin.

"The Bishop and the Rebels." *New York Times (1923–Current File)*, January 26, 1994. http://search.proquest.com/docview/109303258?accountid=11999.

"The Great Failure." *New York Daily Times (1851–1857)*, September 03, 1857. http://search.proquest.com/docview/95924121?accountid=11999.

"The Homestead Meeting." *New York Daily Times (1851–1857)*, May 28, 1852. http://search.proquest.com/docview/95783528?accountid=11999.

"The I.C.C. Dies." *New York Times (1923–Current File)*, January 03, 1996. http://search.proquest.com/docview/109596927?accountid=11999.
The New Oxford American Dictionary (2001) New York: Oxford University Press.
The Oxford English Dictionary, 2nd edn (1989). Oxford: Oxford University Press.
"The Preteen Sexual Harasser." *New York Times (1923–Current File)*, January 09, 1999. http://search.proquest.com/docview/110081216?accountid=11999.
The Random House Dictionary of the English Language (1966). New York: Random House.
"The Voice of the People." *New York Times (1923–Current File)*, December 30, 1923. http://search.proquest.com/docview/103131435?accountid=11999.
"The Year of the Yuppies." *New York Times (1923–Current File)*, March 25, 1984. http://search.proquest.com/docview/122360285?accountid=11999.
[Think: Commissioners; Allea], *Morning Olympian*, 21(224) December 5, 1911, p. 2.
Tiemstra, J. P. (2008) "Rethinking the Costs of Economic Growth. Association for Social Economics Presidential Address 2008," *Review of Social Economy*, 66(4) 423–435.
Tierney, J. "Not in the Kennedys' Backyard." *New York Times (1923–Current File)*, January 17, 2006. http://search.proquest.com/docview/93050789?accountid=11999.
"To Repeal the War Tax Law." *New York Times (1857–1922)*, April 20, 1900. http://search.proquest.com/docview/95984493?accountid=11999.
"To Sell Himself at Auction." *New York Times (1857–1922)*, December 23, 1911. http://search.proquest.com/docview/97189277?accountid=11999.
"Too High for Clark's Man." *Omaha World Herald*, January 13, 1900, p. 7.
"Trails of Blood, Seeds of Doubt." *New York Times (1923–Current File)*, January 27, 1995. http://search.proquest.com/docview/109406913?accountid=11999.
Tucker, I. B. (2008) *Economics for Today*, 5th edn. Mason, OH: Thomson, South-Western.
Turner, J. R. (1919) *Introduction to Economics.* New York: Charles Scribner's Sons.
Twenge, J. M. and Campbell, W. K. (2009) *The Narcissism Epidemic: Living in the Age of Entitlement.* New York: Free Press.
"Unable to Carry Out Big Contracts." *New York Times (1857–1922)*, February 17, 1906. http://search.proquest.com/docview/96604573?accountid=11999.
Van Staveren, I. (2009) "Communitarianism and the Market: A Paradox," *Review of Social Economy*, 67(1): 25–47.
Van Tuinen, H. K. (2011) "The Ignored Manipulation of the Market: Commercial Advertising and Consumerism Require New Economic Theories and Policies," *Review of Political Economy*, 23(2): 213–231.
Von Mises, L. (1977) *A Critique of Interventionism.* New Rochelle, NY: Arlington House.
Von Neumann, J. and Morgenstern, O. (1953) *Theory of Games and Economic Behavior*, Princeton: Princeton University Press.
Walsh, V. (1996) *Rationality, Allocation, and Reproduction*, New York: Oxford University Press.
Webster's New International Dictionary 2nd edn. (1956) Springfield, MA: G.& C. Merriam, Inc.
Welch, P. J. and Welch, G. F. (2007) *Economics: Theory and Practice*, 8th edn. John Wiley & Sons, Inc.
"What Free Market?" *New York Times (1923–Current File)*, January 22, 1992. http://search.proquest.com/docview/109015828?accountid=11999.
White, M. D. (2006) "Multiple Utilities and Weakness of Will: A Kantian Perspective," *Review of Social Economy*, 64(1): 1–20.

"Who are Truly Needy?" *Bangor Daily News*, February 18, 2011. http://search.proquest.com/docview/852722492?accountid=11999.

"Who Owns a Trade Secret? No One is Sure–Yet." *New York Times (1923–Current File)*, March 22, 1963. http://search.proquest.com/docview/116632573?accountid=11999.

Wight, J. B. (2002) *Saving Adam Smith: A Tale of Wealth, Transformation, and Virtue*, New Jersey: Prentice-Hall.

"Willkie Hits Big Government." *New York Times (1923–Current File)*, February 17, 1940. http://search.proquest.com/docview/105150377?accountid=11999.

"Winant Leaves Geneva." *New York Times (1923–Current File)*, July 04, 1940. http://search.proquest.com/docview/105246833?accountid=11999.

Yezer, A. M., Goldfarb, R. S., and Poppen, P. J. (1996) "Does Studying Economics Discourage Cooperation? Watch What We Do, Not What We Say or How We Play." *Journal of Economic Perspectives*, 10(1): 177–186.

Young, M. (1958) *The Rise of the Meritocracy, 1870–2033.* London: Thames & Hudson.

Zezima, K. "The Very Last Tutor." *New York Times (1923–Current File)*, April 23, 2006. http://search.proquest.com/docview/93078280?accountid=11999.

Index

Page numbers in *italics* denote tables.